IRAN AND THE WORLD

IRAN AND THE WORLD

Continuity in a Revolutionary Decade

Shireen T. Hunter

INDIANA UNIVERSITY PRESS
Bloomington & Indianapolis

The paper used in this publication meets the minimum requirements of American
National Standard for Information Sciences—Permanence of Paper for Printed
Library Materials, ANSI Z39.48-1984.

⊗ ™

Manufactured in the United States of America

Library of Congress Cataloging-in-Publication Data
Hunter, Shireen T.
    Iran and the world : continuity in a revolutionary decade / Shireen T. Hunter.
    p.   cm.
    Includes bibliographical references.
    ISBN 0-253-32877-2. — ISBN 0-253-20590-5 (pbk.)
    1. Iran—Foreign relations—1979–   I. Title.
  DS318.83.H86   1990
327.55—dc20

                                                                89-45918
                                                                CIP

        1 2 3 4 5   94 93 92 91 90

Contents

Preface   vii
Introduction   1

1.   Determinants of Iran's Foreign Policy   6
2.   The Evolution of Iran's Diplomacy   21
3.   Iran's Islamic World View and Its Impact on Foreign Policy   36
4.   Iran and the Superpowers: *The United States*   46
5.   Iran and the Superpowers: *The Soviet Union*   79
6.   Iran, the Arab World, and Israel   98
7.   Iran and Its Neighbors: *Pakistan, India, and Turkey*   131
8.   Iran and Europe   139
9.   Iran, East Asia, and the Pacific   157
10. Iran and the Third World   165
11. Iran and International Organizations   169
12. Terrorism and Subversion: *Impact on Foreign Policy*   174

Conclusions   184
Epilogue   190
Statistical Appendix   193
Notes   197
Selected Bibliography   241
Index   247

Preface

Alexis de Tocqueville wrote that "a simple but false idea will always have a greater weight in the world than a true but complex idea." This observation characterizes very well most Western theories about the external behavior of Third World states and their motivating impulses—theories such as "nation-building," "modernizing dictators," or "outlaw nations". The reverse has also been true, as many Third World nations have resorted to simplistic theories of imperialism, neo-colonialism, external intervention, and grand conspiracies to explain their domestic problems and the behavior of other states toward them.

Of course, it would also be incorrect to suggest that such theories have no basis in reality or provide no valid explanation for aspects of both Third World and Western behavior. Rather, it is merely to emphasize that these explanations tell only part of the story. Indeed, their attraction lies in their simplicity and their capacity to absolve all concerned of the need to take responsibility for the impact that their actions have in shaping the behavior of others. The result of applying these simplified theories, however, has been the persistence of an intellectual and emotional barrier, deriving from a deep lack of understanding between most Third World nations and the West. These theories have also hindered the development of a comprehensive notion of state behavior that, in its essentials, can have general validity.

This erroneous mode of approach and its consequences can be observed very clearly in the case of Iran. With a few notable exceptions, most Western analysts of Iranian affairs have explained Iran's external behavior, in both the pre- and post-revolutionary periods, largely in terms of a few national traits or the idiosyncracies of individuals. Thus during the late 1960s and 1970s, Iran's foreign policy was often explained in terms of Persian hegemonism or the Shah's imperial megalo-mania. Likewise, during the post-revolutionary period, Iran's foreign policy has often been explained in terms of Shi'a expansionism, religious fanaticism, or the Ayatollah Rouhollah Khomeini's quest for a new Islamic world order.

No doubt, Iran's national character and the personality of its leaders have deeply affected its behavior. Yet this has been true of many other states, without receiving the kind of emphasis that is applied in Iran's case. Indeed, underlying forces affect state behavior in a more universal manner than is often assumed. By the same token, it is most constructive to analyze state behavior in light of the multiple and complex sets of factors that motivate it rather than to invoke one simplistic and overarching paradigm.

Such is the ambition of this volume: to analyze Iran's behavior during the last decade in light of basic factors that affect state behavior in general, and of certain specific characteristics unique to Iran, and to do so by placing experience during this period in its proper historical context. The hope is that, in this way, some of the most simplistic notions about Iran's behavior will be dispelled and some of the more enduring impulses motivating its actions will be highlighted.

Many readers are likely to disapprove of this approach. Those in Iran who have portrayed its foreign policy as the pursuit of pure and undiluted revolutionary principles will frown at the suggestion that, more often than not, other less lofty motives or necessities of national and regime survival have determined its course. Similarly, both Iran's Islamic leaders and supporters of the Pahlavi regime will likely reject the notion that similarities exist between Iran's pre- and post-revolution foreign policies.

At the same time, those Westerners who have portrayed Iran as an outlaw nation—whose foreign policy has consisted of terrorism and a fanatical pursuit of an Islamic dream and which has been the source of virtually all of the West's problems in the Islamic world—will dismiss any suggestion of normality in Iran's behavior. They are also likely to dismiss the proposition that Iran has not been responsible for all of the West's troubles and, even more so, that at times Western attitudes toward Iran have contributed to those aspects of Iran's behavior most abhorrent to the West. Other observers may object to the questioning of some prevailing views—myths, really—such as Iran's expansionist thrust in the Persian Gulf or its absolute guilt in engendering difficulties with the Arab world during the past 40 years. But these are necessary risks in an effort to understand, analyze, and explain Iran's past and present behavior.

In pursuing the goal of this book, in addition to normal research tools I have drawn on my personal and professional experience as a child growing up in the turbulent Tehran of the 1950s, as a student at Tehran University's Faculty of Law in the early 1960s—at the time of the critical religious-secular dichotomy in Iran—as a member of the Iranian diplomatic service during the heady days of the 1970s, and as an analyst of Iranian affairs and follower and teacher of Middle East and Third World trends in the 1980s. I have had the good fortune of talking to many of diplomats, businessmen, journalists, and scholars who are either expert on Iran or in charge of the conduct of their countries or their firms' relations with Iran. These include individuals resident here in the United States and those met during my travels to Europe, the Soviet Union, China, Japan, India, and various countries in the Persian Gulf and elsewhere in the Middle East. They have provided me with information and intelligent analysis, and I feel deeply indebted to all.

I could not have completed this book without the assistance of a string of young, intelligent, and energetic interns who sacrificed their summer holidays and many long hours in dusty libraries among piles of paper. My heartfelt thanks go to all of them and to the CSIS staff members who went through innumerable drafts of the manuscript, and especially to Brenda Blackburn and Kazuko Campbell.

The patience, encouragement, and sound critique of my husband, Robert Hunter, sustained me throughout this effort, and I am forever indebted and thankful to him. Despite all the assistance I have received in the course of preparing this book, all errors of fact or judgment are mine alone.

Shireen T. Hunter

IRAN AND THE WORLD

Introduction

In February 1979, the triumph of revolutionary forces opposed to the rule of Shah Mohammad Reza Pahlavi ended a 2,500-year tradition of monarchy in Iran. The collapse of the monarchy did not lead to the immediate establishment of an Islamic regime, although Ayatollah Rouhollah Khomeini emerged as the uncontested leader of the revolution. Nominally, for nearly a year, political power rested with the provisional government of Prime Minister Mehdi Bazargan and his secular and nationalist colleagues.

In reality the provisional government was not in control of events, and the country plunged into chaos. Islamic extremists and a mixture of leftist and Islamic-leftist groups challenged the government's authority, and the Revolutionary Council undermined its ability to govern. The ideological battle lines were soon clearly drawn, and it became clear that three basic groupings—secular-nationalist, Islamic, and leftist—held radically different visions of Iran's future.

During the referendum of March 30–31, 1979 that was held to decide the nature of the new regime the secular-nationalist forces called for the establishment of a democratic or Islamic-democratic republic, while the Islamic groups demanded a purely Islamic republic. With the blessing of the Ayatollah Khomeini, the latter prevailed. The Iranian people were offered only the choice of voting either for or against the creation of an Islamic republic.

Given this narrow choice, the majority chose an Islamic republic. After this initial victory, Islamic elements intensified their fight against secular nationalists. Their first victim was Mehdi Bazargan. His government fell on November 4, 1979, as a result of that day's seizure of the U.S. embassy and the beginning of the hostage crisis. The final victory for the religious forces came in June 1981, when President Abol-Hassan Bani-Sadr fled to exile in Paris.

During this period of intense power struggle, the leftist forces suffered heavily. These included the Islamic-Marxist Mojahedin-e-Khalgh, which had cooperated with the religious groups against the secular nationalist forces. After a ruthless crackdown by the government, they were eliminated from the political scene and went underground or fled to neighboring countries. Because of its support for Khomeini, the communist Tudeh Party was tolerated for a longer period. But it, too, was outlawed in 1983, and its leaders were imprisoned.

Even before the complete subjugation of their rivals and the consolidation of their political power, Islamic forces embarked on a process of Islamizing Iranian society. They purged and restructured Iran's political, educational, and judicial systems according to Islamic principles. They also launched an Islamic cultural revolution and attempted to eliminate from Iran's national culture any non-Islamic and anti-Islamic elements; they glorified the role of Islam in Iran's national development; and they attacked Iranian nationalism and Iran's pre-Islamic heritage. Initially, Khomeini and his disciples neither referred to the concept of an Iranian nation nor did they appeal to the Iranians' sense of nationhood. Everything was done in the name of Islam.

Islam also became the principal influence in forming the character of Iran's relations with the outside world. Islamic notions of nation, state, and interstate relations—as interpreted by the Ayatollah Khomeini—shaped the Iranian leaders' world view. The spread of revolutionary Islam's message became the primary focus of Iran's foreign policy.

But the regime's Islamization program did not proceed as smoothly as its leaders had expected. Instead, it generated considerable popular dissatisfaction and vocal opposition, especially among the secularized middle classes. Popular disapproval was unable to arrest the Islamization program, but it moderated its most extreme aspects. The Iranians' sense of nationalism and their attachment to symbols of their pre-Islamic culture proved tenacious, forcing the government to ease its antinationalist crusade.

The Iran-Iraq war enhanced nationalist tendencies in Iran. Thus, in a move that suggests a parallel with Stalin's Russia during 1941–45, Iran's religious leaders resorted to the concept of the Iranian nation and appealed to the Iranians' sense of nationalism, although they qualified Iran and the Iranians as Islamic. This trend illustrated the enduring quality of Iran's historical and cultural realities to which its Islamic leaders had to adapt.

A similar process of adjustment to external realities also took place in foreign policy. Geopolitical and historical forces, economic and commercial necessities, and international reactions to Iran's revolution forced it to adjust its policies, and the ideological content of its foreign policy became diluted. However, Iran's Islamic ideology still affects its world view, its aspirations, and its external behavior thus, producing a tension between ideologically inspired goals and a pragmatically prescribed course of action. Different elements within the Iranian leadership still disagree on the proper mix of ideology and pragmatism in the conduct of Iran's foreign policy. Nevertheless, faced with internal and external pressures, Iran has had to bend its ideological principles. As with other revolutionary governments, Iran's ideology has increasingly served to rationalize policies, adopted for practical reasons, rather than to determine them.

The influence of pragmatic considerations and the influence within Iran of forces other than Islam have resulted in a significant degree of continuity in the underlying patterns of its pre- and post-revolution external relations, despite some dramatic departures from past patterns of behavior. The extent of continuity becomes particularly apparent if it is borne in mind that many aspects of Iran's pre-revolution foreign policy did not reflect popular preferences but rather the views of the ruling elite. Thus, some of the post-revolutionary changes—such as the severing of links with South Africa and Israel and the ending of the close alliance with the United States—were in response to broad popular preferences; indeed, they were introduced by the government of Shapour Bakhtiar as part of efforts to save the monarchy. In this, as in many other respects, the Islamic regime's policies have been afflicted by the same flaw, in that to a disproportionate degree they have reflected the views of the Ayatollah Khomeini and the clerical leadership.

There is no scientific way of proving this contention. Neither in the Shah's time nor since the revolution has a systematic survey of popular Iranian views on the nation's foreign policy been conducted. The lack of a truly independent legislature and press, both in pre- and post-revolutionary periods, has made an accurate assessment of public views difficult. But the views of opposition groups, veiled comments by those individuals inside Iran who oppose some government policies, and general complaints by the population have always provided hints about the existence and extent of a gap between government and public attitudes.

Yet despite the fact that, during the last six decades, Iran's foreign policy has to a disproportionate degree borne the imprint of a few individuals, in the final analysis the determining element has been Iran itself: the land mass, the people, and the culture. Thus, Iran's geopolitical, historical, and economic realities, as well as factors related to the nature of the regional and international systems, have most often dictated its basic foreign policy options, irrespective of its leaders' preferences. Often changes in Iran's foreign policy have followed rather than preceded changes in the constellation of these forces. Thus the tendency among many analysts to explain Iran's foreign policy primarily in terms of the ambitions or idiosyncrasies of its leaders has not been totally justified. It has overlooked the underlying forces and impulses that, throughout Iran's history, have affected its behavior. Despite its ideological aspirations, the Islamic regime has not escaped the influence of these factors.

The content of its ideology, as applied to foreign policy, is also more mixed than official rhetoric has indicated. Officially, Islam provides all the guiding principles for Iran's domestic and foreign policies. The regime's spokesmen use Qor'anic verses and the sayings of Muslim greats to legitimate and rationalize their policies. No doubt, Islam is the core ingredient of the Iranian leaders' ideological makeup, yet not all members of the current leadership are influenced by Islam to the same degree. Likewise, they do not have the same interpretation of Islamic injunctions. Instead, since the early days of the revolution, the Iranian leadership has been characterized by considerable ideological division within its ranks. Moreover, Islam is not the only ingredient in their ideological make-up and world view, which also reflect Iran's historical experience, the deep imprint of dominant Third World political themes, and modern ideologies.

The influence of these factors frequently filters through statements made by these leaders, although they are often garbed in Islamic terms. But at times they are used in their original versions. Indeed, the exposure of Iranian leaders to secular, Third World ideas has been vital in enabling them to apply Islamic principles to present-day international conditions and to try developing Islam into a comprehensive ideology and an alternative to existing foreign-inspired ideologies.

This influence of Third World political themes on the thinking of Iran's leaders has contributed to patterns of continuity in it's post-revolution foreign policy. Long before the Islamic revolution, Iran's political evolution and political culture were affected by developments in the Third World. At times, developments inside Iran, such as the nationalization of its oil in 1951, have inspired others in the Third World. Likewise, despite their vehement rejection of both the eastern and western blocs, Iranian leaders have been affected by the East-West debate of the last forty years. Thus, while most current leaders favor independence from bloc politics, there are serious differences in approach toward issues of East-West conflict and Iran's relations with the two sides.

In sum, contrary to the prevalent perception that Iran's post-revolutionary foreign policy has been primarily determined by Islam in pursuit of Islamically inspired objectives, a variety of factors has influenced its international behavior. Many are rooted in Iran's history, geography, and political culture. Thus, many aspects of Iran's post-revolution foreign policy are different manifestations of some basic national historical impulses. Other aspects reflect the influence of factors that also determine the external behavior of states in general. Different elements of Iran's revolutionary regime are affected by these factors in varying degrees. Some members of the leadership insist on maintaining as much ideological purity as possible, even in the face of outside pressures. Others are more pragmatically oriented, which explains the often contradictory tendencies and sudden changes witnessed in Iran's foreign policy since the revolution.

For states interacting with Iran, it is important to realize the multiplicity and complexity of factors that have been shaping Iran's behavior and to discern patterns of continuity in its present and past policies. To view Iran's behavior during the last decade as a total breach with the past and a complete aberration from normal state behavior would engender false expectations regarding the course of Iranian behavior in the aftermath of the Ayatollah Khomeini's death or even in the event of a change of regime. This widespread perception of a breach is due to the fact that, understandably, Western observers have focused on Iran's relations with the West. Here, indeed, there have been significant departures from historic Iranian behavior. But Iran has maintained widespread relations with a large group of countries, and in this broader context continuities, despite changes, have been quite significant.

It would be equally erroneous to view the conduct of all Iranian foreign policy as the fanatical pursuit of a millenarian dream or a quest to establish a so-called Islamic world order—both views colored by peculiarities and idiosyncrasies of Shi'a Islam. It would be more appropriate to analyze Iran's behavior during the last decade as that of a revolutionary state at different stages of internal consolidation and adaptation to its external setting. Seen in this light, Iran's external behavior in the post-revolutionary period does not appear much different from that of other states in the early stages of revolution.

Iran's case is especially interesting because pragmatic considerations have crept much earlier into the conduct of its external relations than was true of some other revolutionary countries. Thus, to be constructive, Iran's post-revolution foreign relations should be analyzed in light of those factors that shape state behavior as well as Iran's specific geographic, historical, and cultural peculiarities. One should avoid an analysis of Iran's international behavior based on such supposed traits as Shi'a fanaticism, irrationality, an inordinate love of martyrdom, or Iranian xenophobia—although elements of all of these have had some influence. If there is to be comparison with other states, it should be with the experience of other revolutionary governments and their process of adjusting to external realities and the international political system.

In light of this discussion, this book has several principal purposes:

(1) to demonstrate how a variety of factors—not just Islam—have shaped Iran's international behavior and its foreign policy;

(2) to show that the Iranian world view is neither purely Islamic nor a totally novel phenomenon in Third World intellectual trends;

(3) to illustrate that Iran's behavior has not been a total departure from normal state behavior and, in particular, that of a Third World state at a revolutionary stage of its life;

(4) to illustrate the patterns of continuity in Iran's present and past behavior, including its diplomatic strategies;

(5) to provide a record of Iran's foreign relations during the last decade while placing it in its proper historical context; and

(6) to assess the lessons of the last decade for Iran's future behavior, irrespective of the type of regime that may emerge following the Ayatollah Khomeini's death.

The methodological tools used to achieve these goals will be those of classic diplomatic, historical, and foreign policy-making analysis. The book will draw together different strands—including geopolitical and historical factors, the Iranian resource base, domestic conditions (including the decision-making processes), and systemic factors—in order to analyze their interactions and ultimately their impact on Iran's behavior.

1. Determinants of Iran's Foreign Policy

A sovereign state's external behavior is determined by the interaction of many factors, although at times one or another can acquire a disproportionate importance. Some relate to a state's particular characteristics, such as its geographic location, ethnic and religious composition, historical experience, resource base and economic needs, the character of its political system, and its ideology.[1] Other factors relate to the external setting within which a state has to operate—namely, the regional and international systems.

The impact of some factors is subject to change. A country's economic needs can change with the evolution of its economy and so can its political ideology. Regional and global political systems within which states must operate also change. By contrast, a country's geographic location, its physical characteristics, its historical experience, its cultural traits are constant and account for continuity in a state's foreign policy within a constant dialogue between the forces of change and those of continuity. They help shape a state's national aspirations, color its world view, mold its diplomatic style, and influence its freedom of choice and action.

Iran is no exception to this general description. Thus, understanding its recent behavior requires examining it in the context of the underlying determinants of state behavior.

Geophysical Traits and Geostrategic Setting

In the north, east, and west, Iran is surrounded by land frontiers, and its only access to the sea is through the Persian Gulf in the south. It is thus a semi-landlocked country whose only window to the world is through the Persian Gulf—hence, its historic preoccupation with its position there.

Iran is strategically located along Asia's important commercial and military routes and historically has served as a land bridge between Asia and Europe. Over the centuries, its strategic location has made it vulnerable to migratory forces and to pressures from expanding military powers—as represented by Greek, Arab, Mongol, and several Turkic, and Russian invasions. Meanwhile, Iran's other geophysical characteristics, such as its enclosure by chains of mountains, have enhanced its sense of physical unity, which has enabled it to absorb the ethnic and cultural shocks of recurring foreign incursions and to develop a unique cultural identity.[2] This situation has had practical consequences for Iran's external relations. The persistence of an Iranian identity despite Islamization, plus Iran's Shi'ite character, has deeply affected the nature of Arab-Iranian relations. This Iranian-Shi'ite identity also kept it out of the Ottoman realm.[3]

Yet Iran's success in maintaining its cultural identity has come at a price, for it does not have any natural friends. Those peoples who are ethnically and linguistically its kin—in Afghanistan and Tadjikistan—are separated from it by religious differences; they are primarily Sunni. Iran is separated from the Arab world and Turkey by ethnic and sectarian barriers.

In modern times, this sense of isolation has affected Iran's external behavior. Many aspects of its foreign policy that—both under the Shah and since the revolution—have been characterized as expansionist have instead been efforts to break out of this isolation. Nonetheless, obstacles in Iran's way have become steadily stronger. Any meaningful interaction between Iran and its cultural kindred in Soviet Central Asia and the Caucuses has been effectively blocked by Russian and Soviet power. The Shah's efforts to expand ties with the Indian subcontinent were viewed with misgivings by India. The exclusivist dimensions of Arab nationalism, added to traditional Arab-Iranian rivalry, have effectively blocked Iran's interaction with the Arab world. Even the Islamic Republic's use of Islam to penetrate the Arab world has been only marginally successful.

Given its geographic location, Iran has perennially had to cope with the pressures of migratory forces and expanding powers.[4] The emergence of vastly superior powers in its vicinity during the nineteenth century, while Iran was steadily declining, worsened its security dilemmas. It became the immediate neighbor of a great power, with all that this implies in terms of constraints on foreign policy choices of a contiguous small state.[5]

As the largest land mass separating Russia from the Persian Gulf and as the land access to Britain's prized possession—India—Iran was caught in the Anglo-Russian rivalry. The discovery of oil in Iran and elsewhere in the Persian Gulf enhanced its strategic importance and intensified imperial rivalries. Every aspect of Iran's political life became permeated by requirements of this rivalry. The change of regime in Russia in 1917 and the rise of the United States after World War II did nothing to end great power competition; Iran's geostrategic predicament remained unchanged.

Yet, great power rivalries has not always worked against Iran's interests, for they provided a balancing effect, often enabling Iran to keep a modicum of independence and to avoid disintegration.[6] Nevertheless, Iran's location has made its foreign policy choices and indeed its political destiny exceedingly vulnerable to the vagaries of international politics and to the state of great power relations.

Historical Experience

Nations, like individuals, are largely the product of their past. Memories and experiences color their assessment of present reality, shape their vision of the future, and form their national ethos. Some experiences leave such a deep imprint on a nation's psyche that they affect its behavior for generations. Their influence lingers even if that is no longer justified by external realities.

Iran's history is replete with such traumatic experiences, but those of the last two centuries remain most vivid. These can be summed up in terms of its territorial contraction, its political, economic, and cultural domination by others, and its national humiliation.

Most traumatic has been Iran's encounter with Russia—both imperial and socialist. During a brief period of 24 years (1804–1828), the Russo-Iranian conflict resulted in the loss of Iran's trans-Caucasian territories and was followed by the severing of its political and cultural links with neighboring Central Asia.[7] Territorial losses were accompanied by the loss of political and economic independence and generated acute feelings of national dishonor.

Great Britain's efforts to create territorial buffers around India and to maintain naval hegemony in the Persian Gulf were also achieved at Iran's expense. Because of British policies, Iran's links with Afghanistan were severed and its position in the Persian Gulf was undermined.[8] Britain, too, obtained discriminatory concessions.[9] Iran suffered a fate worse than that of colonies, which had an inherent value for imperial powers: Although exploited, they also derived some benefits. But in the words of Sir Dennis Wright, one-time British ambassador to Iran, "Britain never considered Iran a place worth colonizing," thus indicating that "Persia had no intrinsic value" for Britain. It was only to be denied to the Russians, in order to protect India.[10] Not only did Britain do nothing to help Iran's development, in some cases it actively stood in the way.[11]

Successive territorial losses, growing foreign penetration, and constant humiliation were deeply resented by the Iranians, at times leading to mass resistance.[12] Their experience of domination and exploitation by foreigners has deeply affected their national consciousness, shaping attitudes on such issues as foreign investment and borrowing. Reza Shah Pahlavi made much of the fact that he built the Trans-Iranian railway without any foreign borrowing. Despite its massive economic problems, the Islamic regime prides itself in having eliminated Iran's foreign debt, and it has refused to borrow.[13]

This experience has historically nurtured a strong desire for independence and has often led to unrealistic and emotional policies.[14] Notable in recent years was Dr. Mohammad Mossadegh's nationalization of Iran's oil (1951) and his inflexible approach regarding a settlement with Britain. In similar fashion, despite horrendous devastation and with no reasonable prospect of victory, Iran refused to accept a negotiated peace with Iraq until July 1988.

Events during the last fifty years, such as the Russian occupation of Azerbaijan (1941–46), the establishment of a Russian-dominated communist government there and in Iranian Kurdistan (1945), and the coup d'etat of 1953, assisted by the U.S. and Great Britain, that overthrew Mossadegh's nationalist government, have intensified these national tendencies. The Iranians have thus developed a polarized vision of the world, divided between the dominant and the dominated nations and a deep suspicion of great power intentions. Thus, although most Iranians recognize the need to deal with the great powers, they prefer a low level of involvement.

Paradoxically, Iran's long history of foreign influence has led to a widespread belief that nothing has been, or can be, done in the country without foreign intervention. This belief was weakened after the revolution and particularly after Iran, single-handedly, expelled the invading Iraqis. But with massive foreign support for Iraq and the U.S. naval intervention in the Persian Gulf which led to Iran's defeat, the belief has reemerged.

Suspicion has naturally been greatest toward those powers with the longest and most extensive involvement in Iran, and, during the last fifty years, the gradual reduction of foreign influence—or at least of its most obvious signs—has not eliminated these suspicions. Rather, the belief is that change extends only to the great powers' instruments of influence, not to their ultimate motives. The famous twentieth century Iranian author, Jalal Al-Ahmad, expressed this view graphically: "At the beginning, the Western man was Sahib and his wife Memsahib, but today he is a counselor and adviser or representative of UNESCO. And although he no longer is wearing his colonial hat, his mission is the same."[15]

From the Iranian perspective, in recent years cultural domination has been added to political and economic domination and has become the root cause of Iran's dependent status in relation to the great powers. According to Al-Ahmad, this cultural dependence has sapped the capacity of the Eastern man for independent thinking, creating, or inventing, and turned him into a mere consumer of the products and ideas of Western man, thus establishing a dependent pattern of a relationship between the Western and the Eastern man.[16]

Al-Ahmad's views are widely shared in Iran and among Third World intellectuals, who believe that cultural autonomy is essential for economic and technological self-sufficiency.[17] There is no agreement, however, on which part of a nation's cultural patrimony should be preserved and on what can constitute a reasonable degree of foreign involvement.

In Iran's case, there is not even agreement on the character of its national culture. The present government emphasizes Islam as the core of this culture, whereas others, including the previous government, stressed the pre-Islamic elements. Most Iranians, however, are influenced by both elements and favor a balanced mixing of their Iranian and Islamic heritages. Nevertheless, the Islamic government has justified its Islamic cultural revolution in terms of regaining a sense of cultural autonomy essential for greater economic, technological, and political independence, although so far without success.

The humiliating period of Iran's decline has left the strongest imprint on its national ethos. But memories of a glorious past—real or imagined—have also remained strong. This has made it difficult for Iran to come to terms with its decline and the state of dependency that has followed. It has led it to believe in its legitimate right to be an important political and cultural force in the Middle East and the Third World, thus imbuing its foreign policy with an inherent activism that only appears when circumstances permit. In addition to its desire to break out of ethnic and cultural isolation, Iran's activism has essentially reflected this basic national trait. Its need to be recognized—a trait common to all nations—is similar to what the French call their "besoin de rayonnement."

The interaction of this dimension of Iran's historical legacy with its more recent experience of decline has created contradictory tendencies in its external behavior. At one and the same time, Iran wants to be neutral and disengaged from great power competition and to be an influential regional and international actor, an impulse which inevitably embroils it in such rivalries.

Nationalism and Islam

How a nation defines itself in relation to other national entities affects the character of its external behavior and the nature of its international relations. The most common criterion used to define a nation is that of ethnic, linguistic, or religious affinity. Depending on the relative importance of these elements in a country's national makeup, it generally gravitates toward other countries with which it shares the same religion or the same ethnic and linguistic characteristics, although such affinities have never been a guarantee against conflict.

Nationalism and religion often affect a nation's behavior by influencing its political ideology. Islam's receptivity to politicization and ideologization has made it a particularly potent ideological force during the last fifteen years, symbolized by Iran's revolution and the Islamic revivalist movement.[18] Meanwhile, during the last century and a half, nationalism has also developed into a political ideology.

The relative influence of religion and nationalism on a nation's external behavior is highly dependent on the character of society. A secular state is more influenced by nationalism, whereas religion plays a greater role in more religiously-oriented countries. In some cases, such as Israel and Pakistan, it constitutes the core of the state's identity. In others, nationalism and religion clash, as in the Muslim world since the introduction of modern nationalism in the last century.

Iran is a country faced with a basic tension between the nationalist and religious poles of its culture. The Pahlavi reign saw the triumph of nationalism over religion as the main instrument for legitimating the state's power and for rationalizing its policies. In the present regime, religion has taken its revenge. Historically, extreme shifts in either direction have been directly linked to competition for the gaining, retention, or rewinning of political power and have not appealed to the majority of the people. Consequently, policies based on either purely nationalist or purely religious premises have triggered popular reaction. This was the case during the Shah's rule, and it is still true now.

In reality, religion and nationalism have always interacted in Iran and have shaped its national identity and character and, to varying degrees, its international behavior.

The Nature of Iranian Nationalism

In defining the nature of Iranian nationalism, two elements are particularly important. One is nationalism as a political ideology, both in its liberal democratic and in its totalitarian versions—the latter manifested in Nazi Germany, Fascist

Italy, and some Third World countries. The other aspect of nationalism is a much less well-defined notion of a common loyalty—shared by a group of people with ethnic, linguistic, and religious affinities, and often with a common historical and cultural experience—to a political entity within a more or less well-defined territory. Nationalism in this sense is more relevant to Iran's case.

Some of Iran's characteristics strengthen its people's sense of nationalism, whereas others weaken it. Ethnic and linguistic affinities contribute to the Iranians' sense of nationhood—65 percent of them consider themselves to be Persian. By contrast, about 35 percent of Iran's population is composed of other ethnic groups—mostly Turkic, plus some Arab, Kurdish, and Baluch, although the latter two groups, especially the Indo-European Kurds, are related to the Persians.

Language also makes for national unity in Iran, where most people speak Farsi.[19] Even in the case of those Iranians whose main language is not Farsi, over the centuries it has become the principal medium of literary expression and thus part of their cultural heritage. Yet Iran's ethnic and linguistic diversity undermines its national unity and thus the influence of nationalism. In some cases, the corrosive impact of this diversity is mitigated by religious affinity. Given their Shi'a character, Iran's Turkic Azerbaijanis feel much closer to other Shi'a Iranians than to the Sunni Turkic groups. Religious factors can also be divisive. With their Sunni character, and despite ethnic and linguistic ties, Iran's Kurds and Baluch feel somewhat alienated from the Shi'a Persians.

A highly significant element of Iran's national unity is the common cultural heritage and shared memories of the past. This is particularly important because of the many foreign elements that have penetrated and ruled Iran. Yet even Iran's foreign conquerors—such as the Turkic Safavid, Afshar, and Qajar dynasties—have made its historical and cultural heritage their own, with major practical implications. Iran's historical borders, as they stood at the time of the Arab invasion in the seventh century A.D., have exercised a powerful fascination for later rulers, many of whom have aspired to restore them.

In recent times, the maintenance of Iran's territorial integrity has become the key test of the rulers' legitimacy. Many Iranians hold the Qajar kings in low esteem partly because, under their stewardship, Iran suffered massive territorial losses. Likewise, following Iraq's occupation of Khusistan in 1980–81, the Ayatollah Khomeini reportedly was worried lest his regime should become the first in a century to lose Iranian territory.

Iranian Nationalism and Islam: Conflict or Convergence?

Even the advent of Islam, with its emphasis on the brotherhood of all Muslims and its admonition against racial pride, has not eliminated the influence of the Iranian element in Iran's national identity. Over the centuries, the Iranians have fused Islam with their pre-Islamic heritage and, by embracing Shi'ism, they have carved out a special place for themselves among the Muslims.[20]

The Iranians have always been conscious of their vast contribution to the development of Islamic culture. Even the present regime, despite its anti-nationalist feelings, at times exhibits ethnic pride and refers to Iran's role in the development of Islamic civilization. Consequently, many Iranians and foreign students of Iran have come to believe in the mutual dependency of Iranian nationalism and Shi'a Islam. In any event, after Iran's official adoption of Shi'ism as a state religion, in Shi'a eyes Iran's territorial confines also became the true realm of Islam. Thus a great deal of convergence between Shi'ism and Iranian nationalism became a reality.

The tension between Islam and Iranian nationalism is a fairly recent phenomenon that began in the late nineteenth century and reached its peak during the Pahlavi rule. This tension resulted from Iran's contact with the West, ensuing foreign penetration, and the onset of a steady period of decline, which generated a deep soul-searching among Iranians in order to discover the roots of their decline. Some came to see Islam and the contamination of Iran's culture by Arab and Turkic elements as the principal culprits.[21] Thus they prescribed secularization, cultural purification, and a re-Iranization as remedies. Others saw Iran's decline as the result of disregard for Islamic teachings and recommended a faithful application of Islamic rules as the cure.[22]

At the time, nationalism was the rising ideology in the world, modernization was Iran's main preoccupation, and the Islamic clergy were against reforms. Thus, at first, secularists prevailed. Yet early nationalist efforts to reform Iranian society were limited. They neither altered its Islamic character nor did they challenge the Muslim clerics' privileged position. Moreover, during this period, both nationalist and religious forces faced the threat of foreign penetration and often cooperated to oppose it.

In the Pahlavi period, Iranian nationalism acquired a highly secular and anti-Islamic character, and the exaltation of pre-Islamic virtues and culture reached unreasonable levels. Reza Shah secularized Iran's educational and judicial systems, resurrected old Zoroastrian symbols, and placed emphasis on the celebration of pre-Islamic festivities. These policies challenged Iran's Islamic character and thus the privileged position of its religious leaders.

Feeling insecure domestically, his son first tried to reach a *modus vivendi* with the religious leaders who, concerned about the communist threat, were willing to cooperate.[23] But once he felt strong, the Shah exceeded his father in undermining the role of Islam and the influence of religious leaders. The result was a systematic counteroffensive by religious figures and religiously minded lay intellectuals against nationalism—represented as anathema to Islam—and against Iran's pre-Islamic past.

Thus, open conflict emerged between Islam and Iranian nationalism. Contributing to it was the fact that, under the Pahlavis, Iranian nationalism was transformed from a sense of loyalty to an entity called Iran—with certain ethnic and religious characteristics and a common historical and cultural heritage—into a cult of the monarchy, with the person of the monarch as the repository of highest virtue. In fact, in the Pahlavi slogan of *"Khoda, Shah, Mihan"* (God, King, Country), king takes precedence over country.

This cult of monarchy directly clashed with the Shi'a theory of political legitimacy. Since the time of the Safavids (1499–1722), when Shi'ism became Iran's state religion and a large clerical establishment developed, some tension between the government and the clergy had always existed. But in view of the Safavids' almost fanatical commitment to Shi'ism and the clergy's dependence on the king for protection against external Sunni enemies (the Ottoman Empire), a delicately balanced entente developed between the government and the clergy. In essence, the king and the government drew their legitimacy from their roles as protectors of the faith and appliers of Islamic law. By the mid-nineteenth century, when some timid reforms started in Iran, cracks appeared in the entente between religion and government. But it was during the last decade of Pahlavi rule that relations reached the breaking point and thus deepened the dichotomy between nationalisn and Islam.[24]

The attitude toward Iranian nationalism on the part of Iran's Islamic leaders, especially the Ayatollah Khomeini, should be viewed within this historical context. Khomeini opposed nationalism that is based on the superiority of a particular race, the cult of monarchy, the excessive glorification of the country's pre-Islamic past, and the dilution of Iran's Islamic character. In his view, if nationalism means "To love one's fatherland and its people and to protect its frontiers," then it is acceptable. Thus Khomeini was not against nationalism in the sense of "patriotism," but rather as a political theory based on the parochial interests of a race or state, which is thus a threat to Islamic universalism.[25]

In fact, however, the Islamic forces opposed nationalism primarily because it was used to legitimate and expand the power and control of the state at their expense. By imitation, since the revolution, Iran's leaders have used Islam to legitimate and expand their power at the expense of other forces in the country. Nevertheless, although at different times various parts of the Iranian population have been attracted either to the nationalist or to the Islamic poles, the majority of Iranians have felt loyal both to Iran and to Shi'a Islam.

The relative ascendancy of the nationalist or Islamic poles of Iran's national culture has had consequences for its external behavior, although even at those times both forces exerted some influence. Under the Pahlavis, nationalism and the pursuit of Iran's national interest guided its foreign policy. This, however, led to some policies which offended the more Islamically-oriented Iranians. The Islamic regime's behavior has been much more influenced by certain Islamic aspirations, at times at great national cost. This attitude, too, has generated criticism and dissatisfaction. Indeed, any excess in one direction is likely to be unpopular. A more reasonable approach would be one which recognizes the dual Islamic-nationalist character of Iran's identity. Because of this character Iranians support cooperation with Muslim countries and Muslim causes, but not at the cost of either undermining Iran's national interest or its unique Iranian cultural character. Despite the predominance of Islam, the imperatives of the survival of the nation and regime, plus the strength of nationalism, have in the last several years led to a reemergence of cultural and political Iranianism. However, the nationalist-Islamic dichotomy has not yet been resolved in Iran. And until and unless this is done, some confusion and contradiction will remain in the Iranians' view of themselves and their role and place in the world and thus in their external behavior.

The Role of Ideology

Until the emergence of modern ideologies and the post-World War II era, *raison d'etat*, rather than transcendental ideals, tended to determine the behavior of states.[26] The keys to this concept were the maintenance of a state's frontiers, territorial expansion, economic and commercial gain, and the enhancement of prestige—plus the creation or maintenance of a balance of regional and global power that best secured these objectives. Thus, alliances between states were formed and broken as they helped or hindered this pursuit. The concept of *raison d'etat* was sufficient justification and a state did not need to resort to higher values to rationalize its acts, although it occasionally did so. European powers justified their colonial expansion in terms of *mission civilisatrice* or the "white man's burden." But there was no compelling need to do so.

The judgment that, until World War II, ideology had a limited role in determining state behavior is based on defining ideology as a system of comprehensive, well-structured secular values and rules for the organization of a nation's social, political, and economic life and its external behavior. But if ideology is defined as a loosely structured system of values, including spiritual values, then its influence on state behavior extends further back in history. In this sense, some religions that have comprehensive and well-structured rules for societal organization and behavior— such as Islam—could be characterized as ideology. Thus, it is possible to compare religiously motivated state behavior to ideologically determined acts. Good examples are the Crusades and the Hundred Years' War: ideological wars in the modern sense. In Iran's case, during the Safavid period, Shi'a Islam also served as state ideology, affecting its external behavior. The Iranian-Ottoman conflict from the sixteenth through the nineteenth centuries was partly produced by their religious differences.

These limited examples notwithstanding, the term ideology generally refers to the modern, highly structured social, economic, and political theories such as socialism, Fascism, and liberal democracy. During the last several decades and especially after World War II, these ideologies have had a great impact in shaping the direction of Third World countries' development and in determining their external behavior. After gaining independence, most have been primarily concerned with issues of political and economic development. Until recently, many Third World elites have viewed their indigenous, traditional patterns of social, economic and political organization as hindrances to rapid modernization, and they have searched for new models.

With the success of anti-colonial movements after World War II, the traditional pattern of great power rivalry was partly transformed into a competition for the "hearts and minds" of Third World populations. Many of these countries came under tremendous outside pressures—through extensive propaganda, intimidation, or co-optation—to choose one of the ideological camps, identified either with the West or the East, and to adopt the respective economic and political systems.

In fact, these ideas had affected the course of events in the Third World and its intellectual development at a much earlier time. In Iran, some leaders of the constitutionalist movement (1905–06) were deeply affected by the liberal nationalist ideas of nineteenth century Europe.[27] In view of Iran's proximity to Russia and the extensive interaction between northern Iran and southern Russia, the impact of socialist ideology was felt in Iran even before its triumph in Russia. The so-called "jangali" movement of Mirza Kuchek Khan and the creation of a socialist republic in the Iranian province of Gilan in 1918 were largely due to such influences.[28]

Yet in view of the emergence of Islam as an alternative to foreign ideologies in Iran and elsewhere, it is clear that Third World nations have not been passive recipients of this foreign influence. Instead, there has been a fair degree of interaction between modern ideologies and these countries' indigenous value systems and traditional modes of living. This interaction has essentially taken two forms: opposition and efforts to synthesize foreign ideologies with the existing value systems. In the Middle East during the nineteenth and twentieth centuries, Islamic forces strongly opposed the growing influence of foreign ideologies. In Iran, the Western-style, liberal-nationalists' call for a "Hokoumat-e-Mashruteh" (constitutional government) was answered by the Islamic forces' demand for a "Hokoumat-e-Mashrueh" (government by Islamic law).

In other instances, foreign ideologies have acquired a local flavor. In the Arab world, Western ideas of nationalism and socialism were translated into Nasserism and Ba'athism. The Chinese, after the 1949 revolution, developed their own version of Marxism-Leninism. At the international level, the Non-Aligned Movement was the Third World's answer to the two major ideological camps. Nevertheless, to varying degrees, most Third World nations were influenced by one or the other of these camps, a fact that also affected the character of their foreign policies.

In view of the generally authoritarian nature of most Third World governments and the low level of popular political participation, their ideological tendencies have been largely determined by the preferences of ruling elites. These tendencies have not adequately reflected broader intellectual trends or popular preferences. Indeed, a persistent feature of the Third World political scene has been sharp discrepancies between elite and popular ideological preferences and, as a result, differences regarding the direction of each country's foreign policy.

In terms of the specific functions that ideology performs in a state's political life, there is not much difference between Third World and other countries. Ideology serves to legitimate state power and to rationalize its behavior, and it provides a framework for action, both domestically and internationally. It shapes states' perceptions of the outside world, of their place within it, and the external realities upon which they have to act.

The extent to which ideology, as compared to other factors, determines a state's behavior, has been long debated. Hans J. Morgenthau believed that all politics, including international politics, is about power, and thus the main determinant of state behavior is a quest for power. Ideologies serve as disguises. This is necessitated because, without an ideological cover, the state would be in an unfavorable position in regard to other states in a struggle for power. Domestically, in order to rally its people behind its foreign policy, a state must appeal to principles other than the quest for power. In fact, this is the only way a nation can generate popular enthusiasm and gain its people's willingness to sacrifice, without which "no foreign policy can pass the ultimate test of strength."[29]

Other scholars have argued that, in certain instances, states act more out of ideological motives than the mere pursuit of power. They point out that, even if one accepts that the search for power is the principal impulse for state behavior, how a state acquires and uses power is also critical. At this level, ideology becomes particularly relevant because, as Zbigniew Brzezinski has put it, ideology is essentially an "action program."[30] As such, it determines the way states seek to acquire power, and it partly determines their perceptions of national interest.

Empirical evidence shows that both these views—power and ideology—have merit. But it is also clear that, in reality, the dichotomy between ideology and the quest for power is more apparent than real. A state's ideological goals and its search for power are often mutually reinforcing, partly because modern ideologies are flexible and make rationalizations easy for skilled ideologists.

Yet, at times, conflict does arise between the demands of ideological purity and the imperatives of power. In such circumstances, power generally prevails because, as F. S. Northedge remarked, a "state must survive and somehow prosper . . . (and) in the final resort the nation's will to survive is irresistible."[31]

Recent Iranian behavior has demonstrated the multi-dimensional functions of ideology as a legitimating and rationalizing element and as a factor shaping world view and thus the state's external behavior. During the Pahlavi rule, the idea of Iranian nationalism as conceived by the king and the ruling elite served as state ideology. The advancement of Iran's national interests, the vindication of its historic rights, and the enhancement of its prestige were used to rationalize the government's behavior and to harness popular support.

During this period, the other ideological influence on Iran's foreign policy was a strong anti-communism. Thus fighting the Russian-communist threat was long their principal domestic and foreign policy goal. Reza Shah's flirtation with Germany, his son's alliance with the United States, and many aspects of Iran's regional policies stemmed in major part from this preoccupation.[32]

Since the Islamic revolution, the role of ideology in determining Iran's foreign policy has increased. But when the blind pursuit of ideology has threatened national and regime survival, in response to an irresistible will to survive, the government has compromised. Nevertheless, this process of adjustment has been quite slow. The often conflicting demands of national interest and the pursuit of ideological aspirations have created dilemmas for Iran and have led to some contradiction in its external relations. But this is not a novel phenomenon in international relations, and all states at some point have faced tensions and difficult choices in reconciling their ideological and state interests.

Domestic Context: Political System and Public Attitude

If, as Northedge has written, foreign policy is a dialogue between the inside and the outside, then domestic considerations significantly affect a state's external behavior.[33] An important aspect of this interplay of internal and external factors is the way that foreign policy decisions affect public attitudes toward political leaders. Foreign policy choices frequently involve the diversion of economic resources from domestic programs to higher levels of defense spending, thus causing a conflict between the state's external goals and its citizens' economic well-being—a conflict that is especially acute in countries with limited resources. A state's foreign policy involves vital issues of war and peace, potentially requiring the sacrifice of lives.

It is therefore impossible for a state to make foreign policy without bearing in mind the impact on public attitudes. In states with participatory political systems and regular elections, the linkage between foreign policy and the public response is clear and direct. But even in authoritarian systems, such a linkage exists. Often, when foreign policy is totally at variance with public attitudes or is perceived by the citizens as undermining their well-being, ultimately it exacts political costs from the leaders.

In Iran, some of the Shah's unpopular foreign policy choices exacerbated his other problems. The high level of Iran's military expenditures during the late 1960s and the 1970s, which was linked to its foreign policy objectives, was also controversial.[34] Yet despite his authoritarian tendencies, the Shah tried to respond to public preferences by striking a more independent posture on foreign policy. Likewise, in July 1988 the Islamic regime belatedly accepted U.N. Security Council Resolution 598—calling for an immediate cease-fire and the start of negotiations—partly in response to popular opposition to the war and out of fear of the erosion of its base of support.

Another aspect of linkage in Third World states between domestic setting and foreign policy has been the degree of a government's stability and the strength of its base of support. Regimes that lack adequate popular support or face foreign-inspired subversion have often tried to improve their domestic position through foreign policy choices. In Iran during the 1950s, the Shah chose alliance with the United States partly to protect his rule against the Moscow-supported leftist opposition.[35] During the 1960s and 1970s, he improved Iran's ties with the Soviet Union partly to neutralize the leftist opposition by reducing Moscow's support.[36] The same consideration was responsible for his policy of improving ties with radical Arabs.[37]

In a small state like Iran with a social and political system that is highly permeated by external forces, the other side of the coin also applies—namely, the potential impact of a government's foreign policy decisions on the attitudes of competing foreign influences toward it. Thus, some of the Shah's policy choices derived from his concern that external powers would otherwise replace him with a more accommodating figure.

The character of the decision-making apparatus is also very important. In a centralized system, the characteristics and even personal idiosyncrasies of one or a few individuals can be decisive in shaping behavior. This was certainly the case in Iran under the rule of the Pahlavis. In a decentralized system, institutional and personal rivalries and disagreements play a larger role. This case has prevailed in Iran since the revolution, where the lack of centralized decision making, combined with intra-regime differences, has affected the substance and style of its diplomacy.

Resource Constraints

A country's economic, military, and technological resource bases also affect its foreign policy choices. A relatively self-sufficient country has a greater capacity to conduct an independent foreign policy than one dependent on outside sources.

For the last century and a half, Iran has been dependent on foreign military and economic assistance. Early in the nineteenth century, Iran responded positively to Napoleonic France's suggestions for an alliance in order to secure French military assistance.[38] Reza Shah Pahlavi befriended Germany and his son turned to the United States in part to gain assistance for Iran's economic development. During the mid-1960s and 1970s, Iran's growing independence in foreign policy reflected its improved economic and military position.

The same factors have helped shape the Islamic regime's behavior although, rhetorically, it has emphasized economic and technological self-reliance. Yet, given Iran's limitations, it has had to adjust its behavior in order to maintain access to needed material and technological resources. Its need to gain access to capital and technology for its post-war reconstruction will continue to affect its policy choices, although by no means determining them.

External Environment: The Impact of Systemic Factors

In the final analysis, foreign policy is about the management of a state's relations with the outside world in such a way as to maximize gains and minimize losses. In addition to the state's inherent and underlying characteristics, the nature of the external environment—the regional and international systems—within which it operates greatly affects its policy choices. This is so because much of a state's foreign policy consists of responses to the actions of other states that are also trying to maximize gains and to minimize losses.

The choices of small countries are particularly constrained by systemic factors. Also, because of their geostrategic location or other characteristics, some states are more susceptible to systemic changes. A less powerful country that becomes a focus of great power interest or rivalry is even more vulnerable, especially to changes pertaining to the character of relations among principal powers.

During the last two hundred years, Iran's policy choices and at times its national fate have been deeply affected by systemic factors on both the regional and the global level. Thus the rigid bi-polarity of the post-war years largely dictated Iran's alliance policy, although not the character of its allies. Later, the erosion of that bi-polarity and greater superpower accommodation in the late 1960s and 1970s allowed Iran to follow a more independent foreign policy. Yet at the same time, the basically competitive nature of superpower relations shielded Iran from the threat of their collusion, at its expense.

The Islamic regime has benefited from these systemic factors, which have enabled it to follow a more independent foreign policy than was true of its predecessor. Yet the changes in Soviet foreign policy since 1985 under the leadership of Mikhail Gorbachev, the onset of a new era of *détente* in superpower relations, and the opening of possibilities for superpower cooperation on regional issues have made Iran's position more difficult and reduced its ability to manipulate superpower competition. Because of these changes, on occasions when Iran has tried to use these tactics, it has not succeeded, as was the case during the Persian Gulf crisis of 1987–88 when Iran failed to dissuade the United States from reflagging Kuwaiti tankers simply by moving closer to the Soviet Union.

Systemic factors at the regional level and their interaction with global factors also affect a state's policy choices. In Iran's case, the fact that all the areas lying to its north are under Soviet rule thus far has excluded the possibility of affecting conditions on its northern flanks. Iran can exert only a limited influence on its eastern flank because it borders on the Indian subcontinent and is faced with superior Indian power.

During the time of British rule in the Persian Gulf, Iran could not pursue an independent policy. Even after the British withdrawal, the significance of the region to the West and thus its intense interest in the region meant that Iran's policy choices were limited by Western interests and preferences. Thus Iran was able to exert more influence in the Persian Gulf during the 1970s, because this suited Western goals. But whenever these goals collided, as in Bahrain, Iran had to give in.

In general, in those regional subsystems of great interest to principal actors within the global system, purely regional factors are of less importance than larger issues in affecting both the regional balance of power and the political options of regional states. In the Persian Gulf, Iran is the largest and potentially most powerful state in regional terms, but because of the introduction of extra-regional forces, its ability to pursue independent policies is limited. This point was graphically illustrated by the course of developments in the Persian Gulf during 1987–88, with the introduction of U.S. naval power into the region, which drastically altered the balance of power and prevented Iran from pursuing its regional goals. Thus even the Islamic regime, with its propensity to pursue unrealistic goals, had to adjust its behavior to the new realities.

In addition to the presence of global powers, which affects regional settings, during the last several decades the process of increasing linkage and interaction among different regional subsystems and among different zones of regional systems has affected the policy choices of regional states, at times limiting these choices and at times offering new opportunities. With regard to the Middle East, greater linkages between the Persian Gulf, the Arab Middle East, and to some extent the Indian subcontinent have complicated Iran's political calculations and choices by directly introducing extra-regional countries, such as Egypt and Pakistan, into the Persian Gulf power equation. Meanwhile, Iran has become a factor in the political calculations of these states.

This discussion of some of the principal factors that affect state behavior, in general, and some that have shaped Iran's behavior has provided the basic conceptual framework for what follows. This study will begin with a brief survey of the evolution of Iran's diplomatic strategies under the influence of the factors discussed in this chapter and an account of the salient characteristics of the Shah's foreign policy. Together, these will provide a benchmark for assessing the levels of continuity and change in Iran's foreign policy during the last decade. This discussion will be complemented by an explanation of Iran's Islamic ideology and world view and of their interaction with other enduring determinants of Iran's foreign policy. Thus there will emerge the necessary framework for analyzing and assessing specific aspects of the Islamic regime's involvement with the outside world.

2. The Evolution of Iran's Diplomacy

Iran's principal diplomatic strategies and the underlying patterns of its interaction with the outside world were developed over many years in response to external challenges. They reflected its domestic conditions and the range of options available to it in any particular era. At times, a single strategy would determine the principal directions of Iran's foreign policy, whereas at other times several different strategies would be applied simultaneously.

Since Iran's reemergence as a unified state at the end of the fifteenth century, two themes have dominated its foreign relations: the restoration and maintenance of its territorial integrity and the quest for independence. For the first three centuries, Iran was mainly preoccupied with restoring its territorial integrity and maintaining it against direct onslaughts. In the last 180 years, Iran has also become preoccupied with indirect threats to its independence. From these twin concerns of integrity and independence developed all other political themes, such as modernization and military buildup.

This interplay has continued into the modern age. Many of the Pahlavis' foreign and domestic policies, can only be understood in terms of their personal experience with assaults on Iranian independence and integrity. Reza Shah gained prominence during the chaotic years of World War I, when a militarily weak Iran became, despite its neutrality, a battleground for contending forces. His son was traumatized by the Allied occupation in 1941–45 and the collapse of the Iranian military—a feeling most Iranians also shared. It was not surprising, therefore, that at first the Pahlavis' policy of military buildup enjoyed popular support. It was only after three decades of calm and security—and after the military came to be seen more as an instrument of domestic repression than of defense against foreign enemies—that popular attitudes began to change. Only then did a new generation of Iranians, who did not remember the chaos of World War I, the Allied occupation, or the Azerbaijan crisis of 1946, begin opposing the Shah's emphasis on military modernization.[1]

Yet when Iraq invaded on September 22, 1980, Iran again placed its top priority on maintaining its territorial integrity. Overnight, popular belief in the need for a strong defense force was rekindled.[2]

The Evolution of Strategy

Just as Iran's preoccupation with integrity and then with independence developed over the years, so too did strategies to achieve these goals. For many years, Iran enjoyed relative military and technological parity with its adversaries. Thus it was able to rely on its own military and economic resources. Occasionally, it did form alliances and played rival powers off against one another. But in the period between its reunification and the outbreak of the first round of Russo-Iranian wars in 1804, these options were largely ruled out.[3] In particular, the international political system was centered on Europe, and, despite Dutch and Portuguese naval forays into the Persian Gulf, European rivalries did not extend to Iran's immediate surroundings, thereby offering it few opportunities for diplomatic maneuver. What limited European interest there was in Iran derived from rivalry with the Ottomans, focused on finding ways to use Ottoman-Iranian disputes to divert the Sublime Porte's energies from Europe.

By the end of the eighteenth century, Iran was clearly losing power and influence relative to its adversaries. In particular, Europe entered a new age of industrial and military prowess, while the Iranian decline deepened. As part of the same development, European imperial expansion accelerated, as Napoleon occupied Egypt, Britain took on the mantle of empire in India, and Russia undertook an imperial thrust. With this new assertiveness toward the outside world, European imperial rivalries extended to Iran's vicinity, drew it to the attention of leading states, and made it a factor in their calculations of relative power, presence, and purpose. The combined effect of this dramatic shift in power and Iran's gradual integration into that era's global political system faced it with the greatest security challenge since it reemerged as a sovereign state—a challenge that continues today—namely, the same problem of guarding its territorial integrity and independence in the face of superior adversaries.

The Concept of Equilibrium

With the disparities in the rate at which different states were developing economically and accumulating power, by the mid-nineteenth century Iran no longer had the option of effective military resistance to encroaching foreign powers. This had already been dramatized by the outcome of the Russo-Iranian wars (1804–1828) and by Britain's naval supremacy in the Persian Gulf and presence in India.[4]

It became clear to successive Iranian leaders that salvation would depend on the quality of Iran's diplomacy and the adoption of specific strategies to make it effective. Among the first to recognize this need and to respond to it was Mirza Taghi Khan Amir Kabir.[5] He created a strategy of "positive equilibrium" the principal tenet of which was that offering equal privileges to rival powers could shield Iran from the most damaging effects of their competition, such as the preemptive capture of Iranian territory or the carving out of exclusive zones of influence. Amir Kabir and other worthy Iranian leaders understood that this strategy was imperfect, a lesser evil. But they hoped to maintain a state of equilibrium at the lowest possible level of concessions, and they tried to strengthen Iran's place and position in order to make the granting of such concessions unnecessary.[6] Unfortunately for Iran, this strategy was distorted by Amir Kabir's removal from office, the incompetence of most Iranian leaders, and Iran's military and economic weakness. Even though the application of positive equilibrium might have spared Iran an even worse fate, it was effectively divided into Russian and British spheres of influence, thus giving Amir Kabir's strategy a poor reputation in Iranian political culture.

During the 1930s and 1940s, a modified version of this concept appeared in the Iranian left. It argued that Iran should recognize a sphere of security influence for the Soviet Union because of its proximity to Iran, and, given British control of Iran's southern oilfields, similar privileges should be granted to the Soviets in the north. Aspects of the Shah's foreign policy also reflected the influence of this concept, when in the 1960s he tried to befriend the Soviet Union by giving it significant economic stakes in Iran and when he used the same tactic in the 1970s to try co-opting European powers.

A refinement of the concept of equilibrium and of the balancing of contending powers reappeared in the late 1940s in the form of Dr. Mohammad Mossadegh's strategy of "negative equilibrium." In this version of the basic method of diplomatic maneuver, the strategy was to balance the influence of two contending powers by denying both of them excessive privileges or—by denying privileges to all— effectively refusing to favor one side over the other. Not surprisingly, this concept enjoyed wide popular support and easily eclipsed the more demeaning positive equilibrium. Mossadegh even saw Iran's developing a neutral position, on the model of Switzerland.[7] Yet this was not to be. Only countries with sufficient military and economic strength can successfully practice such a strategy. Iran did not meet the test and thus failed in its effort to practice negative equilibrium.

Developments in the outside world contributed to this failure. Most important was the emerging bipolarity of the international system, the all-or-nothing nature of U.S.-Soviet competition, and the superpowers' pressure on small states to choose one of the two camps. Nevertheless, the basic principle behind "negative equilibrium" remained popular among small states, whose populations found nationalism and non-alignment to be most appealing. These competing developments— superpower pressure and popular resistance—were also evident in Iran. After the fall of Mossadegh, the newly restored Shah opted for alliance with the United States and developed a theory of his own, which he called "positive nationalism," as a response to what he believed had been the weaknesses of negative equilibrium or, as he characterized it, "negative self-destructive nationalism." In creating his new strategy, he was out of step with most Iranians.[8] But beneath the surface of the Shah's approach, it was clear that he, too, had been influenced by Mossadegh. The Shah's "independent national policy," introduced in the mid-1960s, was in fact a far less ambitious version of his rival's negative equilibrium strategy.

The Shah had better luck, however. Improvements in Iran's domestic economic conditions were coupled with systemic changes generated by the erosion of rigid bipolarity in global politics and the changing nature of superpower relations from a zero-sum competition to a limited peaceful accommodation. These developments were propitious for the practice of such an independent national policy. Thus seizing on these opportunities, the Shah maintained his alliance with the United States but also improved relations with the Soviet Union.

This trend toward greater independence continued in the 1970s, as both domestic and foreign developments made possible the pursuit of a relatively independent policy, leading one analyst to characterize Iran's policy in this period as *de facto* non-alignment.[9] This is an exaggeration, however. Because the Shah's independent policy did not challenge Iran's alliance with the United States, most Iranians remained highly skeptical about the "independent" nature of the "national policy." Indeed, despite the failure of negative equilibrium—failure represented by the Western powers' decisive intervention in Iran—for most Iranians, Mossadegh's strategy was the local version of non-alignment and, as such, remained synonymous with independence and the absence of foreign influence. Against this background, therefore, the Islamic regime's strategy of "neither East nor West—only Islam," takes on a historical cast and can be seen as a more activist variant of the negative equilibrium strategy.

The Third Power Strategy

During the time when it was developing and experimenting with the strategies of both positive and negative equilibrium, Iran also sometimes employed another diplomatic technique, known formally as "the third-power strategy." Its essence was to balance the presence of the two rival powers by invoking that of a significant third power, thereby gaining a source of military, political, and economic assistance.

The third-power strategy was first developed in the late nineteenth century, but it proved difficult to put into practice. By its very nature, it could only be successful if a third, and preferably distant, power became sufficiently interested in Iran to be prepared to play the role of balancer. Yet, according to the theory, the perceived or actual interest of this third power must not become so great that it would be drawn into deep competition with the two principal contenders. If that happened, Iran would likely gain no benefits. Try as it might, Iran was never capable of finding a third power that met all the relevant criteria. The United States, Iran's first choice to play this role, was not then interested in it.[10] Nor did any of the European powers that might have balanced Russia and Britain have much interest in Iran. During the 1930s, Germany became the favored third power, but it quickly became embroiled in competition for influence, both within Iran and elsewhere.

After World War II, the polarization of the international political system made the practice of the third-power strategy even more problematic for Iran. Despite his advocacy of negative equilibrium, Mossadegh also applied a variant of third-power strategy when, without much success, he tried to use the United States to balance Soviet and British influence and to enlist U.S. support in Iran's struggle against Britain over the nationalization of the oil industry. Aspects of the Shah's policy, too, reflected the influence of the third-power strategy. Because of the changing nature of the international system, as reflected in the emergence of new economic and political powers, he had a greater chance of success. Thus, in the 1970s the Shah used ties with China, Japan, and European countries to reduce Iran's dependence on the United States and to increase its security and economic options.

The Islamic regime has at times also pursued a variation of the third power strategy, using the same countries for similar purposes, with considerable effectiveness. China has served as a counterweight to the Soviet Union at a time of U.S.-Iranian estrangement, and Turkey has provided a bridge to the outside world, thus reducing Iran's economic dependence on the Soviets at a time when its southern ports were damaged or overburdened by the Iran-Iraq war.

Alliance with a Great Power

These strategies all had as their *leitmotiv* an effort to provide benefit for Iran without becoming dependent on other powers. From time to time, it also tried a classical approach to statecraft by forging alliances with different great powers. But Iran's historical experience with alliance politics has been negative. During the first round of the Russo-Iranian wars (1804–1813), it allied itself with France: France would help Iran militarily against Russia, and Iran would keep Russia occupied on its southern front and later would ease Napoleon's passage to India. But in July 1807, Napoleon and Tsar Alexander met at Tilsit and made peace. The Franco-Iranian alliance was ended and French military advisers were withdrawn, precipitating Iran's defeat by the Tsar's forces.[11]

Iran had a similar experience with Britain, which, in the early nineteenth century, sought an alliance in order to prevent Russia or any other European power from reaching India. But British policy was based on a faulty assessment of Iran's military potential and thus of its ability to act as a strong buffer for India. The assessment changed following Iran's dismal performance during the first round of Russo-Iranian wars. Britain abandoned the idea of using Iran as a buffer, began both to weaken it and to bring under direct control its outlying areas closest to India, and then applied the same strategy in the Persian Gulf. Britain's concerns over Iran's reliability as an effective buffer were justified, and a change in strategy made perfect sense in terms of its interests, but the consequences for Iran were devastating.

The result of the Iranian experience with the French and British was a mistrust of unequal alliances. Furthermore, forging a great power alliance is not an easy choice for a small country like Iran that has had a powerful neighbor like Russia in its different incarnations. The option of alliance with the neighbor is not appealing because of the overwhelming disparity of power, which could mean domination or absorption; alliance with a distant power—most recently the United States—is also risky. Not only do large disparities in power tend to produce a client relationship, but ties to the far-off state can fail to deter the neighboring rival and even prompt preemptive aggression. Meanwhile, the neighboring great power generally has a permanent interest in the small state, although this may fluctuate. Yet the interest of the distant great power is more subject to change. Thus if a small state's alliance policy is to be successful, it must hold some intrinsic economic or strategic value for the distant country.

Historically, the interest that distant great powers have taken in Iran has largely been negative—namely, to deny it to a rival rather than to value it for its intrinsic nature. Britain was interested in Iran as a buffer for India, and the United States found it to be a useful buffer against Soviet access to Arabian oilfields—in which the United States does have an intrinsic interest.[12] Iran's collective experience, therefore, is that distant powers have been quite ready, sometimes even eager, to make a deal with the neighboring great power (Russia) at Iran's expense.

As a result, alliance with a great power has never held much attraction for Iran.[13] Yet changes in the world produced by World War II, the growing Soviet threat to Iran, and the dynamics of domestic competition for political power led Iran to look for an alliance relationship with the current distant power, namely the United States. This essay in pragmatism did not sit well with most Iranians, however, in view of past disappointments. Thus in the following decades, as the intensity of the Soviet threat and the Cold War subsided, Iran tried to adopt a more independent policy and to broaden its political options. And the Islamic regime has gone even further and denounced the alliance strategy.

Given a choice, Iran has always tried to avoid a formal alliance or even too close a relationship with any of the great powers. Yet if its security and vital interests are seriously threatened by one of them, it might have no choice but to seek an alliance with another. An intense domestic competition for power could also lead one or another political faction to seek an alliance relationship as a means of winning at home. This consideration was certainly evident in the Shah's alliance with the United States in the 1950s, and it may reappear following the Ayatollah Khomeini's death.

Such an option may not always be open to Iran, however. That would especially be the case if the nature of U.S.-Soviet relations changed from competitive to cooperative regarding Iran, or at least to mutual disengagement. If that were to happen, Washington and Moscow could reach agreements at Iran's expense, ignore it, or use it for their own purposes.

Regional Dimensions of Iran's Foreign Policy

For the first three centuries after it again become a unified state and nation, Iran's regional policy was limited to meeting the competitive challenge of the Ottoman Empire. Then, for the next two centuries, the emergence of the British imperial presence in the Indian subcontinent and the Persian Gulf, plus Russia's southward expansion, stifled the kind of independent interaction between Iran and its surroundings—both immediate and more distant—that for many previous centuries had been open to it. It was only in the 1920s and the 1930s that Iran was able again to develop truly regional dimensions of its foreign policy.

Well into the 1950s, this new Iranian regional policy was focused on immediate neighbors and sought to resolve border disputes and delineate borders with Turkey, Afghanistan, and Iraq—though with mixed success.[14] The most important positive development stemmed from a sense of common vulnerability to Soviet pressures that provided the impetus for Iran, Turkey, and Afghanistan to resolve or at least to contain their differences.[15]

Then in the 1950s, changes taking place beyond Iran's borders caused regional dimensions of Iran's foreign policy to become more important and to take on added complexity. The process of decolonization in the Middle East led to the emergence of new, independent states with interests and policies of their own to pursue. East-West conflict permeated the region as the superpowers competed both for influence and for allies. Like other states in the region, Iran did not remain immune to the impact of these changes. Most important, it joined Turkey, Pakistan, and Iraq in the Baghdad Pact—which, after Iraq's withdrawal following its revolution in 1958, was renamed the Central Treaty Organization (CENTO)—Iran at least indirectly became embroiled in intra-Arab politics, an involvement which did not end with the dissolution of CENTO.

Even so, regional dimensions of Iran's foreign policy remained subordinated to broader imperatives, particularly the need to be attentive to the two superpowers. Indeed, the Baghdad Pact was not the result of independent actions taken by its regional members, based on their assessments of common defense needs and security interests. Rather, it was created at the initiative of Britain and the United States, pursuing their own security interests within a Cold War context. Yet, despite the manner in which the Baghdad Pact came into being, these arrangements were significant as an indication of the new pattern of Iran's interaction with its regional neighbors.

The trend of developments within the area intensified during the 1950s and 1960s, thus enhancing the importance of the regional dimension of Iran's foreign policy. The nearly-complete process of decolonization and the rise of nationalism at one and the same time created greater scope for cooperation among regional states and increased the risk of conflict. From Iran's perspective, the latter element was especially important. The rise of extreme Arab nationalism brought with it irredentist, expansionist, and exclusivist dimensions. It also began increasingly to focus on the Persian Gulf—as exemplified by the activities of Egypt's Gamal Abd-al-Nasser. Naturally, this development posed serious security concerns for Iran on its southern front, and the Indo-Pakistani conflict reduced political stability to the East.

Changes taking place in the international political system also served to sharpen the regional focus of Iran's foreign policy. By the early 1960s, competition between the superpowers increasingly came to include attempts to manipulate the internal politics of regional countries, plus a more frequent use of proxies. For Iran, ever attentive to its northern neighbor, this was a mixed blessing. While the threat of a frontal Soviet attack subsided, that of subversion by pro-Soviet and Soviet-supported regional states increased, requiring the development of new instruments to deal with these challenges.

The trend away from direct involvement by the great powers was strengthened in the 1970s. Britain ended its East of Suez policy and thus withdrew its formal military presence from the Persian Gulf. The United States enunciated the so-called Nixon Doctrine that sought to secure U.S. interests through the actions of regional states, and these two events together fostered interaction among the states of the region, which caused Iran's foreign policy to accordingly highlight regional issues. Meanwhile, Iran's improving economy and increasing military strength allowed it to pursue a more active regional policy, which went beyond its immediate surroundings.

Aspects of Iran's regional policy in this period resulted from its efforts to find a way out of its ethnic and political isolation, especially in the face of growing Arab economic and military power. The Shah's somewhat unrealistic hope of forging close relations with India, Pakistan, and Afghanistan, in the context of what he perceived to be an "Aryan" renaissance, reflected Iran's inherent isolation and its desperate efforts to break out of it.[16] Since the Islamic revolution, the regional dimensions of Iran's foreign policy have become even more important than before because of Iran's revolutionary ambitions and the responses of the regional states. The most dramatic crystallization of this action and response was Iraq's invasion of September 1980 and the ensuing eight-year war. Iran's increasing regional focus has also been made manifest in its involvement in Lebanon and in the Afghan civil war.

In the process of adjusting to the unique characteristics of the current regime, Iran's approach to its surroundings has undergone some fundamental changes. The instruments of its regional policy have also changed, to include aggressive propaganda and at times subversion. But continuities with past policies have also been significant, as will be demonstrated in relevant chapters. Some old ideas for regional cooperation have reappeared in new guises. Moreover, the most dramatic changes that have taken place in the way Iran interacts with other regional states have been largely the result of actions by other countries, notably Iraq's invasion, which has shaped the character of Iran's relations with most of the Arab world.

Third Worldism in Iran's Foreign Policy

In recent decades, Iran's growing involvement within its own region has been closely related to its view of the phenomenon of the Third World. Certainly, Third World dimensions of Iranian foreign policy have been greatly accentuated since the revolution. Yet the widespread view that this was a totally new development is incorrect: This dimension of Iranian foreign policy had long been important. Indeed, for several decades, Iran has been a trendsetter in Third World political movements. Its constitutional movement was the earliest in Asia. Mohammad Mossadegh's theory of negative equilibrium was a forerunner of the Non-Aligned Movement, and his nationalization of Iran's oil industry in 1951 was the harbinger of emerging Third World economic nationalism. Likewise, the Shah had the image of a Western surrogate rather than of a Third World leader. Yet during the 1960s he regularly spoke out on economic problems of Third World countries. The importance of this aspect of the Shah's policy was underscored when Iran decided to join the Organization of Petroleum Exporting Countries (OPEC) as a founding member, despite significant political problems it had with some OPEC members, especially Iraq.[17] The Shah also advised other raw material exporting countries to follow OPEC's example.[18]

Further—unlike all the Arab members of OPEC, except Algeria—during the 1970s Iran became a vocal champion of reforming the international economic order and of other issues that were of special concern to the Third World, at considerable cost to its ties with Western industrial countries.[19] Thus the Third World aspects of Iran's foreign policy that are practiced by the current regime may be more militant than in the past, but they certainly have deep roots.

Salient Features of the Shah's Foreign Policy

These essential components of classical Iranian foreign policy, from the long standing preoccupation with integrity and independence to the more recent development of a special outlook on regional affairs and beyond them to the Third World, provide the backdrop to more detailed examination of the period before the revolution: the basic foreign policies practiced by the Shah.

Given developments taking place elsewhere in the region and in the world, the thirty-seven years of the Shah's rule covered a remarkable period. Not surprisingly, his foreign policy went through several stages, reflecting external realities facing Iran, its domestic economic and military conditions, and, most important, the state of his hold on power at any moment.

Yet despite shifts in the substance and style of Iranian foreign policy during the Shah's lengthy rule, many characteristics remained constant and permeated all other aspects of policy. Particularly important, throughout this period Iran—as a territorial and national expression—was the principal unit of foreign policy; and this policy was consistently nationalist and statist in that its basic objective was the advancement of Iran's national interest, as defined by its leadership, rather than any particular cause or transcendental ideal. That, indeed, is the most significant difference in the pattern of foreign policy behavior between the pre- and post-revolution periods. Under the Islamic regime, Iran's ideological aspirations have competed and conflicted with its state interests.

In addition, throughout the Shah's rule, there was a direct link between the requirements of the regime's survival and foreign policy. In this respect, similarities between the two periods are greater than the differences. There was also a progressive centralization of decision making around the Shah, which further promoted considerable consistency in Iran's foreign policy. This consistency was achieved, however, at the cost of a growing rift between public preferences and state policy. Since the revolution, by contrast, the Iranian regime has been characterized by a diffusion of powers among institutions and individuals, often with different philosophies and conflicting ambitions and with no well-established mechanisms to resolve differences, reach consensus, or sustain a decision over a reasonable period of time. The indications are that this situation is changing in the aftermath of the Ayatollah Khomeini's death, with greater centralization of power. This development would inevitably affect the formulation and conduct of foreign policy.

1941–1953

The last Shah came to power in 1941, but it was some time before he put his personal stamp on Iranian foreign policy. Centralized decision making was not yet in his hands. The parliament, the prime minister, and other centers of power exerted influence on the formulation of Iran's foreign policy. External factors and domestic constraints set the agenda, and the main preoccupation—as so often in the past—was to maintain Iran's territorial integrity and a modicum of political independence.

During this early period of the Shah's rule, Iran's diplomacy was reasonably successful: In the 1943 Tehran Declaration, the Allied Powers recognized its independence and territorial integrity. And in 1946, Soviet troops were forced to withdraw from Iran, as a response to U.S. pressure and United Nations Security Council Resolution No. 1. However, this success owed as much to the skill of Iranian diplomacy as to emerging international realities, especially the U.S.-Soviet rivalry.

After foreign troops left Iran in 1946, it refocused its goals on enlarging the margins of its political and economic independence, as best illustrated by Mossadegh's nationalization of Iranian oil and his determination to end Anglo-Russian domination of Iran's economic and political life. The Anglo-Iranian oil dispute overshadowed all other aspects of Iran's foreign policy. All its diplomatic moves, from efforts to enlist U.S. support to its appeals to the United Nations were connected to this overriding objective. Yet the conduct of Iran's foreign policy suffered because of another classic difficulty: internal political divisions and competition for power, especially between the Shah and Mossadegh.

1954–1963

By 1954, with U.S. and British assistance, the Shah had won the competition for power and had begun to purge his opponents. Not unnaturally, the overriding objective of his domestic and foreign policies was the consolidation of his rule. His principal challenges came from the domestic left, leftist forces within the region, and their superpower patron, the Soviet Union. In response, the Shah adopted a three-part approach: domestic repression, cooperation with like-minded regional states, and alliance with the United States. This approach paid off, as he gradually consolidated his position and enhanced his decision-making powers. Yet he still faced competition from other political forces, especially from powerful prime ministers, such as Ali Amini.

Despite Iran's alliance with the United States, America's commitment to the Shah was not always a foregone conclusion. He sought, therefore, to make himself useful to the Americans and to curry favor with them. His willingness to forge close relations with Israel, despite considerable domestic pressure and against the advice of many of his aides, was prompted by his desire to gain favor with the United States and the help of the powerful U.S. pro-Israeli lobby in obtaining economic and military assistance.[20]

The Shah's preoccupation with being useful to the United States had domestic implications, however. His highly controversial reform policies, which dogged him to the end of his days, were adopted in response to U.S. pressures. At the same time, despite the myth of a close alliance, the United States did not reciprocate adequately, and U.S.-Iran relations were often strained over the low level of U.S. economic assistance, its refusal to provide Iran with adequate military supplies, and its failure to help in protecting regional states, such as Iraq, Pakistan, and Oman, against domestic or foreign enemies.

Partly in response, the Shah occasionally tried to use the possibility of developing closer relations with the Soviet Union to consolidate Iran's position with the United States and to produce greater benefits from the relationship. But given the Soviet Union's underlying animosity toward the Shah's regime and his dependence on the United States, these tactics were only marginally successful with Washington.[21] Nevertheless, his sense of an unbalanced relationship led him to try finding other ways to achieve his and Iran's goals.

This search intensified as regional issues became a greater source of concern to Iran. In particular, interaction with the Arab world increased as the focus of Arab nationalism shifted to the Persian Gulf. Indeed, it was during this period that the underlying pattern of Arab-Iranian interaction took shape. Put simply, Iran forged limited cooperative relations with Arab states that were pro-Western and that shared its fears of communism and other forms of radicalism, while its relations with radical and pro-Soviet forces in the region remained hostile. But Iran's policy options were constrained by what was happening elsewhere, especially the slightly improving state of superpower relations, its limited economic and military resources, and the narrow popular base of its government.

1963–1973

In the early 1960s, several domestic and foreign developments came together and produced significant changes in Iran's foreign policy. The Shah won his competition against Amini. He successfully weathered the disturbances that followed his agrarian and other reforms—his so-called White Revolution—and he gradually concentrated the decision-making process in his hands.

Having thus silenced his enemies—though not totally defeating or converting them—the Shah began planning and implementing an ambitious policy for Iran's economic development and social modernization. The pace of this process was slow, however, because of several resource constraints. It was only in 1968, as a result of tight oil markets and the limited beginning of OPEC actions, that Iran's revenue picture began to improve. The first major breakthrough came in 1971 with the signing of the so-called Tehran Agreement between the Persian Gulf oil producers and the oil companies, considerably increasing Iran's oil income.

The Shah's thinking about foreign policy also evolved partly in response to new international and regional developments and partly in reaction to Iran's experience. He had often wondered about the value of his U.S. alliance. It was true that American support brought him back to power. Gradually, however, alliance with the United States became more of a liability and further eroded his nationalist credentials and political legitimacy. He had increasing doubts about the efficacy of this association as a shield against domestic threats to his rule. These fears had begun with the fall of Iraq's monarchy in 1958 and reached their peak during the Kennedy administration, when the U.S. president made no secret of his preference for Prime Minister Amini.

The Shah's misgivings about the efficacy of the U.S. alliance to protect Iran against regional challenges also deepened. The lack of U.S. support for Turkey over the Cyprus issue and for Pakistan during the 1965 Indo-Pakistan war dramatized CENTO's ineffectiveness against regional sources of conflict. Meanwhile, the thrust of a direct Soviet penetration—against which the U.S. alliance could be valuable—began to diminish. But the Soviet threat continued in an indirect form, through what the Shah saw as a policy of promoting regional subversion and encircling Iran with pro-Soviet radical states. He saw proof of his assessment in Moscow's friendship treaties concluded with India (1971) and Iraq (1972), in its domination of South Yemen, and in its support for anti-Shah elements through its regional allies, such as Libya, Syria, Iraq, and the PLO. The combined impact of these developments required a rethinking of Iran's foreign policy strategy. The result was the introduction of the so-called national independent foreign policy. Although the alliance with the United States remained at the core of Iran's foreign policy until the end of the Shah's rule, he tried to strike a more independent posture and increase Iran's options. Thus he improved relations with the Soviet Union, expanded ties with Europe, and became active in regional politics. In the Middle East and South Asia, he pursued a pragmatic policy aimed at checking radical inroads. He made tactical alliances in the Arab world with conservative governments against Arab radicals. Yet he was also willing to make deals with the radicals, provided that they refrained from subverting his regime.

Turning to South Asia, the Shah tried to stabilize Iran's eastern flank by resolving its differences with Afghanistan, by bolstering Pakistan's security after the trauma of 1971, by mediating regional disputes, and by offering new models of regional cooperation. Thus in 1964, Iran, Turkey, and Pakistan formed the Regional Development for Cooperation (RCD), an ambitious effort to bring together their combined resources. Later, the Shah proposed expanding it to include Afghanistan and Iraq and even suggested the creation of an Asian Common Market.

After 1968, however, a basic shift in great power involvement in the region propelled Iran into assuming a role of a magnitude that even the Shah had not envisaged. As dramatically as it had abandoned its position in the Near East and Southeast Europe a generation earlier, the British government announced its decision to withdraw militarily from the Persian Gulf by 1971. The "East of Suez" policy was over. Yet in large part because of the Vietnam War, this time the United States was most reluctant to assume British security responsibilities. Instead, it developed a strategy of relying on friendly local powers to assume responsibilities for regional defense, in the context of the Nixon Doctrine. At that time, no Arab state in the Persian Gulf had the military and human potential to perform the security task. Iran, therefore, became the first test of the Nixon Doctrine's validity.

These regional and international necessities forced a more active role on Iran. But its new role also appealed to a sense of pride—both Iran's and, even more, the Shah's. This combined with the Shah's fear that the newly developing Soviet-American *détente* could lead the United States to sacrifice Iran's security interests for the sake of reaching broader agreements with Moscow. Thus he concluded that Iran must itself assume greater responsibility for regional defense—both to meet its own interests and to be useful to the United States.

He could not limit his purview to the Persian Gulf, however; again, the subcontinent intruded. Particularly worrying was the Indo-Pakistan war of 1971. The separation of Pakistan's east wing came at a time of Western retrenchment from direct military commitments and a more aggressive Soviet push for influence. The Shah thus extended Iran's so-called security perimeter to include the Indian Ocean.

As this reach and responsibility increased, so Iranian foreign policy became increasingly concerned with issues of national prestige and international standing. The extreme aspect of this concern reflected the Shah's taste for power, but it was also rooted in a basic national impulse, the need for recognition. Nevertheless, the extension of Iranian foreign policy to new fields became a serious domestic liability for the Shah. Despite his emphasis on the independence of his foreign policy, many Iranians believed that the assumption of new responsibilities was done on U.S. instructions and to protect U.S. interests. This view was confirmed when, as a price of becoming the major regional power, the Shah felt compelled to make unpopular concessions to his superpower sponsor, such as relinquishing Iran's claim to Bahrain.

Meanwhile, many Iranians associated the intensification of Iran's arms buildup with its new regional role and resented the diversion of resources from domestic needs.

1973–1978

During the final years of the Shah's rule, all the trends of earlier periods were intensified. Increased oil income freed Iranian diplomacy from financial restraints, made it more independent and activist, and extended its reach. For the first time, it embarked on financial diplomacy, using economic aid as an instrument of foreign policy. Because of its ambitious development plans, Iran's diplomacy became increasingly concerned with issues of access to raw materials and potential export markets.[22] And it became a major participant in the debate between industrialized and developing countries about restructuring the international economic system as, even more than before, an outspoken defender of Third World views.

This increased Iranian activism had its regional price. It exacerbated frictions in relations with several Arab countries and increased radical Arab subversion against the Shah. Even the Persian Gulf Arabs became uneasy with Iran's role as the regional "great power"—however much they benefited from the added security and support for their own prosperity. Iran's activism, its increasing propensity to independent action, its outspokenness on global economic debate, and its hawkishness on oil prices also strained relations with its Western allies, eventually leading them to reassess its value to them. Likewise, Iran's regional policies annoyed the Soviet Union because they were aimed at undermining leftist, and often pro-Soviet, governments and forces. The Soviets were particularly disturbed by Iran's activities in Afghanistan and its ties with China.[23]

At home, Iran's ambitious and activist foreign policy created domestic problems and widened the gap between elite and mass perceptions of its interests and the best means of protecting them. The popular belief that Iran was essentially acting as the West's surrogate deepened. Thus a paradox developed. Many Western experts perceived that Iran was becoming a hegemonist power; but most Iranians interpreted the same set of facts as meaning that Iran had become a proxy for the West. Given the common Iranian belief that the interests of Iran and the West did not coincide, the Shah's contribution to maintaining a regional status quo favorable to the West, so much praised by many Western analysts, became a serious liability.

Not all aspects of the Shah's foreign policy, however, were oriented to the status quo. Indeed, in many ways it was change oriented. The Shah tried to change the direction of Afghanistan's policy away from dependence on the Soviet Union. He tried the same strategy with Somalia. Because these changes were in line with, and supportive of, Western interests, they were welcomed abroad, but most Iranians felt that they were unnecessary, a diversion of Iranian attention and, even more important, of resources, at a time when Iran's own economic needs were so enormous.[24] This controversy intensified after the economic slump of 1976 and contributed both to the alienation of the masses and elites from the regime and to its downfall.

The initial reaction of the revolutionary regime was a total rejection of the Shah's foreign policy and its basic frame of reference and rationale—namely, Iran as a nation state pursuing its national interests. Yet because these policies had not merely been a product of the Shah's personality and ambitions but also reflected the impact of more fundamental forces, many of the underlying patterns have survived and reappeared—albeit at times in a different guise and with new Islamic rationalizations.

3. Iran's Islamic World View and Its Impact on Foreign Policy

Since the Islamic revolution, Iran's foreign policy has been more deeply affected than before by ideological considerations, as a relatively well-defined set of beliefs has guided its actions. The Iranian leadership has been divided over the interpretation of different components of this broad ideology, but no key political figure has challenged the validity of the basic framework. Because of its principal motivations, the Islamic regime has seen itself as representing not just Iran's state interests but also those of a much broader Islamic movement. Thus, in the process, it has acted not only as a state but often as the spokesman of a cause.

The importance of these two factors in shaping Iran's foreign policy after the revolution means that some understanding is needed of the Islamic regime's ideological frame of reference, the tension between Iran's state interests and the regime's ideological aspirations, and the way it has coped with this tension.

The Islamic government's ideology is essentially based on the Ayatollah Rouhollah Khomeini's interpretation of Islam as it applies to the structure of society in all aspects; to the management of societal relationships; and to the conduct and management of the society's relations with communities abroad.

Yet only since 1981 has this ideological framework become the principal guide for action, the sole instrument for legitimating state power, and the means of rationalizing its behavior. In the early days of the revolution, other political forces were vying for control over Iran's future. For a brief period, some of these forces, including those identified with Prime Minister Mehdi Bazargan or President Abol-Hassan Bani-Sadr, held nominal power and exerted some influence over the conduct of national affairs. They either adhered to a set of values and guidelines different from that of the clerics, accepted some components of the current ideological framework, or held fundamentally different interpretations of the same principles. By mid-1981, these forces were effectively eliminated from the Iranian political scene. But their political ideas and concepts have retained influence in Iranian society and with some Islamic leaders.

Although largely based on one man's interpretation of Islam—the Ayatollah Khomeini's—Islamic Iran's ideological framework has not been immune to other influences. Khomeini based his views on Islam, but he was also very much the product of Iran's particular conditions and historical experience, as well as the broader social, political, and historical milieu of the Middle East and the Third World. His views on the nature of the current international system and the world order, although expressed in Islamic terms, are almost identical to secular Iranian and Third World political themes. Thus in their diagnosis of the state of the world and of Iran's predicament, there is little difference between Khomeini and secular Iranian intellectuals or, indeed, most Third World intellectuals. What separated Khomeini from the others has been their different prescriptions for dealing with these ills. Here, too, therefore—in diagnosis if not in prescription—there is continuity with Iran's past and similarity to other Third World philosophies.

Iran's World View

Islamic Iran's vision of the world is polarized along several lines. The first division concerns power. According to Khomeini, the world is divided into two camps: those countries and peoples who have power and use it to dominate and exploit others—namely the "arrogant" or "oppressors" (Mustakbarin); and those who lack power and are exploited and oppressed—namely, the "downtrodden" or the oppressed (Muztasafin). Translated into the outside world, the oppressor-arrogant camp consists of the two superpowers and a few other great powers. In the camp of the oppressed-downtrodden are the Muslim countries and most of the Third World.

The second division is along ideological lines. In this sense, the world according to Khomeini is also divided into two camps: those countries that follow the United States' capitalist line—namely, the Western camp; and those that follow the Soviet Union's socialist line—namely the Eastern camp. In Khomeini's scheme of things, the so-called Non-Aligned countries have no place because he believed that their non-alignment is a sham. Only the Islamic Republic of Iran is truly independent.

A third line of division could be characterized as moral or spiritual. Khomeini believed that the world is divided into those who follow the "right path," the "path of God and belief," and those who follow the "corrupt path," the "path of Satan and disbelief."[1] In his view, the right or divine path is that of Islam and the Qor'an. Here, too, the Islamic Republic stands alone as the only country whose society and government is based on Qor'anic principles and is striving to follow the divine Islamic path. That is why Khomeini and his disciples have so often expressed Iran's struggles, whether with Iraq, the United States, or others, as the fight between what he called *"Haq va Batel"*—truth and righteousness—against falsehood.

Khomeini's polarized vision of the world and the inherent duality in his thinking reflected the traditional Islamic view, with its division of the world into "Dar-al-Islam" (the realm of peace and belief) and "Dar-al-Harb" (the realm of war and disbelief). Khomeini's polarized world view also reflected the influence of Iran's history and culture, as well as the realities of the international system during the last several decades, which has been polarized along East-West and North-South lines.[2]

A polarized vision of the world also fits with pre-Islamic Iranian thinking. Ancient Iranian prophets, from Zoroaster to Mani, saw all of creation and human destiny as the enactment of a cosmic battle between good and evil.[3] Man is not a powerless bystander in this battle, but by his actions he contributes to the final and inevitable victory of good over evil and righteousness over falsehood.

In addition, many aspects of pre-Islamic Iranian philosophical and spiritual ideas have influenced the evolution of Shi'ism and, in particular, Shi'a philosophy and mysticism. To be sure, it is an exaggeration to say, as some Iranians do, that Shi'ism is nothing but a reinterpretation of pre-Islamic Iranian spiritual concepts into an Islamic framework.[4] But the reluctance of some Shi'a clerics to admit to Iranian philosophical influence on the development of Shi'a philosophy and mysticism is also not justified.[5] And as a scholar, philosopher, and mystic, Khomeini was the product of this philosophical-spiritual tradition of Iranian Shi'ism.

Iran's historical experience during the last two hundred years has also engendered a polarized vision of the world, divided between those who have power and those who don't; those who dominate and those who are dominated. Many of the Ayatollah Khomeini's statements and those of his disciples show that he was a product of this experience. Thus in July 1988, Iran's president, Hodjat-al-Islam Seyyed Ali Khamenei, commented to the visiting West German foreign minister how the historic insults suffered by Iran in the last one and a half centuries at the hands of the great powers led the Iranian people to welcome slogans of independence and the philosophy of "neither East nor West."[6]

As a result, most non-clerical and secular Iranian intellectuals have a polarized vision of the world, seeing it as divided between dominating and subjugated, rich and poor, and technologically advanced and backward countries. These views are quite common throughout the Third World. For the Iranian author Jalal Al-Ahmad, the world is essentially divided into two sets of countries: those that have mastered the "machine" (Al-Ahmad's metaphor for technology), and those that have not. For him, this fact determines the essence of the relationship between the two groups—namely, the second group's economic dependency on the first.[7] In Al-Ahmad's view, widely echoed in the Third World community, by maintaining this state of dependency, the advanced countries ensure their own continued economic prosperity and superiority.[8]

In the view of the Ayatollah Khomeini and his disciples, the instruments through which this state of dependency and subjugation is created and perpetuated are the corrupt rulers and political elites of Muslim countries. His yardstick for judging the independence of Muslim leaders from the arrogant powers is their adherence to what he considered to be the true Islamic path. His view is not unique. Here, too, Khomeini's underlying idea regarding the role of ruling elites has been espoused by Iranian lay intellectuals. During most of the Qajar period, for example, the Iranian ruling elites were regularly at the service either of the British or of the Russians. Those who demurred were either killed, sometimes as the result of foreign intrigues, or kept out of power.[9]

Most notable in Iranian history was the fate of two nineteenth century Iranian prime ministers, Ghaem Magham Farahani and Mirza Taghi Khan Amir Kabir, who championed reform and independence. Both men resisted foreign pressures and tried to curb the privileges of the court, and both were murdered on the king's orders. In more recent times, Mohammad Mossadegh met a comparable fate for similar reasons.[10]

In addition to these philosophical and historical dimensions, Khomeini's view of the world was conspiratorial. He believed that, for several centuries, there has been a great conspiracy against Islam by the arrogant powers. He believed that the destruction of the Ottoman Islamic state was the result of a conspiracy to divide and weaken the Muslims in order to dominate them and plunder their wealth.[11]

Again, this underlying theme is shared by lay Iranian intellectuals, as elsewhere in the Third World. Theories of imperialism, neo-imperialism, colonialism, and neo-colonialism are all based on the idea of the advanced countries' need for economic resources and markets in the Third World and thus the need to control these resources. Whether these theories correctly explain all of the Third World's problems is beside the point. Most Third World peoples believe they do. Thus, despite the centrality of Islam in Khomeini's world view, he was also very much the product of his time and environment.

The ideology of Iran's Islamic leaders has not been immune to the influence of principal global ideologies, especially socialism. This is reflected in their differing views on the details of the structuring of Iran's society and its external behavior. Khomeini viewed the current world order as inherently unjust because it is not based on what he called "divine rules." Its essence is the domination and oppression of the weak by the strong. Again, while Khomeini expressed these views in Islamic terms, he has not been alone in his diagnosis of the nature of the current world order. The idea that this order and its rules primarily reflect unequal power between the advanced and non-advanced countries is widespread in the Third World. So is the view that present international rules and regulations are aimed at preserving this unequal pattern of relationships.

The Third World view of the international system and its rules and regulations has perhaps been best described by the Guatemalan leader, Juan Jose Arevalo, in his book, *The Shark and the Sardines*. While Arevalo's work focused essentially on relations between the United States and Latin American countries, as well as on the legal and political foundation of the Inter-American system, many of its ideas apply to the global order. Arevalo referred to what he called "the imperial origins" of international law and its allegiance to what he called the "shark"—a metaphor for the great powers: " . . . The shark smiled, because at this moment he discovered the deepest secret of law—its imperial origin . . . its Mephistophelean function, *its allegiance to the sharks*" [Emphasis added].[12]

It is also this view of the current global order which has been at the root of the Third World nations' calls for the creation of a New International Economic Order and a New International Information Order, as well as their efforts to strengthen the role of the United Nations General Assembly, where they are in a majority.

The Ayatollah Khomeini's prescriptions for rectifying the unjust characteristics of the present world order also bear considerable similarities to other reformist Third World themes, although his prescriptions were developed within an Islamic framework and expressed through Islamic symbolism. He focused on the Muslims, but he believed that their problems and dilemmas are relevant to other oppressed peoples. In his view, the source of the Muslim world's problems is its estrangement from the divine path of Islam, its adoption of corrupt ways of either the East or the West, and its disunity, which is partly due to the intrigues of the oppressors. Their salvation is in a return to Islam, the establishment of truly Islamic governments, and overcoming divisions and achieving unity. He often said that " . . . nobody could defeat one billion Muslims if they were united."[13] Thus the Muslims and other oppressed groups and nations should cooperate in order to change the global balance of power and to put an end to their subjugation and exploitation.

Yet Khomeini's views were not as innovative as they seemed. The idea of Islamic cooperation or "pan-Islamism" was advanced as early as the mid-nineteenth century by Seyyed Jamal ed-din Assad Abadi (known as Al-Afghani) who called for Islamic cooperation to uproot British colonial power from Muslim lands.[14] More recently, the Ayatollah Abol Ghassem Kashani called for the unity of the Muslims so that they could serve as a third force between the East and the West.[15] Furthermore, the idea that Iran should cooperate with other Muslim and Third World nations has not been a creation of the clergy. Writing about nationalism and neutralism in Iran in 1957, L. P. Elwell-Sutton noted that the average Iranian favors association with other small Asian and Muslim powers, feeling that this is probably the only way for these countries to counter the pressure of the great powers.[16]

Furthermore, the idea of pulling resources together in order to balance the inordinate influence of great powers is not peculiar to Muslims. The Non-Aligned Movement was formed to balance East and West and to mitigate the conflictual aspects of the superpower relationship. Ideas such as "South-South cooperation" and "collective self-sufficiency," which were particularly current in the Third World during the 1970s and early 1980s, emanate from the same concerns. Many of the non-clerical members of Iran's revolutionary leadership have also used these Third World themes to explain Iran's foreign policy goals and objectives. At the 41st session of the U.N. General Assembly, the Iranian foreign minister expressed dismay that the old colonialism has been replaced by a more dangerous one, namely neo-colonialism: thus the domination of great powers over weaker states has continued. He added that technical and industrial backwardness, plus the economic underdevelopment of most states, were responsible for the establishment of a new system of domination and neo-colonialism.

Standard Bearer

An important aspect of the vision presented by Khomeini and the Islamic Republic is Iran's international role. The Ayatollah believed that, by virtue of being the only truly Islamic and non-aligned country, Iran has a special duty to help both

Muslim and other oppressed nations achieve similar status. Iran should assume the vanguard of an Islamic revolutionary movement, albeit without the use of force, particularly the initiation of aggressive wars. Khomeini said: " . . . When we say we want to export our revolution we mean we would like to export this spirituality which dominates Iran . . . *we have no intention to attack anyone with swords or other arms* . . . [emphasis added]."[17] This reluctance to export the revolution by force of arms has deep roots in the Shi'a theory of war and peace, which holds that wars to spread Islam can only be waged by the Imams. And since the Shi'a world has been without an Imam since the Twelfth Imam was occluded, no expansionist wars can be waged.[18]

Next to spreading Islam's revolutionary message, in Khomeini's view another principle is of importance for Iran: working for the political, economic, and cultural unity of the Islamic world, which clearly points to an activist foreign policy agenda. Yet the Islamic dimension of Iran's revolution is not the only reason for Iran's activism; it is also due partly to the nature of revolutionary movements, virtually all of which have had universalist dimensions and an irresistible urge to proselytize. Thus, some of the non-clerical and even seminationalist leaders of the Iranian revolution also believed that Iran should speak up in defense of Islamic causes and various underprivileged groups. In an article published in his paper *Enghlab-e-Islami* (Islamic Revolution) in August 1979, Bani-Sadr urged active Iranian involvement in southern Lebanon: " . . . by not paying attention to what is happening there, we will not be helping the advancement of our revolution." Indeed, "in order to advance our revolution, it is imperative that we go beyond our frontiers and to confront the enemies" of Islamic countries wherever they may be, because "if we do not go out of Iran to help the revolution, others will come to our country to plot against us."[19]

Bani-Sadr's comments reflect another common propensity of states: to seek a political milieu that is congenial to their political views and aspirations. This propensity is based on the often incorrect assumption that countries that share the same ideological values do not threaten each other.[20] Indeed, in recent decades, both Western and Soviet foreign policy has put heavy emphasis on creating or maintaining a congenial international environment from the perspective of their particular interests. The same has been true of many Middle Eastern countries, notably Egypt, Iraq, Syria, and, in particular, Saudi Arabia, which has promoted its own version of Islam (Wahabism) in order to spread its influence and enhance its prestige as the so-called custodian of Islam's holy sites.

In Iran during the time of the Shah, the same motives were important in shaping foreign policy, in terms of the nation's interests as he perceived them. Likewise, Islamic Iran's efforts to strengthen other revolutionary forces and to spread its revolutionary ideas are mostly aimed at creating a more congenial and safe regional environment, although, of course, one state's safety is often another state's insecurity!

In general, therefore, Islamic Iran's behavior is not much different than that of any other state. Its claim that its actions are motivated by concern for the good of the Muslims is not correct. Likewise, those who make sweeping claims that attribute Iranian behavior to Islamic messianism, Shi'a hegemonism, or an inherent Iranian tendency for expansionism are equally incorrect. Instead, Iran is moved by the same impulses that move other states, and it uses the same rationalizations. The perceived self-interest, and thus the foreign policies of the Soviet Union and the United States, involve spreading either socialism or liberal democracy and the market economy. Yet both claim that their main goals are world peace and sharing the virtues of their particular system with others. And the same applies to China, the European powers, and the Arab states—which tend to justify every policy in terms of Arab nationalism and Arab unity.

Iran's current activism also reflects a principal Iranian psychological trait: the belief that its history, culture, size, and population—and since the revolution, its special Islamic credentials—entitles it to play an important role both regionally and internationally. By emphasizing its role as the champion of the deprived, Iran has aspired to attain a status that its material wealth and strength do not otherwise entitle it. The Iranian prime minister told a group of Lebanese students that "we feel that we are a spiritual superpower."[21] But in this respect, too, Iran is not alone. Indeed, many regional countries, including some of Iran's neighbors, aspire to a political role that outstrips their material and human resources.

Impact on Foreign Policy

The practical consequences of Iran's world view for its external behavior cannot be resolved in absolute or abstract terms, mainly because there is no agreement within its leadership on how the principles that underlie the world view should be applied to specific cases. Moreover, under the impact of geopolitical imperatives, economic realities, and both regional and international responses to its actions, Iran's position regarding this point continues to evolve, although not in a consistent direction.

In recent years, there has been a major effort outside Iran to discern the beliefs of different members of its leadership, coupled with debate about the existence or absence of a division of opinion that could be characterized as "moderate" versus "radical." Many observers argue that there are no real ideological differences within the Iranian leadership, and that apparent disagreements derive from personal rivalries among leaders and factionalism centered around principal political personalities. That view is incorrect. Indeed, there is a broad division within the leadership that applies both to domestic issues and to foreign policy.[22]

To be sure, differences of opinion are subject to limits set by an Islamic ideological framework. None of the differing opinions challenge the legitimacy and centrality of either Iran's Islamic system of government and society or its Islamic vision and world view. Labels such as "radical" and "moderate" do not adequately define different tendencies. Moreover, there are different grades of moderation and radicalism within each group of leaders. Nevertheless, two broad tendencies do exist.

Each has its own interpretation of the basic ideological framework and thus a separate agenda for Iran's domestic organization and foreign policy.

One tendency takes a traditional view of Islam. It emphasizes that Islam sanctions private property and thus favors an economic system based on private enterprise and a limited role for the state. Some members of this group are relatively tolerant of dissent, provided that it does not challenge the regime's underlying legitimacy. This group also believes in the consolidation of the revolution's gains, gradually normalizing social and political life and easing the most stringent of revolutionary social codes.

In foreign policy, it adheres to a non-aligned posture based on the philosophy of "neither East nor West". But this group is also more suspicious of the Soviet Union than of the West and believes in trying to balance Soviet geographical proximity by establishing reasonable relations with European countries, China, Japan, and others. It does not even rule out the possibility of normalizing ties with the United States. This group does favor the strengthening and expanding of Iran's relations with Islamic and Third World countries and the spreading of Iran's revolutionary message. But it also prefers to do so through traditional channels of diplomacy and interstate relations, and it emphasizes the value of state-to-state relations and the importance of Iran's active involvement in international diplomacy.[23]

The second tendency takes a revolutionary view of Islam, emphasizing its egalitarian aspects and its injunctions against the undue accumulation of wealth in a few hands. This group therefore favors massive land reform and near total state control over the economy, with little room for the private sector. It is intolerant of dissent and believes in maintaining the revolution's purity and fervor.

In foreign policy, this group also subscribes to a nonaligned posture for Iran, but takes a basically benign view of the Soviet Union, favoring close cooperation with Eastern bloc countries. It is vociferously anti-American and opposes the normalization of ties. It also believes in an active policy on exporting the Islamic revolution, even if this creates problems in state-to-state relations.[24] In fact, this group maintains that Iran's foreign policy should focus on the world's "peoples" rather than on its governments.

Because of these differences within the Iranian leadership and the lack of adequate constitutional or other mechanisms either to resolve them or to reach a workable compromise, Iran's postrevolution foreign policy has acquired a dualistic and contradictory character. It has been handicapped by periodic and at times sudden shifts of direction.

It has been particularly difficult for the Iranian leadership to decide on a proper mix of ideology and pragmatism in the conduct of its foreign relations. At times, the regime has behaved more like a revolutionary movement than like a state, at considerable cost to Iran's national interests. Yet the requirements of survival, plus demands imposed by pressing economic and political needs, have forced most Iranian leaders to become political practitioners and statesmen rather than pure ideologues or idealists. In the course of the last decade, they have painfully discovered that the outside world will not easily yield to Iran's ideological aspirations. Rather, those countries that feel threatened resist these aspirations and, by prompting both regional and international responses, exacerbate Iran's problems and even make the achievement of its domestic revolutionary goals less certain. This linkage between Iranian aspiration and international response has been brought home to the regime's leaders by events such as Iran's international isolation following the American hostage crisis; the Iraqi invasion and the broad support which Iraq received, despite its initial aggression; and periodic Western and Arab economic, political, and military pressures on Iran.

For some time, Iran's leaders talked as though they thrived on such responses, and they took pride in the fact that so many powerful countries opposed Iran because they feared its revolutionary impact.[25] Not all Iranians, nor even all Islamic leaders, shared this attitude, however, because they realized the destructive consequences for Iran of ideological extremism. The 1988 U.S.-Iranian confrontation, with its devastating effects, offered these individuals an opportunity to voice their concerns. Even such leaders as Ayatollah Montazeri and Speaker Rafsanjani acknowledged that Iran had made unnecessary enemies.[26]

As a result of these experiences, coupled with a learning process in running the country, Iranian leaders have had to reassess some of their views on the conduct of Iran's external relations. They have slowly realized that it cannot operate outside the international system, no matter how corrupt and unjust that system may be. In effect, Iran has been going through the same process of adjustment to the international system that other revolutionary governments have experienced. This adjustment has not meant the abandonment of revolutionary goals; but it has often meant putting the requirements of national survival first and adapting revolutionary goals to them.

Iran has discovered its limitations and realized that it does not have the economic and military means to pursue its revolutionary goals indiscriminately. It has learned that the external environment has been unreceptive to its ideology. Its failure to generate mass Islamic uprisings, even among the Shi'as of Iraq, has been both sobering and disappointing. Iran's call for Muslim unity has also gone unheeded.

Yet these experiences have not affected all factions to the same degree. Some radicals still resist the process of adjustment, and thus there can be a resurgence of emphasis on ideology in Iran's foreign policy. Yet even some radicals recognize the heavy cost of ideological rigidity. As a result, disputes between the "moderate" and "radical" factions has become focused not so much on the relative weight to be accorded to ideology as opposed to state interests but rather on the choice of Iran's political and economic partners. Thus, resource constraints, external resistance, the massive problems of economic reconstruction, and the lack of receptivity to Iran's message have relegated ideological goals to long-term aspirations.

The following chapters will present the unfolding of this long, uneven, and painful process of adjustment by surveying Iran's external relations. Yet it is possible here to reach some conclusions. The Iranian leadership, including the Ayatollah Khomeini, finally recognized the need to end Iran's international isolation and its aggressive assertion of its international presence. In a famous speech in October 1984, the Ayatollah Khomeini set the tone by pointing out that the Prophet considered it necessary to establish relations, that not having relations with other states was contrary to Islamic precepts, and that Iran must have ties with everyone, with only a few exceptions—including Israel, the United States, and South Africa.[27]

Khomeini also attacked the proponents of the "people-to-people" approach to foreign relations and characterized the view that "Iran must not have links with governments but should establish links with people" as irrational.[28] He insisted, however, that Iran's new relations "must be friendly, rather than relations between a master and his servant." And he stressed "that lack of relations with other countries is irrational, that it ends in nothing but extinction and annihilation. . . . "[29] Other Iranian leaders also began to speak along these lines.[30] Thus, despite the view that the existing international organizations are dominated by the great powers, Iran has recognized the need to be engaged in them and to exploit their potential usefulness.

There is one condition, however—namely, that state-to-state relations must not be pursued at the expense of Islam and its influence, either in Iran or internationally.

In sum, Iran has not abandoned its revolutionary goals, but under internal and external pressures it has been pursuing them more cautiously. The tension between Iran's state goals and ideological aspirations persists. But it is gradually coming to resemble other revolutionary countries, where ideological objectives are basically subordinated to state interests.

In the immediate aftermath of the Ayatollah Khomeini's death, the more moderate trend seemed to gather strength. Statements by Iran's new leaders, including its President, Rafsanjani, indicated a more realistic approach to the conduct of the country's foreign relations and the abandonment of elusive ideological goals. However, their position was by no means unchallenged. Thus the possibility of a reassertion of a more ideologically determined posture remained considerable—especially as different factions disagreed on the interpretation of the Ayatollah Khomeini's spiritual legacy.

Nevertheless, Iran's domestic difficulties and an unresponsive external environment argued against ideological rigidity and in favor of a moderate and realistic approach to relations with the outside world and hence the acceleration of the process of Iran's adjustment to the international system.

4. Iran and the Superpowers

The United States

Introduction to Superpower Relations

The Islamic revolution changed the nature of Iran's relations with the superpowers toward a strictly non-aligned posture, symbolized by the slogan "Neither East nor West—only Islam." Yet non-alignment did not mean equal treatment of the two superpowers: U.S.-Iranian relations suffered more, changing from alliance to confrontation. Under the Shah, Soviet-Iranian relations had stabilized along correct lines. During the 1980s they developed erratically, vacillating between measured hostility and limited cooperation—on balance, reflecting a tilt in Iran's superpower relations, in the Soviets' favor. Whether this tilt continues or even intensifies will depend on the evolution of Iranian politics in the aftermath of the Ayatollah Khomeini's death. Developments in the immediate aftermath of his death tended to intensify this tilt as Soviet-Iranian relations vastly improved and the U.S.-Iranian estrangement continued.

Iran and the United States: Historical Background

Iran's relations with the United States have a relatively short history, but they have made up in emotional intensity what they lack in duration. They have inspired more commentary than any other aspect of Iran's recent involvement with the outside world, including an outpouring of books and articles on the causes of the U.S.-Iranian rift.

Two themes have predominated among explanations for recent U.S.-Iranian difficulties: First, the U.S. "original sin" for partaking in the 1953 *coup d'etat* which toppled the government of Mohammad Mossadegh. According to this view, the U.S. role in the British plot sowed the seeds of Iranian resentment which yielded the bitter harvest of the hostage crisis of 1979–80; second is "Soviet-centeredness" in U.S. foreign policy. According to this view, U.S. preoccupation with the Cold War and the Soviet threat distorted its policy toward Iran. This led it to support the Shah, regardless of his domestic excesses and external ambitions. In the process, the United States became identified with an illegitimate and repressive government, thus triggering Iranian resentment.

Both of these theories have merit. But neither fully explains the intensity of the estrangement, partly because both views are based on hindsight and do not adequately account for the impact of broader developments in the region and the world.

Original Sin

Implicit in the theory of original sin is the notion that the United States would have had few problems with Iran had it not toppled Mossadegh's government. This is a bold assertion, based on the assumption that Mossadegh would have been able to resolve Iran's problems and to guarantee its smooth development within a national democratic framework.

Mossadegh was a sincere nationalist leader, but it is unlikely that he would have succeeded, given the magnitude of Iran's social and economic problems. Moreover, had he undertaken far-reaching and indispensable reforms, he, too, would have faced opposition from such quarters as the landowners, the clerical establishment, and the bazaar merchants. He, too, would likely have had to choose between reform or compromising some of his liberal democratic principles. With his nationalist credentials, perhaps Mossadegh would have better withstood these pressures. Yet the experience of other nationalist leaders argues otherwise. Legitimacy derived from a leader's anti-colonial, revolutionary, or nationalist actions generally has had a limited life span. After a time, legitimacy depends on the tangible results of a leader's policies for the public well-being. Thus it is unlikely that Mossadegh would have succeeded both to meet public expectations and to avoid creating powerful enemies, causing his legitimacy to suffer.

Original sin analysis is also flawed by the assumption that opposition in Iran to the Shah—and by way of association, to the United States—developed solely because of the repressive nature of his regime and his failure to achieve economic and social justice. It is true that the unequal distribution of the fruits of economic development, the Shah's autocratic rule, his unresponsiveness to popular wishes, and his disregard for basic human liberties were the main causes of his problems. But his woes also derived from his successes. Indeed, opposition to the Shah should be analyzed at least partly within the context of Iran's experience with economic development and in light of the so-called revolution of rising expectations.

This is not to absolve the Shah of his mistakes, but to draw attention to the broader causes of his problems, rooted in Iran's social and economic transformation and their disruptive impact on its traditional social and political order. It is also important to strike a balance between the two sets of factors, personal and systemic.

Indeed, balance has been often lacking in assessing the role played by the Shah and his policies in shaping U.S.-Iranian relations. Many Iranian and American analysts have either put the Shah on a pedestal and attributed to him all conceivable virtues—such as that of a staunch ally and a force for stability—or they have portrayed him as the embodiment of all evil, such as a murderous dictator or an imperialist "jerk." Moreover, their analysis of Iran's social and political conditions has, to a disproportionate extent, been colored by their views of the Shah and not by actual evidence.

Soviet-Centeredness

Closely related to original sin theory is the argument that America's "Iran problem" resulted from the Soviet-centered nature of its post-war foreign policy. No doubt, over the years U.S. over emphasis on the Soviet threat hurt its policy and damaged its position in the Third World. But recognition of this fact does not, and should not, lead to the conclusion that the Soviet Union did not pose a serious challenge to U.S. interests and a serious threat to such countries as Iran and Turkey. Nor does admitting the existence of such a threat imply the endorsement of U.S. policies devised to deal with them. It is not necessary to underestimate the leftist-Soviet threat to Iran in order to argue against the U.S. decision to topple the Mossadegh regime. Indeed, a strong argument can be made that the best response to Soviet-leftist efforts to dominate Iran during the 1950s would have been to support nationalist forces. The same argument applies to U.S. policies during the following decades—namely, that the fault lay not so much with the U.S. assessment of the Soviet factor than with the means used to cope with it.

The limitations of the theories of original sin and of Soviet-centeredness show that a full explanation for the U.S.-Iranian rift must be found in a much more intricate and complex set of factors and interactions, of which the following are the most important.

Romanticism Gone Sour

Until the *coup d'etat* of August 1953, most Iranians had a romanticized vision of the United States, viewing it as a benevolent, non-exploitative power which, given its own history of anti-colonial struggle, supported other struggling nations. From the early years of U.S.-Iranian contacts, therefore, Iran looked to the United States as the favorite counterweight to Anglo-Russian involvement and as a potential source of assistance.[1]

Yet the United States' interest in Iran, insofar as it had any, was, in reality, similar to that of other powers. Thus it did develop an interest in Iran as a potential export market—indeed, the 1856 U.S.-Iranian Treaty of Friendship and Commerce granted to the United States the same privileges obtained by other great powers.[2]

But the fact is that, historically, the United States has never had a strong intrinsic interest in Iran, only derivative, as when the U.S. representative at the Ottoman court viewed Iran as a "serviceable potential ally against Great Britain."[3] During the nineteenth century and the first half of the twentieth century, its interest was limited to the protection of its nationals. The United States may have welcomed trade and other economic opportunities in Iran, but it was not willing to take risks or to become over-involved. Because of this lack of direct U.S. interest, Iran failed to enlist U.S. support for domestic reform efforts or for its resistance to Anglo-Russian pressures. Nevertheless, on two occasions prior to the post-World War II period, in 1919 and in 1943, the United States did intervene on Iran's behalf.[4]

With the onset of the Cold War and Soviet-American global competition, U.S. interest in Iran increased. But even then, U.S. motives, like those of Britain before it, were negative and derivative rather than positive and direct, being principally concerned with denying Iran to the Soviet Union. The United States was prepared to do what was necessary to achieve that goal, but beyond that it was not willing to commit itself.

This U.S. attitude toward Iran stands in sharp contrast to its appraisal of its interests in two other Middle East countries—Saudi Arabia and Turkey. Since the early 1940s, American access to Saudi oil has been considered an intrinsic good and thus worthy of constant attention and effort. Unlike Iran, therefore, even in the absence of the Cold War and U.S.-Soviet rivalry, the United States would have had an interest in Saudi Arabia.[5]

At the same time, the United States has had a positive strategic interest in Turkey as the southernmost flank of the North Atlantic Treaty Organization (NATO). From the U.S. perspective, including Turkey in Western defense strategy, rather than just simply seeking to deny it to the Soviet Union, has been the overriding objective. Thus, in the context of NATO, the United States has made security commitments to Turkey that it did not make to Iran, even during the height of their friendship, as illustrated by U.S. reluctance to sign a formal security treaty, despite the Shah's insistence.[6]

The history of the U.S.-Iranian arms supply relationship also reflects this basic U.S. attitude. For a long time, the United States disagreed with the Shah's assessment of Iran's security and military needs and refused to provide it with large amounts of arms.[7] It was only after 1968 and the change in U.S. global strategy from direct military involvement overseas to greater reliance on regional proxies that it reversed course on arms supply.

Because of its lack of intrinsic interest in Iran, beyond a certain limit the United States has not been willing to commit time and money to it. Thus, despite its being an American ally, between 1953 and 1961 Iran received less U.S. aid than did India, which was a non-aligned country with a pro-Soviet tilt. Even Nasser's Egypt received about a third as much assistance as Iran.[8] These disparities enhanced Iranian resentment toward the United States, contributed to the erosion of America's positive image, and intensified domestic opposition to alliance with the United States. Many Iranians argued that a non-aligned posture should gain Iran more economic benefits.

This U.S. unwillingness to commit sufficient financial resources to Iran also contributed to the failure of its policies aimed at political and economic reforms in that country. For example, during the early 1960s the Kennedy administration pressured the Shah to introduce rapid and far-reaching reforms, including large-scale land reform. Meanwhile, it showed a distinct preference for Prime Minister

Ali Amini, which worried the Shah about U.S. intentions and strained his relations with Amini. Yet the United States refused to provide the Amini government with the financial support it needed to cover its budget deficit. Amini was left to carry out reforms, outmaneuver the Shah, and enforce an austerity program. It is no wonder that he failed.[9]

Neglect and Over-Involvement

The lack of direct U.S. interest in Iran has engendered policies that have vacillated between neglect on the one hand and active interference and the imposition of unreasonable burdens on the other. This U.S. vacillation has also partly reflected a basic duality of the American political culture and a deep national division about the ultimate purposes of U.S. foreign policy—namely, the dichotomy between the United States' idealist and imperialist impulses, perhaps best illustrated by two early twentieth-century presidents, Woodrow Wilson and Theodore Roosevelt. There have been practical consequences of this dichotomy in Iran, especially in changing the image of the United States.

Most Iranian and American scholars of U.S.-Iranian relations have traced the change in Iranian attitudes toward the United States to the *coup d'etat* of 1953—i.e., they tend to support the original sin theory. No doubt, Mossadegh's fall marked the end of American innocence in Iran. Yet the erosion of America's image and the rise in Iranian resentment were less a product of any "original sin" than of later U.S. attitudes and policies. Particularly important was the U.S. neglect of Iran's domestic scene. Once the communist threat was reduced, America's interest in Iran's internal developments waned. Had it adopted a different approach, it might have redeemed its role in toppling Mossadegh. Indeed, while most Iranians were saddened by the *coup* and the defeat of the liberal experiment, they were also relieved by the return of law and order. Mossadegh enjoyed great legitimacy and respect as a symbol of Iranian nationalism, but by 1953 skepticism about his abilities as a politician and chief executive, plus concern over his capacity to outmaneuver the communists and their Soviet patrons, had increased.

The importance of order and calm—even if oppressive—for a people like the Iranians should not be underestimated, because their experience of frequent foreign incursions, wars, and tribal unrest has left them with an endemic sense of insecurity. In general, it is only after reasonably long periods of order—as was the case of the two Shahs—have the Iranians tended to become restless and yearn more for freedom than for order.

During the early 1950s, when the Allied occupation and the Azerbaijan crisis were fresh in their minds, and when the streets of Tehran were the daily battleground between communists and brown-shirt fascists, the Iranians' fear of disorder grew steadily. Immediately after the *coup* of 1953, the sense of relief in Iran was stronger than the sense of outrage against the foreign role in restoring order. It was the

Shah's later policies and the seeming U.S. acquiescence to them that deepened anti-American resentment over the Mossadegh affair.

Toeing the American line in foreign policy also exacted a price. The Shah manipulated his U.S. links for his own purposes, but on major issues he followed the American lead. To understand this point has led to much misunderstanding. Many scholars have attributed shifts in Iranian diplomacy to the Shah's growing confidence and independence. Often, however, these shifts resulted from changes in America's strategic outlook and global and regional priorities—following, rather than preceding, U.S. changes.

At the same time, too much U.S. intervention in and experimentation had negative consequences for Iran and for U.S.-Iranian relations. U.S. intervention and experimentation occurred in sudden bursts, without due consideration for the consequences. For example, the Kennedy administration's pressure on the Shah to implement far-reaching reforms reflected its conclusion that containing Soviet influence in the Third World required the implementation of social and economic reforms and the improvement of living conditions. Iran was to be the first test case.

This was a correct diagnosis, and Iran was a legitimate candidate. But what was missing in the Kennedy administration's approach was a clear idea of how these reforms should be carried out, what the social repercussions would be, and how much potential there was for political disruption. Under U.S. pressure, the Shah introduced reforms, including land reform and voting rights for women, that drastically altered Iran's social and political structure and caused major difficulties for him in his relations with powerful sectors of Iranian society, especially the clerical establishment. But then the United States left him alone to cope with the consequences.

This U.S. attitude was an inevitable result of its lack of intrinsic interest in Iran. By contrast, in Latin America, where U.S. interests are far more deeply involved, the United States was much more cautious in encouraging similar experiments, although it was generally agreed that the success of President Kennedy's Alliance for Progress depended on such fundamental reforms.[10]

Likewise, in 1977, after nearly ten years of complacency concerning the Shah's domestic policies, the United States began to experiment with Iran, this time as a test case for President Carter's human rights policy. No doubt, a more active and positive U.S. policy on human rights issues in Iran was long overdue. But in this particular case, the policy was implemented without a correct understanding of the Iranian situation and without according it the kind of sustained bureaucratic analysis and attention that the policy needed to succeed. Even at the height of the Iranian crisis in the fall of 1978, the U.S. administration paid surprisingly little attention to Iran, in part because it was preoccupied with the Arab-Israeli conflict during and after the Camp David summit.[11]

At times, the United States made demands which have contributed to Iran's internal problems and thus damaging U.S.-Iranian relations. The most far-reaching of these demands was the role assigned to Iran during the 1970s to safeguard

Persian Gulf security in the context of the Nixon Doctrine. Most Western and Iranian analysts have interpreted the Shah's policy in the Persian Gulf during the 1970s, as well as the zeal with which he played his role of Western surrogate, as proof of Iran's imperial impulses and the Shah's megalomania. No doubt, the Shah relished the role of the Persian Gulf's policeman. He was an enthusiastic participant and in the late 1970s went even beyond his assigned role. Nevertheless, the United States and other Western countries fed the Shah's ego for as long as they needed him, and then they used this characteristic to discredit him.

It is questionable whether the Shah could have refused the task assigned to him, for at the time, unlike the late 1970s and the 1980s, there were no viable regional alternatives to Iran. Indeed, in 1968, with the British withdrawal looming on the horizon, the U.S. preoccupation with Vietnam, the continuing tide of Arab radicalism, and the fragility of Persian Gulf Arab states, Iran was the only regional country available to fill the vacuum. Most Iranians understood this fact and resented the United States for demanding this role from Iran and the Shah for playing it.

Iran's military buildup during the 1970s was also not just a product of the Shah's insatiable appetite for military hardware. Even more, it was a direct result of the shift in U.S. strategic priorities and of the new role assigned to Iran. Indeed, the Shah's appetite had long existed, and for twenty years he pleaded with Washington for military supplies, without much success. Most Iranians perceived this connection and resented it.

In sum, U.S. policy toward Iran has been determined on the basis of other more important priorities globally and in the Middle East. For instance, the United States took a different approach to countries like Egypt and Saudi Arabia. Since 1979, Egypt has received several times the aid that Iran received in twenty-five years. But the United States has neither demanded that Egypt perform security tasks on behalf of the West which could be politically costly nor has it demanded that Saudi Arabia be forthcoming on the Arab-Israeli issue to an extent that would cause the regime serious political problems. Turkey has also been expended from such burdens.

The U.S. Global Role

Beyond events in U.S.-Iranian relations, the tremendous expansion of U.S. economic and military power during the post-war period, plus its achievement of a global presence, helped to change its idealized image in Iran, as was true in most of the Third World. By replacing other European powers in many regions of the Third World and by becoming the leader of the West, the United States unwittingly assumed the burden of Western history and the legacy of European colonialism. Thus many Third World nations transferred their resentment of European colonial powers to the United States. In the Middle East, the Arabs seem to have forgotten the British role in the creation of the state of Israel or the Anglo-French invasion of Egypt during the Suez crisis, and they have focused their frustrations and resentments on the United States. The expansion in the activities of U.S. transnational companies and the spread of American culture also made the United States the new "imperial" power and therefore the new focus of Third World frustrations and resentment. Often, an increase in the American presence contributed, however unfairly, to anti-Americanism,[12] and Iran was one of the Third World countries where the American presence was greatest.

Meanwhile, caught in the Cold War trap during the 1950s, the United States often equated Third World nationalism, the yearning for social and economic justice, and the desire for non-alignment as signs of communist infiltration. Consequently, during the 1950s, the United States often worked to undermine nationalist, reformist movements and non-aligned tendencies in the Third World. Events such as the *coup* against Mossadegh in Iran, the ouster of Jacobo Arbenz in Guatemala in 1954, and disapproval of Nehru were examples of this approach. The net result was the erosion of the U.S. image in the Third World as a benevolent power.

The coming of the Kennedy administration generated widespread hopes in the Third World that U.S. idealism had been reawakened. President Kennedy's support for the Algerian independence movement, plus his initiation of programs such as the Peace Corps and the Alliance for Progress, raised Third World expectations for the American role. Had U.S. policy developed along these lines over a reasonable period of time, it might have recovered its earlier image. Instead, the United States became mired in the Vietnam conflict—with devastating consequences for its image and prestige in the Third World, Iran included.

During the 1960s and 1970s, U.S. involvement in the politics of the Arab-Israeli conflict also played an important role in generating anti-American feeling among Iran's clerical establishment and among religious-minded laymen. But secular Iranian intellectuals were also affected because the Palestinian issue is not only a religious issue but, for many Third World peoples, one of the last remaining colonial issues. Many Iranian intellectuals shared the view that Israel was an outpost of the Western imperial powers.[13] Thus, as Israel's principal supporter, the United States suffered in Iran as it did in the rest of the Middle East and in some other parts of the Third World. As Israel's involvement in Iranian affairs increased, particularly in such activities as the setting up and training of Iran's security services, U.S.-Israeli links contributed to anti-American feeling in Iran.

These tendencies to judge the United States harshly were reinforced by leftist propaganda depicting the United States as a world-devouring, imperial power, and at the root of all Iranian and Third World problems. Throughout the post-World War II period, leftist propaganda explained the growing U.S. presence and influence in Iran as a natural evolution of the old colonial impulse. Although simplistic, this explanation convinced many people.[14] And in the post-revolution period, leftist forces in Iran have enhanced this anti-American feeling.[15]

In addition to factors specific to the U.S.-Iranian relations, there is also an inherent, underlying source of tension between Iran and the United States—also applying to Iran's relations with other great powers—that derives from their respective positions as a global superpower and as a core regional power. For most of the post-war period, because of Iran's economic and military weakness, this tension in its relations with the United States was latent. But it came to the fore in the 1970s, when the interests of the two countries clashed regarding oil prices. The United States became uneasy with Iran's growing power, with its growing propensity for independent action, and with aspects of its regional policies—although in essence they were supportive of U.S. strategic interests. For his part, the Shah increasingly came to see himself as an ally rather than a surrogate and asked to be treated as such.

U.S.-Iranian Relations in the Post-Revolution Period

Following the Islamic revolution, two sets of factors have determined the shape of U.S.-Iranian relations: Iran's power struggles and intra-regime divisions and differences of opinion within U.S. policy-making circles on five principal issues: the extent of the Soviet threat to Iran and to U.S. interests in the Middle East; the extent of the Iranian threat to U.S. interests—including Iran's role in international terrorism and subversion against the United States' Arab allies; the relative importance of Iran and Iraq in the regional setting; future possibilities for a U.S.-Iranian dialogue; and diametrically opposed political agendas in the Middle East, *e.g.*, the spread of Islamic revolution versus its containment.

U.S.-Iranian Relations:
The Transition Period, February 1979—November 1979

The success of the revolutionary forces in February 1979 did not immediately cause the rupture of U.S.-Iranian relations. During the life of Mehdi Bazargan's provisional government (February 5 to November 4, 1979), Iran and the United States tried to stabilize bilateral relations. By February 1979, the two countries had both concluded that their past tight embrace should be loosened. Indeed, this shift had already been indicated by the Bakhtiar government's basing the future course of Iran's foreign policy on the principle of non-alignment.[16] Some of the most dramatic departures from past patterns of Iranian behavior—such as withdrawal from CENTO, the severing of links with Israel and South Africa, and the abandoning of Iran's security role in the Persian Gulf—were undertaken by Bakhtiar (who was appointed January 6, 1979). In fact, the Bazargan government's position on these issues was almost identical, especially while Karim Sanjabi was foreign minister.[17] This was not surprising, since Bazargan, Bakhtiar, and Sanjabi all belonged to the same Mossadeghist tradition, and their foreign policy outlook was that of moderate non-alignment. They shared a healthy apprehension of Soviet power and proximity as well as suspicion of Soviet intentions, and they recognized Iran's need for reasonable relations with the United States. They had all been critical of the Shah's overly active, and at times provocative, diplomacy and were against

Iran's striking such a posture in the future. In short, their foreign policy outlook was acceptable to the United States.

Other secular personalities involved in the Iranian revolution, such as Ibrahim Yazdi, Abol-Hassan Bani-Sadr, and Sadegh Ghotbzadeh, also came from similar traditions, although other influences were important in shaping their views. Bani-Sadr was the product of French leftist intellectualism, combined with his own Islamic-clerical family background—a mixture which had also produced Ali Shari'ati. Ibrahim Yazdi had a more radical and activist vision of Iran's future regional role. Nevertheless, all were Iranian nationalists and fearful of the Soviet Union. Thus, although they preferred less close relations with the United States, they also recognized the need for non-antagonistic U.S.-Iranian ties—although some of their regional policies might have strained relations with the United States.

It is difficult to document, but the diverging and shifting positions of secular nationalist members of Iran's revolutionary government on the issue of U.S.-Iranian relations were inextricably linked to their own personal power ambitions. Thus their various stances fluctuated depending on whether they held top positions. Nevertheless, as long as the Bazargan government was in power, the severing of ties with the United States was never considered. Rather, all indications, including contacts between Iranian officials and the U.S. Embassy in Tehran, pointed in the opposite direction, despite the existence of some difficulties in bilateral relations.[18] To be sure, there were some mob attacks on the U.S. embassy, but these were instigated by leftist forces.[19]

There was nothing in either U.S. or Iranian behavior to indicate that such problems were unsolvable. The United States seemed to have accepted the Iranian revolution, wanting Iran to develop in a moderate direction and to regain its stability. President Carter expressed America's desire to maintain cooperative relations with the new regime, and the United States recognized the Bazargan government. If anything, the United States and Iran could be faulted for wanting to move too fast to consolidate bilateral ties, an attitude that may have contributed to the downfall of the Bazargan government. As evidence of this haste, analysts have pointed to the meeting between Iranian Foreign Minister Ibrahim Yazdi and the U.S. secretary of state, Cyrus Vance at the United Nations in September 1979, and to the meeting between National Security Advisor Zbigniew Brzezinski and Mehdi Bazargan in Algiers that November.

Meanwhile, other forces in Iran were determined to eliminate the U.S. presence. Their efforts culminated in the American hostage crisis, the fall of the Bazargan government, the break in U.S.-Iranian relations, and an all-out U.S.-Iranian confrontation.

Given the forces at work in Iran at the time, it is difficult to see what the United States could have done differently or refrained from doing that would have prevented the breach. Some actions of the United States Senate, however, may have hurt relations and provided the opponents of reasonable U.S.-Iranian ties with further ammunition. These actions included a Senate resolution condemning the execution of former officials and other prominent figures from the Shah's regime. In principle, a U.S. Senate expression of distaste and concern for these executions was not out of the ordinary. But it was occasioned by the execution of a prominent Jewish businessman with close links to Israel. Members of Iran's religious circles interpreted the Senate protest as a sign of collusion between what they perceived to be U.S. imperialism and international Zionism.[20]

The Senate resolution undercut Bazargan's efforts to normalize U.S.-Iranian relations and forced it to refuse agreement to the U.S. ambassador-designate to Iran. According to Richard Cottam, America's lack of an ambassador in Tehran deprived it of an opportunity to try changing the stereotype of the United States held by some influential religious-political figures.[21] That may have been so. But given their ideological views and foreign connections, Iranians who were determined to eliminate U.S. influence would not have been easily deterred by the presence of a U.S. ambassador or by the lack of U.S. Senate condemnation.

The Hostage Crisis and the Rupture of U.S.-Iranian Relations

Those Iranians who were opposed to the U.S. presence in Iran finally succeeded by taking over the U.S. embassy on November 4, 1979 and by holding its diplomats and employees hostage for 444 days. This action not only prevented the consolidation of a working relationship between Iran and the United States, but, by wounding American national pride, it left a bitter legacy that continues to poison the atmosphere of U.S.-Iranian relations and that has colored every U.S. approach toward Iran.

The period of the hostage crisis, efforts made to gain the hostages' release, the process of policy making in the United States, and the impact of Iran's domestic power struggle on the continuation of the crisis have been well discussed elsewhere and need not be examined here in detail.[22] Yet analysis of key aspects of this crisis is needed in order to draw attention to points that are particularly germane in explaining Iranian foreign policy, then and since.

The hostage-taking operation has often been explained as the result of specific U.S. actions—most important, the admission of the Shah to the United States on October 22, 1979, for medical treatment. Some observers have argued that revolutionary forces in Iran saw this U.S. action as ''part of a larger pattern'' and of U.S. efforts to regain its lost position in Iran.[23] The U.S. decision to admit the Shah clearly did heighten Iranian suspicions of U.S. intentions, and it may have been the event that triggered a set of actions that had previously been prepared. But it is difficult to accept the thesis that, without it, the crisis would not have happened and the embassy would not have been seized. An operation such as the seizure of the U.S. embassy would require considerable time to plan and implement. With only two weeks between the two events, there must be some doubt about a direct cause and effect relationship. This does not mean that admitting the Shah to the United States was a wise political decision, but rather to question the assumption that it caused the hostage crisis.

This explanation also does not take sufficiently into account the objectives of those who directed the hostage-taking operation. These were primarily to influence developments in Iran and to prevent the consolidation and normalization of U.S.-Iranian relations. At that time, religious factions, a variety of leftist forces, and even some secular-nationalists had, for different reasons, one goal in common: to bring down Bazargan's government. Leftist and religious opposition to Bazargan was based on ideological grounds and derived from diverging visions of Iran's future, although the power ambitions of some key individuals also played a role.[24] Their principal purpose was to tear down completely the existing system in order to build a new one. Part of their strategy was to make governing impossible for Bazargan and to create a general sense of turmoil and unease.

Following Lenin's dictum that "The worse it gets the better it is," leftist forces were particularly active in creating this atmosphere, while religious forces, through the creation of revolutionary committees, crippled Bazargan's ability to govern. Thus an alliance of convenience was forged between leftist and religious forces in opposition to the secular nationalists, each calculating that the defeat of the nationalists would eventually lead to its own victory.

Moreover, both religious and leftist forces were committed to eliminating the U.S. presence from Iran. The anti-Americanism of these groups was qualitatively different from the more general sense of disillusionment and resentment. The popular feelings stemmed from a combination of specific U.S. actions and the impact of the more general forces discussed earlier, but the attitudes of the leftist and religious groups had deep ideological roots. The former viewed the United States as the arch-imperialist and the main obstacle to the achievement of their goals in Iran and throughout the Middle East. Religious forces agreed, although for different reasons. And their combined sentiments and objectives were shared by regional allies, including Libya, Syria, and different factions of the PLO, such as George Habash's communist PFLP, which, after the revolution, had infiltrated into Iran.[25]

Thus, because of the character and long-term goals of the hostage takers, it is difficult to see how anything that the United States could have done or refrained from doing would have prevented the crisis. For similar reasons, the thesis that Iranian revolutionaries somehow stumbled into the crisis because of a lack of precautions on the part of the U.S. Embassy, and, later, U.S. policy mistakes, is not logically defensible. The resolution of the hostage crisis was also delayed because of the possibilities that different Iranian groups and personalities saw in it to advance their goals. The Left, for example, correctly judged that as long as the hostage crisis continued, there could be no normalization of U.S.-Iranian relations.

Meanwhile, the Ayatollah Khomeini saw in the crisis an opportunity to humble the United States and to undermine its image and prestige, thus encouraging other Muslims to rise up against America. This fitted with his long-term objective of demonstrating that the United States was no longer omnipotent and that Muslim nations should not fear challenging its supremacy. As Richard Cottam has aptly put it, Khomeini wanted to show that a "shift in power" had occurred against the

United States in favor of the Muslims and, in general, all of those peoples that the Ayatollah and his disciples saw as the oppressed of the earth.[26] The fact that the United States imposed limits on its use of military force against Iran, coupled with the failure of the rescue attempt in April 1980, further convinced Khomeini that the United States was a declining power. Indeed, the United States' concern over the safety of its citizens and the possible Soviet reaction, including an invasion of Iran, foreclosed the use of major military force in order to gain the release of the hostages.

Both these concerns were later justified. In December 1979, the Soviets invaded Afghanistan and then massed troops along their borders with Iran. In the event of U.S. military action against Iran, the Soviets could have invoked Article Six of the 1921 Soviet-Iranian treaty and moved troops into Iran as a defensive measure against a supposed U.S. threat to Soviet security. The hostage crisis happened long before the age of Mikhail Gorbachev and his "New Thinking" in Soviet foreign policy. By the end of the year, the East-West *détente* of the early 1970s was dead, and East-West competition was still being conducted as a "zero-sum game." Of perhaps equal significance within the region, by the time of the hostage crisis the Soviet Union had not yet given up the hope of seeing the Iranian revolution turn into a true socialist revolution.

The United States was aware of the Soviet outlook and was unwilling to take any undue risks. Nevertheless, it did formulate the so-called Carter Doctrine—a commitment to use all means necessary to counter the projection of Soviet power farther into the region.[27] While couched in these general terms, the doctrine was specifically designed to deter a Soviet invasion of Iran. Beyond overall concerns of U.S.-Soviet competition, the United States was worried about a basic shift in strategic relations as well as the vulnerability of the region's oilfields, which required keeping the Iranian buffer out of Soviet control. Yet instead of seeing U.S. reluctance to use military force against Iran as a manifestation of wider issues between the superpowers, Iranian leaders interpreted it as part of a divinely sanctioned trend of growing American weakness and increasing Muslim power, perceptions that persisted in the following years and led to miscalculations about U.S. power and determination to project it.

Just as it is difficult to see what the United States could have done to prevent the taking of hostages, it is difficult to see what additional actions it could have taken to gain their release, because the crisis was essentially about the struggle for Iran's political direction and leadership. It is instructive, for example, that neither the Soviet invasion of Afghanistan nor, initially, the Iraqi invasion of September 1980 prompted Khomeini to end the hostage crisis.

Indeed, some leftist elements might have welcomed a limited Soviet intervention in Iran as a means of gaining power. Others seemed to believe that the Soviet Union would be deterred from invading Iran because of the fear of U.S. retaliation. Paradoxically, the enunciation of the Carter doctrine may have enhanced Iranian unwillingness to deal with the United States by reducing the risks of a Soviet invasion. In fact, until 1988 Iran seemed to believe that Soviet-American rivalry would protect it against direct military intervention by either side.[28]

Only after the first round of Iran's internal power struggle was almost over did it finally agree to end the crisis, which came to an end on January 20, 1981, on the basis of the Algiers Agreement. Most important from Iran's perspective, the United States pledged not to interfere in its internal affairs, directly or indirectly. The agreement also served as the principal document for resolving outstanding disputes between the two countries during the absence of official diplomatic ties.

U.S.-Iranian Relations, 1981–1984

During the months that followed, the religious forces in Iran consolidated their power, and the radicals gained ascendancy. and showed their determination to prevent the return of U.S. influence to Iran. Indeed, the radicals' vision for Iran's future economic and social structure resembled socialist concepts, and they held a relatively benign view of the Soviet Union, favoring closer ties with the East bloc.[29]

But more consequential for Iran's approach toward the United States was the world view of the Ayatollah Khomeini, especially his concept of the global role of the "arrogant powers." Within this frame of reference, the United States occupied a special status as the "Great Satan." The intensity of his animosity toward the United States derived from three basic factors: the U.S. connection with the Shah; Khomeini's view of the United States as the greatest enemy of Islam; and U.S. relations with Israel. In particular, Khomeini considered the state of Israel to be an enemy of the Muslims because, in his view, it has usurped Muslim lands and holy places and has worked to undermine Islam and the influence of Muslim clergy in Iran and throughout the Middle East. Indeed, Khomeini's hatred of the Shah was based partly on the latter's ties to Israel, which seemed to be one reason for the Shah's anti-Islamic policies.[30]

For the Islamic experience to succeed, therefore, Khomeini believed that the U.S. presence must not return to Iran; indeed, for the Muslims to liberate Jerusalem and to achieve true independence, the U.S. presence and influence must be eliminated from the Islamic world. As the vanguard of the Islamic revolution, Iran must begin an all-out campaign against the U.S. presence. It could not be safe if it were surrounded by hostile governments supported by the United States.

As a result, after the resolution of the hostage crisis, the essence of Iranian policy toward the United States became defiance and challenge, and its principal goal the demonstration of U.S. impotence to stem the rising tide of Islam. Understandably, during the next few years, this Iranian attitude would have a determining impact on the U.S. approach to Iran, to the war in the Persian Gulf, to Iraq, and to a host of other Middle East issues. Iran's challenge to the United States in the Muslim world would harden U.S. determination to contain the Iranian revolution, by bolstering the security of America's Middle East allies and by administering some form of defeat to Iran in order to demonstrate the failure, and thus the irrelevance, of its example for other Muslims. This U.S. attitude is reminiscent of the British approach toward Mossadegh: He and his nationalization had to be defeated because otherwise they could set the wrong example. The fact that such lessons are generally lost on those for whom they are intended—as Nasser's nationalization of the Suez Canal illustrated—was not a consideration. As one former official of the U.S. National Security Council told me, dealing effectively with the question of Iran would become an issue of "American manhood."

Yet despite its determination to win the contest with Iran, the United States faced a serious dilemma—namely, how to contain or defeat Iran without either pushing it into the Soviet orbit or causing it to disintegrate, which could also lead to Soviet inroads. Indeed, after Iraq's invasion of Iran in September 1980, officials in Washington were fearful of both possibilities.

Iran, meanwhile, suspected the United States of having instigated the Iraqi invasion. No doubt, the Americans had reasons to do so, most notably to help free their citizens held captive in Tehran. By this reasoning, the United States might also have hoped that Iraq's invasion would topple the Islamic regime. Yet there are countervailing arguments. First, the U.S. fear of Soviet influence in Iran and the danger of Iran's disintegration argued against U.S. support for any action that could cause such developments. Second, the United States could not be sure that Iraq's goals in Iran would be limited to changing the Khomeini regime. Likewise, given the state of U.S.-Iraqi relations, could the United States be confident of controlling Iraq once it had resolved its problem with Iran. Third, because of the nature of the Ba'athist regime and Saddam Hussein's ambitions, the United States did not relish the prospect of Iraq's gaining preponderance in the Persian Gulf and possibly throughout the Middle East.

With the ongoing hostage crisis, the United States was not particularly alert to the possibility of an Iraqi invasion nor, once it happened, highly motivated to stop it, assuming it could have done so. The U.S. attitude at the time was quite understandable. Nevertheless, it deepened the Iranian regime's suspicions of U.S. intentions.

Throughout the war, the United States adopted an official policy of neutrality. But in practice, from time to time, it shifted its posture in favor of one or the other party, depending both on the balance of forces between the two combatants and on its calculations about the nature and source of threat to its interests. Early in the war, the United States feared that, in desperation, Iran might turn to the Soviet Union, and thus it permitted indirect delivery of some U.S.-made weapons and spare parts. Some analysts have attributed this U.S. attitude to the Soviet-centeredness of Reagan's foreign policy, particularly during his first term, and to its effort to roll back Soviet advances.[31] There is merit in this analysis, because in Iran's case the Soviet threat was real—not just an application of ideology—and U.S. concerns were justified.

Meanwhile, Iran's preoccupation with its internal conflict and then with the war had stalled its aggressive and systematic export of revolution. Despite the fact that the Gulf Arab states still felt threatened with revolutionary contagion, they had successfully dealt with its initial infection. They had also forged greater cooperation in security affairs with each other—in the framework of the Gulf Cooperation Council—and with the United States. Thus, during this period, the Soviet threat to Iran and the risk of Iran's disintegration seemed to the United States to be more serious than Iran's threat to Persian Gulf security. Moreover, an Iraqi victory would have made Israel's security more precarious and tipped the Arab-Israeli military balance against it. Therefore, the United States adopted a dual policy of containing Iran while also trying to avoid its disintegration, its domination by the Soviet Union, or its swift defeat by Iraq. Washington indicated that it did not favor any territorial changes in the region, and in May 1982 Secretary of State Alexander Haig said that the United States favored a settlement to the war that would "preserve the sovereignty and territorial integrity of both Iran and Iraq."[32]

Beyond this consideration, not much attention was paid in Washington to developing a coherent policy toward Iran, partly because of the United States' other preoccupations in the Middle East and partly because, with the breach in relations, Iran had no bureaucratic constituency in either the State or Defense Departments. Cynics have argued that—together with its regional allies—the United States found the war easy to accept as long as it was confined to Iran and Iraq, since it tended to weaken both parties. During 1981–82, some American officials may also have hoped that fear of Iran would induce moderate Arabs to join the United States and Israel in the grand alliance of "strategic cooperation" envisaged by Haig. But most important, this U.S. attitude of general neglect of what was going on in the Islamic Republic and in the war showed the lack of intrinsic interest in Iran. As long as the Soviets were out of the Persian Gulf and the oil was flowing, the United States could wait to see how diverse Iranian forces fared, while occasionally toying with possibilities of using Iranian exiles to counter the Khomeini regime.

By the summer of 1982, however, circumstances had begun to change in the Middle East, prompting a gradual reassessment of threats to U.S. interests. Iran repelled Iraqi forces, and the clerical forces consolidated their internal position. The Soviet Union became bogged down in Afghanistan, and the threat of a Soviet military invasion of Iran subsided. Soviet-Iranian relations, which had improved significantly during 1981–82, became strained, thus reducing U.S. anxieties over indirect Soviet control of Iran. Meanwhile, Iraq felt increasingly vulnerable and became more accommodating toward the United States and the Persian Gulf Arab states. Iran's military successes intensified their fears over its intentions in the event of a victory over Iraq, which no longer seemed impossible. It was in this period that the first signs of the U.S. tilt toward Iraq became apparent. The United States removed Iraq from the list of states that supported terrorism and granted it loans and credits.[33]

Events in Lebanon and Iran's activities there also prompted the United States to reassess the "Iran factor" in affecting its regional interests and thus its approach toward Iran. The Israeli invasion of Lebanon in June 1982 offered Iran an opportunity to develop a foothold. Emboldened by its success in the war with Iraq, it embarked on an aggressive and sustained policy of exporting revolution and of challenging the U.S. presence in the Middle East. Lebanon was the first test case. The new Iranian aggressiveness was best illustrated by the bombing of the U.S. Marine barracks at the Beirut International Airport in October 1983. While no Iranian national was involved in carrying out the attacks, strong circumstantial evidence indicated Iranian involvement.[34]

The bombing of the Marine barracks faced the Reagan administration with its first important challenge from terrorism. During the 1980 presidential campaign, Ronald Reagan had severely criticized President Carter's handling of the hostage crisis. The Reagan administration later promised a policy of "swift retribution" toward the terrorists and their sponsors. Thus, how the United States responded to the Marine barracks attack would be a major test of the administration's ability to deal with terrorism. It soon discovered, however, that implementing the policy was not easy. In the event, the United States did not retaliate against either Iran or Syria, the two states implicated in the bombing. Then, under domestic pressure, in February 1984 the United States withdrew its forces from Lebanon, which meant abandoning the hope of putting in place a stable government that would be willing to make a lasting peace with Israel.[35]

Among outside forces, Syria was chiefly responsible for the failure of U.S. policy, but for understandable reasons Iran became the focus of American resentment and was targeted for punishment. The United States was unwilling to antagonize Syria unduly because of the impact this could have on U.S. peacemaking efforts in the Arab-Israeli conflict, in the context of the "Reagan Plan, of September 1982" as well as on U.S. hopes that Syria could play a positive role in pacifying Lebanon. Thus, there was pressure within the State Department against taking a harsh stand toward Syria. The search for an alternative also coincided with a change in leadership at the State Department, as George Shultz replaced Alexander Haig and the bureaucratic indifference that had affected the U.S. approach toward Iran. Both Secretary of State Shultz and Secretary of Defense Caspar Weinberger were more sensitive to Arab concerns than Haig had been. While they disagreed on most aspects of U.S. policy in Lebanon and in the Middle East, generally, as one former official of the National Security Council told me, a "punitive policy on Iran was the only policy they could agree on." In his words, Iran thereby became the whipping-boy for U.S. Middle East frustrations. This is not to suggest that the U.S. did not have valid reasons to want to punish Iran. It simply means that bureaucratic factors also played an important role.

Meanwhile, Arab allies of the United States, especially Egypt, were lobbying for a stronger U.S. response against Iran and greater support for Iraq. Egypt wanted to return to the Arab fold, from which it had been excluded since signing the Camp David Accords, and hoped to facilitate its reentry by proving its influence with Washington. Meanwhile, Iranian-inspired terrorism enhanced anti-Iranian sentiment and increased U.S. determination to punish Iran. On December 12, 1983, there was an attempted truck bombing of the U.S. embassy in Kuwait, and on

January 23, 1984, the U.S. secretary of state designated Iran as a terrorist state. As a result, the United States imposed controls on the export to Iran of a large number of items, including all goods and technical data subject to national security control if destined for military end-use.[36]

While Iran's rhetoric remained defiant, it was evident that its leaders feared a U.S. military strike.[37] But when this did not happen by the end of January 1984, the tone of Iranian commentary became more strident. In an interview, the Iranian Prime Minister dismissed U.S. accusations of terrorism against Iran as an election-year ploy and said: " . . . we remind him [President Reagan] of the events of Tabas ["Desert One"] and we warn that Reagan may face the same fate that befell Carter. . . . "[38]

The United States refrained from taking direct military action against Iran, because of its fears about the possible Soviet response, uncertainty over the effects of military action on the security of Persian Gulf states, and the possibility of increased Iranian terrorism or suicide bombing of vital Gulf installations. Yet at the same time, there was increasing pressure in the United States, and especially at the State Department, for a tilt toward Iraq in the war. Some U.S. officials began arguing for a more active U.S. role in trying to undermine the Khomeini regime by, among other things, supporting Iranian opposition forces.[39] The U.S. debate on policy toward Iran was not totally resolved until 1987, but by the beginning of 1984 the United States had tilted toward Iraq, re-establishing diplomatic relations with that country and providing it with economic assistance in the form of agricultural credits. There were no direct U.S. military supplies to Iraq, but U.S. arms may have reached it via Egypt and Jordan, and the United States did provide Iraq with intelligence information.[40] At the same time, the United States began to put heavier pressure on Iran.

1984–1986: Public Confrontation: Secret Reconciliation

Another source of friction in U.S.-Iranian relations was added when Iraq began the tanker war in late 1983, potentially threatening the flow of oil from the Persian Gulf in order to internationalize the war and to stimulate outside pressure on Iran to negotiate. In an effort to frustrate these Iraqi aspirations, Iran threatened to close the Strait of Hormuz.[41] The United States and other Western countries responded that they would keep the strait open, if need be, by military intervention. Despite inflammatory rhetoric, however, Iran's sense of pragmatism prevailed. Recognizing its own need to export oil and its vulnerability to punitive military actions, it made no efforts to close the strait. Ironically, even tragically, the hardening of U.S. policy toward Iran during this period coincided with the emergence of more moderate and pragmatic tendencies in Iran's foreign policy. Although U.S. academic experts on Iran drew attention to this development, it was largely ignored by U.S. officials.[42] The Bureaucratic factors discussed above contributed to this lack of attention. The fact was that the U.S. had already moved toward a more punitive policy regarding Iran, which may have been partly responsible for the official dismissal of such warnings from the academic community.

Iran's new pragmatism did not extend very far in terms of dealing with the United States, however. Its rhetoric remained defiant and abusive, and the radicals' influence persisted. It is understandable, therefore, that the United States did not want to make overtures to Iran that would run a high risk of being rebuffed. It is also possible that a conciliatory U.S. attitude would simply have emboldened the radicals. Yet high-ranking Iranian officials did comment that Iran would be prepared for reconciliation with the United States, provided it changed its ways. Rafsanjani, the speaker of the Iranian parliament, said that U.S.-Iranian hostility should not last until "doomsday." Many analysts broadly interpreted the condition that the United States must "change its ways" to include abandonment of its support for Israel. But most probably, the Iranians meant abandonment of U.S. support for the Iranian opposition and for Iraq. In any event, the United States never seriously tested Iran's intentions, and the lack of a positive response to the fledgling moderation of Iran's attitudes may have undermined the chances that this moderation could become entrenched.

The United States continued to apply pressure on Iran and to present it as the principal threat to U.S. regional interests. In 1984, it launched its "Operation Staunch," designed to dry up the supply of weapons to Iran.[43] Yet beyond that effort, the United States paid little attention to developing an overall policy toward Iran based on a mixture of pressures and incentives.[44] Not only was there Arab lobbying, closer U.S.-Iraqi ties, and a lack of bureaucratic interest in Iran, but also by 1984 the United States was convinced that the threat of a Soviet military invasion of Iran had declined sharply. With the Iranian regime's 1983 crackdown on the Tudeh Party and the deterioration of Soviet-Iranian relations, so had the threat of indirect Soviet control of Iran.

Later, changes in the Soviet approach toward the Third World, plus the priority that a new Soviet leader, Mikhail Gorbachev, gave to the improvement of East-West relations over other policy goals, freed the United States even more from concern over the possibility of increased Soviet influence in Iran. Indeed, within the U.S. administration—especially at the State Department—the view developed that Islamic fundamentalism, not communism, had become the most serious threat to stability in the Middle East and U.S. interests. Thus Iran, not the Soviet Union, was America's principal concern in the region.

No doubt, the nature of the Soviet challenge had changed considerably since the 1970s and early 1980s. Islamic fundamentalism had emerged as a serious rival to leftist ideologies as a magnet for frustrated and radicalized groups in the Middle East. But the thesis was flawed because it did not distinguish between the Soviets' military threat and their political and diplomatic challenge. Nor did it recognize the difference between the seriousness of the Soviet challenge in areas such as Iran, Afghanistan, and Pakistan on the one hand and in the Arab world on the other. And it did not appreciate the important buffer role that Iran had always played in checking Soviet influence. Thus the thesis concerning the primacy of a threat from Islamic fundamentalism did not correctly assess the cost to the United States if the Soviets came to dominate Iran.

At the same time, there was an inadequate recognition in the U.S. government of Iran's contribution to the success of U.S. policy in fighting the Soviet presence in Afghanistan, through Iran's support for the Afghan Mojahedin and its hosting of more than 2 million Afghan refugees, without any outside assistance. In effect, both sides were reluctant to acknowledge the fact that in Afghanistan, they were strategic allies. And U.S. attitudes also did not take into consideration Iran's reasonably good relations with Pakistan and Turkey, two U.S. allies.

The negative U.S. assessment of Iran was partly influenced by efforts of officials and others outside the government to lead the United States toward a more actively pro-Iraq policy. Only in this way, they argued, could the United States contain Iran and force it to compromise.[45] Moreover, a pro-Iraq policy was a convenient way of compensating for the lack of U.S. support for Arab concerns in the Arab-Israeli conflict.[46] Following this logic, the hardliners on Iran dismissed the chances for improved U.S.-Iranian relations before Iran's political regime changed fundamentally. And they rejected a dialogue before Iran accepted a negotiated end to the war and unequivocally renounced terrorism and stopped destabilizing Persian Gulf Arab states.[47]

This view was not shared by all U.S. government officials. Among the National Security Council staff and in the intelligence community, there was a greater appreciation both of the Soviet factor and of Iran's internal fragility. These officials seemed to be aware of the diverging views within Iran's leadership regarding the direction of its foreign policy. As a result, they believed that it was important for the United States to establish some contacts with Iran, not because they were unaware of Iran's threat to U.S. interests or that they did not want to pressure Iran into changing its behavior. Rather, they believed that a policy of pressure and containment did not exclude exploring possibilities for accommodation. The impact of this viewpoint can be seen in the fact that, despite a punitive policy, the United States did not try to isolate Iran completely. Rather, it encouraged third countries, such as Japan, West Germany, and a few others, to play a diplomatic role in Iran as counterweights to the Soviet Union.

The ill-fated Iran-Contra affair has been almost universally condemned as a blunder. No doubt, much was wrong with it, morally as well as politically, including the attempt to trade arms for hostages and the deceiving of Congress.[48] But insofar as U.S. secret dealings with Iran related to establishing some kind of dialogue and exploring ways through which the United States could influence Iran to move in a moderate direction, they represented a valid expression of U.S. interests. This was particularly true in the context of both the potential role of the Soviet Union in Iran and U.S.-Soviet competition in Southwest Asia.[49] Indeed, in his first television address to the nation on the "Irangate" affair in November 1986, President Reagan put the strategic case for what he had done. What went wrong in the Iran initiative was not the goal of establishing a dialogue with Iran but the fact that other concerns, such as the release of the hostages, acquired an urgency and importance that eclipsed other long-term policy concerns.[50]

The View from Iran

Understanding the evolution of U.S.-Iranian relations since the revolution also requires an analysis of Iranian motives for seeking a dialogue with the United States and the identification of which Iranians were involved in these contacts.[51] The most pressing motive was, indeed, to obtain U.S. arms. U.S. Marine Corps Colonel Oliver North identified Iranian motives in the following terms:

> The Iranians . . . are under extraordinary military pressure from Iraq and are, by their own admission, subject to regular overflights of Iranian territory by Soviet aircraft. They currently have no capability to deal with this affront and find themselves in an increasingly desperate situation toward Iraq. . . . [52]

This assessment was correct. The Iraqi bombing of Iranian cities and economic installations was becoming increasingly effective, bringing tremendous psychological and economic pressures to bear. Iran experienced increasing difficulty in obtaining arms. In this regard, the moderates and the radicals were in agreement.

There were other, long-term reasons for Iran's mild overture to the United States. Very likely, the leadership wanted to convince the United States to change its attitude toward the war and the conditions for ending it: to accept, for example, Iran's request that the United States and other nations join in condemning Iraq's aggression. The leadership may have wanted to persuade the United States to stop assisting Iranian opposition groups. Furthermore, several major figures within the Iranian leadership shared concerns regarding Soviet influence.[53] With an eye to the post-Khomeini era, they may have wanted a dialogue with the United States as a prelude to eventual reconciliation. They were aware of Soviet influence among the radical wing, and, to balance that influence, they may have wanted to establish links with the United States in anticipation of a power struggle after the Ayatollah's death. Indeed, this conjecture best explains why Mehdi Hashemi, a noted radical, leaked knowledge of the secret U.S.-Iranian contacts to the Syrian newspaper, *Al-Shi'ra*. The disclosure—and most important, the fact of Israel's involvement—achieved its purpose, namely to torpedo U.S.-Iranian rapprochement.

Nevertheless, until December 1986 the supporters of a dialogue tried to salvage it. Hodjat-al-Islam Rafsanjani tried not to close the door to all contacts with the United States.[54] In a speech at Tehran University in late November, Foreign Minister Ali-Akbar Velayati argued that having relations with other countries—presumably including the United States—did not mean accepting their hegemony. Meanwhile, however, the radicals counterattacked and vowed that they would block the return of U.S. influence to Iran.[55] Thus, given the atmosphere in Iran, coupled with the hardening of the U.S. position as a result of the Iran-Contra affair, the moderates also adopted a hard-line posture in order to protect their position and redeem their revolutionary credentials. Their statements regarding contacts with the United States became gradually harsher, and the two countries headed toward another confrontation.

1987–88: Final Confrontation

As the dust settled after the Iran-Contra affair, it became clear that it had had ramifications for both the foreign policy issues involved and for U.S. domestic politics and the decision-making process in Washington. It created a major controversy between the executive and legislative branches and significantly reduced the flexibility of the U.S. administration to deal with Iran, because of the glare of publicity. The Iran-Contra affair reduced the influence of the proponents of an opening to Iran, and it increased that of officials who were more concerned about Iran's threat to America's Arab allies than about either the role of the Soviet Union or Iran's internal developments. This group supported a decisive tilt in Iraq's favor and exaggerated the impact of the United States' Iranian dealings on its relations with the Arabs, who suspected that Israel wished to reestablish contacts between Iran and the United States in order to sow discord in U.S.-Arab relations.[56] And the public outrage over the ''arms-for-hostages'' deal also forced the administration to adopt a more hard-line posture on the question of dealing with terrorists, and thus Iran.

Nevertheless, as late as the end of January 1987, the United States was still trying to keep the door open for a future dialogue. This time, however, it insisted that Iran unequivocally change its policies. Secretary of State Shultz acknowledged Iran's importance in the region and referred to the historic, common U.S.-Iranian strategic interest in containing the Soviet Union. He noted Iran's critical stand on Afghanistan, another common interest. He admitted that the United States had an ''obvious stake in better relations with Iran,'' and he reiterated that the United States recognized Iran's revolution as a ''fact of history'' and bore ''no malice toward the Iranian people.'' He also stressed, however, that ''American interests are directly threatened by the Iranian government's pursuit of its war with Iraq, by its sponsorship of terrorism, and by its collusion with terrorist forces elsewhere in the region.'' Furthermore, Shultz warned that the United States ''cannot hope for progress without fundamental changes in Iranian policy and practice,'' and could not pursue better relations with Iran ''to the detriment of our many other interests and commitments in the region.''[57]

From this point, the United States would also insist that any contacts with Iran be in open discussions with authorized and official representatives. These U.S. conditions were not unreasonable. But given Iran's domestic politics, U.S. insistence on them made the pursuit of a dialogue impossible. In Iran, the moderates' position had been eroded and the radicals and their Lebanese allies tried to preempt any further dialogue by kidnapping three American nationals in Beirut. Thus internal developments in Iran, as well as in the United States, precluded any chance of sustaining a dialogue.

In Iran, however, the shift in the balance of power in favor of the radicals was not decisive. The moderates soon recovered their influence and demonstrated it by trying and executing Mehdi Hashemi, the man most responsible for leaking information about U.S.-Iranian contacts. But the moderates' gradual recovery did not help U.S.-Iranian relations because, partly as a reaction to Irangate and its many ramifications, by the spring of 1987 U.S. policy had shifted toward active support for Iraq and a vigorous effort to drive Iran to the bargaining table, with punitive actions, if necessary.

The United States soon found the opportunity to implement this policy. In September 1986, Kuwait had turned to it for help in protecting its fleet of oil tankers against Iranian attacks. The United States' initial response was not enthusiastic. On January 13, 1987, Kuwait again approached the United States and asked it to reflag up to eight oil tankers and to provide naval protection. The U.S. government initially agreed only to escort Kuwaiti tankers. Later, however, it agreed both to the reflagging and offering naval protection, in part because, after first being rebuffed by the United States, Kuwait had appealed to the Soviet Union, which agreed to lease three tankers to Kuwait. In Washington, this move was seen as affording the Soviet Union an opportunity to increase its influence in the Persian Gulf. Also important, unlike September 1986 when it had been pursuing the option of an opening to Iran, U.S. Persian Gulf policy had become totally focused on the Arab states.

At different times, the U.S. government cited six basic reasons for accepting the Kuwaiti request: to prevent Soviet domination of the Persian Gulf; to protect freedom of shipping; to prevent the spread of the war to other "non-belligerent" countries; to support Iraqi morale; to reassure Arab states of the Persian Gulf that arms-dealing with Iran had been an aberration; and to help bring the war to an end.[58] It argued particularly that, in the absence of a positive U.S. response to Kuwait's request, the Soviet Union could make significant inroads in the area.

There was some contradiction, however, in U.S. views on the seriousness of the Soviet threat to the region. On the one hand, the United States maintained that the principal threat to Middle East stability and U.S. interests was Islamic fundamentalism. But on the other hand, the potential leasing of three Soviet tankers to Kuwait was considered a critical threat to U.S. interests. Furthermore, while exaggerating the potential Soviet threat in the Persian Gulf if Moscow established better ties with Kuwait, the United States systematically underplayed the possibility that Iran would turn toward the Soviet Union in response to increased U.S. naval activity in the Persian Gulf and strong support for the Arab position in the war.[59]

The administration's argument that international shipping was threatened was also not convincing. According to all accounts, the tanker war involved fewer than one percent of ships plying the Persian Gulf and had hardly affected world oil supplies.[60] Also, more than 70 percent of attacks on shipping had been carried out by Iraq, not Iran, as part of Baghdad's policy to try internationalizing the war.

Indeed, on several occasions Iran had expressed its readiness to end attacks, provided Iraq did the same, and both Iran and the United States, along with all other oil producing and consuming states, had a common interest in ending the tanker war.

In discussing its role in the Gulf, the United States also argued that Iran's acquisition of Chinese-made Silkworm missiles as posing a new threat to shipping, particularly the danger that Iran might use the missiles to close the Strait of Hormuz. But this argument ignored both the physical difficulty of closing the strait, along with Iran's vulnerability to counterattack, and its own vital interest in keeping the strait open.

The risk that the conflict could spread to other "non-belligerent" countries of the Persian Gulf was also exaggerated by the U.S. administration and the Gulf Arabs. Indeed, by 1987 Iran was in its weakest state militarily and economically and was in no position to threaten the Gulf states. Infrequent Iranian attacks on Kuwait's shipping were not of a magnitude to threaten either its security or its oil income.[61] Furthermore, if Iran were capable of posing a serious threat to the Gulf Arabs, it would have done so long before, especially in view of their active support for Iraq.[62] Among other inhibitions was Iran's knowledge that such an action would trigger a Western response. The delivery of Silkworm missiles had not changed this basic political calculation.

These arguments were essentially designed to quell misgivings of members of Congress who feared that the reflagging operations could put the United States in another impossible situation, as had happened in Lebanon. The debate, however, was settled when, on May 17, 1987, an Iraqi Exocet missile hit the *U.S.S. Stark,* killing thirty-seven and injuring twenty-one U.S. servicemen. The *Stark* incident was accepted as an accident, and no hard evidence was found to prove otherwise. However, without it the administration would have had a more difficult task of convincing the Congress of the wisdom of its reflagging operations. The incident certainly accomplished what the tanker war had failed to, namely to internationalize the Persian Gulf war.

Iran's response to the U.S. decision to reflag the Kuwaiti tankers was a mixture of rhetorical bravado and practical caution—a combination not often well understood in the United States. There was a debate within the Iranian leadership. The radicals argued that Iran should mount all-out attacks on the United States, including suicide bombings. They believed that raising the risk of high American casualties would rally U.S. public opinion against involvement in the Persian Gulf and would force a U.S. withdrawal, as had happened in Lebanon. As part of this tactic, in August 1987 Iran held a series of naval maneuvers, code-named "Martyrdom." But the pragmatic trend prevailed, and Iran did not embark on an even more self-destructive policy. Lacking a military riposte that would do more good than harm, Iran tried to affect political debate within the United States, particularly between the Congress and the administration, by threatening large-scale terrorist actions against U.S. interests throughout the Middle East. Also, partly as a tactic to dissuade the United States from reflagging the Kuwaiti tankers, Iran warmed up relations with the Soviet Union and leaked rumors of an impending Soviet-Iranian friendship treaty. Theoretically, Iran did have a Soviet card to play. Had it been willing to stop its criticism of the Soviet Union and to help it resolve the Afghan problem, Moscow might have taken more risks to prevent the projection of U.S. naval power into the Persian Gulf. Some factions in Iran did argue for cooperating with the Soviets, but others were opposed, not least because such a move would have undermined Iran's Islamic credentials.

Following its decision to reflag the Kuwaiti tankers, the United States at first moved with caution in the Persian Gulf, which was reciprocated by Iran. In July 1987, the first reflagged Kuwaiti tanker, renamed the *Bridgeton,* hit a mine, but the United States did not retaliate against the presumed source, Iran. By contrast, on September 22, while Iran's president was speaking at the United Nations in New York, U.S. helicopters attacked the Iranian vessel *Iran Arj* on the grounds that it was being used as a base for laying mines. It was the Iranians' turn to take the lead in exercising caution by only attacking a Liberian-flagged, albeit U.S.-owned, tanker in Kuwaiti waters. Then, on October 16th, a missile struck the U.S.-flagged Kuwaiti tanker, *Sea-Isle City.*[63] This time, the United States retaliated, on October 19th, by bombing one Iranian oil platform and boarding another, destroying its communication system. The U.S. government characterized its action as a measured response; the Iranians seemed to agree with that characterization and did not retaliate. On October 26th, however, the United States followed up by imposing a total trade embargo on Iran.

To parallel its reflagging policy and naval operations in the Persian Gulf, the United States took diplomatic initiatives at the United Nations. With the support of Britain, in the spring of 1987 it began pressing other members of the U.N. Security Council to pass a resolution on the Iran-Iraq war that would include the threat of sanctions in the case of non-compliance by either of the belligerents. These efforts succeeded. On June 22, the Security Council unanimously passed Resolution 598.

The United States had expected that Iran would reject the resolution, and this may have even been its design.[64] If so, the U.S. strategy backfired. Iran conditionally accepted the resolution, thereby making problematic the immediate imposition of an arms embargo. But despite Iran's willingness to consider a negotiated peace and to accept an unofficial U.N.-sponsored cease-fire, provided some changes were made in Resolution 598—especially on the timing of a process to determine the aggressor in the war—the United States insisted that it accept Resolution 598 unconditionally. In fact, Iran's greater flexibility on the issue of peace, a reflection of its deteriorating military and economic situation, encouraged the United States in its punitive policy. However, it still moved cautiously. After the incident of October 1987 in the Persian Gulf, the U.S.-Iranian military confrontation had stabilized. The United States continued to provide Iraq with valuable intelligence regarding Iran's military operations and troop movements, and massive Iraqi bombing and use of chemical weapons weakened Iran's position in the war. Nevertheless, the U.S. presence failed to force Iran to the negotiating table.

The lull was broken on April 14, 1988, when the *U.S.S. Roberts* struck a mine.

After some initial doubt, the United States determined that the mines had been recently laid and retaliated by attacking an Iranian oil platform with an export capacity of 150,000 barrels per day. This time, Iran opened fire on U.S. Navy vessels. In retaliation, the United States destroyed three Iranian warships and declared that it would protect all neutral shipping.[65] This series of events represented a major escalation and reflected growing U.S. confidence that Iran could not retaliate in any meaningful way.

The Soviets were also unlikely to take any undue risks on Iran's behalf. It is unclear whether there was an explicit understanding between the United States and the Soviet Union. But given the interest of both countries in containing Iran, plus Tehran's inability to play the Soviet card effectively, the Soviet Union certainly acquiesced to U.S. actions. It may also have calculated that a U.S. military attack on Iran would, in the long run, force it to look to Moscow. Indeed, Iranian radicals, especially within the Revolutionary Guards, were widely suspected of having laid the mines because they were unhappy about the cautious and non-provocative posture of their government toward the United States.[66]

Moreover, before the incident, Iran's Deputy Foreign Minister, Mohammad Javad Larijani, had told the U.N. secretary general that it wanted to talk to the United States. Washington reportedly expressed orally its willingness to meet with Larijani, but the *U.S.S. Roberts* incident made this difficult.[67] No doubt, skepticism was legitimate, but it also undermined the ability of the United States to test Iranian sincerity in seeking a dialogue. U.S.-Iran confrontations in the Persian Gulf also played into the hands of the Iranian radicals.

U.S. military attacks certainly had a traumatizing effect on the Iranian public and leadership by raising the specter of a wider conflict with the United States. This factor, together with fear of further Iraqi gains and the debilitating impact on Iranian morale of Iraqi use of poison gas, marked the beginning of a process which would lead to Iran's unconditional acceptance of Resolution 598.

The Iranian response to the U.S. attacks in April 1988 was limited to complaints to the U.N. Secretary General and requests that the Security Council investigate U.S. aggression. Then, on July 3, 1988, surface-to-air missiles fired by the *U.S.S. Vincennes* struck an Iran Air passenger aircraft, killing 290 people. Iran claimed that the attack was premeditated; yet, remarkably, it took no retaliatory action against the United States. Initially, there was harsh rhetoric. The Ayatollah Khomeini declared that " . . . we must be all prepared for a real war and go to the war fronts and fight against America and its lackeys."[68] But Hodjat-al-Islam Rafsanjani was more conciliatory, arguing against seeking "a swift revenge." Iran had more to gain, he said, by keeping international sympathy on its side.[69] Thus Iran concentrated its efforts in international organizations and tried to have the United States condemned for the incident, failing in both the International Civil Aviation Organization (ICAO) and the United Nations.[70] Then, on July 27, Iran's Deputy Foreign Minister called on the United States to end its hostile attitude; denied that Iran wanted to export its revolution "with a gun;" reiterated its interest in regional cooperation for security in the Persian Gulf; complained about Iraqi sabotage against

Iran; and said that Iran could help gain the release of American hostages if the United States ended the difficulties that it had created for Iran. Under the circumstances, these statements were conciliatory and, in an oblique way, they met some of the U.S. conditions, such as denouncing terrorism and subversion in the Gulf.[71]

The official response of the U.S. government was firm, even harsh. While it expressed its regret for the loss of civilian life, it extended no apology nor any immediate offer of compensation. The United States maintained that, while regrettable, the incident was basically Iran's fault and the inevitable result of tensions in the Persian Gulf, caused by Iran's intransigence, unwillingness to accept a negotiated peace, and aggressive policies.[72] Vice President George Bush called the incident an act of self-defense.[73] This official U.S. attitude was not shared by all Americans, however. Many analysts attributed the incident to a provocative U.S. posture.[74] The ICAO report also blamed the United States for gross negligence in shooting down the airplane.

Post-Confrontation Period: Hope and Uncertainty

The long-term effect of American military confrontation on U.S.-Iranian relations cannot yet be adequately assessed. It is likely that U.S. intervention in the Persian Gulf on Iraq's side, along with its efforts in the United Nations that effectively precluded consideration of Iran's grievances, will leave a bitter memory in Iran. Through a process of mythologization, it could acquire a symbolism as significant as that of the *coup d'etat* against Mossadegh.

The immediate impact of these events, however, was salutary because they dramatically demonstrated to Iran the disastrous consequences of its policies. They punctured the Iranian belief that the United States was incapable of using its massive military power in defense of its interests. They also demonstrated that sooner or later Iran would have to come to terms with the United States. On July 20 Iran accepted a cease-fire under Resolution 598, and it took effect on August 22—an ironic byproduct of a tragic incident. For the United States, the use of military force against Iran had a cathartic effect. It partially expiated the humiliation of the hostage crisis, and it revenged the deaths of more than 300 U.S. servicemen in Lebanon.

The *Vincennes* incident did not initially produce a radical backlash in Iran. Instead, the position of the moderates was strengthened by the demonstration of the consequences of radical policies. Thus, shortly after the incident, there were increasing rumors of U.S.-Iranian contacts and the possibility of some kind of dialogue. The United States' official response was that it had no such intentions.[75] It also reiterated its conditions for starting a dialogue and offered no concessions. During this period, some private individuals tried to mediate between Iran and the United States, including efforts to gain the release of American hostages in Lebanon. But, burned by the Iran-Contra episode, both sides agreed that any contacts should be limited to official channels. For the next several months, the U.S. government's ability to respond to Iranian overtures was also constrained because of the presidential campaign, in which memories of the Iran-Contra affair figured.[76]

This stasis in U.S. policy was unfortunate, however, because the period between July and November 1988 proved to be the most propitious time to achieve some kind of breakthrough. However, domestic considerations prevented both sides from taking steps to promote a dialogue. In Iran, the radical opposition blocked efforts to gain release of the American hostages. The United States, for its part, still did not pay compensation for the victims of the airline tragedy, nor did it agree to the release of some Iranian funds as an inducement for Iran to work harder for the release of U.S. citizens. In January 1989, however, President Bush said in his inaugural address that Iranian good will would generate U.S. good will—yet he offered no concrete actions. Iran reacted favorably to this statement but it, too, took no practical steps, and the mutual paralysis in U.S.-Iranian relations continued.

From the U.S. side, the lack of effort to explore the possibility of changed relations with Iran—indeed, the possibility of influencing the development of Iranian politics at a time of great flux—can be attributed in part to continuing disagreements within the U.S. government. Debate centered around two themes: the relative importance of Iran versus Iraq, both within the region and from the perspective of U.S. interests; and the extent to which the United States should risk antagonizing Iraq and its Arab allies in order to promote a dialogue with Iran.[77] Judging from the evolution of U.S. policy toward Iran, the proponents emphasizing Iraq's greater regional importance prevailed.

According to this point of view, Iraq's larger oil reserves and its stronger military position enhance its importance, whereas Iran's economic and military weakness and its uncertain political future reduce its importance. Meanwhile, the reduction of the Soviet threat undermined Iran's significance as a strategic buffer.[78] Favoring ties with Iraq would increase the chances of obtaining its cooperation on Arab-Israeli peacemaking.

In the course of the U.S. debate, key Arab allies, especially Egypt, lobbied against any shift in U.S. policy preferences away from Iraq. Thus the United States took no action that could encourage an Iranian response and improve the chances for a dialogue. Quite the contrary. In August, the U.S. House of Representatives proposed legislation to impose sanctions on Iraq for using chemical weapons, but the State Department intervened and the bill was watered down to the point of being meaningless.[79] Nor, despite Iran's earlier hopes, did the United States help with the full implementation of Resolution 598.

It was, of course, difficult for the United States, especially in the midst of an election campaign and then during a transition of government, to make any positive gesture toward Iran. This was especially so because of the continued captivity of U.S. citizens, but while justified and understandable, this posture undercut the position of those Iranians who wanted to develop a dialogue with the United States. Since Iran accepted the cease-fire, there had been a continuing debate on the issue of hostages and U.S.-Iranian reconciliation. Radicals who opposed normalizing relations resisted mediation to gain their release. As during the hostage crisis of

1979–81, they understood that, as long as U.S. citizens were held hostage, no significant improvement in U.S.-Iranian relations was possible. By contrast, the pragmatic moderates realized that their policy of opening up to the West could succeed only if Iran reached some understanding with the United States, which could lead to the lifting of the trade ban and the releasing of Iranian assets. They were also aware that Iran would need U.S. acquiescence if it were to try borrowing from the World Bank and the IMF.

Strikingly, there was considerable open debate over the reestablishment of ties with the United States. Those who favored better ties with the West recognized the need for Iran to establish a working relationship with the United States, but they were ambivalent about moving decisively, fearing a backlash by the radicals, who believed that Iran had already made enough concessions. Given Iran's U.S.-oriented military and economic infrastructure, the radicals feared that the resumption of diplomatic relations would again lead to Iran's economic and political dependence on the United States.

In the middle of this debate, which was also a struggle for domestic political ascendance, controversy broke out in the Islamic world over the novel *Satanic Verses,* written by the Indian-born, British author Salman Rushdie. Reaction among Muslims was almost universal—that the novel was blasphemous. The West's support for Rushdie's right of free literary expression was interpreted by many Muslims as reflecting insensitivity or a revival of a condescending attitude toward the Muslim world. It took several weeks before the focus of opposition among Muslims moved to Iran—there had already been protests from others, including Pakistan and Saudi Arabia—but, when it did, the world spotlight shifted to the Ayatollah Khomeini, who called for Rushdie's death. Khomeini's statements and those of other clerics also became part of the struggle for power in Iran. Quite rapidly, the pragmatists were isolated, and the radicals were in the ascendant. Even though the Bush administration responded to Khomeini's condemnation of Rushdie in low-key terms, the window of opportunity for dialogue with the United States, which had already narrowed because of what the Iranians viewed as the meager payoffs of their policy of opening to the West, closed completely.

Indeed, with the ascendance of Iranian radicals opposed to reconciliation with the United States, the threat of another U.S.-Iranian crisis loomed on the horizon. In April 1989, Iran declared that it had uncovered a U.S. espionage network and accused the United States of having violated the terms of the Algiers Agreement.[80] The United States responded that it did not know what the Iranians were talking about. However, it later transpired that the U.S. had indeed infiltrated Iran's military establishment and, as a result, had received detailed information about Iranian military planning.[81] Yet neither side was willing to unduly escalate the affair.

In a departure from past U.S. attitudes, the Bush administration also refrained from reacting too strongly to provocative statements by Rafsanjani, which amounted to an incitement of the Palestinians to take terrorist actions against Western nationals. This approach has had the great merit of not exacerbating already acute problems and making future reconciliation more problematic.[82]

The death of the Ayatollah Khomeini in June 1989 intensified internal debate in the United States. In view of growing Soviet-Iranian rapprochement, there was some criticism that U.S. policy toward Iran was simply drifting. This view was countered by proponents in and outside the government of a policy of waiting patiently until Iran took the initiative in approaching the United States. They argued that Iran would have no choice but to do so.[83]

Soon after, however, another crisis loomed in U.S.-Iran relations, this time prompted by Israel's abduction of a Lebanese Shi'a cleric, Sheikh Abd-al-Karim Obeid, on 28 July 1989, believed to be one of the leaders of the radical Shi'a group Hizbulallah. The Lebanese radicals demanded that Israel free Sheikh Obeid and threatened that if he was not freed, they would kill Colonel William Higgins, who was in captivity, since February 1988. Israel refused to free Sheikh Obeid, and the Hizbulallah declared that it had killed Colonel Higgins in retaliation.[84] It also threatened to kill another U.S. hostage, Joseph Cicippio, if Sheikh Obeid was not freed.

This situation put the United States and Iran's newly elected president Rafsanjani in a difficult position. The United States could not allow the killing of another of its citizens, but it was also aware of the delicate position of Iran's new leader. This time the United States succeeded in developing a response which, while firm, was not unnecessarily provocative or rigid.

The United States, in a diplomatic note, warned Iran that it would hold it responsible if "any additional U.S. hostages were harmed or put to death" and made it clear that it would not shirk from using military force against Iran if any U.S. hostages were killed. To make this threat credible, the United States moved its warships to the close vicinity of Iran.[85] However, it also made it clear that it did not want to have to resort to military force. Indeed, this time the United States showed a greater awareness of the limits of Iran's influence over the Lebanese radicals as well as the fact that other players such as Syria were equally important, although official U.S. statements continued to focus on Iran.[86]

This time the United States was also more willing to acknowledge signs of a positive role played by Iran, as illustrated by the comment of the spokeswoman of the State Department that the United States did not have any reason to believe that Iran was not serious about trying to spare the life of Joseph Cicippio.[87]

During a Friday prayer sermon on 4 August 1989, directly addressing himself to the White House, Rafsanjani indicated that the problem of hostages and Lebanon had peaceful solutions.[88] He also admitted that the behavior of the Bush administration was "wiser" than that of the previous administration.[89] This attitude reflected both his own inclination, as well as the fact the Iran could ill afford a military confrontation with the United States.

He also again renewed his offer that Iran would use its influence to gain the release of U.S. hostages if America released Iranian assets and ended its hostile attitude toward Iran. The U.S. response again was more forthcoming than in the past. President Bush reiterated his earlier promise that Iranian "goodwill" would beget U.S. goodwill. But the Bush administration was no more able than the Reagan administration to enter into any arrangement which could be interpreted as a trade-off on the hostages and a compromise of the U.S. principle of not dealing with the terrorists.[90] Domestic political constraints also hampered Iran from being more forceful in achieving the freedom of U.S. hostages, assuming that it could have done so.

As noted, Iranian hard-liners had always feared that the release of hostages would open the way for eventual normalization of U.S.-Iran relations, which they wanted to prevent. Thus they tried to argue that any compromise on this issue would mean the betrayal of the Ayatollah Khomeini's legacy. His son, Ahmad, vocalized this view and his fears by saying that " . . . today the United States thinks that since the Imam is no longer among us it can accuse our officials of having contacts with it."[91]

In view of the restraint shown by both Iran and the United States, an immediate crisis was averted. No other hostages were killed, although Sheikh Obeid remained in captivity, and no military encounter took place. Indirect contacts on this issue also, in effect, created a dialogue between the two countries, which seemed to become well established through the intermediary of Pakistan.[92]

Relations in the Absence of Relations

Throughout this remarkable period, it is reasonable to inquire about the means by which the United States and Iran sought to understand one another and to make their views known. Indeed, despite the lack of official diplomatic relations, they have communicated through a number of channels. The first was the so-called Hague Process, created by the Algiers Agreement of 1981 to settle U.S.-Iranian claims. By all accounts, Iran's behavior at the Hague has been professional. It has tried to depoliticize the process, despite domestic criticism from several sources, including some members of parliament. It is significant that through mid-1989, between 80 and 85 percent of all cases have been resolved in favor of U.S. claimants. But the Iranians realized that their business and financial credibility depends on their respecting their obligations. Iran's attitude has also been influenced by the Islamic emphasis on the sanctity of contract. And, despite earlier doubts, Iran seems to have become convinced of the basic fairness of the Hague Process.[93]

The second venue for U.S.-Iranian contacts has been through the Swiss and Algerian governments, which represent U.S. and Iranian interests, respectively. These contacts have been limited to consular affairs, especially related to U.S. citizens living in Iran. The Swiss have avoided being used as a channel for political messages. Iran has used the Algerian channel primarily to transmit official protests over issues such as U.S. overflights of Iranian airspace or intrusions into Iranian territorial waters. But these protests have generally been delivered at least several days after the incidents, apparently just for the purpose of putting a protest on record.[94]

Political messages have been exchanged through other third parties, in particular

West Germany, Japan, and, occasionally, Turkey and Pakistan. Until October 1987, when the United States imposed a total trade ban, some trade was conducted between the two countries, consisting mostly of U.S. purchases of Iranian oil. In addition, large numbers of Iranian students continued to study in the United States.

Conclusions

U.S.-Iranian difficulties during the last decade have represented the culmination of a long process. The intensity of U.S.-Iranian animosity has been the inevitable result of a too tight embrace, as well as of high expectations turned into resentment. Iran's core problem in dealing with the United States, both before and after the revolution, has derived from the fact that the United States has no intrinsic interest in it, thus allowing the Americans to take risks with Iran that they have not taken with other, more intrinsically valuable, countries, thus making Iran vulnerable to changes both in U.S. domestic politics and in U.S.-Soviet relations.

Meanwhile, Iran's competitive nature as a core regional power has created underlying—albeit often dormant—tensions in U.S.-Iranian relations. This was true under the Shah, and it has come violently to the fore since the revolution. Meanwhile, Iran's geostrategic location and the existence of a degree of continuing common strategic interest between it and the United States have excluded the option of total disentanglement, even if the alternative proves to be confrontation.

U.S.-Iranian relations have been affected by the political ethos of the two countries, their diplomatic styles, and their internal contradictions. In Iran's case, the traditional emotional and unrealistic streak of its political culture, its inability to tailor its aspirations to its abilities, and the bravado of its diplomatic style have contributed to its difficulties with the United States. This has been true under the Shah and under the Islamic regime. Another source of difficulty has been the lack of a broad national consensus in Iran regarding its domestic and foreign policies. This became particularly important after the revolution, with the fierce factional in-fighting that has plagued the country.

In the United States, certain contradictions in its regional interests, plus difficulties involved in simultaneously pursuing them, have affected U.S.-Iranian relations. U.S. economic interests have been more tied to the Arabs than to Iran, whereas U.S. strategic interests in Southwest Asia are more tied with Iran. Yet the United States has been unwilling to recognize this situation, for example, failing to give Iran credit for its role in Afghanistan. Also, Arab and Iranian ambitions and aspirations have often clashed. In the past, the United States had the traditional great power problem of maintaining its influence with two sets of competing allies. Since the revolution, oversensitivity to Arab concerns has precluded a more balanced U.S. policy toward Iran.

Likewise, U.S.-Iranian relations have been affected by the U.S. dilemma in reconciling its ties with both Israel and Arab states. Indeed, the United States' inability to satisfy Arab demands with regard to the Arab-Israeli peace process was partly responsible for its policy of punishing Iran in the late 1980s. The United States has also encouraged Arab-Iranian tensions in order to entice them to reach a *modus vivendi* with Israel.

Furthermore, there has been an inherent tension between two American impulses—idealist and *Realpolitik*—along with the bureaucratic divisions in Washington that emanate partly from the dichotomy between regionalist and globalist approaches to foreign policy. The ascendance of the regionalist outlook within the U.S. policy-making apparatus after the Iran-Contra affair accentuated the Arab-centeredness of its Persian Gulf policy and thus its approach toward Iran. This may have reduced U.S. flexibility in responding to opportunities for ending its confrontation with Iran. The personal idiosyncrasies of the two countries' leaders have also played an important role.

In the future, none of these underlying determinants of U.S.-Iranian relations is likely to change rapidly, if at all. In particular, Iran's political debate on its domestic and foreign policies, especially in regard to ties with the U.S. is unlikely to be settled decisively any time soon. Nor are differences of opinion in the United States regarding relations with Iran likely to be quickly resolved. The inherent conflict between Iran as a potential core regional power and the United States as a global power will also continue. Growing U.S. dependence on imported energy would mean that the Arab world will remain more important for the United States, especially if a reemergence of past U.S.-Iranian friendship is unlikely and if East-West *détente* continues to intensify.

Some strain in U.S.-Iranian relations, even at the best of times, is inevitable. Yet the confrontation of the last decade has been neither necessary nor healthy, and there are no compelling reasons that it continue. But before U.S.-Iranian relations can be put on a new footing, Iran's political scene will have to stabilize in the post-Khomeini era. As in the past, U.S.-Iranian ties will also be affected by broader changes in global politics, especially in Soviet policies and in the nature of U.S.-Soviet relations.

Regardless of what the future holds for Iran and for global politics, reconciliation between Iran and the United States will have to be based on mutual respect and understanding of each other's interests, and it must include mutual efforts to meet each other's concerns.

5. Iran and the Superpowers

The Soviet Union

Iran and the Soviet Union: Historical Background

The historical legacy of Russian-Iranian interaction still largely determines the psychological setting and underlying patterns of their relationship. The intense interaction of the two began after the fall of the Safavid Empire, when Iran entered a long period of decline while Russia began a period of progress and expansion under Peter the Great. The underlying shape of Russian-Iranian relations, characterized by Russian's expansion and Iran's contraction, was established early in this era, as Russia took advantage of Iran's turmoil and occupied its northern provinces.[1]

During the eighteenth century, Russia's rivalry with the Ottomans and later with other powers, affected its strategy toward Iran. As a rule, Russia tried to block any rival power that threatened Iran while it sought advantages for itself. Failing that, it sought to accommodate the rival power at Iran's expense.[2] The domination or partition of Iran by Russia and the Ottomans was averted by the emergence of Nadir Shah Afshar and by the death of Peter the Great, which temporarily slowed Russian expansion.

Yet the Russo-Iranian wars of 1804–1828 revived and consolidated a pattern of Russian expansion and Iranian contraction, completely opening Iran to Russian penetration.[3] Under the Treaty of Turkmanchai, known in Iran as the "Shameful Treaty," Iran ceded all of its trans-Caucasian provinces to Russia and granted it extra-territorial rights, significant trade concessions, and heavy war reparations. Russia also received a veto over the succession in Iran.[4] Turkmanchai shaped the basic Iranian attitude toward Russia, an attitude of fear and suspicion, and Russia's southward expansion created new geopolitical realities for Iran—namely, a 1,500-mile border with the Russian Empire.[5]

During these years, an enduring framework for Russo-Iranian interaction was developed, based on Russian expansion and Iranian decline, Russian proximity to Iran, great power politics, the state of international politics, and domestic conditions in both Russia and Iran. Russian objectives toward Iran acquired a lasting dualistic character: the maximalist goal of dominating Iran and the minimalist goal of preventing its domination by a rival power, or at least securing a share for itself.

The Russian Revolution of 1917

The Bolshevik revolution of 1917 introduced new complexities, most notably ideology, to Russo-Iranian relations. But its immediate impact on Iran's destiny was positive because it ended the Russo-British entente. The new Russian government opened negotiations for the withdrawal of Soviet troops from Iran, and Leon Trotsky both denounced the Anglo-Russian agreement of 1907 and helped procure the removal of British troops.[6] As a result, a strong sense of relief and sympathy for the Bolshevik government developed in Iran, as illustrated by a graphic observation at the time: "Two enemies, each pulling one side of a rope, were trying to strangle a man. Suddenly one of them let the rope go and said 'Poor man, I am your brother,' and the unfortunate man was released. The man who let the rope go from our throat was Lenin."[7]

Thus, at first, the Russian revolution saved Iran's independence and territorial integrity.[8] Russia had by no means abandoned its desire to dominate Iran, but this time would try by revolutionizing it, as witnessed by Russian involvement in setting up the socialist Republic of Gilan in northern Iran.[9] The Russian revolution also introduced a new pattern into Russo-Iranian relations—namely, that of acquiring influence through co-optation. Yet, over time, Bolshevik Russia reverted to the imperial style of behavior, best illustrated by the Nazi-Soviet Pact of 1939, which recognized "the Asiatic area to the south of the Soviet Union as Russia's sphere of influence"; by the Soviet refusal to withdraw from northern Iran after the end of World War II; and by its efforts to establish autonomous Communist governments in the Iranian provinces of Azerbaijan and Kurdistan. Naturally, Iran's good will toward Russia following the Bolshevik Revolution was dissipated; its old fears were reaffirmed. During the 1950s, 1960s, and 1970s, Soviet-Iranian relations developed erratically and vacillated between outright confrontation and limited cooperation, partly because of events external to the region—especially the course of the Cold War—and in part because of a duality in the Soviet Union's approach to Iran.[10] It conducted its diplomacy at two levels: state to state and Communist Party to Communist Party. Moscow tried to forge economic ties and politically beneficial relations with Iran, while simultaneously seeking to subvert the Shah's regime and to preserve Soviet links with Iranian leftists and other opposition forces. This dual-track policy imposed some costs on the Soviet Union, however. Its willingness to deal with the Shah's regime eroded its prestige and enhanced its image with the Iranian Left as a selfish imperialist power, and its dealings with the Shah's opponents limited the scope for Soviet-Iranian cooperation.

Thus, from Peter the Great to the modern Soviet state, the past has produced in Iran an image of a Russia that is an opportunistic and exploitative great power, whether Tsarist or socialist, and it produced an acute awareness of Russian proximity and power. But some positive memories linger, and pro-Russian sentiments exist in Iran, particularly among the Left and autonomist minorities.[11] In the Soviet Union, meanwhile, the legacy of the past has produced a perception that Iran is within the natural sphere of Soviet influence and that it has flexibility to pursue both minimalist and maximalist goals there.

Revolutionary Iran and the Soviet Union:
The Transitional Period, February-November 1979

As the Islamic regime was established, its initial approach to the Soviet Union was shaped largely by the character of its leadership and internal power struggles. But for the Islamic regime, political philosophy was also important. In particular, Prime Minister Mehdi Bazargan subscribed to Mossadegh's theory of negative equilibrium and believed that Iran should have reasonable relations with all countries, especially its neighbors. As products of Iran's historical experience with Russia, Bazargan and his colleagues both recognized the need to accommodate the Soviet Union and feared its intentions. Initially, therefore, Iran made no significant departures from its policies toward the Soviet Union.

For its part, the Soviet Union's attitude toward Iran was determined by calculation of the likely impact of Soviet policies on the course of the Iranian revolution, the balance of power among different political factions, and the chances for dramatically increasing Soviet influence in Iran. It welcomed changes in Iran's foreign policy that reduced the influence of the United States.[12] But it was also uncertain about the future course of this novel, revolutionary regime. Thus, the initial Soviet reaction to the Iranian revolution was a mixture of apprehension and expectation. The Russians feared that the revolution would lead to turmoil and prompt U.S. intervention, perhaps leading to the establishment of another docile, pro-American government in Iran. They were also suspicious of the true character of the new Iranian regime, having difficulty in believing that the United States had allowed the Shah's fall without assuring that the successor regime would be equally responsive to U.S. interests. Noting U.S.-Iranian disagreements on various issues, they suspected U.S. complicity in Iran's political changeover and viewed the new regime as yet an unknown quantity.[13]

These suspicions were partly justified. Mehdi Bazargan, his National Front colleagues, and figures such as Ibrahim Yazdi, Sadegh Ghotbzadeh, and Abol-Hassan Bani-Sadr, were not committed anti-Americans.[14] They all viewed the Soviet Union as a greater threat to Iran's security and independence even if, for purposes of political expediency, they did not openly say so.[15] The meetings between Ibrahim Yazdi and U.S. Secretary of State Cyrus Vance in October 1979, and between Mehdi Bazargan and Zbigniew Brzezinski in Algiers in November, strengthened Soviet suspicions.

The Soviets also had expectations about the Islamic revolution. For example, they were aware of the Left's role in the revolution. Conventional wisdom holds that the Soviet Union was concerned about the Shah's removal and how that would affect its comfortable relations with Iran. Although the Soviets were ambivalent about the Shah's departure, one of their long-term goals had been the replacement of his regime by one more responsive to Moscow, as illustrated by Nikita Khrushchev's famous comment that "Iran is a rotten plum that will fall in our lap." Thus, even when official Soviet-Iranian relations were at their best, Soviet-based radio stations located in Soviet Azerbaijan beamed anti-Shah propaganda and clandestine broadcasts supporting the Shah's opponents. Furthermore, despite recurring purges, the communist Tudeh Party was active underground and in 1978 organized the oil workers' strikes that helped to bring down the Shah. It is unlikely that Moscow was unaware of these activities or disapproved of them.[16]

The Soviets believed in the eventual transformation of bourgeois revolutions—including Iran's Islamic revolution—into true Socialist revolutions. Their hopes were reflected in early Soviet commentaries on the role of religion in social transformation and on Islam's progressive potential. The Soviet Commentator Leonid Medvedko wrote about the recognition in Marxist-Leninist classics that, like nationalism, religion historically has two aspects: Although it has been mostly at the service of the ruling classes, religion has on occasion been used by the oppressed to protest against national or social oppression.[17] Referring to one of Lenin's works, "A Draft Programme of Our Party," Medvedko noted that "Political protests in religious guise are common to all nations at a certain stage of their development." This stage, according to Lenin, is one of upheaval, in which "the old order has been turned upside down," but one cannot yet see what kind of a new order is taking place.[18] This, in Medvedko's words, was precisely what was happening in what he called the "newly-free dependent capitalist countries where the historical breakdown of the pre-capitalist socio-economic structure is taking place." His article also emphasized Islam's revolutionary potential, criticized the Western assessment of Islam as a submissive and fatalistic creed, and noted that:

"... ideas of equality, abstention from extravagance, and condemnation of corruption, theft, and usury preached by Islam ... are expressive, in a religious form of the need to establish just relations among people, a concept social in form and progressive in character."[19]

Meanwhile, the Soviets suspected the Bazargan government of bourgeois nationalism. This perception led them to criticize it and to praise the revolution and the Ayatollah Khomeini. They were not wrong, for although Bazargan's philosophy did not lead him to turn against the Soviet Union, he had no enthusiasm for closer ties with the Soviet Union. It had, indeed, been heavy-handed regarding issues of special concern to Iran, particularly by insisting on the validity of Articles V and VI of the 1921 Soviet-Iranian Treaty, under which the Soviets could invade Iran under certain circumstances to protect their interests.[20]

There was also suspicion of Soviet attitudes toward Iran's ethnic minorities. Depending on the state of its relations with Iran, the Soviet Union has sometimes seen fit to manipulate Iran's minorities, believing that fragmentation along ethnic lines would enhance its influence and could lead to gradual Sovietization.[21] Thus, after the revolution, when disturbances occurred among Iran's Turkmen and Kurdish minorities, Moscow attributed them to imperialist plots and cautioned the Kurds. But as it became disappointed with the Bazargan government, it began to support the Kurds and criticized the Iranian government's handling of the nationality problem.[22]

Soviet involvement in Afghanistan posed particular concerns. The Communist coup of April 1978 had disturbed the Shah, but he could do little about it. The new Iranian regime criticized Soviet intervention in Afghanistan, and the Ayatollah Khomeini, in a meeting on June 12, 1979, warned the Soviet ambassador against such interference. And the regime was not pleased with the Soviet-Iraqi connection. After the Iranian revolution, Iraq agitated among Iran's Arabic-speaking minority in Khusistan and enticed it to rebellion.[23] Given the Soviet Union's attitude toward Iran's ethnic minorities and its close relations with Iraq, the Islamic regime became suspicious of Soviet involvement in Iraqi subversive efforts.

The U.S. Hostage Crisis and the Bani-Sadr Government

As 1979 progressed, the Bazargan government came under increasing pressure from Islamic factions, leftist forces, and such Islamic-nationalist figures as Sadegh Ghotbzadeh and Bani-Sadr. The opposition of the political figures stemmed from personal power ambitions. The opposition of the first two groups was based on ideological and policy grounds, especially Bazargan's efforts to stabilize U.S.-Iranian relations. These pressures made governing extremely difficult for Bazargan. Finally, the seizure of the U.S. Embassy by a group of radical students ended his premiership.

There are no hard facts concerning the Soviet Union's involvement in these events, but circumstantial evidence indicates that it may not have been totally innocent. The person widely believed to have masterminded the hostage operation, Hojat-el-Islam Khoeiniha, is known as Moscow's man, or as the French call him, "Le Mollah Rouge." The pro-Moscow Tudeh Party took a positive attitude toward the embassy seizure. In an interview with Eric Rouleau, Nureddin Kianuri—the Tudeh's secretary general—expressed the main reason for his and Moscow's pleasure with the hostage events: "As long as the hostages are in Iran, normalization of relations with the United States . . . will not be possible."[24] And the Tudeh and the Soviets expected that Bazargan's fall would help transform Iran's revolution into true socialism. According to Kianuri, the period following the revolution's victory was characterized by a dualism of power, symbolized by the revolutionary center headed by Ayatollah Khomeini and by the government of the liberal "opportunistic bourgeoisie." The revolutionary center around Ayatollah Khomeini opposed any compromise with U.S. imperialism and favored fundamental economic change, benefiting the working masses. But the liberal bourgeoisie obstructed the revolutionary movement for the sake of its own economic interests.[25]

As the hostage crisis progressed, the Soviets apparently began to fear U.S. military intervention in Iran, possibly leading to the installation of a pro-American government and thereby undoing what they had gained from the U.S.-Iranian estrangement. In January 1980, Leonid Brezhnev warned the United States that the Soviet Union would not tolerate any outside interference in Iran's internal affairs. Coming after the Soviet invasion of Afghanistan, however, this warning alarmed rather than reassured the Iranians. They had always suspected that the December 1979 Soviet invasion was a prelude to Soviet advances into Baluchistan. At that time, Iranian leaders had warned the Soviet Union that, with Soviet troops only 30 miles from its borders, Iran could not remain silent in the face of threats to its frontier region. After becoming president in February 1980, Bani-Sadr asked for Soviet assurances that there would be no military intervention beyond Afghanistan, and Khomeini warned the Soviets against helping Iran's Baluch and Kurdish autonomists.[26] Indeed, they feared that the Soviet Union would seize on a U.S. threat as a pretext to invade Iran. Consequently, Iran's ambassador to Moscow informed Soviet officials that it could defend itself alone, and it would not allow a single foreign soldier to enter its territory, on whatever pretext, and by virtue of whatever friendship treaty.[27]

Beyond these security concerns, Iran's position on Afghanistan was determined by a sense of Islamic solidarity. Thus, notwithstanding its problems with the United States and Soviet support for Iran in the hostage crisis, it condemned the Soviet invasion and withdrew from the 1980 Moscow Olympics. Khomeini even called the Soviet Union the "other Great Satan."

Yet despite tensions over Afghanistan, during 1980 other events led Iran and the Soviet Union to expand their economic and trade relations. The Western economic embargo against Iran in retaliation for the hostage crisis increased the importance of the Soviet Union and some East European countries as trading partners. Thus in April 1980, the Iranian Minister of Economy and Finance visited Moscow and concluded agreements on transit, trade, and other subjects.[28] The American hostage rescue mission also exacerbated Iranian fears of U.S. military intervention and cautioned them against alienating the Soviets further.

Suspicions continued, however, especially following Iraq's invasion in September 1980. Many Iranians saw the Americans behind it, and some saw the West Europeans and even the Soviet Union.[29] According to Sadegh Ghotbzadeh, the major powers wanted to use Iraq to isolate Iran: the United States so that it could regain its influence and the Soviet Union so that it could force Iran to enter the Eastern camp. And there were fears of a Soviet-American agreement to divide Iran into spheres of influence in the traditional pattern of Russo-British agreements.[30] The Soviet Union tried to dispel these suspicions, without success.

The Fall of Bani-Sadr and Soviet-Iranian Rapprochement

At the beginning, the Soviet Union had viewed Bani-Sadr's assumption of the presidency as a victory for the progressive elements over the liberal bourgeoisie, but it soon grew disappointed with him and with some of his colleagues, especially

Foreign Minister Sadegh Ghotbzadeh, who was a vocal critic of Soviet policy in Afghanistan.[31] Thus the Soviets came to see the Bani-Sadr government as similar to the bourgeois nationalists, and when challenged by the clerical factions and their allies—which were mostly gathered within the Islamic Republican Party—the Soviets and the Tudeh Party supported the latter. After Bani-Sadr's flight from Iran in June 1981 and, later, Sadegh Ghotbzadeh's arrest and execution, Islamic factions consolidated their power. Soon, the new leadership embarked on the elimi-nation of leftist forces, but the Tudeh Party was spared. Both sides had valid reasons for this tactical cooperation.

Islamic forces perceived the non-Tudeh left, particularly the Islamic-Marxist Mojahedin-e-Khalgh, as their most formidable rivals, and, until two years after Bani-Sadr's fall, the radical and relatively pro-Soviet faction of the Iranian lead-ership was ascendant.[32] For their part, the Tudeh Party and the Soviet Union rated as slim their prospects of generating a socialist revolution and gaining power in Iran and thus saw cooperation with the Islamic leadership as the best way to enhance their influence. They also perceived other leftist forces to be greater rivals and believed that their success would dim the chances of the Tudeh, which was more subservient to Moscow than the other leftists. And besides, the Tudeh had adopted a strategy of penetrating bureaucratic and military organizations, then seizing power from within at an appropriate time, in cooperation with the radical pro-Soviet elements.[33]

These factors, plus Iran's economic and military needs, led to Soviet-Iranian rapprochement. As a result, Soviet-made arms reached Iran through Libya, Syria, North Korea, and some East European countries.[34] According to some reports, Soviet advisers became involved in training the Revolutionary Guards and in or-ganizing Iran's intelligence services.[35] Trade and economic relations expanded, although the issue of Iranian gas exports to the Soviet Union, which were interrupted after the revolution over price disputes, was not solved.[36] The number of visits by Soviet and Iranian dignitaries to each other's countries also increased.[37] But the Soviet military presence in Afghanistan continued to hinder further cooperation.

Erratic Fluctuation: 1983–1988

The Soviet-Iranian rapprochement of 1981–82 was limited and short-lived. For several years afterwards, relations went through periods ranging from severe de-terioration to relative improvement and limited cooperation. As in the past, these fluctuations reflected the impact of the shifting balance of power within the Iranian leadership; changing Soviet assessments of the nature of the Iranian regime, es-pecially its "progressive potential"; Iran's economic and military situation; the state of Iran's relations with the West; shifting Soviet foreign and domestic prior-ities; and the overall evolution of Middle East politics and the Soviet Union's perceptions of its broader regional interests.

By the end of 1982, the Soviet-Iranian rapprochement had stalled, primarily because Iran was less in need of the Soviet Union. This was particularly so after the lifting of the Western economic embargo and Iran's adjustment to the loss of Khoramshahr. Iran had also forced the withdrawal of invading Iraqi forces and had resumed its oil exports, earning nearly $20 billion during 1982–83. Thus Iran's financial situation improved and enabled it to expand its trade relations with Japan, Europe, and Third World countries. Meanwhile, the Soviets' attitude toward the Iran-Iraq war changed, resuming arms deliveries to Iraq and reassessing the Iranian revolution. In the early days after the clerics consolidated their rule, the Soviets had an optimistic assessment of Islam's progressive role. In the Iranian context, Soviet analysts measured the progressiveness of the new regime and its usefulness to the Soviet Union by the extent of its anti-Americanism. For example, the Soviet scholar Yevgeny Primakov preferred the fundamentalist clerics to Bani-Sadr and his supporters because they were oriented toward the the West, whereas the former, according to him, adopted favorable positions on a wide range of issues.[38]

Yet some Soviet scholars noted that the clerical factions' anti-Americanism did not translate into pro-Soviet sentiments, and they argued that this should not be the only criterion for assessing Iranian developments. Alexander Bovin perceived that the clerical factions' struggle "against the Western devil" appeared together with "a struggle against the Eastern devil."[39]

Furthermore, the emergence of an uneasy balance between two tendencies of the Iranian leadership, with growing influence on the part of conservative clergy, had prevented the implementation of radical economic and social programs. As a result, the Soviets' assessment of Islam's progressive potential became less optimistic and they began to view this new brand of Islam as a challenge and rival to socialism more than as an accomplice and ally.[40] And they began to worry about its potentially disruptive impact on their own Muslim republics.[41] The Soviets did not give up on Islam's progressive potential, however, and their commentaries on the situation continued to distinguish between progressive and reactionary Islam.[42] But their estimate of its progressive potential and expectation of its usefulness to advance Soviet regional goals has been lowered.

Some aspects of Iran's foreign policy affected Soviet policy even more than did the disillusionment with Islam. Iran continued to condemn the Soviet invasion of Afghanistan and argued that the Afghan Mojahedin should be direct participants in any negotiations designed to resolve the conflict. It also financed and armed eight Shi'a Afghan guerrilla groups and played host to nearly 2.3 million Afghan refugees.[43] Assistance to the Afghan Mojahedin at times led to skirmishes between Iranian military forces and those of the Kabul regime and the Soviet Union, arousing Soviet anger. Yet, given its preoccupation with the Persian Gulf war and its awareness of Soviet power and proximity, Iran carefully calibrated its relations with the Mojahedin in order to minimize provocation. It has kept a tight reign on Afghan refugees and the the Mojahedin.

At times, some Iranian leaders argued that, in light of Western support for Iraq, Iran should make a deal with the Soviet Union over Afghanistan.[44] Yet the adoption of such a pragmatic stand was not possible, for Iran's ideological constraints and its position as the self-proclaimed defender of Islam made it impossible to betray the Afghan Mojahedin without damaging its Islamic credentials. It also had to be conscious of the potential impact that such a deal would have on its relations with Pakistan and the West. The regime's anti-Soviet members opposed this step, despite periodic rumors about a Soviet-Iranian deal.[45] The Geneva Accords of May 1988 and the Soviet decision to withdraw its troops from Afghanistan reduced Iran's ability to use the Afghan issue as a bargaining chip in relations with Moscow. Nevertheless, as long as the political situation in Afghanistan is not stabilized and factional rivalries continue, Iran can use its influence with some Afghan groups to help or hinder Soviet goals in that country.

Meanwhile, in its assessment of Iran's value to them, the Soviets also became displeased with Iran's reasonably friendly relations with Pakistan and Turkey.[46] By 1983, the Soviet Union began to have doubts that the Iranian revolution would improve their position in the Persian Gulf. Initially, Moscow had hoped that the Iranian revolution would, besides reducing the American presence, weaken the Arab regimes of the Persian Gulf and create new opportunities there. These hopes did not materialize, although the Soviet Union did make some significant inroads in the Gulf by establishing diplomatic ties with Oman and the United Arab Emirates in 1985 and with Qatar in August 1988. Instead, fear of contagion by the Iranian revolution intensified Arab cooperation and in 1981 led to the formation of the Gulf Cooperation Council. By enhancing the Arab need for a U.S. protective shield, the revolution consolidated their American ties.

Despite the growing Soviet disillusionment with the Islamic revolution, it was Iran and not the Soviet Union that initiated the rift in 1983. In April, Iran expelled eighteen Soviet diplomats on charges of spying, acting on the basis of information supplied by Britain, which had obtained it from a Soviet defector, an ex-vice consul in Tehran and senior KGB official, Vladimir Andreyevich Kuzichkin. He also disclosed the extensive penetration of Iranian revolutionary organizations, bureaucracy, and the military by Tudeh members and Soviet agents, thus alerting Iranian authorities to a serious Soviet threat and leading to extensive purges.[47] The extent of penetration by the Tudeh indicated the Soviet Union's despair that the Islamic regime had not become a "progressive pro-Soviet" state and that Tudeh was positioning itself to seize power after Khomeini's death.[48]

Following these purges, the Tudeh Party was banned and its leaders arrested and tried. During televised trials, they confessed to spying for the Soviet Union, to having infiltrated the bureaucracy and the military, to collaborating with the Kurdish rebels, and to planning to seize power.[49] The purpose of this public trial was to demonstrate the Tudeh's foreign links and to undermine its legitimacy. This was encapsulated by the Tudeh leader Kianuri's confession that "no leftist trend should infiltrate into Iran as it means affiliation to foreigners . . . [and] is the mother of all treason."[50]

The Soviet Union reacted sharply to the treatment of the Tudeh members, in contrast with its past behavior, when it had overlooked similar treatment of members of the Communist Parties of Egypt and Iraq. Soviet commentators attacked the

Iranian government, but focused their criticism on "the conservative wing of the Shi'ite Muslim clergy . . . ", accusing them of being the allies of the "bourgeois and land-owning" elements.[51] Both directly and through intermediaries, they warned Iran against the execution of Tudeh leaders, warnings that were serious and effective. Executions did not take place, and the trials stopped. Meanwhile, the discovery of Tudeh activities generated a wave of anti-Soviet sentiment in Iran.[52] Iran closed Soviet cultural offices and terminated language classes, nationalized Soviet banking and insurance, and took over a hospital run by the Soviet Red Cross.[53]

Nevertheless, both sides kept open lines of communication and did not let relations deteriorate dangerously. The Soviet Union withdrew its technical experts under the pretext that Iraqi bombings made the situation unsafe, an action that caused serious disruptions in electric power installations and that led Iranian authorities to accuse the Soviet Union of using these technicians to pressure Iran. But Moscow did not curtail transit and other trade, and Soviet broadcasts to Iran, while critical of aspects of Iranian policies, emphasized the benefits of closer Soviet-Iranian economic cooperation.

For its part, Iran tolerated some Soviet activities on its eastern borders with Afghanistan, reflecting the unique character of its relations with the Soviet Union, where proximity imposes constraints on Iranian behavior.[54]

By June 1984, events in the Iran-Iraq war led to a lessening of Soviet-Iranian tensions. Iraqi attacks on Persian Gulf shipping were growing; the United States was warning against Iranian disruption of the flow of Persian Gulf oil and delivering Stinger anti-aircraft missiles to Saudi Arabia; and in May, Saudi Arabian F-15 fighters shot down an intruding Iranian F-4 aircraft. Iran feared these events were a prelude to U.S. intervention and tried to enlist Soviet cooperation to deter the United States. As a result, the director general of the Iranian Foreign Ministry, Mohammad Reza Sadr, visited Moscow and met with Foreign Minister Andrei Gromyko.[55]

The Soviets shared Iran's fears and wanted to prevent the United States from using the Persian Gulf crisis to establish a military presence in the region.[56] Thus, the Soviet-Iranian communique at the end of Sadr's Moscow visit stressed the two sides' opposition to foreign intervention in the Persian Gulf. Other visits to Iran by low-level Soviet energy officials followed, and the two countries agreed to resume work on a number of projects.

As Soviet-Iranian relations evolved during the mid-1980s, two additional factors also played important roles: Iran's economic and financial situation and its relations with other countries. During 1982–83, Iran's oil revenues increased, and the country experienced a mini-boom. Although the situation began to change by 1984 because of falling oil prices and Iraqi bombings, the effects of the boom were still felt in 1984. That year, Iran also adopted an active diplomacy to end its international isolation, and the moderate trend within the regime reasserted itself. That summer, the West German foreign minister, Hans-Dietrich Genscher, visited Tehran and reported his impression that Iran might be prepared to open up to the West.[57] In

1985, Rafsanjani visited the People's Republic of China and Japan, visits that improved Iran's diplomatic position and economic options, while his trip to Beijing provided access to new sources of military supplies. Also during this period secret U.S.-Iranian contacts began.

As a result, while efforts to reduce tensions with the Soviet Union continued, Iran had become less dependent on it, and there were no major breakthroughs in relations with Moscow. Most Soviet and Iranian visitors to Tehran and Moscow were middle-level technical and economic experts. Their talks focused on reactivating the joint Soviet-Iranian Economic Commission and projects such as joint shipping in the Caspian Sea and the exploration for gas and oil in border areas.[58] An exception was the visit of Soviet first deputy foreign minister, Georgi Kornienko, to Tehran in February 1986, who received a mixed reception. Iran's prime minister, Mir Hossein Musavi, and its president, Ali Khamenei, stressed the positive and cooperative aspects of Soviet-Iranian relations, while the speaker of parliament, Hashemi Rafsanjani, focused on the Soviet presence in Afghanistan.[59] Nevertheless, agreements about economic and commercial relations were reached in principle, and the joint Soviet-Iranian economic commission resumed its work.

By the spring and summer of 1986, oil prices fell, and Iraqi bombing took a devastating toll on Iran's economy, necessitating a new strategy,[60] including the enlistment of Soviet cooperation in efforts to regulate oil markets and to resume the export of natural gas to the USSR. In August, Iran's oil minister visited Moscow where, as a goodwill gesture, the Soviets agreed to reduce their oil exports by 100,000 barrels a day. They did not, however, respond to Iran's request to resume gas exports, apparently expecting to use this issue in the future as leverage to gain more concessions.[61]

Iran-Contra Affair: Impact on Soviet-Iranian Relations

After the outbreak of the Iran-Contra affair in October 1986, the position of Iranian moderates was weakened, and the radicals gained the opportunity to attack them, questioning their revolutionary credentials. The radical, pro-Soviet faction was strengthened, and anti-American rhetoric mounted. For political protection, even the moderates took part in this rhetoric. Yet despite the radicals' fury over the dealings with the United States, as long as there was hope to salvage this dialogue, there was no immediate change in Soviet-Iranian relations. Thus, speaking at Tehran University in November, Velayati stressed that having relations with the superpowers does not mean "accepting their hegemony," and he added that "Iran will never accept Soviet domination."[62] In response, *Izvestia,* on December 7, expressed surprise that such a comment should come from "an Iranian official in whom such lofty powers in the foreign policy field are vested."[63] But as these hopes of salvaging the U.S.-Iranian dialogue faded by the beginning of 1987, the Soviet-Iranian rapprochement accelerated. High-level Iranian and Soviet officials exchanged visits, including Foreign Minister Velayati, who visited Moscow in February.[64]

The shift in U.S. Persian Gulf policy in the spring of 1987 that brought the reflagging of Kuwaiti tankers and the projection of American naval power into the Gulf accelerated the new Soviet-Iranian rapprochement by generating serious anxieties in both Moscow and Tehran. Iran feared U.S. military strikes against its oil and military installations. The U.S. bombing of Libya in 1986 had punctured Iran's belief that the United States was unwilling to use military force against Third World countries because of its experiences in Vietnam and Lebanon. Now, Iranian leaders worried that the United States might use its military presence in the Gulf to topple the Islamic regime.

The Soviets both shared these fears and manipulated them. Whatever problems Moscow had with Iran, it opposed more the return of a pro-American regime. The Persian Service of Radio Moscow warned that, all along, the U.S. objective had been to establish a subservient government in Iran, which was the U.S. goal in its attempt to land commandos in Tabas and in sending White House representatives Robert McFarlane and Oliver North to Tehran.[65] Moreover, the Soviets worried that the Americans could obtain permanent military bases in the Gulf Arab states, which would stall Moscow's strategy of penetration. Moreover, given the proximity of the Persian Gulf to Afghanistan and the Soviet Asian republics, the entrenchment of a U.S. military presence in the Persian Gulf was alarming to Moscow.

Thus, once more a commonality of interest developed between Tehran and Moscow—namely, the prevention of the consolidation of the U.S. military presence in the Persian Gulf and the promotion of its departure. Moscow also tried to curry favor with Iran by manipulating its fears of U.S. intentions. In May, however, two incidents risked the disruption of Soviet-Iranian relations. On May 6, Iranian speedboats fired on the Soviet diesel ship, *Korateyev,* and on May 18 a Soviet tanker hit a mine. The Iranian attacks seemed to be in retaliation for the Soviet leasing of three tankers to Kuwait and the USSR's increased military assistance to Iraq. Iranian commentary accused the Soviets of collusion with the United States and said that Soviet policy in the Persian Gulf amounted to a declaration of war on Iran.[66] Moscow reacted mildly to these events, thereby avoiding serious damage to the relationship.

By June 1987, as the U.S.-Iranian confrontation intensified, a series of high-level Soviet-Iranian contacts began, and in mid-June Yuli Vorontsov, Soviet deputy foreign minister, visited Iran. On several occasions, both sides expressed their common view on the Persian Gulf and called for the withdrawal of foreign navies.[67] Iranian officials, including the generally suspicious Rafsanjani, admitted that Moscow had adopted a "correct approach" toward the Persian Gulf.[68] Meanwhile, the Soviet Union seized on the precarious situation of Iran regarding the United States to forge long-term links with it. The two countries reached agreements on the export of Iranian oil through Soviet territory; the building of a trans-Iranian railroad linking Sarakhs on the Soviet-Iranian border with Bandar Abbas in the south; the joint exploration for oil and the setting up of a joint shipping line in the Caspian

Sea; dam-building over border rivers; and joint industrial projects.[69] If completed, these projects would increase Iran's economic dependence on the Soviet Union and the latter's political leverage on Iran.

Furthermore, in October 1987, Aeroflot resumed its weekly flights to Tehran, and the Soviets supplied Iran with badly needed oil products in exchange for crude oil. But the most significant result of the new Soviet-Iranian rapprochement, produced by U.S. military and political actions, was Moscow's willingness to help delay the passage of a United Nations Security Council resolution calling for the imposition of an arms embargo on Iran. This resolution was designed by Iraq and its supporters, including the United States, to be a follow-up to U.N. Security Council Resolution 598.

Although Iran had not rejected Resolution 598, instead making its acceptance contingent upon certain changes, Western countries saw its behavior as foot-dragging and urged the council to impose an arms embargo. The Soviet Union took advantage of the opportunity thus provided and argued that Iran and the U.N. secretary general should both be given more time to ensure the application of Resolution 598. Some observers believed that the Soviets hoped to emerge as the logical mediators and to sponsor a peace conference, similar to the Tashkent Conference of 1965 that ended that year's Indo-Pakistani war. Following this Soviet initiative, during the summer and fall of 1987 there were widespread rumors about Soviet-Iranian negotiations on a friendship treaty,[70] and there was talk of an exchange of visits by Rafsanjani and Shevardnadze.[71]

By late 1987, however, the climate changed. Iran began to show less enthusiasm for improving relations after the Iran-Contra affair and the onset of direct confrontation with the United States. After their initial setback, Iranian moderates had recouped some of their influence. Also, the U.S. reflagging operation had not fundamentally changed the course of the war, nor had the U.S.-Iranian military clash in October, when the United States bombed two abandoned Iranian oil platforms. Thus, the Soviets had not succeeded in keeping the United States from projecting its power into the Gulf. For Iran, therefore, the Soviet connection was clearly of limited benefit.

The Soviet Union's position also changed, and it began talking about the possibility of its joining in acceptance of an arms embargo against Iran. It was clearly frustrated by the slow pace at which relations with Iran were improving and by the persistence of major disagreements, especially regarding Iran's rigid stance on Afghanistan. Arab criticism of Soviet policy also mounted.[72] Perhaps more important, Mikhail Gorbachev was beginning to embark on his major diplomatic venture to transform East-West relations, conclude arms control agreements, and improve Soviet standing globally. As a result, the Soviets were becoming concerned lest disagreements over regional issues derail progress in other areas as the U.S. expressed its unhappiness over Soviet tactics.[73] Thus, to keep the arms embargo issue from disrupting relations with the United States, the Soviet Union changed its tactics and began focusing on problems of enforcement. It questioned whether it could be sure that secret arms deals on the model of the Iran-Contra affair would not be repeated, and it suggested the creation of a U.N. naval force, presumably with the participation of Soviet naval forces, to enforce the embargo.[74]

This proposal was unacceptable to the West because it favored the Soviets and entailed legal and technical problems. Implied in the proposal was the withdrawal of the bulk of Western navies from the Persian Gulf, which risked undoing U.S. and Western gains with the Gulf Arabs; it was therefore dismissed as a delaying tactic.

The Soviets chose these complex tactics primarily to balance two objectives: they did not want to undermine their chances of improving their position in Iran by agreeing to an arms embargo, but they also wanted to counter Arab and U.S. criticism. Obviously, Moscow judged the chances poor of replacing U.S. influence with the Gulf Arabs. Had it thought this possible, it might have risked damaging relations with Iran and gone along with the embargo. Moreover, the Arabs' ability to penalize the Soviet Union for its strategy was limited because of their need for Soviet help on the Arab-Israeli issue.

The Soviet Union's complex position on the embargo was also apparently designed to help it in two other ways. First, it was interested in promoting a positive U.S. attitude on an Afghan settlement and thus was unwilling to give up all its bargaining leverage in the Gulf. It rightly assumed that the United States also had a stake in improving East-West relations which limited its capacity to press the Soviet Union too far on regional issues.

Second, it may have used the arms embargo issue to pressure Iran into cooperating on the Afghan question. Indeed, Iranian commentary hinted at such a possibility under certain conditions.[75] But despite periodic rumors, it reached no understanding with Iran linking the Afghan issue with Soviet policy in the Persian Gulf. First, a number of Iranian leaders did not favor closer Soviet-Iranian cooperation; moreover, upon reflection, the Soviets may have concluded that whatever service Iran might render in Afghanistan would not be worth jeopardizing ties to Iraq or risking an Iranian victory. Nor could the Soviets trust Iran to honor its commitment. Instead, they feared that, if victorious, Iran would become more actively involved in Afghanistan.

The Soviets' position on the arms embargo provided them with little benefit. But the U.S.-Iranian military confrontation in April 1988 offered them another opportunity to improve their position in Iran. They could not fully exploit it, however, because of Soviet military supplies to Iraq. This became a particularly significant irritant when Iraq began massive bombing of Iranian cities in March 1988, using Soviet-supplied missiles whose range had been extended. The Soviets denied that they had helped Iraq make such improvements to their equipment. Nevertheless, Rafsanjani accused them of "pursuing a policy of hypocrisy and duplicity."[76] Moreover, after Iran had captured Faw in February 1986, the Soviets delivered nearly $2 billion worth of weapons to Iraq in a major rearmament effort.

Even with the opportunity offered by the severity of the U.S.-Iranian confrontation, the Soviets remained unwilling to jeopardize ties with the United States by overreacting to U.S. military action against Iran. This Soviet attitude provoked an editorial in *Keyhan,* which recited a litany of Soviet Russian hostile deeds against Iran and then expressed regret that the Soviet Union had not taken

> . . . stock of the advantages and gains of having the most anti-American country in the world for a neighbor . . . and not shown its gratitude and appreciation towards Iran for dismantling . . . U.S. installations in the Caspian Sea region to spy and monitor Soviet activities.[77]

The Soviet Union tried to limit damage to its ties with Iran by pushing for an end to the so-called "war of the cities," and it made a proposal in the United Nations which was welcomed by Iran.[78] It offered to mediate an end to the war, and, in April, the foreign ministers of both Iran and Iraq visited Moscow, but nothing came of these talks. Later, when Iran accepted U.N. Resolution 598, the Soviets offered to organize direct talks between the two parties. Iran refused this proposal and opted for U.N. mediation. This attitude partly reflected Iran's unhappiness with the Soviet Union's mild reaction to the U.S. downing of the Iran Air jet on July 3. Admittedly, during a visit to Tehran on July 20, Vorontsov had strongly condemned this incident as an "act of barbarism."[79] But the Soviet Union's public reaction in the United Nations and elsewhere was more restrained, and it did not help Iran to obtain international condemnation of U.S. actions.

Post-Cease-fire Developments

Moscow welcomed Iran's acceptance of a cease-fire under Resolution 598 and offered to organize peace talks between Iran and Iraq. But again, Iran chose to conduct such talks under U.N. auspices. The Soviets also said that they would like to make up for past support of Iraq and to help with Iran's reconstruction.[80] Iran took note of these gestures and, as part of its policy of trying to end its international isolation, moved to improve ties with the Soviet Union. The Soviet Union took part in the Tehran Trade Fair, and Iran opened a trade exhibition in Moscow. The two sides agreed on the resumption of Iran's gas exports to the Soviet Union and on the return of Soviet experts to Iran. The Soviet-Iranian economic committee met twice.[81] However, during the first few months after the cease-fire, Iran focused its energies on improving relations with the West, especially because the position of the moderates improved with peace and because public criticism mounted over the negative consequences from past extremist policies.[82]

Yet, by late 1988, the improvement in Iran's relations with the West had stalled and the radicals were regaining some of their lost influence. As a result, beginning in early 1989, the pace of Soviet-Iranian rapprochement accelerated. On January 5, an Iranian delegation headed by the Ayatollah Abdollah Javadi Amoli met with Mikhail Gorbachev.[83] Soviet and Iranian commentary on each other became increasingly positive,[84] and both sides said that the end of the Iran-Iraq war and the Soviet withdrawal from Afghanistan had eliminated all barriers to better Soviet-

Iranian relations. And the Soviet Union admitted that, since it withdrew its forces from Afghanistan, Iran had acted to prevent a bloodbath.[85]

In February, the outbreak of the Salman Rushdie controversy, the Ayatollah Khomeini's call for his execution, and the resulting crisis in Iran's relations with the West gave the radicals their chance to undermine the moderates' reconciliatory posture toward the West. Thus, new importance was accorded to the visit to Tehran of the Soviet foreign minister, Eduard Shevardnadze, which had been agreed upon in 1987, and especially to his meeting with the Ayatollah Khomeini, a rare occurrence. There were also rumors about an arms deal which generated criticism from the United States.[86]

Iran's disappointment with the results of its Western strategy also contributed to a shift in the Soviets' direction. In particular, the Western countries were unwilling to put any pressure on Iraq to withdraw its remaining troops from Iranian territory or to be more flexible at the negotiating table. Iran thus asked the Soviet Union to put pressure on Iraq; and the Soviets agreed to play a more active role in the Iran-Iraq peace process.

The prospects for better Soviet-Iranian relations improved further in the spring, when Mikhail Gorbachev said that the Soviet Union viewed Iran as a desirable partner and invited Rafsanjani to visit Moscow. Soviet-Iranian official contacts also increased and their content became more substantive and the Soviet Union offered Iran 1.2 billion rubles in credit.

On 20 June Rafsanjani visited Moscow and was given the red carpet treatment. In a meeting with him, Mikhail Gorbachev said that " . . . we explicitly declare that our country supports your anti-imperialist revolution" and added that "we are ready to go as far as Iran is ready to meet us."[87]

In response, Rafsanjani said that Gorbachev's fresh approach to foreign policy and to the Soviet Union's Muslim population has created a new atmosphere for Soviet-Iranian relations.[88] An important event during Rafsanjani's Soviet trip was his visit to Baku, the capital of Soviet Azerbaijan, and the delivering of a sermon during the Friday prayer ceremonies. Not since the separation of that region from Iran in 1828 had a high-ranking Iranian official as Rafsanjani visited Baku. In his sermon Rafsanjani praised Gorbachev and called him one of the greatest world leaders. During Rafsanjani's trip the two sides signed a broad agreement setting the framework for Soviet-Iranian cooperation until the year 2000.[89]

This much warmer Soviet embrace of Iran also reflects the fact that after several years of ambivalence about Iran, and efforts to expand their influence among the moderate Arab states, the Soviets seem to have concluded that 1) Iran is vital to their national interest politically and economically. Politically Iran can help Russia to deal with its Muslim populations. Better economic relations with Iran would help revitalize Soviet Asian republics. 2) They cannot hope to compete with the West for influence with the moderate Arabs. Thus, it would be wiser to consolidate their influence in Iran rather than pursue an unattainable objective in the Arab world.

For Iran, in addition to the reasons noted earlier, the U.S. Afghan policy and those of its allies, especially Saudi Arabia, of exluding Iran and the Iran-based Mojahedin from any arrangements for Afghanistan's future, and the aggressive Saudi-Wahabi proselytizing campaign in the region generated a degree of commonality of strategic interest between Iran and the Soviet Union, namely to prevent the consolidation of Western-Saudi domination in the region.

Better relations with the Soviet Union also offerred Iran the possibility of a greater presence among Soviet Muslims. The result of this Soviet-Iranian rapprochement was an even greater softening of Iran's politions on the future shape of an Afghan government, which could include certain elements of the current regime. The Soviet foreign minister, visiting Tehran in August 1989, clearly stated that Iraq should withdraw from any Iranian territory that it still occupied at that time.[90]

The Iran-Iraq War: Impact on Soviet-Iranian Relations

In reviewing the complex, often contradictory, development of Soviet-Iranian relations in the 1980s, it is important to have a clear understanding of one special factor in Iranian foreign policy, the Iran-Iraq war. In particular, it is important to understand the extent to which the Soviet attitude toward the war either did, or did not, determine the course of Soviet-Iranian relations.

Throughout the war, the Soviet Union adopted an official policy of neutrality. In practice, however, its position fluctuated, depending on its assessment of the war's impact on its interests. In particular, Iraq's invasion in September 1980 faced the Soviet Union with a dilemma. On the one hand, the 1972 Soviet-Iraqi Friendship Treaty provided for Soviet assistance to Iraq in the "removal" of threats to its security. Iraq viewed Iran as a security threat, and thus the war inevitably raised the issue of Soviet assistance. On the other hand, in 1980 the Soviets had competing concerns, made more important by the fact that Soviet-Iraq relations had cooled because of Iraq's increasing orientation toward the West, including evidence of contacts with the United States.[91]

At that time, the Soviet Union still hoped for the transformation of the Iranian revolution and the expansion of its influence in Iran. This positive Soviet move stemmed in part from the fact that the revolution had eliminated the U.S. presence, and Moscow feared that Iran's defeat could lead to a change of regime and a return of U.S. influence.[92] Soviet commentaries accused the West, especially the United States, of having provoked the conflict by exacerbating Iraq's fears of Iran and by indicating that it would not oppose Iraqi ambitions, including the creation of a Republic of Arabistan.[93] Furthermore, the Soviet Union has traditionally opposed territorial changes along its borders, unless directed by Moscow, and it had therefore to be concerned lest Iran disintegrate under the Iraqi onslaught. Initially, therefore, the Soviet Union tilted toward Iran, it stopped arms deliveries to Iraq; offered Iran weaponry; and helped to set up its internal security system.[94] These Soviet offers were not received enthusiastically, and even after the rapprochement of 1981–82, Iran refused direct delivery, although Soviet-made arms indirectly reached Iran.

Moscow's attitude changed in the summer of 1982, after the withdrawal of Iraqi troops from Iran, and it was first signalled by the Tudeh Party's call for an end to the war and the conclusion of a peace treaty. When Iran refused to negotiate, the Soviet Union resumed arms deliveries to Iraq. This time, Iraq, rather than Iran, appeared to be threatened by territorial disintegration. The Soviets disapproved of a drastic increase in Iranian power and influence, which would make Iran both less willing to accommodate Soviet wishes and better able to spread Islamic fundamentalism to the Soviet Asian empire. And the Soviets were clearly disappointed with the evolution of events in Iran and irritated over Iranian intransigence on Afghanistan.

Nevertheless, the Soviet tilt toward Iraq did not become pronounced until 1983, after the serious deterioration in overall Soviet-Iranian relations. Even then, the decision was only reached after considerable debate within the Soviet leadership.[95] The Soviet Union's tilt also derived from its perception that developments in the Middle East, generally, offered opportunities to expand its influence and undermine the U.S. position at a time of the Lebanon crisis and the gradual unraveling of U.S.-Israeli plans, when U.S. prestige and credibility in the Middle East were at an all-time low. The Soviets could calculate that the benefits they would gain in the Arab world from supporting Iraq would outweigh losses in Iran.[96]

This Soviet attitude reflected its traditional behavior. As a superpower with global interests, it has always accorded priority to pursuit of its broader regional and global ambitions, based on a calculation of costs and benefits, even if this has meant tensions in relations with Iran. It had had the same motive in the Soviet-Iraqi Friendship Treaty of 1972.[97]

The Soviets' tilt toward Iraq did exact a price, however. Their assistance to Iraq and unwillingness to address the issue of some kind of punishment for its invasion of Iran reduced their ability to capitalize on the U.S.-Iranian estrangement and weakened the position of pro-Soviet elements within the Iranian leadership. Yet occasionally the war and its impact on Iran's relations with the United States and with some Gulf Arab countries offered the Soviet Union opportunities to improve its position in Iran, as during the Iranian-Saudi military encounter of May 1984 and the U.S.-Iranian confrontation of 1987–88.

With the war over, this record of Soviet behavior in the Iran-Iraq war could cast a shadow over future relations and exclude close Soviet-Iranian ties. Nevertheless, compared to Western treatment of Iran, the Soviet position, especially during 1980–82 and 1987–88, was more cognizant of Iranian grievances, even at the risk of damaging Soviet relations with Iraq and other Arabs. Thus, if other factors work in the Soviet favor in Iran, as they seemed to be doing as of mid-1989, the Soviet record may not be an insurmountable barrier to a better relationship.

Conclusions

Neither the Iran-Iraq war nor Soviet support for Iraq altered the underlying patterns of Soviet-Iranian relations. The Soviet Union has been pursuing a two-track policy, keeping channels of communication open and maintaining cooperation with the existing Iranian government. The Soviets also promoted the pro-Soviet, Islamic radicals and other leftist elements and urged a coalition between them.

The Soviet Union still determines its policy toward Iran in light of its broader regional and global goals and on the basis of an analysis of costs and benefits. Since 1985 and the introduction of the so-called new thinking and risk aversion in Soviet foreign policy under Mikhail Gorbachev—especially as it applies to the Third World—the Soviet Union has accentuated its focus on broader goals in its dealings with Iran. The Soviets are still concerned about Iran's regional influence and try to check it. However, in 1989 domestic economic and political considerations seemed to be playing a greater role in determining the Soviet approach toward Iran.

At the same time, Iran's behavior toward the Soviets is also remarkably similar to that in the past—namely, a mixture of deep suspicion (although not shared to the same extent by all), occasional provocative rhetoric, and keen awareness of the need to accommodate Soviet power and proximity. Yet, as in the past, the fact of Soviet proximity and Iran's fear of total subjugation have acted as a break on meaningful Soviet-Iranian cooperation, which remains limited to economic areas. In the past, Iran's ideological rigidity and its political divisions prevented the Islamic regime from effectively playing a Soviet card, thereby leaving it far more vulnerable to U.S. and other Western pressures. Meanwhile, because of fears of Islamic revivalism and because of its other domestic and international priorities, the Soviet Union missed opportunities to co-opt Iran. Indeed, occasional Soviet gains in Iran have stemmed more from Western (especially U.S.) mistakes than from Soviet diplomatic dexterity.

All this may be changing, however. If, under Mikhail Gorbachev, the Soviets continue in their non-threatening posture toward Iran, if their internal reforms reduce Iranian fears that their economy and society will be Sovietized, and if the West remains unresponsive to Iran's basic grievances, then the possibilities for qualitatively different Soviet-Iranian relations will increase. Indeed, the outlook for closer Soviet-Iranian relations looks brighter than ever in the immediate aftermath of the Ayatollah Khomeini's death as Iranian leaders claim that such a move is what was desired by the Imam.

6. Iran, the Arab World, and Israel

Iran's relations with the Arab world best illustrates both the changes that the Islamic revolution has introduced into Iranian foreign policy and the persistence of underlying patterns and their basic determinants. The latter was made most evident by the Iran-Iraq war, which reflected the long history of Iran's involvement with the Arabs.

Ethnic and Religious Differences

Since Iran's defeat by the Arabs in the seventh century, A.D., ethnic and religious differences have provided a background of tension to Arab-Iranian relations. Despite Islamization, Iran was not Arabized. It retained its ethnic and cultural distinctiveness, and in the third century after the Arab invasion, it experienced a linguistic, literary, and political renaissance.[1]

Islam itself became a divisive rather than a unifying factor between Iran and the Arabs. It provided a universalist message which transcended ethnic and racial barriers. But after Mohammad's death, the Arabs forgot Islam's universalist and egalitarian dimensions, viewed its Arab origins as proof of their racial superiority, and discriminated against non-Arab converts. This practice enhanced particularist tendencies among new converts and led them to dissociate themselves from the religious beliefs of their rulers.[2] The Iranians' attraction and later conversion to Shi'ism enhanced their sense of distinctiveness and deepened the Arab-Iranian chasm.[3]

Iran's Islamization gave rise to a cultural competition between Arabs and Iranians, which became particularly significant in the twentieth century with the rise of modern nationalism in the Middle East.[4] To be sure, ethnic and sectarian antagonisms alone have not determined the character of Arab-Iranian relations. But they have formed a backdrop and have exacerbated the divisive impact of other factors. Such antagonisms have been manipulated by Arab and Iranian leaderships alike in order to harness public support. For example, faced with Iran's revolutionary challenge, conservative Arab states have argued that Iran's experience is irrelevant and alien to the Sunni Arab world because it is a purely Persian-Shi'a phenomenon.[5] Yet no such charges were made against the equally threatening ideologies of Gamal abd-al Nasser or Muammar Qadhafi. These charges are not even well-directed at Iran, whose revolutionary message has found sympathetic echoes among some non-Shi'a Arabs, although ethnic and sectarian barriers have limited its reach among the Arab masses.[6]

Likewise, the Islamic regime's policy of downgrading Persian nationalism has been only marginally successful in changing Arab perceptions of Iran or in the public attitudes of Iranians.[7] Iraq succeeded in gaining support for its war against Iran by using Arab nationalism and racially charged symbols.[8]

Competing Nationalisms

The rise of modern nationalism in the Arab world and Iran has added a political dimension to their ethnic and cultural differences. From the Iranian perspective, two characteristics of Arab nationalism—namely, what Professor Majid Khaduri has called its "irredentist" and "romantic" dimensions—have been particularly ominous.[9] Arab nationalists have wanted to unite Arab lands and to liberate those areas they consider to be part of the Arab homeland—areas that have included Bahrain and the Iranian province of Khusistan. This form of pan-Arabism has viewed Iran as a principal obstacle to achieving its goals.[10] Indeed, with considerable success they have even tried to change the historic name of the Gulf from "Persian" to "Arabian," and successive Arab governments have periodically challenged the legitimacy of Iran's presence there.[11]

The Arab nationalist ethos has affected Iran's relations even with otherwise sympathetic Arab countries, because all Arab regimes are attracted to some degree to Arab nationalism's irredentist and romantic aspects. Moreover, open divergence from this ethos could be politically costly, as witnessed during the 1960s and 1970s, when the commitment of Persian Gulf Arab states to Arab nationalism—coupled with their vulnerability to radical Arab propaganda and subversion—hindered their cooperation with Iran despite common security concerns.[12]

Meanwhile, during the last several decades Iranian nationalism has been preoccupied with reasserting Iran's position in the Persian Gulf and maintaining its rights. Although for two centuries Iran has been retrenching in the Persian Gulf, both territorially and politically, this has often been interpreted by Arabs and Westerners as proof of Iran's expansionism.

On coming to power, the Islamic regime formally rejected Iranian nationalism, yet, in fact, its perceptions of Iran's interests in the Persian Gulf and its regional role are identical to those of the Iranian nationalists, and statements made by the Islamic Republic's officials about the Persian Gulf echo those of the Shah.[13] Therefore, during the post-revolution period, the antagonistic forces of nationalism have remained divisive in Arab-Iranian relations. Indeed, the Islamic regime had a taste of the potency of Arab nationalism when the Arab summit (23–26 May 1989) unanimously endorsed Iraq's claim of sovereignty over the Shat-al Arab. This generated bitter commentary in the Tehran press against Algeria. They questioned how Algeria, which had mediated the agreement of 1975 that divided the waterway, could have endorsed Iraq's claim.[14]

The Regional and Global Political Systems

Arab-Iranian relations have clearly been affected by broader changes that have taken place in the international and regional (political) systems, including post-war polarization. During the 1950s and 1960s, Iran was primarily preoccupied with the Soviet threat, thus turning to the United States and joining the Baghdad Pact. Many Arab states, meanwhile, were concerned with the challenge from Israel and mindful of U.S. support for it, and therefore turned to the Soviet Union. Thus, Iran's alliance with the United States and the Arabs' inclination toward the Soviet Union—in other words, their superpower connections—deeply affected Arab-Iranian relations.

During the 1970s, changes in the Middle East, including the complete integration of the Arab side of the Persian Gulf into the Arab world, enhanced Arab-Iranian interaction. This process had begun in the 1950s, partly because of the shift of the Arab nationalist focus to the Persian Gulf, especially by Egypt and later by the Ba'athists. Extreme Arab nationalists viewed the Persian Gulf as a bastion of Western influence and the Gulf regimes, both Arab and Iranian, as Western surrogates. They believed that this Western domination had deprived the Arabs of the oil revenues which should have been used for their development.[15] Thus, the elimination of the West's influence and its regional supporters was their primary objective. Iran, the largest Persian Gulf country and Western ally, was therefore viewed by Arab extremists as the principal obstacle to realizing their objectives. A change in its leadership would be necessary.

For its part, Iran viewed Arab extremists as a serious threat both to its own security and to that of the region. Not surprisingly, therefore, during the 1960s the Persian Gulf became an arena of Egyptian-Iranian competition, to be followed in the 1970s by Iraqi-Iranian rivalry. Meanwhile, the common threat of Arab radicalism drew Iran and conservative Arabs closer together.

Intra-regional linkages and Arab-Iranian interaction intensified in the 1970s, following the Arab-Israeli war of 1973 and the ensuing oil shock. Because of its activist policy in the Persian Gulf and in the Middle East, Iran became a particular target of Arab extremists' subversion. During the last decade, the process of extending Arab-Iranian interaction and regional ties has intensified. Iran's anti-Israel, anti-Zionist, and anti-imperialist rhetoric; its emphasis on Islamic brotherhood; and its downplaying of Persian nationalism—all have enabled it to reach Arab masses to a larger, albeit still limited, degree. Yet the essence of Iran's Persian Gulf and Middle East policies have remained the same. Iran still wants to safeguard its shores in the Persian Gulf; to maintain an adequate economic, commercial, and political presence on the Arab side of the Gulf; and to create a regional environment congenial to its interests. But after the revolution, achieving these goals has meant reducing Western influence and creating like-minded Islamic regimes. This has strained Iran's relations with conservative Arab regimes and improved relations with extremist forces.

Intra-Arab Politics: Impact on Arab-Iranian Relations

These changes in the regional system have made Arab-Iranian relations vulnerable to developments in intra-Arab politics. Besides the Arab nationalist ethos, divisions among Arab states and rivalries for prestige and leadership have affected Arab-Iranian relations, as various Arab states have used Iran as a tool for affecting the balance of power among themselves. Iran has also forged tactical alliances with particular Arab countries in order to create a regional environment congenial to its interests. During the 1950s, Iraq cooperated with Iran, and during the 1960s, Saudi Arabia did the same, both in part because of their rivalry with, and concern over, Nasser's Egypt. And during the 1970s, Saudi Arabia and Iran jointly fought Middle East extremists, despite their competition in the Persian Gulf and elsewhere.[16]

A similar situation has prevailed since the Islamic revolution, as Syria has aligned with Iran because of its rivalry with Iraq, and Syria and Libya have used Iran to strengthen the position of the so-called Arab rejectionist front. Meanwhile, Egypt has manipulated the Iranian challenge as a means of easing its way back into the Arab world, posing as a counterweight to Iran.

Territorial Disputes

A number of territorial disputes, notably the Arab-Iranian dispute over Bahrain and Arab claim on the Iranian province of Khusistan, have also affected Arab-Iranian relations.[17]

The Bahrain dispute was settled in 1970 when Iran relinquished its claim, although many Iranians have not come to terms with this loss and feel that, at least, Iran should have been able to retain a strong presence. This lack of influence in Bahrain is particularly difficult to accept given the fact that the island, especially after the completion of the causeway linking it to Saudi Arabia, has become a Saudi appendage in all but name.[18] By contrast, the Arab claim to Khusistan has never been clearly settled. Arab governments have recognized Iran and established diplomatic ties, an act which implies their recognition of its borders. In practice, however, many Arab countries have kept alive their collective claim toward Khusistan, and hostile Arab governments periodically have used the Khusistan issue to justify anti-Iranian postures and subversion of different Iranian regimes.[19] Indeed, the desire to vindicate the Arab claim to Khusistan was one of the principle reasons that Iraq invaded Iran—the most dramatic example of the impact of territorial disputes on Arab-Iranian relations—and during the early days of the war the Gulf Arabs welcomed its liberation. They have also repeatedly laid claim to the three Persian Gulf islands of Abu Musa and the Greater and Lesser Tunbs, and Iraq claims total sovereignty over the Shat-al-Arab (Arvand Rud).

Although territorial disputes have been significant underlying irritants, however, in the final analysis they have not determined the character of Arab-Iranian relations. Whether they have been used actively against Iran by individual Arab governments or have instead been conveniently ignored, has depended on other factors. In 1971, Libya was in the forefront of Arab attacks against Iran's military takeover of the disputed Persian Gulf islands, but it supported Iran in its war against Iraq. Significantly, however, neither Libya nor Syria has renounced the Arab claim either to Khusistan or to the islands.

The Impact of Ideology

During the last four decades, the presence or absence of ideological affinity has been most influential in shaping Arab-Iranian relations. Under the Shah, Iran's anti-Communism and its alliance with the United States resulted in cooperative relations with conservative Arab countries and to strained ties with radical, pro-Soviet Arab states.[20] Similarly, revolutionary Iran's anti-Americanism partly explains its closer ties with Syria, Libya, and South Yemen, and its strained relations with pro-Western Arabs.[21] With changes in the nature of U.S.-Soviet relations and the continued erosion of the East-West conflict, however, the ideological factor may lose its importance as a determinant in Arab-Iranian relations.

The Israel Factor

In the past, the Arabs have often cited Iran's close relations with the state of Israel as the primary cause of Arab-Iranian tensions. No doubt, in time this closeness became a major irritant, but such an Arab view mistakes cause for effect, ignores Iran's motivations for establishing links to Israel, and provides no explanation for the Arab claims to Khusistan and ambitions to turn the Persian Gulf into an Arab lake. Indeed, Iran has always basically supported the Arab position on Palestine. At the United Nations in 1947, it voted for the minority plan which envisaged a federated state of Palestine composed of two autonomous Jewish and Arab states, and it voted against the partition plan that was adopted. Furthermore, during the 1940s and 1950s, there was a large measure of support for the Arab cause in Iran that largely derived from the common anti-British dimensions of Arab and Iranian nationalism.[22] Similarly, during the 1960s and the 1970s, many Iranians opposed close ties with Israel because they saw it, as Professor Ali Mazrui has said, as an outpost of Western imperialism in the Third World.[23]

At heart, two sets of considerations have been most important in determining Iran's approach toward Israel and the Arab-Israel conflict: first, the nature and intensity of the Soviet threat to Iran and thus Iran's sensitivity to the attitude of regional states toward the Soviet Union; and second, Arab attitudes toward Iran. During Israel's early days of existence, the Iranians were not sure of its political orientation and were especially worried about its Soviet ties and the Zionist movement's socialist leanings.[24] These doubts dissipated as the United States became

Israel's principal supporter, leading Iran to value Israel as a barrier to Soviet penetration of the Middle East. Meanwhile, the new Arab nationalists, such as Gamal
abd-al-Nasser, chose the Soviet camp, in part because of Western support for Israel.
Indeed, had Israel and the Soviet Union maintained close ties and had the Soviet
Union become Israel's protector, the Arabs would likely have turned to the West.
Under those conditions, Iran would have cooperated with the Arabs in order to
contain joint Soviet-Israeli influence in the region. As matters developed, however,
a basic conflict developed between Iran's principal security concern, which was
the Soviet Union, and that of many Arabs, which was the state of Israel.

As Iran's views developed on the nature of the Soviet threat and on the factors
contributing to the expansion of Soviet influence, so did its policy toward the Arab-
Israeli conflict. By the early 1970s, Iran believed that the Soviets were less likely
to attack it than to encircle it with radical, pro-Soviet states. Iran also saw the
festering Palestinian problem as a catalyst for Soviet inroads in the Middle East,
and it was convinced that a satisfactory resolution of this problem was essential to
prevent Soviet penetration. After the war of 1973, these changing perceptions led
Iran to take a more pro-Arab posture on the Arab-Israeli conflict and to develop
its so-called Arab option. Indeed, this change in Iran's Arab policy made the Israelis
unhappy with both it and the Shah and may have changed their assessment of Iran's
value to them.[25]

Arab attitudes toward Iran also deeply affected its relations with Israel. As Arab
nationalism evolved from an anti-colonial movement into an irredentist, expansionist, and exclusivist ideology, Iran felt seriously threatened. Thus it was natural
for it to develop another basis for a common strategic interest with Israel—namely,
to contain extreme Arab nationalism. Yet Iran's cooperation with Israel merely
intensified negative Arab attitudes toward Iran, based on other factors. This conclusion is dramatized by the lack of similar Arab reaction toward Turkey's ties with
Israel. Indeed, Turkey recognized Israel *de jure* soon after its creation and has had
diplomatic ties and discreet security cooperation with it. If the mere recognition
of Israel were truly responsible for the anti-Iran dimensions of Arab nationalism,
Turkey should have become an equally important target of Arab animosity, which
did not happen. In striking contrast, Iran only accepted Israel (from 1950 onward)
de facto.

It could be argued that Arab-Iranian relations would have been less acrimonious
if Iran had not developed close ties with Israel, but far more relevant is the fact of
diametrically opposed Arab and Iranian perceptions of threats to their security, as
well as the inherently irredentist and exclusivist dimensions of Arab nationalism,
which made a forging of close ties between Iran and Israel almost inevitable. By
contrast, had the Arabs come to terms with Israel, they would have effectively
foreclosed the Iranian option of cooperating with it. In other words, the Arab
attitude has been, throughout, the pivotal factor determining the state of Iran's
relations with Israel.

The Arab variable has been the single most important factor in shaping Israel's
posture toward Iran. Had the Arabs accepted Israel and made peace with it, it would

not have had to devise its so-called "peripheral strategy", based on cooperation with non-Arab states in the region. Indeed, after the signing of the Egyptian-Israeli peace treaty and especially after the Iranian revolution, the development of a hostile Iranian attitude toward Israel, plus the rise of the challenge of Islamic fundamentalism, helped create support in Israel for an "Arab option".

Many Israeli scholars and politicians have questioned the validity of David Ben Gurion's "peripheral strategy" and urged Israel to support the Arabs against Iran—thereby, supposedly, prompting an Arab compromise with Israel on the Palestinian issue. This Israeli debate became particularly focused during the Iran-Iraq war, when a growing number of experts argued in favor of supporting Iraq. According to this view, if the Arabs were willing to make necessary compromises, Israel would side with them against Iran. But since this did not happen, the debate produced no fruit: Israel opted for a policy of maintaining a balance between Iran and the Arabs while trying to weaken both sides.

The limited impact that Iran's position on Israel and the Arab-Israeli conflict has had on its relations with the Arabs is underscored by the failure of alterations in Iranian policy to change the Arab response. Thus, despite a considerable pro-Arab shift in Iran's policy on the Palestinian issue during the 1970s, the Palestine Liberation Organization (PLO) continued its anti-Shah activities, including the training of anti-regime guerrillas in its camps. Even as early as 1969, the Shah had tried to reach a modus vivendi with the PLO, but he was rebuffed by Arafat.[26] By the same token, those Arab states which considered good relations with Iran to be in their interest were not deterred by Iran's ties with Israel.

Furthermore, the Islamic regime has followed a totally pro-Arab policy on the Palestinian issue and has gone further than many Arab states by supporting the liberation of the whole of Palestine. This attitude has been costly, particularly in terms of Iran's relations with the West. Yet it has not been enough to secure Arab, or even Palestinian, amity toward Iran. Even post-revolutionary Iran's limited secret dealings with Israel, including the obtaining of arms and the Iran-Contra episode, have been largely a function of the Arab attitude toward Iran and Israel. If Iraq had not invaded, there would have been no Iranian purchases of Israeli arms and no need for Israeli intercession with the United States on Iran's behalf. Similarly, had the Arabs compromised with Israel, it would have lost interest in Iran.

In short, Iran's position on Israel and the Palestinians has had little to do in shaping Arab-Iranian relations. More basic and enduring factors have exerted a more powerful and lasting influence. Under the Shah's rule, they limited the extent of Arab-Iranian cooperation. After the revolution, they have intensified Arab opposition and animosity toward Iran.

The Iran-Iraq War

Iraq's invasion of Iran and the Arab reaction to the war best illustrate the impact of underlying, sublime factors in shaping Iran's relations with the Arabs. Few observers disagree that Iraq started the war,[27] but opinion is divided concerning the primary impulse behind Iraq's action. One school of thought holds that it was prompted by fear of the contagious effect of the Islamic revolution, whereas another school considers ambition to have been a more powerful motive.

Iran's revolution had indeed aroused Shi'ite passions in Iraq and had accentuated the problems faced by the narrowly based, Sunni-dominated, secular Ba'athist regime of Saddam Hussein al-Takriti. No doubt, Iranian revolutionaries were calling on the Iraqis to overthrow Saddam's regime, and Iraq blamed all acts of Shi'ite violence on Iran.[28] Also, Iran believed in the validity of its revolution for other Muslim countries, but there is no evidence that it intended to try imposing its ideology on others by force. More important, by the time of the invasion, neither Iraq's Shi'a opposition nor its Iranian supporters were strong enough to seriously threaten the survival of Saddam's regime. Indeed, after the arrest and execution of Imam Muhammad Baqir as-Sadr by the Ba'athist government in April 1980, the Iraqi Shi'a movement was in disarray, while Iraq was at the pinnacle of its economic and political power.[29] Meanwhile, Iran's military forces had largely disintegrated, its new revolutionary guards were composed of untrained ideological zealots, the American hostage crisis had isolated it politically, Western sanctions had sapped its economic strength, and factional divisions and political rivalries had virtually paralyzed its government.

Moreover, this view that fear motivated Saddam Hussein does not adequately consider the impact of the expansionist and exclusivist dimensions of Arab nationalist ideology on his behavior. His statements and actions during the period between the fall of the Shah and the outbreak of the war clearly reflect these influences. Saddam Hussein warned Iran that any revolution that called itself Islamic must be friendly to the Arab revolution; he demanded that Iran return to the Arabs the three disputed Persian Gulf islands; he nullified the Algiers Agreement of 1975 that divided the Shat-al-Arab on the basis of the median line; he sent arms to agitate Khusistan's Arab minority; and he called for the restoration of rights to Iran's oppressed minorities.[30] Furthermore, given the Arab claim to Khusistan province, the implications of Ba'athist pan-Arabism for Iran's territorial integrity are obvious.

Statements by Iraqi officials just prior to the invasion also belie fear as the strongest motive. The Iraqi minister of culture, for example, said in an interview with the Danish newspaper, *Berlingske Tidende,* that the Ayatollah Khomeini was a madman, a lunatic, who was not dangerous. He also said that a country like Iran which lacks an army and is in chaos could not threaten a country like Iraq which has a strong army, leadership, and economy.[31]

At the regional level, Iran's collapse and Egypt's isolation following its peace treaty with Israel had created a vacuum of power and leadership, and thus an irresistible temptation for Iraq to try dominating the Persian Gulf and, potentially, becoming the leading state in the Middle East. Thus, Iraq's ambitions, as the emerging regional power and as custodian of the Arab nationalist mantle, and Iran's weakness created an irresistible temptation and triggered the war.

Evolution of the War, 1980–84

When it invaded, Iraq clearly expected a quick victory, leading to a change of regime in Iran and the conclusion of a treaty that would ensure its total sovereignty over Shat-al-Arab. Iraq also hoped for the separation of Khusistan or even Iran's disintegration into its ethnic components, as reflected in a comment by Tariq Aziz, its prime minister, that "Five small Iran's would be better than one big Iran." At the beginning, Iraq successfully launched a three-pronged offensive in Ghasr-e-Shirin in the north, Mehran in the center, and Susangerd-Khoramshahr in the south, occupying a large part of Khusistan and Bakhtaran.

By contrast, in Iran the chaotic state of the military, preoccupation with internal ethnic unrest and factionalism, and the commitment of a large portion of its troops and tanks to the Soviet border led to early defeats. The rapidity of Iraq's successes caused an upsurge of nationalism in Iran and allowed President Bani-Sadr to release some well-trained Iranian pilots. Iranian air and naval forces bombed Iraq's oil installations and for a brief period stopped its oil exports.

But Iraq continued its advance, and by November 1980 occupied a third of Khusistan. Meanwhile, disagreements between Bani-Sadr and the Islamic Republican Party and its selected prime minister Rajai undermined Iran's war efforts.[32] In fact, only after Bani-Sadr's ouster would Iran put up a credible defense. In June 1981 Bani-Sadr left Iran and by that fall, the tide of the war turned in Iran's favor. During the fall and winter of 1981 and the spring of 1982, Iran recaptured some of its lost territory, using a series of massive offensives and human-wave tactics.

In April 1982, in protest against assistance provided by Saddam Hussein to Syria's dissident Muslim Brethren, Syria shut off the Iraqi oil pipeline to the Syrian port of Banias. On 30 April, Iran launched an offensive in Khusistan, which was a prelude to the famous battle of Khoramshahr on 21 May. Three days later, Khoramshahr fell to the Iranians; its recapture marked the end of the first cycle of the Iran-Iraq war, although Saddam Hussein did not withdraw Iraqi troops until June 20. By June 30, however, except for some insignificant pockets, Iraqi troops had withdrawn from the bulk of Iranian territory.

This period of Iranian advance between May and July 1982 provided opportunities to end the war. After Iran's victory in Khoramshahr, Iraqi Shi'as rioted, causing anxiety in Iraq and setting off a flurry of activity among Arab states. Meanwhile, after the liberation of Iranian territory, some Iranian leaders—including the communist Tudeh Party and former Prime Minister Mehdi Bazargan's Freedom Movement—called for a negotiated peace. Moderate elements of Iran's leadership also favored this option and opposed moving into Iraqi territory, warning that invading Iraq would erode Muslim sympathy and good will toward Iran. However, peace efforts pressed by a variety of sources ended in failure.

In particular, Iran's leadership miscalculated both the ability of Saddam Hussein's regime to survive a military defeat and the determination of outside powers to help Iraq. Iran was convinced that Iraq could not long hold, and in view of its poor performance in the war after initial victories, the inefficiency of the Iraqi air force, despite its sophisticated equipment, the large numbers of army desertions and prisoners of war, and finally the withdrawal of Iraqi forces, Iran opted to continue the war.[33] Extremist leaders, especially, believed that Iraq's defeat would open the Persian Gulf and the Middle East to Iranian revolutionary influence.

The Shi'a riots in Iraq led Iran's leaders to wrongly calculate that a move into Iraq would trigger a popular uprising against Saddam Hussein, much as Iraq had miscalculated the reaction of Khusistan's Arabs. Iraq's deteriorating economy, while Iran's was improving, also helped convince the Iranians that victory was at hand. Indeed, while they launched several attacks against Iraq in 1982–83, particularly the effort to capture Basra in July 1982, the changed economic picture led Iran to rely upon a war of economic attrition. It expected its larger population and Iraqi economic problems to cause its collapse, and Iranian attacks were designed essentially to accelerate this process. During the balance of 1982 and 1983, Iran advanced into Iraqi territory, once as close as seven miles from Basra. But it could not hold onto captured territories because it lacked adequate equipment and logistical support, while political infighting continued between regular Iranian armed forces and the Revolutionary Guards and volunteers.

The war was not being conducted in a vacuum, however. Once Iran adopted an offensive posture, the flow of arms to it slowed, but assistance to Iraq increased. In particular, the Gulf Arab states increased their financial assistance. Jordan and Egypt provided military equipment, advisers, and fighters, while other Arab states sent volunteers. In October 1983, France delivered Super Etendard aircraft and Exocet missiles, and the Soviet Union resumed sending military supplies, thus beginning to create an overwhelming Iraqi air superiority that would prove decisive in the war.

1984–1986:
Tanker War, Chemical Warfare, and the Iranian Capture of Faw

By 1984, Iran's war of economic attrition had failed to topple the Iraqi regime which, with sophisticated weapons, had launched its own economic warfare on Iran by attacking its oil terminal at Khargh Island and tankers calling on its ports. There was merit in Iraq's tanker war strategy, designed both to cripple Iran's oil exports and draw in outside powers by endangering the flow of oil. Iran was totally dependent on the Persian Gulf to export oil (vital to earn revenues for the war effort), while Iraq exported its oil by pipelines through Saudi Arabia and Turkey. As Iraq expected, the tanker war revived the fears that, in retaliation, Iran would close the Strait of Hormuz. At the very outset, therefore, Western powers declared that they would do everything necessary to keep the strait and the sea lanes open.[34]

Iran had indeed said that, were it to be prevented from exporting its oil, no one else would be allowed to do so either. But it had never seriously considered closing the Strait of Hormuz, because it would have suffered most. Indeed, the speaker of the parliament, Rafsanjani, said that Iran would not close the strait, provided it could export even half of its oil.[35] Yet despite improvisation to cope with the effects of the tanker war, Iran soon realized that its strategy of economic attrition had backfired and that it now faced merciless economic warfare.

Meanwhile, since 1983, Iraq had been using its air superiority to strike at Iran's civilian centers.[36] Facing indiscriminate Iraqi bombings and growing economic pressures, Iran began launching a series of land offensives. In 1984, the first major offensive began on 14 February. On the southern front, Iranian forces attempted to cut the Baghdad-Basra road, while a second offensive was concentrated in the area west of Mehran and southeast of Baghdad, again aiming at Basra. At this point in the war, Iran had to rely primarily on ill-trained and poorly armed volunteers who, after some advances, were pushed back with massive casualties. Yet Iran continued its offensive, attacking Iraq across the Hawizah marshes north of Basra until, after suffering horrendous casualties, it could only hold the man-made Majnoon islands which contained oil wells with estimated reserves of 7 or 8 billion barrels.

The year 1984 was a bad one for Iran. It suffered heavy casualties, its economic situation deteriorated, and it encountered greater difficulties obtaining arms, partly because of the U.S. "Operation Staunch." Iran's position was further undermined by its continued reliance on untrained paramilitary forces and volunteers, by the lack of cooperation and coordination within its diverse military forces, and by the massive flow of sophisticated weaponry to Iraq. Meanwhile, Iraq's use of chemical weapons nullified Iran's numerical superiority as a factor in the war.

The situation did not improve in 1985. Iran's human losses and the domestic political repercussions forced it to abandon human wave tactics and to rely more on probing offensives on several fronts. It tried to improve the training of the Revolutionary Guards and to use its regular armed forces more effectively, but with little success, despite some minor gains on the northern front near Kurdish areas. In March 1985, Iran launched another big offensive in the south which briefly cut the Basra-Baghdad highway, but, as before, it could not hold onto its gains. Meanwhile, by using Saudi and Kuwaiti air space, Iraq's bombing of Iranian economic installations became more effective.

In addition, the Gulf Arabs increased their economic pressure on Iran and their assistance to Iraq. The Saudis provided Iraq with intelligence gathered by their U.S.-supplied Airborne Warning and Control Aircraft (AWACs) and created an extended air and sea defense zones in order to prevent the tanker war from expanding to their shores. This step intensified the pressure on Iran because it could not attack ships in those areas in retaliation for Iraqi strikes on its shipping. Furthermore, because Iran has a long coastline and Iraq has virtually none, Iraq could declare the Iranian coast a war zone and thus bomb ships calling on Iranian ports with impunity. Yet any Iranian retaliatory actions were characterized by Iraq and the world community as attacks on neutral shipping.

For the rest of 1985, Iran tried to consolidate its gains in the marshy areas and focused its attention on the northern front. It forged cooperative relations with two Kurdish rebel factions headed by Jalal Talebani and Massoud Barzani who, after resolving their differences in late 1985, joined Iran.

Iran hoped that a northern front strategy would both put enough pressure on Iraq to force it to thin its defenses in the south and would stop Iraqi oil exports through Turkey and perhaps even capture Kirkuk and Mosul. Whether that strategy could have succeeded militarily will never be known, because Turkey stepped in.

With its large Kurdish minority, Turkey had been concerned about the upsurge of Kurdish autonomist activity in Iraq and Iran and especially about the occasional infiltration of Kurdish areas in Turkey by Iraqi Kurds. Ankara did not relish the prospect either of Iranian control over these areas or financial losses deriving from the interruption of Iraqi oil exports. Likewise the Turks looked askance at an Iranian victory that would shift the balance of regional power and help spread the Islamic revolution. Thus, by taking military action against the Iraqi Kurdish rebels and sending messages through diplomatic channels, Turkey warned Iran that actions which threatened these basic Turkish interests would not be tolerated. As a result, Iran's northern strategy was stillborn.

The year 1986 began differently. In February, Iran scored a major victory by capturing the Faw peninsula, thereby alarming the Persian Gulf Arab states and other supporters of Iraq, about a collapse of Iraqi morale and increased Iranian pressures on Kuwait to stop helping Baghdad.

In response to the loss of Faw, Iraq seized the Iranian city of Mehran in the northern front, but Iranian forces soon retook it. Nevertheless, Iran's successes failed to achieve their ultimate objective—namely, to break Iraq's resistance and to topple Saddam Hussein. Instead, the Iraqi air force continued to pound Iranian cities and economic targets. And the Persian Gulf Arab states—including Oman and the UAE, which had reasonable ties with Iran—on 5 March 1986 issued a stiff communique warning Iran that an attack on any of the GCC countries would be considered an attack on them all.

1987–88

After the capture of Faw Peninsula, Iran was widely expected to launch a massive offensive. But because of its difficulties in obtaining weapons and recruiting new volunteers, the offensive did not materialize. Instead, in January 1987 Iran attacked Basra, hoping to exploit the psychological impact of Faw and either to capture Basra or to force out its inhabitants. Had this attack succeeded, Basra would have been effectively cut from the rest of the country, thus putting great pressure on Saddam Hussein, although not necessarily ending his rule. But despite some initial gains at the price of 30,000 casualties, Iran failed to break through Basra's defenses, thus marking its last major thrust on the southern front. In Kurdish areas, joint Iranian-Kurdish operations had some success, but it was halted both by Turkey's role and by Iraq's massive use of chemical weapons, most graphically demonstrated in Halabja, against its own civilian Kurds.[37]

Meanwhile, Iraq continued its massive and indiscriminate bombing of Iranian cities, oil installations, and industry. The Gulf Arab states, especially Kuwait, also increased their involvement on Iraq's behalf. But the most dramatic event of 1987–88, as discussed in detail in previous chapters, was the U.S. reflagging of Kuwaiti tankers and the augmentation of the U.S. naval presence in the Persian Gulf. Throughout the war, Iran had used tactics ranging in character from friendly persuasion to subversion to dissuade Kuwait from helping Iraq, but to no avail. In 1986–87, Iran increased its attacks on Kuwaiti ships, which, in response, made its requests for help to the United States and others. Kuwait argued that Iranian attacks threatened its oil exports and thus its economic well-being, yet at no time had this been true. Indeed, the principal purpose of Kuwait's reflagging strategy was to involve the great powers in the Gulf war, a variation on, and complement to, Iraq's strategy of internationalizing it. Given the shift in U.S. policy toward the Iran-Iraq war and the U.S. tilt toward Iraq after the Irangate episode, Kuwait's strategy succeeded where the tanker war had failed. U.S. intervention in the Gulf further weakened Iran and bolstered Iraq. As a result, in April 1988 Iraq achieved a number of military victories, including the recapture of Faw.[38] All these developments finally culminated in Iran's acceptance of U.N. Security Council Resolution 598 in July 1988, and a cease-fire was declared on 20 August of the same year.[39]

Mediation Efforts in the War

During the early stages of the war and as long as Iraq seemed to be winning, there were no serious efforts by the United Nations, the Non-aligned Movement (NAM), the Organization of the Islamic Conference (OIC), or any other organization to end the war, to condemn Iraq's aggression, or to call for the withdrawal of its forces from Iranian territory. Serious efforts began only after the tide of war turned against Iraq. Even then, none of the mediation efforts addressed Iran's principal demand, that Iraq be condemned for its aggression. The lack of early action by the international community and, later, its unwillingness to chastise Iraq, became a significant cause of the failure of mediation efforts and the prolongation of the war.

The United Nations and the Iran-Iraq War

Early in the war, the United Nations Security Council did not act forcefully to stop the conflict. The first Security Council resolution on the war, adopted on 28 September 1980 (R. 479), called for ''an immediate end to the use of force and a peaceful settlement to the dispute and urged both sides to accept any appropriate offer of mediation.'' It did not refer to Iraq's aggression nor call for the withdrawal of Iraqi troops from Iranian territory. This failure would handicap the United Nations in its later mediation effort. It convinced Iran that the Security Council would not treat its grievance fair-mindedly, and it strengthened Iranian extremists, who favored a military solution. However, in view of U.S.-Iranian hostility, Iran's subsequent involvement in Middle East terrorism, and the general fear of the spread of Islamic fundamentalism, it is difficult to see how the U.N. Security Council could have acted differently in the face of the opposition of most of its permanent members and their anti-Iranian biases.[40]

The council's later resolutions enhanced Iran's distrust. For example, on 12 July 1982 after Iran had occupied Iraqi territory, the council adopted Resolution 514, calling for the withdrawal of all forces to the internationally recognized borders. At Iran's request in 1983, a United Nations team investigated damage done to civilian areas by Iraqi bombing. It duly reported extensive damage, but, despite Iran's request, the Security Council resolution adopted on 31 October refused to mention this point. Similarly, in the following years the United Nations refused to condemn unequivocally Iraq's massive use of chemical weapons, despite repeated Iranian complaints and the visit of a U.N. team to Iran.[41]

During the tanker war, U.N. resolutions only condemned Iranian attacks on shipping, as in Resolution 552 of 11 June 1984, leading Iran to accuse the Security Council of "pandering to Iraq and its Gulf allies while ignoring a deliberate effort by Iraq to internationalize the conflict by escalating the 'Tanker War'."[42] Even more telling, in 1985 Iran responded favorably to an eight-point plan presented by the U.N. secretary general for a step-by-step approach to peace. This plan was never made public and was rejected by Iraq, which wanted an immediate cease-fire.[43]

It is difficult to assess whether the United Nations could have ended the Persian Gulf war earlier. Nevertheless, it is possible that the inability or unwillingness of the U.N. to take a fair and principled position contributed to the war's prolongation. Even in 1987, the intransigence of the Security Council, largely under U.S. pressure, delayed the application of Resolution 598. This was especially true of Iran's willingness to accept the resolution, provided that the committee to investigate the origins of the war was convened before the cease-fire. Later, Iran accepted the simultaneous declaration of a cease-fire and the setting up of the commission proposed by the Soviet Union. But the council took the position that Iran must accept the resolution "as is" or face the consequences. Ironically, after the cease-fire and despite Iran's request, there was no pressure to implement other provisions of the resolution.[44]

The Non-Aligned Movement (NAM)

In October 1980, the Non-Aligned Movement's coordination office agreed in principle to form a ministerial committee to end the Iran-Iraq war and to carry out a fact-finding mission on the roots of the conflict. During the NAM foreign ministers' meeting in Belgrade in November 1980, Cuba was asked to contact Iran and

Iraq, but the NAM's Peace Committee did not visit the area until April 1981. Nor, so long as Iraq was winning, did it pronounce itself on Iraq's aggression or advance proposals on how to end the conflict.[45] The NAM's peace activities increased after the summer of 1982, but nothing came of them. A proposal made by the group did not meet Iran's conditions: withdrawal of Iraqi forces from Iranian territory, payment of reparations, the return of Iraqi refugees, and the identification and punishment of the aggressor. Iraq, for its part, repeated its condition for peace—namely, that it "should preserve Iraq's legitimate rights."[46] These "legitimate rights" were never spelled out, however. Indeed, Iraq would apply that term to mean establishment of its total sovereignty over the Shat-al-Arab.

Whether a different approach would have helped the NAM's efforts is hard to judge. But its failure to condemn Iraq doomed its efforts. The apparent fragility of the Iranian regime and the apparent strength of Iraq, the economic and political weight of the Arab bloc, Iran's negative international image, and the fear that some members of the NAM had of Islamic fundamentalism prevented it from taking a principled stand and eroded its credibility as a mediator.

The Organization of The Islamic Conference (OIC)

The Organization of the Islamic Conference also attempted to mediate. Early in the war, Pakistan's president, Zia-ul-Haq, visited Tehran and Baghdad, followed by the OIC Secretary General, Habib Chatti. And during its Taif summit meeting in February 1981, the OIC formed a "peace committee," initially chaired by the president of Guinea, Ahmad Sekou Toure.

A year later, in March 1982, the OIC presented a two-part peace plan, the first consisting of general principles, such as respect for the sovereignty and territorial integrity of each country, the non-acquisition of territory by force, non-interference in internal affairs of each state, settlement of differences by peaceful means, and freedom of navigation. The second part dealt with issues of policy, including a cease-fire and creation of a temporary regime for the Shat-al-Arab. Iran rejected the plan, however, arguing that the Shat-al-Arab issue had been settled by the 1975 Algiers Agreement. It called instead for the immediate withdrawal of Iraqi forces and noted that the plan contained no mechanism for investigating Iraq's aggression. Iraq also rejected the plan, insisting that it would not withdraw before Iran recognized Iraq's sovereignty over the Shat-al-Arab.[47] The OIC's unwillingness to condemn Iraq, despite an appeal to Muslims by the Ayatollah Khomeini, was particularly galling to the Islamic regime.[48] However, given the configuration of forces within the OIC, its attitude was quite in character.

The GCC, Arab League, Palme Mission

Mediation efforts by the Gulf Cooperation Council began in the spring of 1982, following Iran's military success. The initiative was taken by the UAE, the Gulf country with the best ties with Iran, under the leadership of Sheikh Zaid, who was well respected in Iran. The GCC plan took concrete shape in June 1982, by which time Iraqi forces had withdrawn from most of Iranian territory.

In its essential features, the GCC plan resembled other mediation efforts, calling for an immediate cease-fire, withdrawal to borders demarcated by the Algiers Agreement, negotiations with third parties to resolve other disputes, and the establishment of an international reconstruction fund to which the GCC countries would be major contributors. But this plan also failed because it came too late and did not address the issue of war guilt and the identification of the aggressor. The GCC's peace activities were most intense in 1982–83 and then after the initiation of the tanker war and increasing fears that the war would expand. As these efforts met with no success, however, the GCC gradually drifted into a policy of pressuring Iran.

Palme Mission

The other significant mediation effort in the Iran-Iraq war was undertaken as early as November 1980 by the Swedish prime minister, Olaf Palme, in his capacity as personal representative of the U.N. Secretary General. Palme, like Sheikh Zaid, enjoyed considerable credibility and respect in Iran, which also distinguished between the U.N. Security Council and the Secretary General's office. The Iranians were not well-disposed toward Kurt Waldheim, however, and became responsive to the secretariat's efforts only after the election of Alfonzo Perez de Cuellar. The essence of Palme's efforts was a step-by-step approach while at the same time trying to create a legal and political framework for a final resolution of conflict, based on such principles as the non-acquisition of territory by force, respect for the sovereignty and the territorial integrity of all states, and non-interference in internal affairs.

Such an approach, it was hoped, would answer some of each party's basic concerns, without facing them at once with the political dilemma of accepting or rejecting peace.[49] Palme's efforts were handicapped, however, by two factors: as with other mediators, he was unable to address the issue of Iraq's aggression and to call for troop withdrawals; and he faced fierce political infighting in Iran and the lack of a clear decision-making center.[50] Palme continued his efforts through 1982, always focusing on limited measures that gradually could build an atmosphere conducive to peace. For example, he made suggestions for opening up the Shat-al-Arab to navigation. Later, he expanded these partial proposals to other areas which, together, formed the basis of the Secretary General's eight-point plan, which itself became the basis of Resolution 598. Again, Iran accepted the plan, but Iraq, fearing that Iran would gain breathing space to prepare fresh attacks, rejected it.

There were other peace initiatives undertaken by a variety of sources, such as the Arab League, Japan, and China, all of which were short-lived and unsuccessful.[51] The failure of these peace efforts has been principally attributed to Iran's intransigence, its internal disarray, and expansionist ambitions. But also important were the regime's ignorance of facts of international life, its naive belief in such notions as the trial of war criminals—on the Nuremburg model—and its expectation that similar procedures should apply to Saddam Hussein, and, most of all, its despair at getting a fair hearing from international organizations or other intermediaries.

Iranian-Gulf Relations

Because of geographical proximity and a long history of interaction, relations between Iran and Arab states of the Persian Gulf have acquired special characteristics and dynamics of their own. In recent decades, they also have become increasingly affected by the general dynamics of Arab-Iranian relations. Since the creation of the GCC in May 1981, there has been a tendency to view its relations with Iran as though it acted as a single organ with total unity of views. In reality, behind the facade of joint communiques, there have been considerable differences in the approach taken by individual Gulf Arab states toward Iran and thus in the character of Iran's relations with them.

Beginning with Kuwait's independence in 1961, several specific factors have affected Iran-Gulf relations, such as the Gulf states' ethnic and religious makeup, their power ambitions, and the nature of their relations with one another. For example, during the Shah's era, the presence in Kuwait of a large Palestinian community with extreme Arab nationalist tendencies was a principal cause of tensions with Iran.[52] The same factor contributed to Kuwait's support for Iraq in the Persian Gulf war, because many of these Arab nationalist Palestinians are pro-Iraqi and sympathetic to the Ba'ath. By contrast, the existence of Shi'a communities in these countries, or communities of Iranian origin, has been of less importance in Iranian-Gulf relations than is generally believed. Instead, in some cases the existence of large, long-established Iranian communities has contributed to good relations.[53] The Wahabi view of the Shi'as, however, as being worse than infidels, has contributed to tense Saudi-Iranian relations.

The nature of relations among the Gulf Arab states has also affected their ties with Iran. For example, states such as Oman and the UAE have been subjected to Saudi territorial and other ambitions and have also resented Saudi heavy handedness in the Persian Gulf and in the Arabian peninsula. As a result, they have developed relatively good ties with Iran. Bahrain, by contrast, depends on Saudi Arabia financially, and thus has had more strained relations with Iran. This has been true both under the Shah and the Islamic regime.

Since the revolution, three other factors have affected Iran-Gulf relations: the Gulf states' fear of contagion from the Iranian revolution; the Iran-Iraq war and the Gulf states' stance; and Iran's domestic conditions, especially factionalism within its leadership.

The Gulf States and the Fear of Islamic Revolution

The Gulf Arabs' initial attitude toward the new government in Iran was a mixture of apprehension and expectation. Despite having benefited from the Shah's regional policies, they resented Iran's role as the Persian Gulf's great power, as well as its ties with Israel. Sensitive to these views, the new government of Mehdi Bazargan announced that Iran would no longer play the role of the Gulf's gendarme; it would pursue good neighborly relations with the Gulf Arabs; and it would sever all ties to Israel. These statements were welcomed by the Gulf Arab states.

In their most optimistic moments, they even hoped that Iran would return to Arab sovereignty the three disputed islands of Abu Musa and the Greater and Lesser Tunbs.[54] But they soon realized that these expectations did not reflect Iranian realities. Indeed, although many Iranians opposed aspects of the Shah's Persian Gulf policy, they did not doubt the legitimacy of Iran's claims. The Gulf countries also soon realized that the Iranian revolution was just one manifestation of a deep-rooted Islamic movement which could threaten their own governments. This fear was enhanced during 1979–81, when Shi'a riots broke out in Saudi Arabia, Kuwait, and Bahrain; even more disturbing, the Grand Mosque in Mecca was seized in November 1979, albeit by a group of Sunni fundamentalists. Meanwhile, Iran began to promote its revolutionary ideas among the Gulf Shi'as and exhorted them to emulate its example.

During the premiership of Mehdi Bazargan and even as long as figures such as Abol-Hassan Bani-Sadr and Sadegh Ghotbzadeh exerted some influence on Iranian politics, Iranian-Gulf relations had a dualistic and contradictory character. Iran's government subscribed to a policy of good neighborliness based on mutual respect and non-interference in the internal affairs of others, while Muslim revolutionaries propagated their ideas. These activities seriously strained Iran-Gulf relations, as was the case in 1979 when Ayatollah Sadegh Rouhani declared that he would lead a movement to annex Bahrain unless its rulers adopted an Islamic form of government.[55] Although expressed in religious terms, this statement reflected Iranian unhappiness with the Shah's relinquishing of Iran's historic claim. However, the Bazargan government swiftly reassured Bahrain that Ayatollah Rouhani's call did not represent its policy and denied any Iranian territorial claims against the Gulf Arab states.[56] Since then, no similar statements have been made, although Iran has been implicated in subversive activities in Bahrain and has supported the Islamic Front for the Liberation of Bahrain, established in 1977.[57]

Two other revolutionary clerical figures, Hodjat-el-Islam Hadi-al-Modaresi and Hodjat-al-Islam Abbas Mohri, who had lived in exile in Kuwait, agitated among the Shi'as in Bahrain and Kuwait. As a result, in September 1979, Kuwait expelled the whole Mohri family, and Hadi Modaresi was expelled from Bahrain. In addition, during the next few years, Kuwait expelled thousands of Iranian immigrants, regardless of whether they were involved in subversive activities. Charges about Iranian subversion increased in later years as did a series of bombings and assassination attempts. It has been far from clear, however, to what extent Iran has been behind the problems that the Persian Gulf Arab states have had with their Shi‘a communities.

No doubt Iran's Islamic revolution acted as a catalyst for the eruption of Shi‘a disturbances in the Gulf Arab states. But, as in the laboratory, the Iranian catalyst succeeded only because all the other ingredients necessary to generate a certain reaction were present. The overwhelming majority of the Gulf Shi‘as felt economically and socially underprivileged and politically disenfranchised.[58] Thus, it was inevitable that their frustrations would eventually surface. Shi‘ite disturbances in the Gulf states were also another manifestation of a growing self-awareness, in general. Paradoxically, in fact, Iran's revolution may have rendered the Gulf states a service by forcing them to focus on their Shi‘a populations and to avoid long-term disaster by improving the Shi‘a's economic and political conditions. Partly as a result of these efforts, along with the Gulf Shi‘as disillusionment with the Iranian revolution, by 1983–84 the Shi‘ite threat in the Gulf had substantially subsided.

The war with Iraq led Iran to reduce its agitation among the Gulf Shi‘as, in the hope of convincing the Gulf governments to reduce their support for Iraq. Thus, by 1982 a relationship was established between the attitude of individual Gulf states toward the Iran-Iraq war and the extent of Iran's manipulation of their Shi‘a problems.

Nevertheless, some Persian Gulf Arab states continued to use the fear of subversion by Iran to justify hostile policies toward it. In fact, contrary to general perceptions, the Gulf Arabs' attitude toward Iran gradually stiffened, not because their fears of Iran intensified but rather because they sensed Iran's weakness and limitations. Had Iran's direct or indirect threat to the Gulf Arabs' security been as great as is often suggested, the Gulf states would have been much more willing to accommodate to Iran than has been the case. The issue of Iranian subversion against the Gulf states should also be judged in light of Arab support for Iranian opposition forces and autonomist movements.[59] In recent years, almost all subversive actions in the Gulf have been attributed to Iran. Yet other countries, including Iraq and Syria, have also been involved. Iraq used subversion in Kuwait and Bahrain to keep them from changing their position toward the Gulf war or from accommodating Iran.[60]

Some Gulf Arabs have also not been responsive to Iran's reassurances. In a speech on 21 December 1981, Iran's prime minister, Mir Hossein Musavi, said that Iran did not have any designs on the Gulf Arabs' independence, integrity, or even their dollars. On another occasion, speaker Rafsanjani said that the Gulf Arab states " . . . can even benefit from the AWACs planes in defending their skies," stressed that Iran had no intention of attacking them, and said that "we would not even allow Iraq to attack Kuwait's borders."[61] These assurances did not have much impact on Kuwait and Saudi Arabia, but the UAE did respond positively. As a result, despite occasional problems, the two countries have maintained reasonably good relations. During the war, the UAE's assistance to Iraq was not significant, and it continued its lucrative trade with Iran. For these reasons, the Iraqis accused the UAE, especially Dubai, of treason. Iran developed a similar pattern of relations with Qatar and, after some initial friction, with Oman, despite the fact that Oman is a close ally of the United States and was also close to the Shah. Oman has acted as a mediator between Iran and the Gulf states, and at times, as a messenger between Iran and the United States. And on several occasions, the Omani foreign minister has visited Tehran.

In view of these successes, the question therefore arises why Kuwait and Saudi Arabia did not reach similar understandings with Iran. Part of the explanation lies in the fact that Kuwait was vulnerable to Iraqi pressures and that Saudi Arabia was also determined to contain Iran, meaning, in its view, helping Iraq. But the contradictory nature of Iran's Gulf policy also contributed to this failure. For example, while some Iranian authorities were reassuring Gulf Arab leaders of Iran's good intentions, Iranian radio broadcasts were blasting them as reactionary, anti-Islamic, and at the service of U.S. imperialism. Likewise Iran was not willing to abandon unequivocally the goal of exporting its revolution. Thus the Gulf Arabs legitimately felt that they could not abandon Iraq because they could not be sure of Iran's next move once it had defeated Iraq. Nevertheless, it is also true that the Gulf Arabs never seriously tested Iran's sincerity to compromise, even after the danger of Iraq's collapse had disappeared.

The Iran-Iraq War and Iran-Gulf Relations

The Iran-Iraq war greatly affected Iran-Gulf relations. Initially, the Gulf reaction to the war was one of ambivalence: They hoped that Iraq's invasion would topple the revolutionary regime in Iran and thus eliminate the threat of contagion.

As Arab nationalists, they also welcomed the prospect of Khusistan's liberation. In fact, as a foreign diplomat based in Manama told me at the time, after the Iraqi invasion, the mood in Bahrain was jubilant. Yet, the Gulf Arabs also did not relish the prospect of Iraq's preponderance in the region. By September 1980, it had moderated its positions and had distanced itself from the Soviet Union, but for at least the previous year, Iraq had been behaving much like the region's Great Power, setting guidelines for Arab policy and behavior.[62] Despite the Gulf Arabs' misgivings, however, because of fear of the Iranian revolution, Iraq's good prospects for victory, and the impact of the Arab nationalist ethos, they sided with Iraq.

The result was tension between Iran and the Gulf states which would later intensify as Iraq became dependent on their financial and military assistance, such as intelligence and the use of Kuwaiti and Saudi territory and air space.[63] Indeed, given the extent of Saudi and Kuwaiti support for Iraq, they almost became co-belligerents, a fact that should be borne in mind in assessing Iranian subversion against them.

Indeed, throughout the war Iran knew that it could not challenge the Gulf states militarily, partly because such an attack would trigger a Western response. Thus, there was never a serious direct Iranian military threat to the Gulf Arabs. Moreover, on several occasions Iran suggested to the Persian Gulf states to separate broader issues of Persian Gulf security from the Iran-Iraq war.[64] Iran's attitude was partly in response to Iraqi efforts to internationalize the war and partly the result of the gradual emergence of a pragmatic trend within its leadership, including a gradual softening of conditions for ending the war.

The Gulf Arabs refused to accept this suggestion, however, and continued to link Persian Gulf security to the ending of the war, while adamantly refusing to consider Iran's demand that Iraq be condemned for its aggression. This unresponsiveness strengthened the position of the proponents of the aggressive export of revolution and forced Iran to manipulate the disaffected Shi'a elements in the Gulf in order to pressure their governments to change their attitude.

In Kuwait, subversion allegedly sponsored by Iran took the form of a series of bombings, with targets including the U.S. embassy in Kuwait City on 13 December 1983.[65] Saudi Arabia's physical distance from Iran, plus the lack of any significant Iranian influence among Saudi Shi'as, made Iranian subversion difficult. But Iran used the Hadj ceremonies to undermine the Saudi regime. Iranian and Saudi views of the Hadj and its functions had differed diametrically; the Saudis see the Hadj as a spiritual experience and as an occasion for all Muslims to gather together in peace and harmony, not as an occasion for political bickering. The Iranians, by contrast, have considered the Hadj a unique opportunity for Muslims to discuss their problems and to mobilize resources to fight their enemies.

Irrespective of the intrinsic value of the Saudis' position that Islam and politics should be separated, it is inconsistent with their own practice of using Islam for purposes of gaining domestic legitimacy and enhancing its international prestige and influence. By the same token, Iran's purpose has not been just to discuss Muslims' problems but rather to use the Hadj to spread its revolutionary message and to undermine conservative Arab regimes. Saudi-Iranian differences over the Hadj have often strained their relations. In 1981, skirmishes took place between Saudi police and Iranian pilgrims when Hodjat-al-Islam Khoeiniha, one of the Islamic regime's most radical figures, was in charge of Iran's Hadj affairs. The Hadj ceremonies of 1982 were also particularly tense because of Iran's victories against Iraq and Israel's invasion of Lebanon.[66]

Disagreements over the conditions of Shi'a shrines in Saudi Arabia and difficulties of access to them have been another source of strain. Saudi authorities did repair some of these shrines and made them more accessible, although it is not clear whether they did so to accommodate Iran or to co-opt the Saudi Shi'a population. During the period 1985–86, there was a degree of thaw in Iran-Saudi ties, and it seemed as though the Hadj problem could be resolved. Iran removed the radical Hojat-al-Islam Khoeiniha from the Hadj Committee as a friendly gesture toward the Saudis. Following the Iran-Contra affair and the Kuwaiti reflagging operations, however, Iran's relations with the Gulf states entered a new phase of confrontation, leading in the summer of 1987 to a worse Saudi-Iranian conflict during the Hadj.

At the time, the U.S. naval presence in the Persian Gulf posed a difficult dilemma for Iran—namely, whether to take on the United States and face massive military retaliation or to do nothing and admit to impotence in the face of the joint U.S.-Arab challenge. The Iranian government prudently did not challenge the United States, but it felt pressured to show somehow that it had not been intimidated. It used the Hadj ceremonies to do so. As in the past, Iranian pilgrims marched and chanted slogans, but, emboldened by the U.S. presence in the Gulf, this time the Saudis were not in a tolerant mood: Indeed, this was the time of growing pan-Arab pressure on Iran. It is not clear how the behavior of Iranian pilgrims in 1987 differed from previous occasions, although Saudi Arabia claimed that they carried knives and attacked the police. Perhaps some pilgrims carried small arms, but the question is whether this time they posed a qualitatively different threat. The Saudis judged that they did, and the Saudi police opened fire on Iranian pilgrims. The Saudis denied that they fired and maintained that all the 400 Iranian pilgrims who died were killed in the stampede that followed police intervention. However, Iranian authorities later proved that firearms had been used by showing the bullet wounds in the victims' bodies.

The Iranian government charged that the United States was behind the incident, and it also vowed to take revenge on the Saudis.[67] But there was no retaliation. This reflected the shift of the regional balance of power against Iran and its growing problems. Following the events of the Hadj, Saudi Arabia severed diplomatic relations with Iran and, much to Saudi relief, Iran boycotted the Hadj ceremonies in 1988.

Saudi Arabia Flexes Its Oil Muscle

Saudi Arabia also used its oil power to weaken Iran. Saudi-Iranian interests on oil prices and OPEC policies have usually clashed, a situation which has reflected their different economic needs and oil reserves. With the oil slump of 1983–86, the Saudi oil minister, Sheikh Zaki Yamani, concluded that the only way out of the slump was for oil prices to plummet in order to boost global demand. Iran, by contrast, felt that tighter supply was the solution, to maximize revenues for each barrel sold.

Between 1985 and August 1986, Saudi Arabia and Kuwait put downward pressure on oil prices which, by the summer of 1986, fell to seven or eight dollars per barrel with five dollars looming on the horizon. This Saudi policy was devastating to Iran, whose exports had fallen because of Iraqi bombings. Whether or not the desire to hurt Iran economically was the principal motive behind the Saudis' oil policy, they could not miss its devastating impact on Iran, coming at the time of the Iranian capture of Faw and growing Saudi anxiety about Iraq's fate. Whatever the Saudi motives, the Iranians saw this policy as principally aimed at weakening them, and they accused Saudi Arabia of "dealing a severe blow to OPEC by glutting the oil market and forcing down prices'' and of being ''guilty of the greatest treason ever committed against the oppressed and deprived countries. . . . ''[68]

Iran's realization of Saudi oil power, however, prompted it to reach an accommodation with the kingdom. Saudi Arabia also came under great pressure from other OPEC and non-OPEC oil exporters, including Egypt, which had been suffering because of lower oil prices. At an OPEC meeting in August 1986, Iran and Saudi Arabia thus agreed to stabilize oil prices at about $18 a barrel. Meanwhile, their political relations also seemed to be improving, a process which had started in the summer of 1985. At the time, there had been talk of Rafsanjani's visiting Saudi Arabia, and in 1985 the Saudi foreign minister had visited Tehran, but disagreements on the Iran-Iraq war and also differences of opinion within the regime prevented a meaningful accommodation. However, in the final analysis, the inability of Saudis and Iranians to reach a compromise has derived from their competition for leadership in the Persian Gulf and the Muslim world.

The Iranian View of the GCC

In regional terms, one of the important consequences of the Iranian revolution has been the creation of the Gulf Cooperation Council. The idea of creating a regional security framework embracing all states of the Persian Gulf dates from the 1960s. Such an organization was made both unnecessary and unrealizable, however, by the Iranian-Iraqi rivalry, the exclusivist dimensions of Arab nationalism—which made an organization incorporating both Iran and the Arab states an unrealistic proposition because of territorial and other disputes around the Persian Gulf and by Iran's role as the protector of regional stability.

The Iranian revolution and the Iran-Iraq war changed this calculation both by eliminating obstacles and by providing a strong motive—namely, the containment of the Islamic revolution. The Gulf Cooperation Council, without either Iran or Iraq, was created in May 1981. For a variety of reasons, however, Iran took a negative view of the organization. To begin with, Iran viewed the GCC as an anti-Iranian military pact because there was no reason to believe it was directed against Israel.[69] Iran was also concerned about the exclusive nature of the GCC, viewing it as a ploy to keep Iran out of Persian Gulf affairs. Iranian concerns were heightened by the GCC's behavior, which portrayed its creation as a first step toward broader Arab economic and political integration. Admittedly, this was aimed at silencing Arab criticism of the GCC as a ''rich man's club'' and against the ultimate goal of Arab economic unity.[70] Nevertheless, the fact is that other Arab countries are involved in pan-Arab projects in the Persian Gulf, while the Gulf Arabs are active participants in other pan-Arab institutions. Thus, there is an organic link between collective Gulf Arab institutions and the rest of the Arab world. Under these circumstances, it was natural for Iran to feel isolated and excluded from the economic and political life of the Persian Gulf region—and also to worry about occasional calls to include Iraq in the GCC.[71]

Third, Iran viewed the GCC as a cover for the expansion of Saudi influence. This is not totally justified, but it is a concern shared by some of the Gulf states.[72] Iran also viewed Saudi efforts to sign bilateral agreements with GCC members on cooperation on internal security matters as proof of Saudi intentions to control the GCC states.[73] In addition, Iran viewed the GCC as an instrument of U.S. policy in the Persian Gulf, much the way radical Arabs viewed Iran under the Shah.[74] And while not clearly stated, Iran's difficulties with Iraq led it to be apprehensive about the emergence of another Arab power bloc in the Persian Gulf. Most important in explaining Iran's negative view of the GCC, however, was the fear that it could have aggressive intentions against Iran. In fact, some Iranian officials said that they did not object to the GCC as long as it remained a defensive organization and was willing to live with Iran.[75]

Despite these fears and the fact that, to some degree, the GCC has adopted common positions toward Iran, its creation has not dramatically affected Iran's relations with the Gulf states, because it has failed to develop into a tightly knit political and military organization. Instead, GCC members have in practice followed their own independent approach to ties with Iran.

Iran-Gulf Relations after the Cease-Fire

The August 20, 1988, cease-fire eliminated the most serious irritant in Iranian-Gulf state relations. Iran's weakness and Iraq's overconfident behavior after its military victories in 1988 led the Gulf states to begin reverting to their traditional policy of balancing off Iran and Iraq. The latter's heavy-handed policy toward Kuwait forced the tiny state to move closer to Iran. Almost immediately after the cease-fire, Kuwait resumed full diplomatic relations with Iran. In September, the foreign minister of Oman visited Tehran. Later, Iran and Oman established a joint economic commission to expand economic relations, and Iran established a permanent trade exhibition in Dubai.[76] Even the Saudis made some conciliatory remarks. But, because of the Hadj incident, continued disagreements about the number of Iranian pilgrims, and Saudi-Iranian competition for regional influence, their relations would take longer to mend.

For their part, Iranian officials expressed their desire to improve ties with the Gulf states. Some Iranian commentators, however, said that if the Persian Gulf Arabs wanted better relations with Iran, they had to "compensate for their previous unfriendly behavior and assume a more active role in the conduct of the peace talks. . . . "[77]

In sum, despite the dramatic effects of the Iranian revolution and the Iran-Iraq war, in their underlying characteristics post-revolution Iranian-Gulf relations show considerable continuity with the past. With the end of the war, and provided Iran's foreign policy evolves in a moderate direction, traditional patterns of interaction—especially the Gulf states' desire to balance relations with Iran, Iraq, and, in the case of some, with Saudi Arabia—will reappear even more strongly.

Iran, Syria, and Lebanon

In some respects, the Syrian-Iranian alliance represents a significant departure from past patterns of Arab-Iranian interaction. Paradoxically, this alliance also fits well within traditional patterns of these relations, in that it illustrates the impact of intra-Arab politics on these ties. Given their fundamental differences, the alliance between Syria and Iran has been intriguing. The former is secular and Arab nationalist, whereas the latter is Islamic and outspokenly anti-nationalist. Syria has a large Islamic movement which it has brutally suppressed, and regional ambitions of the two countries have also been incompatible. Nevertheless, while tense and tenuous, for three basic reasons the Syrian-Iranian alliance has held longer than would logically have been expected:

1. *Ideological affinity.* Despite the sharp dichotomy between Iran's Islamic universalism and Syria's secular Arab nationalism, the two countries share similar views regarding a range of regional and international issues, including the Arab-Israeli conflict and the U.S. role in the Middle East.

2. *The common challenge of Iraq.* The Syrian-Iranian alliance has largely been a function of their concern with Iraq. By 1979, Syria felt at once isolated, exposed, and encircled. The Egyptian-Israeli peace treaty had left Syria exposed to the Israeli military threat, and an increase in Iraq's power had made it subject to Iraqi pressures. Thus, alliance with Iran was one way for Syria to restore the intra-Arab balance of power and to improve its position, a policy in line with the traditional Arab practice. Syria also used Iran to compensate for the loss of Egypt. As the British journalist Patrick Seale has put it, Syria saw Iran as the natural counterweight to Egypt, much as King Faisal had done during the 1960s against Nasser.[78]

After Iraq's invasion, Syria helped Iran to prevent an Iraqi victory, thus forestalling a drastic shift of the regional balance of power in Baghdad's favor. Syria feared that after defeating Iran, Iraq would try to settle scores with Damascus. This Syrian fear was proved justified when following the cease-fire, Iraq declared victory, said that it intended to punish Syria, and began supporting anti-Syrian elements in Lebanon. Yet Syria never favored an Iranian victory, particularly if this would mean the establishment of an Islamic republic in Iraq, because that would have meant a shift in the balance of power in Iran's favor. Syria preferred a situation in which Saddam Hussein's collapse under Iranian pressure would allow it to determine his successor. Indeed, in such an event, it is likely that the Syrian-Iranian alliance would have turned into conflict over Iraq's fate.[79]

Shi'a solidarity, though less important than other factors, should also not be ignored. The fact that Syria is ruled by the Alawites—an unorthodox Shi'a sect—did play a role in the Syrian-Iranian alliance. The Syrian Alawites feel isolated in the overwhelmingly Sunni Arab world, and thus it was natural for them to look to Iran for friendship.[80]

3. *Financial benefits.* Syria's alliance with Iran enabled it to obtain financial concessions from Persian Gulf Arab states by acting as an intermediary between

them and Iran. Syria often claimed that it had used its influence with Iran as a security valve which prevented Tehran from invading other countries in the Gulf region. It also received oil from Iran worth several billion dollars. Occasionally, Syria indicated that it might be persuaded to end its alliance with Iran and repair its differences with Iraq, an attitude that led a number of Arab personalities, especially Jordan's King Hussein, to mediate between Syria and Iraq, without much success. Nevertheless, Syria took part in both the 1986 Islamic summit conference in Kuwait—an event that Iran had tried hard to prevent—and in the Amman Arab summit conference in 1987, which formalized the so-called Arab alliance against Iran.

Syrian-Iranian alliance has been an uneven partnership, in which Syria benefits most. Yet Iran worked to keep this uneven partnership going, in part because of its military needs and—more important—because of its desire to break the unity of Arab ranks and to prevent the Iran-Iraq war from turning into an Arab-Persian conflict. Iran's eagerness to forestall this outcome must be seen in light of its ideological ambitions in the Arab world. It has maintained that its ideology has a universal validity for all Muslims. By minimizing Persian nationalism, exalting Islam and the Arabic language, and by its strident anti-Israeli rhetoric, Iran tried to convince the Arabs of its commitment to friendship with them and their cause. Yet after the outbreak of the Iran-Iraq war, the overwhelming majority of Arabs supported Iraq. This Arab support reflected the tenacity of ethnicity, nationalism, and sectarianism in the Middle East and was a serious blow to Iran's Islamic universalism. Its alliance with Syria was thus designed to prove that only the reactionary and corrupt Arabs sided with Iraq. For example, in a speech to visiting Muslim theologians, in which he denied that there were any anti-Arab feelings in Iran, Rafsanjani said that "the enemies of Islam are raising the issue of the Arabs and non-Arabs." Support by Libya and Syria for Iran seemed to show that this was not so.[81]

Challenge and Opportunity in Lebanon

The Israeli invasion of Lebanon in June 1982 and the Israeli-Western effort to establish a strong Maronite-based government in Beirut posed a challenge both to Syria's security and to its regional ambitions. This event illustrated the shift in the strategic balance that was produced by the Egyptian-Israeli peace treaty. Even in the face of a full-scale Israeli invasion, Egypt did not risk its peace treaty with Israel. Other Arab states, meanwhile, were preoccupied with the Persian Gulf war. Feeling isolated, Syria welcomed Iranian support and the dispatch of three thousand Revolutionary Guards to Lebanon.

For Iran, the Lebanese situation presented a unique opportunity to prove its pro-Arab and anti-Israeli credentials, to propagate its revolutionary ideology, and to develop a core of supporters. Later, however, Syrian-Iranian objectives would clash in Lebanon and strain their relations, principally because of the competition for influence and diverging visions of Lebanon's political future. Syria has always considered Lebanon to be its natural sphere of influence and thus it did not approve of Iran's growing presence there. This presence made it more difficult for Syria to practice its traditional role of playing off different Lebanese factions against one another.

The character of the Lebanese political system of government was never the Syrians' principal concern as long as it remained responsive to their interests. But by 1984, Syria became concerned about the spread of Iranian-style Islamic radicalism in Lebanon which, if successful, would have replaced Syrian influence with that of Iran. The establishment of an Islamic government in Lebanon could have become a dangerous precedent for Syria itself. Thus, Syria opposed the creation of any government in Lebanon remotely resembling an Islamic republic. Iran, meanwhile, saw Lebanon as the only place where it could hope to repeat its revolutionary experience.

Although Iran may have had large numbers of followers in Lebanon, especially among the Shi'as, Syria had the military power and was willing to use it, which it demonstrated in 1987 and 1988. In February 1987, Syrian troops moved into Muslim West Beirut in order to stop the fighting between the Shi'as and the Palestinians, and in the course of operations, executed about 22 members of the pro-Iranian Hizbullah, who resisted the advance of Syrian forces. In April and May 1988, during the bloody infighting between two rival Shi'a groups—the pro-Syrian AMAL and the pro-Iranian Hizbullah—the Syrian army demonstrated its superiority.

During this fighting, the Hizbullah, assisted by the Iranian Revolutionary Guards, appeared to be winning the battle. The setbacks suffered by AMAL put Syria in a difficult position. To allow a Hizbullah victory would seriously undermine its image and credibility as the ultimate power broker in Lebanon and would enhance Iranian influence. However, to challenge the Hizbullah, who were reputed to be fierce fighters, would not be easy and Syria would have required a large military force to subdue them.[82]

Iran, too, faced dilemmas. To abandon the Hizbullah to Syria would have made a mockery of its claim to be the champion of Muslim revolutionaries, thus eroding its prestige. Yet to continue its support and to challenge Syria would have jeopardized relations with Damascus, a prospect which, at the time, Iran could not view with a light heart. Thus, Tehran and Damascus tried to work out a compromise and establish a truce between the two Shi'a groups, as Sunni Muslims called for Syrian military intervention to end the fighting.[83] Indeed, the Syrian Defense Minister, General Tlas, threatened to do so.[84]

Iran initially opposed Syrian troop deployments, partly because of concern over Western hostages held by the Hizbullah, worrying that this might transfer control to the Syrians. For some time, Syria had wanted to gain the release of these hostages in order to curry favor with the West. Iran, by contrast, wanted to use the hostages in order to achieve political goals, including making deals with Western countries as was the case with France. Iran's deputy foreign minister, Hossein Sheikholeslam, presented this Iranian concern when he said that Iran would approve a Syrian military intervention in the slums only if the hostage situation is resolved "in a way that serves the objectives for which they were kidnapped."[85]

In the end, Iran had to give in, and Syrian forces entered Southern Lebanon on 27 May 1988, clearly illustrating Syrian superiority there and the inherent difficulties that the Shi'a-Persian country has in expanding its influence in the Arab world. But Syria, too, had to make some compromises; it did not insist on having the hostages transferred to its control.

Difficulties among Shi'a groups in the remaining months of 1988 and 1989 remained a potential source of conflict. During 1989, Iraq's military assistance to the Maronites, especially General Michel Awn, threatened both Syria's and Iran's positions in Lebanon. Iran feared that Syria might succumb to pan-Arab pressures through the intermediary of the Arab League and, by accepting the introduction of an Arab—or international peace-keeping—force, would further undermine Iran's influence there. To prevent that, Iran sent a delegation to Beirut, offered medical and food help for Lebanese victims, and urged AMAL and the Hizbullah to cooperate.[86] However, the Arab League efforts failed and the growing challenge of Iraq and its Christian allies to Syria brought all the Muslim forces and Iran and Syria closer together. Disagreements in Lebanon and their management clearly illustrated both the tenuous nature of the Syrian-Iranian alliance and its importance for them both. Thus, neither allowed the Lebanese problem to destroy the alliance. Other problems have strained Syrian-Iranian relations, including the problem of Iranian tourists in Syria, especially their propaganda activities.[87] Popular reaction to the Iranians was also negative. Thus, in addition to official unhappiness, even at the popular level, the Syrian-Iranian alliance has not led to greater understanding and friendship.

Iran and Lebanon

Of all the Arab states, Lebanon has proved most receptive to Iran's Islamic message and influence. This phenomenon was not a sign of Iran's skillful diplomacy or the appeal of its Islamic message, however. Instead, it resulted from Lebanese internal characteristics and regional developments, especially the Israeli invasion. Indeed, despite the long history of Iran's involvement with Lebanon, it is difficult to see how Iran could have developed a foothold in Lebanon, had it not been for the opportunities that the invasion provided.

The presence of a large, disaffected, and radicalized Shi'a community in Lebanon facilitated Iranian penetration. The historic connection between Iran and the Shi'as of Lebanon is well documented.[88] In more recent times, this connection has been symbolized by the Iranian-born cleric Musa Sadr and his role in mobilizing the Lebanese Shi'a community.[89] The Lebanese Shi'a movement, AMAL, trained anti-Shah activists, some of whom reached high positions in post-revolutionary Iran—e.g., Mustapha Chamran, who briefly became Iran's defense minister.[90]

Its dispatch in 1982 of Revolutionary Guards to Lebanon, who were largely concentrated in the Bekaa Valley, enabled Iran to spread the Islamic revolutionary message, set up a network of social services, and disburse financial aid among the Shi'as.[91] Meanwhile, the presence of the Israeli army in the Shi'a areas intensified anti-Israeli feelings and rendered the Shi'a more receptive to Iranian propaganda. The principal arm of Iranian influence in Lebanon has been the Hizbullah and several small organizations which have been involved in anti-Western terrorism.[92]

Iran has been able to operate in Lebanon because of Lebanese and Syrian complicity. Syria has used Iran and its Shi'a allies in its maneuvers against the Palestinians and certain Lebanese groups. It is also inconceivable that pro-Iranian elements could have carried out their terrorist actions without Syrian complicity. Indeed, when Syria has judged the Iranian presence and influence detrimental to its own ambitions, it has forcefully curbed them. Iran has used its Lebanese allies to advance its foreign policy goals. For example, the attacks on the U.S. and French military headquarters in 1983 and the kidnapping of French nationals in 1985–86 were related to the Iran-Iraq war and French support for Iraq. However, Iran has not been able to control all Lebanese Shi'as, as illustrated by the alliance that AMAL and its leader, Nabih Berri, forged with Syria. Moreover, even Iran's supporters within the Shi'a community have not all shared Iran's vision of Lebanon's political future. For example, the spiritual leader of the Lebanese, Hizbullah Sheikh Fad-al-Allah, did not favor the establishment of an Islamic republic in Lebanon.[93]

Iran's influence over the Lebanese Shi'as has also been a function of its successes or failures in the war with Iraq. The period 1983–86, especially in light of the capture of Faw, was a period of Iranian success and rising hopes that Saddam Hussein's regime would fall, opening the way for an Islamic government in Iraq. This was also the height of Iranian influence in Lebanon. Beginning in the spring of 1987, as Iran's fortunes began to fade in the war, and with the introduction of U.S. naval forces into the Persian Gulf, its standing in Lebanon also suffered. This was further deepened by Iran's inability to prevent Syrian intervention in the southern suburbs of Beirut. Furthermore, Lebanese Shi'a factions have been responsive to Iran as long as Iran's state goals and their local interests have coincided. Otherwise, Iran's ability to manipulate its Shi'a allies has been far more limited than has been generally assumed. For example, during the intra-Shi'a infighting in Beirut in 1988, Iran had difficulty in convincing the Hizbullah to come to terms with Syria and AMAL. Writing in *The Washington Post*, Jonathan Randal said that "the showdown in Beirut may also bring into question just how obedient Hizbullah really is to Tehran's desires." He added that the lengthy "negotiations and the presence there of senior Iranian officials suggests that they, like so many other foreigners before them, *are having trouble controlling 'their' Lebanese*" [emphasis added].[94]

Iran's limitations in getting the Hizbullah to do what it wanted were even more drastically illustrated during the summer of 1988. As part of its new policy of improving ties with the West, Iran tried to get the release of British hostages, but had difficulty convincing the Hizbullah. This Iranian inability reflected in part Iran's own internal factionalism which is also reproduced among its Lebanese allies; the issue of opening to the West and the release of British hostages was a controversial issue in Iran itself. But this inability also showed the divergence between Iran's state interests and those of the Hizbullah. In fact, the more Iran begins to put its national interest ahead of its revolutionary aspirations, the more its influence in Lebanon would diminish.

Iran and the Palestinians

The Palestinians viewed the Shah's Iran as a principal enemy, and different Palestinian groups took an active part in subversion against his regime, including the training of Iranians for urban guerrilla warfare.[95] When in 1978 it became clear that the Shah's regime was in serious trouble, the PLO leader, Yasser Arafat, declared that it would do everything possible to help the revolutionaries.[96] After the revolutionary forces brought down the Shah's regime, their first foreign guest was Yasser Arafat.

The Shah's ouster represented a significant victory for the PLO. Ayatollah Khomeini was intensely anti-Israel, and his regime would make the liberation of Palestine a principal goal. Indeed, during his visit to Iran in February 1979, Arafat demonstrated the links between the PLO and the Iranian revolutionaries and the PLO's assessment of the revolution's importance:

> We consider ourselves an extension of our brother Iranians. . . . They have given to us and we have given to them. However, we will never match what they have given us. Our presence here demonstrates how much they have given us. This revolution has created a new era in the area. . . . [97]

PLO-Iranian amity proved to be short-lived, however, and became a victim of the Iran-Iraq war, which posed serious dilemmas for the PLO. Given the imperatives of the Arab nationalist ethos, Arafat and the PLO could not condemn Iraq. They were also financially dependent on the Persian Gulf Arab states, all of which, to varying degrees, supported Iraq. The war, however, was the test for Iran. Arafat did try to mediate between Iran and Iraq, but then he lacked credibility in Iran.

Iran's refusal to make peace intensified the PLO's resentment. The Palestinians felt that the Iran-Iraq war deflected attention from the struggle against Israel. When differences grew between Yasser Arafat and Syrian President Hafiz al-Assad, Palestinian-Iranian relations also suffered because of Iran's alliance with Syria. When, during the Lebanese crisis, Colonel Abu-Musa challenged Arafat's leadership and chose a pro-Syrian stand, Iran, too, rejected the PLO leader. Iran had, however, always distinguished between the Palestinians and Arafat. While it attacked Arafat, it still permitted the PLO to maintain an embassy in Tehran[98] and instituted Jerusalem Day, during which demonstrations were organized in support of the Palestinian cause. Iran was also concerned about the conflict between the Shi'as and the Palestinians, and on several occasions tried to mediate between them.[99]

Iran's experience with the PLO substantiates the point that underlying forces, including the Arab nationalist ethos, have been more important in determining the state of Arab-Iranian relations than have Iran's position on the Palestinian issue and its ties to Israel.

Iran's Relations with Other Arab States

Regarding Iran's post-revolution relations with other Arab states, with few exceptions, the overall trend has been toward deterioration, with the notable exceptions of Libya, Algeria, and the People's Democratic Republic of Yemen (PDRY). Some commonality of outlook on international and regional issues has brought Iran and these countries closer. Many Iranians have long been attracted to Algeria's revolution and to its militant Third Worldism, and Algeria has found appealing both Iran's new non-aligned policy and its defiance of the superpowers. Indeed, when the Iran-Iraq war began, Algeria adopted a balanced posture. Because of considerations of intra-Arab politics, it did not condemn Iraq, but it also did not join the Arab chorus supporting Iraq, thus retaining its credibility in Tehran. And since the rupture of U.S.-Iranian diplomatic relations, Algeria has represented Iran's interests in the United States.

With Libya, the new Iranian regime shared strong anti-Americanism and anti-Zionism. Like the PLO, Libya also played a role in bringing down the Shah's regime. There have been considerable differences of opinion and interest between Libya and Iran, however. Iran's Islamic ideology is different from Gadhafi's, and in Lebanon they have supported different factions. Libya's role in the disappearance of Imam Musa Sadr has also been a source of tension. Nevertheless, despite these differences the two countries have maintained their friendship and the Libyans provided arms to Iran during the war, although they have denied it.[100] Iran, meanwhile, supported Libya during its confrontation with the United States in 1986 and the Iranians may have assisted Libya's oil industry. Iran also joined Libya and Syria in 1985–86 to block the collaboration among Arafat, Jordan, and Egypt on Arab-Israeli peacemaking.[101]

Iran's friendship with South Yemen is more difficult to explain because of the incompatibility between the two countries' ideologies, one Islamic and the other Marxist. Here too, however, shared antagonism to the West, especially the United States, and hard-line stands on the Palestinian issue brought the two together. Iran also desperately wanted to show that it had Arab friends and thus was willing to compromise its ideological principles.

Meanwhile, Iran's relations suffered with Egypt, Jordan, Morocco, Tunisia, and

Sudan (as long as Numeiry was in power). In each case, Iran had specific reasons for either ending or downgrading its diplomatic relations with these countries, but general causes were also important. To begin with, most of these countries had pro-Western or, more specifically, pro-American governments, had formal or informal security relationships with the United States, and were major recipients of U.S. military and economic aid. Thus, according to Iran's Islamic world view, they were part of the "arrogant-oppressor" camp. There was also a basic ideological conflict between these countries and Iran, which wanted to promote Islamic revolution, against the others' preference for maintaining their essentially secular political structures. Iran's ideological challenge was particularly worrying because of the existence of Islamic revolutionary groups, in each of these countries which had been revitalized by the Iranian revolution. Moreover, these countries suspected Iran of assisting their Muslim dissidents. In 1987, for example, Tunisia accused the Iranian embassy and its staff of undertaking subversive activities and forging links with Islamic fundamentalist groups; it thus broke diplomatic relations.

The Shah's admission to Egypt and its harsh criticism of Iran during the U.S. hostage crisis—which went beyond the general condemnation voiced by almost all nations—contributed to Egyptian-Iranian tensions and to Iranian animosity toward President Anwar al-Sadat. Indeed, in Iran, his assassination by Muslim dissidents was viewed as just retribution, and it raised hopes that an Islamic revolution was imminent in Egypt. By contrast, President Hosni Mubarak did not have the same political legacy as President Sadat and, therefore, there was a chance of halting the deterioration in Egyptian-Iranian relations, but it ended with the Iran-Iraq war and Egypt's siding with Iraq. Egypt also provided aid to Iraq out of fear over the rise of Islamic militancy and the potential impact of an Iranian victory on its Muslim militants. Egypt also wanted to return to the Arab fold and thus, by helping Iraq, wanted to show that the Arab world required its military and political weight.

The same was true of Jordan, which became one of Iraq's staunchest supporters, providing military advice and equipment. More important, Jordan was in the forefront in garnering Arab support for Iraq. Indeed, it was at the Amman summit in November 1987 that the Arab world officially lined up against Iran. Similarly, King Hussein tried hard to bring about a reconciliation between Iraq and Syria. In the case of Morocco, a link to the Shah and his family, as well as Moroccan support for Iraq, played additional roles.

Conclusions

The foregoing has illustrated the validity of past patterns of Arab-Iranian relations, despite some major departures since the revolution. Even in the post-revolution period, ethnic-sectarian divisions have provided a background of tension to Arab-Iranian ties. They have also limited Iran's ability to influence events in the Arab world. The single most important determinant of Arab-Iranian relations has remained their ideological outlooks and their superpower connections. The nature of Iran's ties with Israel has remained of minimal importance in shaping the basic character of its relations with the Arabs. Iran's post-revolution relations with the Arab world, as in the past, has been a mixture of some fundmental conflicts and limited tactical cooperation.

7. Iran and Its Neighbors

Pakistan, India, and Turkey

Historical Background

Iran has had close and long-standing relations with the peoples and cultures of the Indian subcontinent, dating back to the pre-Islamic era.[1] After Islamization, Iran became a principal transmitter of Indian culture and science to the Arabs and of Islam to the Indian subcontinent.[2] This close interaction has led to mutual appreciation and respect rather than to competition.[3]

The British domination of India in the nineteenth century ended the close interaction between Iran and the subcontinent. The establishment of modern diplomatic relations had to wait until the emergence of a reasonably stable government in Iran and India's independence from Britain. When India was partitioned in 1947, three reasons led Iran to develop more extensive and friendly relations with Pakistan: a common border; religious and cultural affinity; and common security problems.[4] During the 1950s and 1960s, the pro-Western stands adopted by both Iran and Pakistan cemented their relations. They joined the Baghdad Pact, and in July 1964 joined Turkey in setting up the Regional Cooperation for Development (RCD).[5]

Yet Iran also maintained friendly relations with India because, in addition to historical and cultural factors, India is a major political and military force in South Asia which Iran could not ignore. Thus even in the 1950s, despite Iran's Western alliance and India's non-alignment, the two countries maintained friendly relations. In September 1959, the Indian prime minister, Jawaharlal Nehru, visited Tehran, and on 4 January 1960 the Shah paid a return visit.[6] India also offered Iran significant opportunities for economic, trade, and technological cooperation, which became particularly important after the 1973 oil revolution. This was partly due to the fact that political differences limited the scope of Arab-Iranian and Soviet-Iranian economic cooperation, as well as the factors summed up in the following comment by an Iranian journalist: "Bound by the USSR to the north and blocked by the Arab-Israeli conflict to the west, Iran is looking East in search of new friends and areas for economic and political activity. . . ."[7]

However, during the 1960s and the 1970s, tensions between India and Pakistan remained a deep source of concern to Iran and a barrier to closer Indo-Iranian relations. Iran had an important stake in Pakistan's survival and in its territorial integrity, because its disintegration could have exacerbated Iran's own centrifugal tendencies. Iran also saw Pakistan as a security buffer against superior Indian military power and a balancing factor in the region. Therefore, Iran viewed the Indo-

Pakistani wars of 1965 and 1971 with great anxiety. The lack of any help from CENTO or from the United States in the 1965 Indo-Pakistani war was a rude awakening for both Iran and Pakistan and forced them to reassess the value of their superpower alliance, particularly as a defense against regional enemies.[8]

Partly as a result of this reassessment, as noted earlier, Iran intensified its regional diplomacy in order to achieve two objectives: to resolve any remaining problems with its neighbors and to mediate between its neighbors and to help resolve their own disputes, as in the cases of Pakistan-Afghanistan conflict over Pakhtunistan and Indo-Pakistani tensions.[9]

Iran's mediating ability was enhanced after 1973, with improvements in its military and financial capabilities. Thus, in order to prevent another Indo-Pakistani clash, Iran " . . . offered its military support to Pakistan to deter India from attacking it, and yet refused to supply Pakistan with weapons, thus reassuring India."[10] In using its oil revenues to achieve its regional security goals, Iran provided Pakistan with considerable amounts of aid and entered into joint economic development programs, particularly in the restive Baluchistan province.

Iran also gave economic assistance to India as a means of reducing Indo-Soviet ties.[11] Iran had been concerned with the signing of the Indo-Soviet friendship treaty of 1971, which was followed by the signing of a similar treaty with Iraq in 1972. It viewed these acts as evidence of a Soviet policy of encirclement. It also tried the same policy toward Afghanistan, with some success. There is some evidence that the alternative offered to Afghanistan by Iran, as well as by Arab aid, led Afghan President Daoud to try distancing his country from the Soviet Union.[12]

The Shah offered a regional alternative to Soviet ties by proposing the expansion of the RCD to include Afghanistan, India, and Iraq. He also proposed the creation of an Asian Common Market. Some commentators believe that this was designed to be the first step toward military cooperation and that it was ultimately aimed at reducing the superpower presence in the Indian Ocean region. In fact, it could be said that the Shah advanced this idea in response to the Soviet proposal for an Asian collective security pact.[13]

Economic factors—including its increasing need for raw materials, technology, and manpower—contributed to Iran's activist diplomacy in the subcontinent.[14] Yet its efforts to develop a congenial environment in the subcontinent faced stiff competition from the Arab states, particularly Saudi Arabia, which offered regional states important economic incentives,[15] of which the latter eagerly took advantage, even when it meant friction with Iran.

During the early 1970s, Libya's Muammar Qadhafi and Pakistan's President Zulfiqar Ali Bhutto developed a close relationship which displeased the Shah. Yet despite its need for Iranian support, Pakistan did not end its Libyan connection. Likewise, after the 1973 oil revolution, Pakistan developed extensive economic relations with Saudi Arabia and other Persian Gulf Arab states; it even assumed a security role in Saudi Arabia by stationing 20,000 of its troops there.[16]

India's trade and economic relations with the Persian Gulf Arab states and Iraq also expanded considerably, and Arab-Iranian competition for regional influence extended to India.[17] Iran's naval build-up and its ambition to become an Indian Ocean power limited the scope of Indo-Iranian cooperation and became a source of tension. In particular, India was concerned about Iran's close relationship with Pakistan. Although weakened and traumatized by the war of 1971 and the separation of its east wing, Pakistan remained India's principal security preoccupation. Thus, despite its efforts to ease Indian fears, Iran remained suspect because India could not be confident that Iran would remain militarily neutral in case of another Indo-Pakistani war. Iran had also improved its relations with China, another major Indian security preoccupation, and both it and Iran shared a common interest in Pakistan. Also, despite considerable improvement in Soviet-Iranian relations, the Soviet Union remained Iran's principal security preoccupation, whereas India had a friendship treaty with the Soviets, received the bulk of its military supplies from them, and considered the Soviet presence in South Asia to be a necessary counterweight to that of China and the United States.

India also was concerned about the expansion of the U.S. military presence in South Asia, a concern that had intensified since the 1971 Indo-Pakistani war and the dispatch of a U.S. naval task force to the Bay of Bengal. Iran, an ally of the United States, was perceived by India to be serving U.S. regional goals, thus indirectly undermining India's security interests.[18] In addition, India's self-image as the leading power in South Asia and its ambition to be a global power clashed with the Shah's ambition to make Iran a major—perhaps the leading—power in South Asia and the Indian Ocean. India could accept Iran in this role in the Persian Gulf but not in South Asia.[19] Yet both countries realized the importance of having workable relations and kept their differences within manageable bounds.

Turkey: Historical Background

Turko-Iranian relations have also extended over several centuries. A long period was marred by Persian-Ottoman rivalry and sectarian differences. But recent history has been marked by a successful reconciliation and cooperation, for several reasons.[20] Under the leadership of Mustafa Kemal Ataturk, Turkey shed its Ottoman past and the territorial and power ambitions that went with it. In Iran, meanwhile, Reza Shah focused on modernizing Iran and on resolving its problems with neighboring states—his good neighbor policy. These developments helped reconcile Turkey and Iran to one another and led to the signing of the Treaty of Saad Abad in 1937.[21] Furthermore, Pahlavi Iran's and Kemalist Turkey's commitment to modernization and secularization created an ideological affinity between the two nations which facilitated their reconciliation. The two countries' common geopolitical concerns, notably their fear of Soviet intentions, was also important in leading them to develop an intrinsic interest in each other's stability. Their membership in CENTO and in the RCD were added incentives to cooperation.

Yet because of a lack of complementarity, Turkish-Iranian economic and trade relations remained limited. Even the 1970s did not alter this situation much, as

Iran looked more to the West and as Turkey found lucrative markets in Arab states. On the contrary, Turkey's balance of payments problems, following oil price increases, created difficulties in its relations with Iran, because the Shah did not respond favorably to Turkish requests for help. Turkey also was not comfortable with Iran's growing military power or with aspects of its Persian Gulf policy— especially the Shah's manipulation of Iraq's Kurdish problems.[22]

The Post-Revolutionary Period

The Islamic revolution introduced new complexities and a greater degree of uncertainty into Iran's relations with its neighbors. Yet in some cases it eliminated some of the old impediments to better relations. For example, Iran's withdrawal from CENTO, its adoption of a non-aligned posture, and its abandonment of the Shah's more ambitious military plans created a better atmosphere for friendly Indo-Iranian relations. Similarly, Iran's emphasis on expanding its ties with Third World countries should have led to a better atmosphere for cooperative relations. However, its Islamic activism strained ties with India. The same developments also changed some of the foundations of Turko-Iranian friendship. Iran's ideology of Islamic revolutionary universalism is anathema to Turkey's secular nationalism. Indeed, Iran has tried to eradicate the Pahlavis' secular legacy, while Turkey—particularly its military leaders—is committed to the Kemalist tradition and opposes Islamic revivalism.

Since the revolution, Iran has had a confrontational relationship with the United States and has tried to undermine Western influence in the region, whereas Turkey is a NATO member and as such, serves U.S. Western regional interests. To a lesser extent, the same applies to Pakistan, which also has close ties to the United States, although because of Pakistan's own process of Islamization under President Zia-ul-Haq, ideological differences with Iran were not as deep as in Turkey's case. But U.S.-Iranian tensions have spilled over onto relations with these countries, especially Turkey. For example, after the Rushdie affair, the worsening of Iran's relations with the West and its claims about the discovery of a U.S. spy ring, Iranian authorities hinted that Turkey had been implicated in these activities. These allegations may have been put forth because Turkey had tried to mediate between Iran and the West. Iran's criticism of Turkey's so-called anti-Islamic measures also increased.[23] The Iran-Iraq war created its own tensions, especially between Iran and Turkey.

Nevertheless, given the fact that many of the geopolitical, economic, and other factors that had led to the development of patterns of interaction have remained unchanged, there has been considerable continuity in Iran's relations with its neighbors. Iran's economic difficulties, caused by the war, soft oil markets, and Western economic pressures, forced it to temper its ideological aspirations, thus contributing some continuity to its relations with its neighbors.

In this period, too, Iran has had closer relations with Pakistan than with India because of common strategic interests. Concerned about the potential impact on its own centrifugal tendencies, Pakistan has feared Iran's disintegration or its domination by the Soviet Union. Initially, Pakistan most feared a direct Soviet military invasion of Iran. In the last several years, however, it has feared that internal and external pressures would force Iran to turn to the Soviets, a development that would have potentially surrounded Pakistan with three pro-Soviet countries and led Iran and India to cooperate against it. In order to prevent such an outcome, Pakistan has shown considerable patience toward the Islamic regime and has argued against isolating or putting excessive pressure on it.[24]

Pakistan has also been willing to nurture friendly relations with Iran because of its sizable Shi'a minority (20–25 percent); Sunni-Shi'a tensions resulting from the Islamization program of the late President Zia-ul-Haq; and the potential for Iran to manipulate Pakistan's Shi'a community and thereby create political problems for the government. Sympathy for Iran in Pakistan has not been limited to the Shi'as, however. Economic and trade opportunities have also argued for maintaining good relations with Iran.

For similar reasons, Iran has overlooked Pakistan's links to the United States and has focused instead on its Islamic character.[25] Both countries were also concerned about the establishment of a Communist government in Afghanistan and the expansion of the Soviet military presence, and both have had problems with Afghan refugees. Furthermore, any change in either country's attitude toward the problem of Afghanistan and the future state of Afghan relations with the Soviet Union would have deeply affected the interests of the other. For example, if Iran were willing to compromise with the Soviet-supported Afghan government, Pakistan's position of supporting Afghan rebels would have become almost untenable— and vice versa. Indeed, during the ten-year Soviet occupation of Afghanistan, differences of opinion have existed between Iran and Pakistan on the Afghan issue. Iran demanded the unconditional withdrawal of Soviet troops and the establishment of an Islamic government in Kabul. It also refused to take part in the U.N.-sponsored proximity talks with the Soviet Union because Afghan rebels were not included. Pakistan did not take this line, and at times, indicated that it might be amenable to a compromise formula, according to which non-Islamic forces, even including the communists, might play a role. Since 1989 Iran has been more flexible on the issue of finding a compromise solution to the Afghanistan problem.

Nevertheless, both sides tried to insulate their bilateral relations from the disruptive effects of these differences, and Pakistan kept Iran abreast of the progress of the proximity talks on the war. But the future of Afghanistan, the type of government to be created after the Soviet withdrawal, and especially the role of the Iran-based Shi'a Afghan rebel groups in such a government, have remained sources of Iranian-Pakistani tensions.[26]

Pakistan has also faced a dilemma in trying to balance its ties with Iran and Saudi Arabia in regard to the Afghan issue. Since the Soviet invasion, Saudi Arabia—through financial and military assistance and aggressive Wahabi proselytizing—has established a significant position among Afghan rebels, intending to translate this position into dominant influence within a future Afghan government. The Saudis have also intended to limit or block any Iranian influence in a future Afghan government. This objective became quite clear during negotiations in 1989 between the Afghan rebel groups, based in Iran and Pakistan, over the level of their respective representation in a future Afghan government. Finally, an interim government was formed only by seven Pakistan-based groups. Saudi Arabia immediately recognized the interim government, while Iran sharply criticized the exclusion of Shi'a groups and withheld recognition. This development put Pakistan in a difficult position. If it were to follow the Saudi line of excluding Iran and its Afghan Mojahedin, it would certainly antagonize Iran.[27] And if it tried to accommodate Iran, its relations with Saudi Arabia would be complicated. However, given Saudi Arabia's considerable economic and political leverage on Pakistan, and more important because the U.S. has also supported Saudi positions, Pakistan has had to go along with the Saudis while trying somehow to placate Iran.

Indeed, on other occasions Arab-Iranian tensions have created dilemmas for Pakistan. Difficulties have mostly arisen from the Arab side, however, while Iran has been accommodating to Pakistan's policy of balancing its ties with Iran and the Arab states, including the issue of the Iran-Iraq conflict. As evidence of Arab concerns, in 1988 the Saudis sent home the 20,000-man Pakistani brigade, arguing that the existence of too many Shi'as among them was a security risk.[28] But other factors were also involved, including Saudi Arabia's fear of a possible military confrontation with Iran, in which it would expect the Pakistani brigade to take part, is something Pakistan could not accept. Furthermore, Egypt's greater involvement in Gulf Arab security as a counterweight to Iran, plus the greater U.S. presence in the Gulf, had reduced the Saudis' need for Pakistani troops.

Meanwhile, the prospect for Pakistani-Iranian cooperation will depend on how Pakistan manages to reconcile its strategic interest in Iran with its Arab—especially Saudi—ties and its financial dependence on them. It is unlikely that the United States will allow close cooperation of Pakistan and Iran. Thus, while there has been speculation about closer cooperation, including in the military field, serious barriers persist. For example, the extent of Iranian-Pakistani cooperation would depend on the state of Iran's relations with the Arab states, including Saudi Arabia and, more important, with the United States. As long as U.S.-Iranian hostility continues, improved cooperation with Pakistan is unlikely.[29]

Meanwhile, as in the past, several factors limited the scope of Indo-Iranian cooperation while others encouraged it. Indo-Pakistani rivalry remained a restricting factor, given Iran's stake in Pakistan's security and territorial integrity, as having differing perceptions of Soviet intentions.

Since the revolution, Afghanistan has been another area of disagreement between India and Iran. The latter categorically condemned the Soviets' invasion and called for the withdrawal of their troops. India, by contrast, did not unequivocally criticize the Soviet Union and equated its military presence with U.S. aid given to the Afghan rebels. After the signing of the Geneva accords in 1988, India said that it did not accept the inevitable fall of the Kabul regime and tried to help prevent such an outcome.[30]

A new source of tension in Indo-Iranian relations has been the treatment of India's Muslims by the government. Especially during Hindu-Muslim clashes, Iranian religious leaders, members of Parliament, and officials have made comments about India's Muslims which have angered Indian officials. Some Indian Muslim leaders have also used Iran as a sounding-board for their grievances.[31] India has been concerned about potential Iranian propaganda among its Muslim community and has made clear its opposition. This warning seems to have been effective, and Iranian activities among Indian Muslims have not become significant.[32]

Meanwhile, several new factors in the revolutionary era have contributed to better Indo-Iranian relations. The end of the U.S.-Iranian alliance and Iran's abandoning its military aspirations in the Indian Ocean have been welcomed by India. In addition, Iran's policy of expanding ties with Third World countries and satisfying a larger part of its economic and technological needs from Third World nations has made India an attractive partner for the Islamic regime as other considerations had done in the Shah's time.[33] In the future, two developments could also improve prospects for Indo-Iranian cooperation—namely, improved Soviet-Iranian relations and growing disagreement between Iran on the one hand and Pakistan and Saudi Arabia on the other regarding the Afghan issue.[34] However, a rise in Hindu-Muslim tensions would certainly cause fresh difficulties.

Regarding Turkey, the post-revolutionary changes in both Iran's international outlook and its foreign policy undermined much of the basis of Turko-Iranian cooperation. The dichotomy between Iran's Islamic and Turkey's secular ideologies has been reflected in frictions over the Turkish government's banning of the Islamic headdress for female students—including foreigners—and the lack of adequate respect shown by Iranian officials for Ataturk.[35] The activities of some Iranian exiles and the presence of nearly one million Iranians in Turkey have not helped.[36] But the most serious threat to friendly Turko-Iranian relations emanated from the Iran-Iraq war and especially from Iran's connection with Iraq's Kurdish rebels.

The Kurdish issue posed several problems for Turkey, related to the impact of Iranian and Iraqi Kurdish insurgencies on its own serious Kurdish problem.[37] In August 1986, several Iraqi Kurdish groups, armed and assisted by Iran and fighting against the Ba'athist regime, ambushed Turkish soldiers. The Turkish air force retaliated by bombing Kurdish sites and, according to some reports, killed more than 200 insurgents.[38] Tehran viewed this action with grave concern. No doubt, the Turks' concern with the Kurdish problem had been real, but their military action was also intended as a signal to Iran that they would not allow it to defeat Iraq through pressure on the northern front, including damage to the Kirkuk oil installations or the Turkish pipeline. Indeed, throughout the war, Turkey viewed an Iranian victory as unacceptable because it would have shifted the balance of power in Iran's favor and encouraged Muslim revivalist forces. In fact, some observers believe that Turkey had serious plans for occupying Mosul and Kirkuk in the event of an Iranian victory in the south.[39]

Whatever the motives for Turkey's actions, Iran viewed them as intervention in the war and as a sign of its territorial ambitions in Iraq. Iranian officials and commentators warned against any territorial designs. In October 1986, Prime Minister Musavi declared that: "The Islamic Republic of Iran strongly defends Iraq's territorial integrity . . . [and] that after Saddam's downfall it should be respected by all countries."[40]

Despite these tensions, however, for a variety of economic and geopolitical reasons, Turkey and Iran have held back from open conflict. Turkey has been keenly aware of Iran's strategic importance and the significance of Iranian events for its security, including its possible disintegration or domination by the Soviet Union. Thus Turkey has avoided backing Iran into a corner, where it would have no choice but to turn to Moscow, and Ankara has advised the Western allies, particularly the United States, against doing so. Turkey has also resisted Arab pressures to cut its ties with Iran.[41]

In Iran's case, economic factors and its greater need for alternative trading routes after the destruction of its southern ports have led it to maintain reasonably good relations with Turkey and to tolerate certain aspects of Turkish policy—including its position on the Iran-Iraq war—at times in the face of domestic opposition.[42]

The future of Turkish-Iranian relations, however, remains uncertain, and their direction will depend largely on internal developments in each country. In Iran, for example, the consolidation of a more moderate, pragmatic trend would benefit Turkish-Iranian relations. By contrast, the strengthening of the radical trend would be harmful, particularly if Iran tries to manipulate Turkey's Islamic forces. In Turkey, an increase in the strength of Islamic forces, a repetition of the political instability of the late 1970s, or even possibly a return of military rule would strain Turko-Iranian relations.[43]

Conclusion

Iran's relations since the revolution with the Indian subcontinent and with Turkey illustrate the diversity of factors, in addition to Islam, that influence its foreign policy. It also offers a good example of patterns of continuity in its behavior despite changes introduced by its revolutionary ideology and world outlook. Indeed, because of the continued importance of geopolitical, cultural, and economic considerations, the underlying aspects of Iran's relations with these countries have remained unchanged.

8. Iran and Europe

Historical Background

Iran's post-revolutionary relations with the countries of Europe cannot be understood without some knowledge of their historical context. If present-day Europe is successor to Greece and Rome, then Iran and Europe have interacted for three thousand years. Yet beyond the circle of specialists, European knowledge of Iran, of its culture, and of its contribution to world civilization is limited. J. H. Iliffe has caught this point very well:

> Considering the tremendous role which Aryan man has played in world history, how unfamiliar to us (his descendants) are his origins and the lands that were the cradle of our race. Hebrew, Greek, and Roman civilization is absorbed more or less by western man with his mother's milk; the vast Iranian panorama in which our ancestors arose and flourished seems as remote to the majority as the moon. For us its early history is restricted to those occasions when it formed part of Israel or of Greece. Our interest and sympathies are enlisted on behalf of Jewish exiles, the drama of Marathon and Thermopylae, the march of the ten thousand, or Alexander's meteoric career; incidental in our minds to these events are the extent of the realm of Ahasuerus, the background to the decree of Cyrus, King of Persia, the initiative shown by Darius on his accession, or the rise of Zoroastrianism.[1]

This lack of intrinsic European interest in Iran has continued into modern times. Such interest as there has been derives from other concerns: dealing with the Ottoman threat, protecting India, gaining access to warm waters, preventing Russian-Soviet expansion, and protecting Arabian oilfields.

The Europeans' lack of knowledge about Iran has been accompanied by distorted images. Europeans have viewed the Persian empire as the archetype of Eastern despotism and the Persians as the barbarians who threatened civilized Athens and Rome. Beyond the circle of specialists, there has been little awareness of Iran's contributions to Western civilization, through what it has imparted directly and what it has transmitted from the other civilizations.

Iran's role as the transmitter of Western culture to the East from India to China has also gone unnoticed. Most Westerners have not been aware or appreciative of Iran's historic role as a barrier between the West and Asian nomads. Yet it was the elimination of this formidable Iranian barrier after the collapse of the Sassanid Empire in the seventh century A.D. which opened the way for the penetration of these nomadic hordes into Mesopotamia and the Mediterranean and brought them perilously close to the European heartland.

For more than 1,300 years Islamic Iran has not been treated any more fairly. Europeans recognize that their cultural and scientific renaissance owes much to Islamic civilization, yet most would identify Islamic civilization with the Arabs, even though, as the renowned British Iran specialist, Edward Brown, has said: "Take of what is wrongly known as Arabian sciences . . . what has been contributed by the Persians, and the best is gone."[2] Paradoxically, the Europeans' neglect and underestimation of Iran has been accompanied by an almost unconscious view of it as a competitor and by a recognition that Iran's challenge to the ancient Western world was not only that of a brute force but also of a highly developed culture and politics. Hence, there is a grudging admission of Iran's achievements and its potential. Yet, because of its steady decline during the last two centuries, an element of disdain has dominated Europe's view of Iran. To its ancient image as the land of barbarians was added that of a spineless, lethargic, decadent, and unjustifiably vain people.[3]

Western overreaction to the Islamic revolution has reflected the impact of these contradictory perceptions. It has conjured up images of Iranian "barbarians" once more threatening civilized citadels of Europe. During the Persian Gulf war, it was often said that Iraq was defending civilization against barbarism, thus justifying the West's support.[4]

Paradoxically, Western overreaction has also stemmed from an implicit admission of Iran's potential to turn Islam into a potent ideological force and to propagate it.[5] Indeed, implicit acknowledgement of Iran's latent competitive potential had affected the European approach toward Iran for more than a century. During the nineteenth and twentieth centuries, a principal aspect of British Persian Gulf policy was to weaken Iran and to strengthen Arab elements, as well as to eliminate its political and cultural influence from Afghanistan and India.[6]

West European reaction to the Shah in his last years, including the Western outcry about Iran's hegemonism in the Persian Gulf, derived from similar factors. The Shah was neither more repressive nor more corrupt than other Western allies, from Ferdinand Marcos to Mobutu Sese Seko. But his country sat at a strategic corner and had the potential of a serious middle-sized power. So, he had to be contained, hence the charges of Iran's expansionism, the Shah's imperial megalomania, and the murderous character of his regime.[7] Likewise, charges about the Ayatollah Khomeini's desire to create an Islamic empire and the placing of greater emphasis on Iran's human rights violations than those of countries such as Iraq, Syria, and Western allies such as Turkey also derive from Iran's competitive potential.

In power terms, this approach is logical. In fact, during the late 1970s, strains in Iran's relations with West Europe and the United States originated largely from the inherent tension in relations between great powers and core regional powers, since even a friendly core regional power is a potential competitor and has ambitions that are not always compatible with those of the greater powers. Thus, despite the Shah's pro-Western orientation, the West disliked his growing ambitions and strength. Likewise, the intensity of European reaction to the Islamic revolution compared with the response to other Middle East radical movements stemmed not only from its ideology but also from the fact that, if successful, it could enhance Iran's regional influence and its competitive potential.

The history of colonialism also affected European-Iranian relations. Many colonizers have developed a tremendous liking and even affection for the peoples and cultures of their ex-colonies, providing tangible economic and political payoffs for some countries. British Arabists have inherited Lawrence of Arabia's romantic vision of the noble Arab nomad, and other Britons retain great affection for India.

But regarding Iran there is no such tradition, although some Britons acquainted with the Persian language may appreciate the wisdom of a Hafiz, the mysticism of a Jalal-ed-Din Balkhi, or the romantic cynicism of Omar Khayyam. Or the French philosopher Montesquieu might entitle a major work *Les Lettres Persannes,* and the German poet Goethe's *Oriental Book* might be influenced by Hafiz of Shiraz. More tangibly, colonial powers have also often contributed to their colonies' development. But in the case of semi-colonies like Iran, the relationship has been mostly an exploitative one.[8]

Thus, whether justified or not, the historical legacy of Iran's experience with Europe has involved an underlying feeling of resentment—shared even by Westernized Iranians—for having always been unfairly treated. Western Europe's support for Iraq—despite its aggression—and its exaggeration of the Iranian threat have enhanced such feelings. Resentment has not determined Iran's approach toward Europe, but beneath the surface, the effect has remained strong and periodically has emerged in waves of national xenophobia and anti-Western hysteria, leading to unrealistic Iranian policies.[9]

The intensity of Iran's resentment toward European countries has been directly related to its experience with individual states. Until the end of World War II, Iran's contacts with Europe were limited to a few countries. In the nineteenth century, its foreign relations were primarily marked by a one-sided involvement with Great Britain and Russia, which had a total of 65 consular offices in Iran, although Iran did have diplomatic ties with some other European countries.[10]

France and Germany illustrate the relationship between Iran's experience and its attitudes. Except for a brief period during the Napoleonic wars, France's presence in Iran has been mostly cultural.[11] Thus not having experienced a semi-colonial relationship, Iran has generally been well-disposed toward it, although this historic good will has been largely eroded because of France's support for Iraq in the recent war. Similarly, German influence in Iran was limited to a short period during the 1930s when Iran used Germany to balance the Anglo-Russian presence, and thus it, too, has retained a positive image.[12]

Europe and Iran: Some Underlying Attitudes

Since the mid-nineteenth century, an important aspect of Iran's diplomatic strategy has been a quest for a counterweight to Anglo-Russian influence, hence, its long-standing interest in expanding ties with European countries. Yet because of Anglo-Russian obstruction and because of the lack of significant European interest, this strategy had little success, except for the period of German influence in the 1930s. The German occupation of Holland and Belgium during World War II interrupted Iran's relations with the Low Countries, and then the Allied occupation of Iran interrupted its ties with Germany and Italy. After World War II, Iran's political instability and Europe's preoccupation with reconstruction kept relations from expanding. But Iran did upgrade some of its missions and opened new embassies in Europe. During the last two decades of his rule, and especially after 1973, the Shah expanded Iran's ties with West European states in order to increase its economic and political options beyond the United States in order to gain greater independence and give Europe a stake in his regime's survival. As the Cold War subsided in the mid-1960s, Iran also expanded its ties with East European countries, although these ties remained limited compared to those with West European states, especially in the cultural field.[13]

Meanwhile, European criticism of Iran's human rights record and the activities of anti-Shah students strained its relations with West European states. European leftists, including members of parliament, attacked the Shah's despotic rule. He complained to their governments for not stopping such criticisms and Iranian student demonstrations. European public reaction to Iranian complaints was negative. Indeed, the more the Shah complained, the more ammunition he gave his detractors, creating a vicious circle of criticism, acrimony, and further strained relations. During his last years, the Shah's arrogant manner and criticism of the Europeans' handling of their own and the world's problems enhanced his enemies' animosity and exasperated his supporters. This process contributed to the erosion of European support, and, because Arab countries offered Europe greater financial and trade advantages, the Shah could not mitigate European opposition with the offer of economic incentives.

Immediately after the revolution and under the Bazargan's transition government, Iran's relations with West European countries did not change much, with the exception of Britain, whose embassy in Tehran was attacked by mobs. In addition to general European fear of the destabilizing effects of the Iranian revolution, and concern over Soviet domination of Iran, several factors have shaped Iranian ties with European countries since the fall of Bazargan in November 1979: intra-governmental differences in Iran; economic necessities; European attitudes toward the Iran-Iraq war; the spillover of U.S.-Iranian tensions; and West European domestic politics. In addition, Iran wanted to curb the Western cultural presence because of fear of its impact on the role of Islam and the creation of cultural dependency. Thus, initially, Iran closed European cultural centers, but recently some have been allowed to reopen. For the same reason—plus unsafe conditions during the Iran-Iraq war and the Iranian economic slump—the number of European experts working in Iran was also reduced. Politics permitting, this situation may change as Iran embarks on reconstruction.

The Islamic government has preferred to expand its ties with smaller European countries. Thus economic and trade relations with Sweden, Denmark, Finland, Ireland, Spain, Portugal, Belgium, and Switzerland have expanded. Because of the low level of economic activity, however, in most cases the total volume of exchanges has not been much greater than during the pre-revolution period. Political relations with these countries have also generally been good. Principal irritants have remained the activities of Iranian opposition groups in these countries, public criticism of Iran's human rights record, and Iran's implication in terrorist activities.[14] Sweden has had particularly good ties with Iran, despite some difficulties because of uncertainties over the fate of pre-revolution Swedish contracts.[15]

Sweden's lack of membership in either of the two major military pacts, plus its balanced approach to the Iran-Iraq war and its non-hostile attitude toward the Islamic regime have been responsible for extensive economic ties with Iran, reasonably good political relations, and extensive contacts between officials. But the expansion of economic relations was slowed because of Iran's financial difficulties and Sweden's unwillingness to take part in certain projects in Iran.[16]

Italy also has been a favorite economic partner because of its basically neutral posture toward the Iran-Iraq war. In 1987, Italy waited longer than other European countries to send ships to support the U.S. Gulf policy, and it recognized that resolving the Persian Gulf conflict required an acknowledgement of Iran's grievances. Thus, after the U.S. bombing of the Iranian oil platform in April 1988, the spokesman for the Italian Ministry of Foreign Affairs characterized it as the "outcome of a rigid military logic." And at a meeting of the Western European Union, the Italian foreign minister called for the condemnation of Iraq's use of chemical weapons.[17] As a result, it is generally expected that Italy will play a large part in Iran's reconstruction plans. Indeed, a few days after the cease-fire was declared on 20 August 1988, a large Italian delegation headed by the Ministry of Industry visited Iran and reactivated the Joint Trade Commission that had not met since 1979.[18] In January 1989, Prime Minister Mir-Hossein Musavi visited Italy and also met Pope John Paul II.[19] In general, however, West European-Iranian relations took a turn to the worse over the so-called Rushdie controversy. The Ayatollah Khomeini's call for his execution led the European countries to withdraw their ambassadors from Iran and to cancel a number of scheduled high-level visits.[20] Iran reciprocated, but the situation was somewhat diffused in April 1989 when some European countries decided to return their ambassadors to Tehran.[21] Like its predecessors, the Islamic regime has looked to the countries of Europe as a potential counterweight to the superpowers—following a diplomatic tactic reminiscent of the third-power strategy, but with mixed results. In the past, Iran's moderates have been concerned that West European pressure on Iran, reflecting compliance with U.S. policy, would result in its dependence on the Soviet Union and the East bloc countries. Thus, during the hostage crisis and the U.S. embargo on Iran, supported by West Europe, the director of Iran's Central Bank, Ali-Reza Nobari, pleaded with West European states not to pressure Iran and force it to turn to the Soviet Union. Nevertheless, given the international reaction to the hostage crisis and the far more important requirement of preserving harmony within the Western alliance, Nobari's pleas were not heeded.[22] During the Gulf crisis of 1987, the requirements of U.S.-European solidarity also overcame any West European concern to play the role of the counterweight.

The Iranian leadership has also been divided over which group of European countries to favor as partners. The radical factions have preferred the East European states and their case has been strengthened by Iran's need for arms.[23] Its economic and financial requirements—caused by the fall in its oil revenues, by its reluctance to borrow, by periodic Western economic restrictions, and by the West European unwillingness to extend credits—have helped promote Iranian ties with East European countries. Consequently, since 1980 the volume of Iranian-East European trade has increased—doubled, according to some sources—and now accounts for 11 percent of the Iranian market.[24] East Europeans have also been involved in a number of industrial and other projects in Iran.[25]

After the Rushdie affair and the worsening of Iranian-West European relations, Iran either reached or was envisioning reaching wide-ranging agreements with East European countries to help it rebuild its economy and military.[26] Political relations with East European countries have also improved and could expand further. In January 1989, Iran's prime minister visited Poland and in February its president visited Yugoslavia and Romania and in June the speaker of Parliament, Rafsanjani, made a tour of East European capitals.[27] Yugoslavia and Romania have been Iran's principal partners, but others such as Poland, Bulgaria, and East Germany have been involved in a number of projects in Iran, and prospects for their greater involvement remain good.[28]

One reason for Iran's look to Eastern Europe in relations has been the fact that these countries are not susceptible to the impact of U.S.-Iran tensions and also do not criticize Iran's domestic or foreign policies, and they are also more willing to do business on a barter basis. Iran was also disappointed with the West European countries' unwillingness to criticize Iraq's use of chemical weapons and their reluctance to help in the full implementation of Resolution 598. Thus, if political tensions between Iran and Western Europe continue, and if the moderate elements fail to consolidate their position, a dramatic shift could occur in the balance of Iran's economic and political relations with Europe in favor of Eastern Europe.[29] However, the evolution of Iranian politics in the immediate aftermath of the Ayatollah Khomeini's death indicated an assertion of a moderate, realist trend, which, together with Iran's economic and technological needs should lead to more balanced relations with both West and East European countries.

Iran and Britain

For more than a century Britain, together with Russia, dominated Iran's political life. The U.S. ascendancy after World War II and British decline didn't eliminate the influence of the U.K., which, until the early 1960s, matched that of the United States, in part because until the 1956 Suez crisis, the United States considered the

Middle East as essentially a British sphere of influence. Indeed, the coup d'etat of 1953 against Mohammed Mossadegh was masterminded by Britain.

The legacy of Anglo-Iranian interaction is somewhat contradictory. Britain has the image in Iran of a manipulative and exploitative power whose policies have hampered Iran's development, undermined its independence, and caused the loss of its territory and influence from the Persian Gulf to Afghanistan. The Iranians still have an exaggerated view of Britain's capabilities, believing that it has compensated for its loss of power with diplomatic shrewdness.[30]

Meanwhile, Britain's long involvement in Iran has left a legacy of a large and intricate—albeit diminishing—network of influence, even with the clerical establishment. Indeed, because of Britain's connections, opponents of the Islamic regime suspected British complicity in toppling the Shah's regime.[31] For its part, Britain defended its pre-revolution links to the clerical factions as "natural," given the latter's importance in Iran's social and political life.[32]

Regardless of the merits of such suspicions, the fact is that, during the late 1970s, Anglo-Iranian relations were strained because of Iran's hawkishness on oil prices, its regional ambitions, the Shah's arrogant manner, and his refusal to renew the oil consortium's agreement. Meanwhile, regional developments had dramatically diminished Iran's value for Britain. In 1978, the Persian Gulf Arab states were rich and stable; Egypt had rejoined the Western camp; and the chances for Arab-Israeli peace had increased. Thus, the prospect of the Shah's being replaced by a more popular and less ambitious Islamic nationalist government had become more appealing.

After the revolution, Britain's links to clerical factions enabled it to maintain a presence until the outbreak of the Rushdie affair in 1989. Thus, despite its role in restoring the Shah to power in 1953, Britain initially did not suffer America's fate. Nevertheless, resentment of the British role in Iran has lingered, and British diplomats and observers of Iran have sensed contradictory impulses in the Iranian public and government regarding ties with Britain. A British diplomat characterized this attitude as a "mixture of attraction and mistrust." On the British side, too, there does not seem to have been a consensus on the appropriate mixture of pressures and incentives to include in policy toward Iran. Britain has had its own version of hawks and doves.[33] Also, British policy toward Iran has been affected all along by their perception of the relative importance of the Soviet threat to Iran and of Iran's challenge to British interests and to those of their friends in the Persian Gulf. Thus, as with the U.S., the hardening of British policy toward Iran in 1987–88 resulted from their calculation that the Soviet threat to Iran had diminished and that they could therefore safely pressure Iran and cement their relations with Persian Gulf Arabs.

These mutual ambivalences resulted in the erratic development of Anglo-Iranian relations. Immediately after the revolution, the element of mistrust predominated. Some religious factions saw Britain as the Shah's accomplice and held it responsible for his actions. The British embassy was attacked, leading the British government to close it and to maintain an interests section in the Swedish embassy.[34] But it continued to use the embassy compound, and for most of the post-revolution period, it kept several diplomats in Iran.

Iran's internal power struggles also deeply affected Anglo-Iranian relations. When the pragmatic and moderate elements were in the ascendancy, relations improved. Indeed, in the spring of 1983, Britain informed Iran of the Tudeh Party's infiltration of its military and civilian organizations.

During 1983–1986, Anglo-Iranian relations remained erratic, though tolerable, partly because the shift in the balance of power in the moderates' favor was never decisive. Thus there was a rear-guard action by the extremists to block further improvement. This was even evident during the summer and fall of 1988, when Iran officially tried to improve its ties with Britain. Thus while Iran's foreign minister made positive statements on Anglo-Iranian relations, the prime minister dampened expectations. In an interview, he accused Britain of having supported American hostility toward Iran, including the shooting down of the Iran Air Airbus, and he cited Britain's past interference in Iran as an impediment to better relations.[35] Nevertheless, between 1983 and 1986, bilateral trade increased. In May 1983, the first post-revolution British trade mission visited Tehran, and the British became optimistic about trade potential, leading Britain to become fourth among Iran's trading partners.[36]

But the spillover of U.S.-Iranian tensions have hurt Anglo-Iranian relations. Periodically, Britain has had to take anti-Iranian measures in support of U.S. policy, as was the case during the 1979–1980 U.S. hostage crisis when Britain imposed an economic embargo on Iran.[37] In 1987–1988, Britain supported U.S. policy, sent minesweepers to the Persian Gulf, and joined the United States in advocating a U.N.-sponsored arms embargo against Iran.[38]

The fallout from the Iran-Contra affair also hurt Anglo-Iranian ties. It hardened Western attitudes and generated a confrontational mood in Iran by undermining the moderates' position. The effects of this process were felt in British-Iranian relations in May 1987, when Britain accused an Iranian diplomat, Ghassemi, of shoplifting. When he refused to appear in court, he was arrested by the police. In retaliation, a British diplomat in Tehran, Edward Chaplin, was arrested and beaten up by the Islamic Revolution Committee (IRC) guards. He was released after 24 hours, but remained under suspicion, and Iran threatened to charge him with espionage. Iran also accused Britain of having fabricated the shoplifting charges against its envoy and linked Chaplin's treatment by Iran to Britain's handling of their diplomat.[39]

The Chaplin incident reflected Iran's internal divisions and the extremists' efforts to sabotage Iran's relations with the West. For example, the IRC guards who assaulted Chaplin reported to the Ministry of the Interior, headed by Ayatollah Mohtashami, Iran's ex-ambassador to Syria and one of its most extreme political figures. The order for Chaplin's arrest was reportedly given by the deputy foreign minister, Hossein Sheikholeslam—another extremist—while Foreign Minister Velayati was out of the country.[40] The British government retaliated by closing down the Iranian consulate in Manchester and expelling Ghassemi. This led to a spiral of expulsions of diplomats, which ultimately left only one diplomat from each country in London and Tehran.

During June and July 1987 the crisis escalated. Extremists in Tehran tried to use this opportunity to force a total break in diplomatic ties with Britain. Iranian newspapers wrote anti-British articles calling Britain the "Mini-Satan."[41] Given the atmosphere in Iran, even the relatively moderate and pragmatic Velayati was forced to make an anti-British statement. For its part, Britain closed the London office of the National Iranian Oil Company, which was suspected of having served as a military procurement office for arms purchases in the European black markets.[42] However, a total break in diplomatic ties was averted.

In addition to these incidents, Anglo-Iranian relations have been strained by the activities of Iranian opposition groups in Britain, by Iranian charges of British harassment of pro-Islamic Iranian students in Britain, by Iranian spying charges against some British nationals in Iran, by the imprisonment of some British nationals, and by Iranian actions against British ships in the context of the Persian Gulf conflict and the tanker war.[43] Furthermore, Iran's involvement in Middle East terrorism has also affected the atmosphere of Anglo-Iranian relations, leading even to disagreement between the two countries about their respective envoys. In 1986, Britain refused *agreement* to Abbas Malaek, Iran's appointed *charge d'affaires*, on the grounds that he was one of the so-called students involved in the seizing of the U.S. embassy. In retaliation, Iran refused agreement to Hugh Arbuthnot, nominated to be the head of the British interests section in Tehran.[44]

By the spring of 1988, as Iran tried to improve its Western ties and to reduce its isolation, Anglo-Iranian relations also benefitted. In June, Britain and Iran agreed on reparation for damages done to their respective embassies, and a British parliamentary team visited Tehran.[45] In negotiations with Iran, Britain set several conditions for full restoration of diplomatic ties: (1) Iran should observe international law and end attacks on Gulf shipping; (2) it should stop its activities in Lebanon and free British hostages; (3) it should stop destabilizing the Persian Gulf Arab states; (4) it should allow British consular officers to visit imprisoned British citizens; and (5) diplomatic ties could only be fully restored on the basis of complete reciprocity, and Britain would only send a senior diplomat to Iran when he could operate under the British flag. Iran's acceptance of UN Resolution 598, followed by a relative improvement in Iranian relations with Gulf Arab states, answered some of Britain's conditions. But the release of British hostages proved more difficult to achieve. At first, British authorities seemed to make allowances for Iran's limitations in trying to obtain the release of their hostages. Thus efforts to normalize relations continued despite the lack of progress on the hostage issue.

By the summer of 1988, British firms were beginning to show a renewed interest in the Iranian market. In September, the foreign ministers of the two countries met in New York, and on 30 September the British foreign secretary, Sir Geoffrey Howe, declared that Britain was resuming full diplomatic relations on the basis of "reciprocity and mutual respect."[46] During the fall of 1988, the issue of hostages and the British prisoners in Tehran—especially the fate of Roger Cooper—continued to mar relations. Britain maintained that it would not send a senior diplomat to Tehran unless British citizens were released from prison. Nevertheless, on 4 December, the Union Jack flew over the British embassy, and in January 1989 the first senior British diplomat, Gordon Pirie, arrived in Tehran. Upon his arrival, Pirie assured the Iranians that Britain no longer had any ambition of interfering in Iran's affairs. Nevertheless, there were no major improvements in relations, although one of the two British prisoners, Nicholas Nicola, was released.

Progress was limited because of the radicals' obstruction, the problem of Roger Cooper and the hostages, and British unwillingness to pressure Iraq or to speed up the implementation of Resolution 598. The radicals opposed improving relations with Britain, partly because of their belief that this would facilitate the normalization of U.S.-Iranian relations. Britain might also have become a source of military supplies, a prospect which was extremely disconcerting to the radicals.

The outbreak of the Rushdie affair resulted in the worst crisis in Anglo-Iranian relations and finally led Iran to break diplomatic relations with Britain on 7 March 1989. This event reflected the victory of the radical factions. On the British side, too, the handling of the Rushdie affair reflected the triumph of the hard-liners in the British Foreign Service, despite desperate efforts by Iranian moderates to distance themselves from the Ayatollah Khomeini's death threat to Rushdie.[47]

As the radicals gained the upper hand in Iran, however, the British government did try to distance itself from Rushdie by saying that it did not share his views, and it emphasized that Rushdie had been equally insulting to Britain by comparing it to Nazi Germany. Yet given their domestic political concerns neither side could make the necessary concessions needed to avoid total estrangement. The Rushdie affair undid the results of nearly ten years of generally cautious British diplomacy toward Iran, because of which, until the Rushdie affair, no irremediable damage was done to Anglo-Iranian relations. But the normalization of relations after the break and, more important, developing extensive economic and other relations will be much more difficult, especially if the radicals retain their influence.

Iran and France

Until recently, the historical legacy of Franco-Iranian relations has been positive, a fact which has facilitated Franco-Iranian reconciliation. Thus when France and Iran resumed diplomatic relations in the summer of 1988, Iran's oil minister, Gholamreza Aghazadeh, said that there could be vast expansion of economic and trade relations: Iran did not feel the same hostility toward France that it did toward Britain and the United States because there was no colonial experience with France.[48]

Yet despite its favorable image and its cultural influence in Iran, until the 1960s Franco-Iranian economic and trade relations were limited compared to those with Britain and the United States. By the mid-1960s, bilateral relations began to expand as Charles de Gaulle's vision of France as an alternative to the superpowers for Third World countries appealed to the Shah, who wanted to pursue a more independent foreign policy.[49] During the 1970s, Iran's improved financial position and ambitious development plan led to a sharp expansion of Franco-Iranian economic relations.[50] Meanwhile, Franco-Arab relations expanded as Arab oil producers became major markets for France and invested heavily there. This intricate economic and financial interaction enhanced France's political stake in these countries. In particular, France developed a special interest in Iraq, deriving from a desire to obtain a privileged position among the oil-producing countries. Iran, Saudi Arabia, the Gulf Arab sheikhdoms, and Oman were all dominated by Britain or the United States. But three revolutions in Iraq—in 1958, 1963, and 1968—had eliminated the Anglo-American presence. The Soviet Union benefitted most from this vacuum, but France also saw opportunities and seized them. Its inroads in Iraq during the 1960s turned into a major economic and trade partnership in the 1970s.

By 1978, France's Arab ties were far more important than those with Iran. Thus, France reacted to Iranian events with complacency. During the post-revolutionary period as well, France's Arab ties have weighed heavily in its approach toward Iran. At the same time, France's hospitality to Ayatollah Khomeini during his years in exile gave it a head start with the new regime in Tehran.[51] Iran seemed to be aware of this French expectation. An Iranian news commentary stated that "the French government hoped to hold the status of a favored nation in Iran, in return for the treatment it meted to Imam Khomeini" and thus "France would be able to gain what the United States used to plunder . . . "[52] But the course of the Iranian revolution, the Iran-Iraq war, the Lebanese crisis, French fears of Islamic fundamentalism, and Iran's role in terrorism soured Franco-Iranian relations. To begin with, those French, especially on the left, who disliked the Shah expected the revolutionary regime to be secular, left of center, and more or less democratic. This expectation was systematically fed by such figures as Bani-Sadr. The fall of Bazargan and Bani-Sadr, the elimination of leftist forces, and the victory of religious elements disappointed French expectations and changed their views of the Iranian revolution. The Socialists' victory in 1981 also affected Franco-Iranian relations. They reacted more strongly to Iran's human rights record and allowed Iranian opposition groups to operate more freely in France. Thus the People's Mojahedin of Iran, former President Bani-Sadr, and the royalist opposition all settled in Paris. Iran accused France of supporting its opponents and, in response, France stressed its tradition as a haven for exile. France's fears of the spread of Islamic fundamentalism and its disruptive impact on Middle Eastern and North African governments—and, by extension, on French interests—increasingly influenced its approach toward Iran and the Iran-Iraq war.[53] It was also concerned about the impact of the movement on its Arab minority.[54] Given Iran's symbolic and active role within the fundamentalist movement, France viewed Iran as a major threat to its interests. Throughout the Iran-Iraq war, France unconditionally supported Iraq, hoping that it would end the Khomeini regime. When the war turned against Iraq, fear of its collapse, and, most important, French investment in Iraq, led France to continue support. At heart, French views on Persian Gulf security were determined more by economic than by geopolitical considerations, and thus

France viewed Iraq and the regional Arab states as more important than Iran. Some French analysts believed that even the loss of Iran to the Soviet Union would not rival the possible collapse of Iraq and its aftereffects. Some French observers even thought that a Communist Iran would be much easier to deal with than a Muslim-fundamentalist Iran.[55]

Many French leaders also believed that support for the Arab states against Iran might prompt them to deal with Israel.[56] The assumption behind this view was that fear of Iran and Islamic fundamentalism was stronger among moderate Arabs than their concerns for the Palestinians. Thus, Western support for moderate Arabs against Iran might consolidate Arab-Western ties better than anything the West could do on the Palestinian issue.

Because of these calculations, when Iraq's military position faltered in late 1982, France supplied it with sophisticated weaponry.[57] The Super Etendard aircraft deliveries put Iran's oil terminal at Kharg Island and other installations within the reach of Iraqi firepower. Naturally, French military supplies generated strong anti-French feelings in Iran. There were calls for the closure of France's cultural institutions; actions were taken against its economic interests; and French sociological and archaeological research was prohibited. Mass demonstrations were held in front of the French embassy. However, economic ties with France were not totally broken.[58]

Events in Lebanon also hurt Franco-Iranian relations. After the Israeli invasion in June 1982 and the creation of the Multi-National Force (MNF)—with French participation—many Lebanese, including the pro-Iranian Shiʻas, saw the MNF and the Western countries as promotors of the political goals of the Israelis and the Lebanese Christians. Thus they and their supporters, Syria and Iran, tried to force the MNF's departure by resorting to terrorism. In October 1983, truck bombings killed 58 French military personnel. The French government retaliated by bombing the military barracks of radical Shiʻas in the Beka'a Valley, which was also the headquarters of the Iranian Revolutionary Guards. Yet, despite assertions that six Iranians had conducted the bombing of the French barracks, France did not directly attack Iran.[59]

France's role in Lebanon and in the Persian Gulf conflict made it a target of attacks by pro-Iranian, Lebanese Shiʻa groups. In 1984, Iraq's use of French-supplied Super Etendards and Exocet missiles to launch attacks on Iranian oil installations initiated the so-called tanker war. As a result, during 1984 and 1985 there were several attacks and kidnappings directed against French nationals in Beirut.[60] The fate of these hostages became a major preoccupation of successive French governments and a burning political issue, leading to a severe deterioration of Franco-Iranian relations.[61]

Conflicting Franco-Iranian interests in Lebanon and Franco-Iraqi support for the Lebanese Christian faction continue to strain relations with Iran. France's policy of total support for Iraq had never won unanimous approval at home. Some voices, albeit muffled, had always argued against this policy undermining historic Franco-Iranian good will.[62] Individuals inside and outside the French government who emphasized geopolitical rather than solely economic factors especially opposed this one-sided policy, including a small group within the French foreign ministry who favored a more balanced policy toward Iran; they were, as one French journalist told me, a small "Iran lobby." Their influence was limited, but nevertheless, several factors forced the French government to reassess its approach toward Iran, thus enabling them to influence policy. Those factors were the longevity of the Islamic regime, which had outlived earlier expectations; the perception of Iraq's vulnerability, especially after Iran's capture of the Faw Peninsula in early 1986; and French domestic politics and the question of French hostages.

The continued captivity of French citizens in Lebanon had become a particularly sensitive issue in France because of a strong popular clamor for the government to act more decisively with the terrorists. Thus, all French politicians felt that the hostages' release was important for their political future. During the campaign for the parliamentary election of March 1986, the socialist government was attacked by the opposition, especially by Jacques Chirac, leader of the Gaullist RPR, for its mishandling of the terrorist problem. The socialists lost the election and Chirac became France's prime minister. He set out to make good on his campaign promises, but he soon discovered that, because of Iran's influence in Lebanon, he needed to normalize ties with Tehran.

Meanwhile, as one French diplomat told me, the Quai d'Orsay wanted to improve ties with Iran for strategic and political reasons. Many French diplomats and analysts felt that France had been trapped (piégé) in its relationship with Iraq, which had started as an opportunity with great promise but had turned into a burden. In order to sell this policy to Prime Minister Chirac, the Foreign Ministry had to present it as the only way to get the release of the hostages.[63]

Iran also wanted to improve relations with France in order to alleviate some of its financial difficulties, as it hoped to obtain some of the $1 billion lent by the Shah to France for the EURODIF Project and to persuade France to reduce its assistance to Iraq and adopt a more neutral position on the war. But according to French diplomats, while Iran regularly referred to this issue, it never made it a central point in the bargaining process.

The first steps in the Franco-Iranian dialogue were taken by private intermediaries, including French businessmen, followed by a French parliamentary delegation which visited Tehran in January 1986.[64] In May, Ali-Reza Mo'ayeri, Iran's deputy prime minister, visited Paris, and in September the Iranian and French foreign ministers met in New York. By June 1986, France and Iran had reached a tentative agreement on a number of issues. Two French journalists who had been kidnapped, Phillipe Rochat and Georges Hansen, were released on 20 June in West Beirut, and France agreed to pay Iran $330 million as part of the settlement of a $1 billion EURODIF loan extended during the Shah's reign. It also agreed to expel the Iranian opposition group, the Mojahedin-e-Khalgh, including its leader, Massoud Rajavi.

This policy of normalizing relations with Iran was controversial. Chirac's political rivals portrayed the opening to Iran as a facade for a deal on French hostages and a compromise on France's principled position of not negotiating with terrorists. The strong pro-Iraq lobby also reacted sharply and warned that an opening to Iran could damage France's Arab ties. In response, the French government denied that the opening to Iran was related to the question of hostages. In a radio interview, Foreign Minister Jean-Bernard Raimond said that: "Given Iran's weight in the Middle East, France would have wanted to normalize relations with Iran even if there were no French hostages in Lebanon."[65] But he also stated that "the resumption of ties with Iran did not imply any change in France's Middle East policy or in its policy toward Iraq. . . . "[66]

Franco-Iranian rapprochement achieved some of the two parties' purposes. But it was short-lived because both had unrealistic expectations. Iran hoped to convince France to halt its arms deliveries to Iraq, and France wrongly assumed that it could simultaneously have a reconciliation with Iran and maintain its support for Iraq. Because of several developments, some not directly related to Franco-Iranian relations, bilateral ties deteriorated and led to the rupture of diplomatic relations in the summer of 1987. According to French diplomats, already by September 1986 the Franco-Iranian reconciliation was stalled because of Tehran's unresponsiveness. As one French diplomat told me: "It was impossible to get any response from Tehran," as though the whole Iranian Foreign Ministry had been paralyzed. In all likelihood, this situation was the result of infighting and countermeasures by the extremists, an analysis supported by the events of early November 1986—namely, the leaking by Iranian extremists of the story of secret U.S.-Iran contacts, which sabotaged efforts at U.S.-Iranian reconciliation.

Franco-Iranian relations were adversely affected by the hardening of the Iranian and Western mood after Irangate and the change in U.S. Persian Gulf policy. An upshot of the Iran-Contra affair was a sharpening of political rhetoric on the issue of dealing with terrorists. In France's case, the handling of the so-called Gordji Affair became the litmus test of the new tough policy on terrorism.

Vahid Gordji was the official interpreter of the Iranian embassy in Paris.[67] French security officials had long suspected him of having ties to terrorists. They viewed him as an *éminence grise* whose official rank did not reflect his real influence.[68] For lack of evidence or other considerations, however, they had not accused him of improper behavior.

In September 1986, several terrorist attacks in France led to widespread public demand for a tougher approach to terrorism. The opponents of the policy of an opening to Iran—especially the powerful pro-Iraqi lobby—also seized on this opportunity. Prime Minister Chirac was put in a delicate position. Politically, he had both to prove that he could be tough on terrorism and to shake off criticism of his handling of ties with Iran. Franco-Iranian relations were thus the casualty of French domestic politics.

French authorities determined that Gordji was involved with the network responsible for terrorist incidents in France, including those which occurred in September 1986, and demanded that he appear before a judge for interrogation. Fearing that this might be a prelude to his indictment, Gordji refused. French authorities then surrounded the Iranian embassy to prevent him from leaving. In retaliation, Iran accused the French diplomat, Paul Torri, of espionage, helping the opposition, and dealing in drugs. Its forces surrounded the French embassy in Tehran and warned France of angry popular reactions, thereby raising fears in Paris that the American hostage crisis might be repeated.[69] By July 1987, the war of the embassies was still continuing; therefore France broke diplomatic relations with Iran and imposed an embargo on the purchase of Iranian oil.

It is plausible that Gordji was involved with the terrorists and terrorist acts. Yet French security officials must have been aware of this much earlier and had chosen not to confront him. Thus to challenge Gordji at that particular time was more likely prompted by a political decision taken in the post-Irangate atmosphere and in the context of the changed Western attitude toward Iran.[70] Some terrorist experts have even disputed whether Gordji, and thus Iran, was responsible for the September attacks in Paris.[71]

During this affair, France ultimately chose a hard-line approach toward Iran. At first, however, the foreign ministry favored a less confrontational posture, having in mind the safety of French nationals in Iran. By contrast, the minister of the interior insisted that Gordji appear before the judge. These differences of view reflected the impact of France's domestic politics and the tensions inherent in its government of "co-habitation."

Franco-Iranian relations further deteriorated when France supported U.S. re-flagging operations and sent warships to the Persian Gulf. The crisis was finally defused in December 1987 when France and Iran agreed to end the war of the embassies. Following the resolution of the Gordji affair, France resumed talks with Iran in order to try gaining the release of its remaining three hostages in Lebanon.[72] Unlike in the past, in this round the foreign ministry's role was limited, and negotiations were handled by French security services. As part of the bargain, France expelled fourteen of the most active members of the Iranian opposition although, under French and international pressure, it had to readmit some of them.[73] This sign of French goodwill brought the release of the French hostages.

By then, the mood of confrontation produced by the Iran-Contra affair had subsided both in Iran and in the West. Iran's setbacks in the war with Iraq also prompted it to mend its Western ties. The Chirac government wanted to gain the release of French hostages on the eve of the presidential elections. Thus, conditions were ripe for a Franco-Iranian deal. As part of the arrangements, France paid Iran another $300 million installment on its $1 billion EURODIF debt and agreed to restore diplomatic ties. The release of the hostages did not help Chirac, however, who lost his presidential bid, but the new prime minister, Michel Rocard, declared that his government would abide by the agreement reached by its predecessor.[74]

On 16 June, diplomatic relations were restored. Shortly afterwards, France lifted the embargo imposed on the purchase of Iranian oil during the crisis of 1987. During the summer and fall of 1988, several Iranian officials visited France, and a number of trade agreements were signed.[75] The Iranian ambassador to France said that there might be scope for a "big boost" in trade.[76] Improvement in political relations, however, was marred by two factors: first was the fate of Annis Nacache, who was accused of attempting to kill the ex-Iranian prime minister, Shahpur

Bakhtiar. Iran maintained that the Rocard government had gone back on Chirac's promise to release him as a part of the deal over the French hostages in Lebanon. Second was France's concern that ties with Iran not affect relations with Iraq.[77]

Despite these difficulties, Franco-Iranian relations continued to develop steadily. On 5–6 February 1989, French foreign minister Roland Dumas visited Iran and a number of other high-level visits were planned.[78] Then the Rushdie affair exploded and halted progress. The French Foreign Ministry's attitude was measured, however, and Minister Roland Dumas opposed hasty action against Iran, saying that diplomacy is not a race against the clock.[79] But the momentum of the affair, the dynamics of intra-European politics, and public reaction in France forced the Foreign Ministry to toughen France's stand against Iran, although it was clear that this would undermine Iranian moderates.[80] Nevertheless, a break in diplomatic ties was averted.

In the future, Franco-Iranian relations will be affected most by the evolution of Iran's political scene. But France's other priorities, especially its deep involvement in Iraq, its support of Maronite forces in Lebanon, and its contributions to the build-up of Iraq's military-industrial base will limit the extent of improvement in Franco-Iranian relations even under the best of conditions.[81]

Iran and The Federal Republic of Germany

Under the Shah, U.S. and British supremacy in Iran kept West Germany from taking advantage of the positive German image in Iran—based on a limited history of contacts—although it did develop lucrative economic ties with Iran. Politically, German-Iranian ties were often strained because of the activities of anti-Shah Iranian students.

Until the outbreak of the Rushdie affair, Islamic Iran's relations with West Germany were good, for several reasons: (1) Islamic elements do not have a particular grievance against West Germany, such as having restored the Shah to power or having trained his secret service; (2) West Germany had shown patience toward Iran and taken a neutral stance on the Iran-Iraq war; and (3) Iran has needed an advanced country as an economic partner. Thus, West Germany has maintained a significant economic presence in Iran, by 1989 controlling 20 percent of Iran's export market.[82]

Politically, the Federal Republic has consistently argued in favor of keeping open lines of communication to Iran and has often served as an intermediary between Iran and the United States. In 1984, when Iran began its first experiment with pragmatic diplomacy, the German foreign minister, Hans Dietrich Genscher, visited Tehran in July. Iranian foreign minister Ali-Akbar Velayati visited West Germany on several occasions, including the spring and summer of 1987 when Iran was trying to gather support for its position on U.N. Resolution 598 and to prevent the imposition of a U.N. arms embargo. Unlike other Western countries, West Germany considered Iran's grievances sympathetically and, during the Security Council ne-gotiations, helped include language in Resolution 598 to make it more acceptable to Iran. The Federal Republic also reacted in a relatively low-key manner toward terrorism allegedly sponsored by Iran. As a result, it did not become a principal target of Iranian terrorism, and its last two hostages in Lebanon were released in September 1988, through Iranian mediation. The West German foreign minister attributed this Iranian action to a "long-standing German policy of maintaining good relations with Iran even while other major Western countries have had severe problems with Tehran."[83] As in the past, however, the activities of Iranian op-position groups in West Germany and public criticism of Iran's human rights record have strained bilateral relations without causing permanent damage.[84]

After the cease-fire in the Gulf war, West German-Iranian relations seemed to be improving rapidly. On 27 November 1988, the West German foreign minister visited Tehran, accompanied by sixty German businessmen. The Federal Republic indicated willingness to consider Iran's request for long-term credits, but it refused more ambitious requests, such as a German reconstruction fund for Iran.[85]

The Rushdie affair, however, caused a serious crisis in German-Iranian relations. In a dramatic departure from its past behavior, West Germany reacted harshly toward Iran and even threatened economic sanctions. But more than the Rushdie affair was involved in the German reaction. First, the foreign minister was angry with Iran over its behavior in the case of Dr. Danesh, an Iranian national and long-time resident of the Federal Republic, who had returned to Iran after the revolution and was rumored to have been killed. West German human rights activists, Iranian opposition groups, and even some members of the Bundestag had been pressing Minister Genscher on Danesh's fate. In contacts with Iranian authorities, Genscher was led to believe that Danesh was still alive and that something could be done for him, only to be told during his trip that Danesh had been executed. Whether the Iranians deliberately lied to the West German foreign minister, or whether they themselves had been misled by security officials the revelation was embarrassing to Genscher.[86] In addition, after revelations about the involvement of German firms in the development of Libyan chemical weapons, Foreign Minister Genscher's policy toward "outlaw" nations, such as Iran and Libya, had come under increasing attack. Reaction to the Rushdie affair was partly due to domestic political consid-erations and in part to counter charges of leniency in handling these states.

As a result, Iran and West Germany recalled their ambassadors, and there were calls in Iran to break diplomatic relations. Iran also was angered by disclosures about Germany's involvement in the development of Iraq's military capabilities. The Iranians also accused the Germans of having been implicated in U.S. espionage activities in Iran, acting as a U.S. satellite.[87] Neither side seemed to be willing to go as far as breaking diplomatic relations, however. The West Germans still hoped to become Iran's leading European economic partner, and Iran also needed German capital and know-how. However, the future of German-Iranian relations seemed more uncertain in the spring of 1989 than it did only a few months before. But their ultimate fate as with other European countries will depend on the outcome of Iran's power struggle and the evolution of Iran's relations with other industrial nations.

Conclusions

Relations between Iran and the nations of Western Europe have witnessed major departures from past patterns, but continuities have also existed. Iran has continued to use European states as counterweights to both superpowers, and it has tried to balance its relations with East and West European countries. Principal causes of strain have also remained Iran's human rights record and the activities of its opposition forces in Europe. Other tensions in Iranian-West European relations have had more basic causes, some of which predate the Iranian revolution, especially Iran's competitive potential. The growing importance of the Arab states for West Europeans, itself a result of the oil revolution of 1973 and the intricate web of Arab-European economic and financial ties, has also affected West Europe's relations with Iran. Because of these ties, European countries have not been willing to respond even to Iran's just grievances, such as Iraqi aggression. Should this European attitude continue, it will limit the extent of improvement in Iran's relations with major West European powers. Nevertheless, the determining factors would be the evolution of Iran's internal politics, its willingness to abandon the subversive dimensions of its foreign policy, and developments in East-West and intra-European relations.

9. Iran, East Asia, and the Pacific

Historical Background

Historically, Iran's longest-standing relationship with an East Asian state has been with China, with which it has had political and cultural ties, albeit with periods of long interruptions, for two thousand years.[1]

Iran has also interacted with Southeast Asia for several hundred years. Iranian merchants, sailors, and religious men were in contact with Indonesia from at least the fourteenth century, A.D.[2] And Iranian religious leaders played an important role in spreading Islam in that area.[3] The same has been true of Iran's relations with Thailand (Siam), and Malaysia.[4]

Relations with Japan are of a more recent origin. The first official contact took place in 1863, when Japan sent an envoy by the name of Yoshida to Iran, accompanied by an interpreter and four businessmen, to sign a friendship treaty.[5] Because of the lack of political leadership in Iran, these contacts were not pursued. But for many decades, Iranian reformists concerned about their country's decline looked to Japan as a model of progress. Japan's defeat of Russia in 1905 enhanced its image, puncturing the myth of European invincibility and encouraging nationalist movements in Asia. In Iran, it heartened the constitutionalists.[6]

Nevertheless, for most of the eighteenth and nineteenth century, Iran's relations with East Asia were either interrupted or remained limited, although there was some similarity of political and economic circumstances. During the nineteenth century, Iran and China both went through a period of decline; were penetrated by competing foreign powers, and lost their political independence. In 1906, Iran had its constitutional revolution, and China followed suit in 1912. During the 1920s, both countries experienced significant social, economic, and political changes.

During the 1920s and 1930s, after Iran's domestic scene stabilized and in the context of its policy of having friendly ties with Asian countries, Iran established diplomatic ties with Japan and China.[7] Relations with other East Asian countries had to wait because most of them were under colonial rule. There was some progress in Sino-Iranian and Iran-Japan relations during this period. Iran and Japan established direct telegraphic and shipping lines, and on 18 October 1939 they signed a friendship treaty. During World War II, Japanese propaganda tried to mobilize Iranian sympathy and support by promoting the idea of Asian solidarity. The Allied invasion of Iran in 1941 interrupted Japanese-Iranian relations, which were only resumed in 1955. During the late 1940s and throughout the 1950s, Japan was preoccupied with internal political reform and economic reconstruction, while Iran struggled with political instability and financial difficulties. These circumstances limited the scope of their relations. Nevertheless, in the late 1950s, a number of high level visits and the signing of economic and cultural cooperation agreements paved the way for the expansion of relations.[8] In the late 1960s, Japan emerged as a major economic power, and Iran's political and financial conditions improved. Together they opened the way for greater Iranian-Japanese cooperation.[9]

The oil revolution of the 1970s and Japan's energy dependency created new incentives—indeed imperatives—for expanded Japanese-Iranian cooperation. Japan was anxious to secure reliable sources of long-term oil supplies, and Iran craved Japanese technology. This complimentarity of economic needs marked the beginning of extensive Iranian-Japanese economic cooperation based on the long-term exchange of Iranian oil for Japan's assistance in Iran's industrial development, best symbolized by the $4 billion petrochemical complex built by the Japanese in Bandar Shahpur (Khomeini).[10]

Although by 1978, Iran was supplying only 2 percent of Japan's oil needs via the Western consortium, it was negotiating for direct sales of its oil and was seeking Japanese help in setting up industries which would enable it in the future to export more semi-finished goods to Japan.[11]

Meanwhile, post-World War II developments in Iran and China resulted in another long period of estrangement. The Chinese communist victory led to the establishment of the People's Republic of China (PRC); the U.S. break in relations with the new government; the creation of a rival Chinese nationalist regime in Taiwan; and the Sino-Soviet alliance. In Iran, the Soviet security and political threat led to closer U.S.-Iranian relations. Given its fears of the Soviet Union, Tehran was concerned at the communist victory in China and the Sino-Soviet alliance. Thus, following the lead of the United States, Iran withheld recognition from the PRC until 1971.[12] China's revolutionary activities in the Third World further contributed to the Sino-Iranian estrangement.

By the early 1960s, the Sino-Soviet rift began to alter the context of Sino-Iranian relations. Despite some improvement in relations, the Soviet Union remained Iran's main security concern. Thus, as two countries bordering the hostile Soviet superpower, China and Iran developed an important common strategic interest. The Sino-Soviet rift also enhanced the Soviet interest in the stability of its southern borders and hence in better relations with Iran, and Iran developed an interest in the continuation of Sino-Soviet differences. Now, China became interested in limiting Soviet influence in Iran, although the impact of the new geopolitical realities was not felt immediately in Sino-Iranian relations.

For most of the 1960s, China remained in ideological competition with both U.S. capitalist "imperialism" and Soviet "social imperialism." It offered its own version of socialism as the ideal model for Third World countries and warned them against Soviet and American hegemonism. The Iranian regime—with its U.S. alliance and willingness to accommodate the Soviet Union—remained a target of Chinese criticism. Chinese commentary accused it of suppressing its workers, peasants, and revolutionary intellectuals, and characterized the Shah's regime as meekly subservient to U.S. imperialism, despite pretensions of reform and independence. And it predicted that the Iranian people would destroy the reactionary regime.[13]

Ideological differences notwithstanding, developments in South Asia, such as Soviet-Indian cooperation, Sino-Indian clashes in 1962, and the Indo-Pakistan war of 1965 caused other common concerns for Iran and China over Pakistan's security and over the Soviet challenge to the region.

Nevertheless, the reestablishment of relations between the two had to await a change in U.S. policy. But Sino-Iranian contacts had started by 1965.[14] The change in U.S. policy happened in 1971. And on 17 August 1971, a Sino-Iranian bilateral agreement on recognition and the establishment of diplomatic relations was announced.

During the 1970s, regional developments such as the Indo-Pakistan War of 1971, the Soviet-Indian treaty of friendship, and increased Soviet naval power in the Indian Ocean intensified Sino-Iranian security concerns and drew them closer while at the same time Chinese support for subversive leftist groups such as the Dhofari rebels in Oman strained their relations. Nevertheless, as China grew more concerned with the Soviet challenge in South Asia and more interested in Iran as a buffer to Soviet influence, it ended its support to the rebels in 1974.

Iran's increasing economic, financial, and military potential also led China to reassess its value as a counter-balance to Indian and Soviet power in South Asia. China viewed with favor Iran's regional policy of mediating between India and Pakistan and between Pakistan and Afghanistan, plus Iranian efforts to reduce Afghanistan's dependence on the Soviet Union. The Chinese commended Iran's support for the so-called united struggle against big-power hegemonism, its efforts to strengthen and develop relations with the countries in South Asia, and its increase in defense capability.[15] Despite growing common strategic interests, however, during the 1970s Sino-Iranian economic relations remained limited.[16]

Meanwhile, during the 1960s and 1970s, Iran established diplomatic ties with a large number of other East Asian countries.[17] Political, strategic, and economic considerations lay behind this policy of opening to Asia. Iran was concerned about the security of the sea lanes through which its oil had to flow, and its development plans required access to export markets and raw materials.[18] And, as an emerging Asian power, Iran felt the need to increase its international presence.

Iran's new Asian orientation was received favorably in the region, where its economic potential and its value as an economic and trading partner were recognized. Iran's eastward-looking policy in the 1970s also led it to increase its contacts with Australia and New Zealand. The Shah visited both countries, and he included Australia in his vision of an Asian common market.[19]

The Post-Revolution Period

Since the revolution, Iran has maintained its best and most extensive relations in East Asia with China, which has been appealing to the Islamic regime for several reasons. China has had a genuinely fundamental socioeconomic and political revolution. It successfully defied the United States for more than two decades, and it later took on the Soviet Union, as well. Despite its defiance of the superpowers, China succeeded in achieving some degree of economic, military, and technological self-sufficiency. Although still far behind advanced industrial countries, China has become a major power, at least in Asia. And, for a long time, China championed Third World causes.

Iran aspires to the same revolutionary goals.[20] Furthermore, China provided Iran with an alternative to the superpowers—an alternative which it has used in a way reminiscent of the third-power strategy. Revolutionary Iran's desire to reduce its technological dependence on the West, plus its shift of emphasis from the Shah's infatuation with Western technology to what in Third World jargon is called "appropriate" technology has also increased the opportunities for greater Sino-Iranian economic cooperation, a development which has not escaped China's attention. China has been even more concerned about Iran's political evolution, especially the possibility of significant Soviet political and economic inroads in Iran.

The Soviets' invasion of Afghanistan and the prospect that they would set up a puppet government in Kabul worried the Chinese. If successful, these developments would have put Pakistan under great pressure, forcing it to accommodate to Moscow. Soviet domination of Iran, especially if it were combined with Soviet control of Afghanistan, would have further damaged China's strategic interests in South Asia. A pro-Soviet Iran could cooperate with India, further pressuring Pakistan and thus enhancing its fears of Soviet encirclement.

Despite these considerations, no major steps for the expansion of Sino-Iranian relations were taken before 1984. Iran had internal political problems and was preoccupied with the war with Iraq. More important, until early 1983 pro-Soviet factions within the Iranian leadership were in the ascendancy. As a result, neither Iran nor China was anxious for closer relations. By 1984, however, the revolutionary regime seemed to have consolidated its hold on power. Although it had not achieved a victory, the war seemed under control. Moreover, the moderate factions had asserted their influence, and, with the blessing of the Ayatollah Khomeini, Iran had embarked on a policy of expanding its international ties. As a result, in July 1985, the speaker of the parliament, Rafsanjani, visited China, during which, he discussed issues related to the expansion of bilateral trade and economic cooperation.[21] Rafsanjani also emphasized the vast potential that existed for economic cooperation between Iran and China, once Iran was freed from the burden of the war with Iraq.

Iran was also interested in Chinese military supplies because of its difficulties in obtaining military equipment from Western, Soviet, or other sources. Iran did obtain some Chinese arms, but the magnitude of the trade is not clear,[22] although it reportedly included missiles.[23] The supply of Chinese Silkworm missiles to Iran, which was first reported during the summer of 1987 during the Persian Gulf crisis, became highly controversial and strained Sino-American relations. The United States threatened to revise its policy of supplying China with sophisticated technology if the arms supply to Iran continued.[24]

The U.S. attitude faced China with a delicate dilemma. On the one hand China could not afford to antagonize the Americans, because of its need for U.S. technology and capital. On the other hand, the Chinese were aware of the dangers of leaving Iran isolated, which could force it into the Soviet orbit. China faced a similar dilemma in 1987–88 regarding a possible U.N.-imposed arms embargo against Iran, following the passage of Security Council Resolution 598. China did not want the Soviet Union to appear to be Iran's only supporter in the council. Thus it too adopted the position that, before an arms embargo were agreed to, the U.N. secretary general should be given more time to find a diplomatic solution. Although this position put China at loggerheads with the United States and aggravated their other disagreements, Beijing refused to go along with the embargo.

The Iran-Iraq War complicated China's relations with Iran and caused a contradiction in its strategic and commercial interests. China has a keen interest in the Arab world, including Iraq.[25] Thus it has tried to maintain friendly ties with it and other Arab states, including supplying weapons—such as the controversial sale of ballistic missiles to Saudi Arabia. Of course, China's desire to counterbalance the Soviets in the Arab world has also been an important part of its policy.[26] If Arab-Iranian animosity had deepened, leading, for example, to the Saudis' use of Chinese missiles against Iran, Sino-Iranian relations would have suffered, thus damaging China's strategic interests in Southwest Asia. The end of the Iran-Iraq war and gradual Arab-Iranian reconciliation, however, at least temporarily resolved this dilemma. During the summer and fall of 1988 and into 1989, Sino-Iranian contacts increased and the two sides reached a number of economic agreements.[27] It was also reported that Iran might buy 100 Chinese-made jet fighters.[28]

China's strategic interest in Iran has largely been a function of its concerns over Soviet intentions and its regional differences with India. It is unclear whether China's interest will remain as high after an improvement in Sino-Soviet relations. China might not be as concerned with preventing Soviet inroads in Iran or in keeping it as a buffer against Soviet penetration of the Persian Gulf. Similarly, a change in Iran's orientation, in either a decidedly pro-Soviet or pro-Western direction, could diminish its interest in China. Improvement in Sino-Indian relations would also reduce Iran's value for China.[29]

It is likely that, for the foreseeable future, both China and Iran will face some degree of Soviet competition, if not outright hostility, in their immediate surroundings. Thus some strategic understanding between China and Iran will continue to exist. Also, unless Iran were to become a Soviet client, it will always need a counterweight to Soviet power. Because it is unlikely that Iran will want to become again dependent on the United States, China will be appealing to Iran as a counterweight to both superpowers.

China's attitude toward Iran during the last several years, including the weapons sales and support in the U.N. Security Council, has generated a great deal of good will. In fact, during the visit of China's deputy foreign minister to Iran in August 1988, Speaker Rafsanjani remarked that China is a "true friend of Iran" and added that "China has been cooperative with Iran during the war and the resulting hardships.''[30] Further, to cement Sino-Iranian relations, Iran's president, Hodjat-al-Islam Ali Khamenei, visited China in May 1989.[31]

The potential for Sino-Iranian economic cooperation will remain considerable, particularly if China's modernization programs succeed and as Iran begins its post-war reconstruction. Thus barring some dramatic domestic changes in Iran and China and in regional politics, Sino-Iranian relations should develop along cooperative lines.

Meanwhile, since the revolution, Iran's economic and trade relations with Japan have continued. To begin with, Iran has needed long-term reliable customers for its oil. For a long time, Japan was the only country willing to enter into such long-term arrangements.[32] Japan has also held a long-term view of the relationship, and it has kept in mind future opportunities for expanded trade and economic relations with Iran. Japan has had a keen appreciation of Iran's geopolitical importance, considering it to be a key to Persian Gulf security and thus to Japan's energy security. This appreciation of Iran's geostrategic importance has been a major reason for Japan to be patient toward the Islamic regime.[33]

Furthermore, Japan is the only country, outside of the United States and Western Europe, with state-of-the-art technology and which, despite its close U.S. ties, is acceptable to the Iranian revolutionaries. And throughout the Iran-Iraq war, Japan was mindful of its long-term economic interests and adopted an essentially neutral position between the two combatants—occasionally even trying to mediate between them. For example, in July 1983 the Japanese foreign minister traveled to Baghdad and Tehran to explore ways of ending the Persian Gulf conflict peacefully.[34] Sensing the difficulties involved, however, Japan delicately abandoned these efforts. Despite this caution, at times Iran considered Japan's call for a peaceful solution to the war as Tokyo's siding with Iraq.

As in the case of Western Europe, U.S.-Iran tensions have spilled over onto Japanese-Iranian relations. For example, Japan's ability to maintain its neutral position in the war was severely tested during the U.S. military intervention in the Persian Gulf in 1987–88. As the United States sought support from its allies and U.S. congressional leaders argued that, because of their greater dependence on oil, the Europeans and Japanese should assume a larger part of the burden of maintaining Persian Gulf security. Japan had to develop an intricate economic package to help finance U.S. Gulf operations.[35] This Japanese participation undermined its image of neutrality in Iran. Washington also has periodically pressured Japan to stop buying Iranian oil, and from time to time, it has complied. For example, in 1987 Japan imposed a ceiling of 200,000 bpd on its purchase of Iranian oil which strained their bilateral relations and triggered Iranian complaints.[36] Dispute over the fate of the Bandar Khomeini petrochemical complex has been another source of tension. Despite these problems, Japan has remained a major trading partner of Iran.[37]

Politically, Japan has stayed on good terms with Iran and has often served as an intermediary between it and the United States during their long period of political estrangement. But the future of these relations remains uncertain as both sides appear to be reevaluating their relations. For Iran, in particular, Japan's attitude toward the completion of the Bandar Khomeini complex or finding a fair way to end this troubled partnership would be very important. For Japan, the most important test may become Iran's political moderation and its position on the oil prices as Japan will grow increasingly dependent on Persian Gulf oil in the 1990s and beyond.[38]

Several principles of Iran's foreign policy, such as the priority that it assigns to the expansion of ties with Islamic and Third World nations and its support for the enhancement of South-South cooperation, has kept Iran interested in South and Northeast Asian countries in the post-revolution period. Yet the revolutionary dimensions of Iran's foreign policy, particularly its desire to export its Islamic ideology, have hampered the expansion of ties with some of these countries. For example, Islam often has been a source of tension in Iran's relations with Malaysia and Indonesia because of their fear of the potentially destabilizing impact of Iranian ideology. These concerns have forced them to limit contacts with Iran despite their desire to avoid friction and to take advantage of economic and trade opportunities. Occasionally, they have complained of direct Iranian interference in their internal affairs through propaganda spread among their Muslim populations. Iran has responded that allegations of interference are imperialist propaganda aimed at undermining its friendly relations with these countries and preventing Islamic solidarity.[39]

On other occasions, other Iranian officials, especially those at the Foreign Ministry, have acknowledged that the activities of certain Iranian elements have damaged ties.[40] Since 1984, the Iranian Foreign Ministry has tried to undo the damage, and as a result, official contacts between Iran and East Asian countries have increased.[41] Partly because of Iran's financial difficulties, trade and economic relations have remained limited, although Iran has become a significant trading partner for some of them.[42] It is, for example, a principal purchaser of Thailand's rice. Economic and trade relations with South Korea are also reasonably extensive. Many South Koreans still work in Iran, and the tone of diplomatic contacts has also remained good.[43] With its preoccupation—to avoid dependence on Western countries and to diversify its sources of military and other supplies—the potential for greatly expanded and more varied economic and technical cooperation between Iran and several East Asian countries remains promising.[44]

A significant departure from the past has been Iran's ties with North Korea. Indeed, during the Iran-Iraq war North Korea became one of Iran's principal sources of military supplies. The tone of political exchanges between Iran and North Korea has also been much warmer than those with other East Asian countries.[45] It is likely that North Korea will become more involved in Iran's post-war military and economic reconstruction. Political relations were also further cemented when Iran's President Khamenei visited North Korea in May 1989. Also, in a similar departure from the past, Iran has expanded contacts with Laos and Vietnam.[46]

Iran's relations with Australia and New Zealand have been limited mostly to the purchase of agricultural products. Diplomatic relations with Australia were downgraded when it recalled its ambassador from Tehran during the American hostage crisis, and they were normalized only in the summer of 1985.[47] Iran has been considering opening an embassy in Wellington. Both island countries remain potentially attractive economic partners because of their advanced technological and industrial development.

Conclusions

The expansion of Iran's relations with East Asia have resulted from changes in Iran's world outlook, especially its Third World dimension, tensions in its relations with the West and at times with the Soviet Union, and its desire to avoid becoming dependent on a few economic partners. This expansion also reflects the growing economic and technological potential of these countries. The eastward thrust of Iran's diplomacy, however, predates the revolution. The post-revolution development of this policy is indeed another indication of a significant degree of continuity in Iranian foreign policy.

10. Iran and the Third World

Historical Background

Even under the Shah, Iran's foreign policy had a strong Third World focus, partly because of a sense of solidarity which was, itself, the result of similar experiences. Thus, during the 1950s and 1960s, Iran was active within the United Nations and worked to accelerate the process of decolonization.[1] Iran's Third World focus also derived from its desire to enhance its international presence and, during the 1970s, from a number of strategic and economic factors as well.

During this last period, Africa became a special focus of Iran's diplomacy.[2] Its principal political and strategic concerns were to prevent Soviet inroads in the continent, the spread of radical ideas, or the establishment of radical governments. Given Iran's preoccupation with the security of its oil routes, it was particularly concerned about the security of the Red Sea and the Horn of Africa.

Since the 1960s, some developments in the Red Sea region had been disturbing to Iran, including the creation in 1967 of a Marxist, pro-Soviet government in Aden, the forging of close relations between Somalia and the Soviet Union, and the building of a Soviet naval base in Berbera. Although Somalia later changed sides, this step was more than balanced by the *coup d'etat* in Addis Ababa and the establishment of a pro-Soviet government. Iran was also concerned about Libya's efforts to destabilize the Muslim African countries.

In order to counter radical challenges, Iran actively supported moderate forces through political, economic, and occasionally military assistance.[3] Yet because of its ambitions to become an Indian Ocean power, it also developed extensive relations with South Africa, including the supply of Iranian oil—thereby undermining its image in Africa and limiting the scope of Iranian cooperation with most other African countries.

For reasons of distance, cultural differences, and the lack of significant common interests or serious conflicts, Iran's relations with Latin America were late in developing. An exception was Venezuela, where the countries' common concern over gaining greater control over their oil resources had led to contacts and some cooperation by the late 1940s. During the 1970s, the Shah established diplomatic relations with Brazil, Argentina, Venezuela, and Mexico in order to enhance Iran's international presence. In 1975, he established diplomatic relations with Cuba, as part of Tehran's national independent policy and its desire to expand ties with all countries, regardless of their social and political systems. Relations were broken in 1976, however, when the Cuban president, Fidel Castro, met in Moscow with the leaders of the outlawed communist party of Iran. This meeting was just the triggering event, given Iran's concern over Cuba's growing activities in the Middle East and Africa in support of radical forces. These activities included Cuba's providing assistance to anti-Shah elements through its Middle East allies, such as the PLO.[4]

Post-Revolution Period

The principal tenets of Iran's revolutionary ideology have included solidarity with Third World countries, support for all the oppressed and dispossessed peoples of the world, and the enhancement of South-South relations. As a result, there has been a marked emphasis in Iran's diplomacy on relations with these countries. In addition, both short- and long-term economic considerations and political factors have contributed to the enhancement of Iran's interests in relations with them. For example, Iran has systematically tried to reduce its technological and economic dependence on great powers and has sought to diversify its sources of supplies. The fact that in the last decade many Third World countries have achieved a significant degree of industrial and technological sophistication has facilitated the implementation of Iran's diplomacy.

Furthermore, political difficulties that have developed in Iran's relations with the great powers have forced it to turn to Third World nations. Relations with Latin America provide some good examples. For example, Iran has reached extensive agreements with Brazil, including help in industrial projects. Relations may possibly expand into the military area.[5] Trade with Argentina has expanded largely because Iran has stopped purchasing U.S. grain.

U.S.-Iranian hostility has also contributed to the forging of close ties between Iran, Cuba, and Nicaragua, marked by frequent visits by Cuban, Nicaraguan, and Iranian officials to each other's capitals.[6] These relations are also interesting because they reflect the ideological flexibility of both sides. Both Latin countries espouse Marxist ideology and are heavily dependent on the Soviet Union—positions which are anathema to Iran's declared policies of self-reliance and strict non-alignment. Meanwhile, despite the fact that the Islamic regime decries Marxism, Castro has supported the Iranian revolution, primarily because of Iran's anti-Americanism. Initially, Cuba must also have noted that the Iranian communists supported Khomeini, hoping, like the Soviets, that religion could play a progressive role and thus permit an alliance between socialism and progressive religious movements.[7]

The extent of Cuba's influence in Iran is difficult to assess. Some analysts believe that it may have helped to train the Iranian Revolutionary Guards. Cuba does have extensive connections in the Middle East, especially with Libya and the PLO, both of which have ties with Iran, and it may have used them to infiltrate Iran. At times, however, Cuba's close ties with Iraq have strained Iranian-Cuban relations, although Cuba has tried to overcome this handicap by helping Iran in the Non-Aligned Movement and in the United Nations.[8]

With both Cuba and Nicaragua, Iran's sense of revolutionary solidarity, shared animosity toward the United States, and a mutual self-perception as revolutions under siege because of superpower pressure has overcome other differences.[9] Iran has provided Nicaragua with oil on credit terms, and there were rumors that some North Korean arms reached Nicaragua through Iran (Iranian authorities denied these reports).

Yet despite greater interaction with certain Latin American states, Africa has been the special focus of Iran's diplomacy in the Third World. Added to the Shah's motives has been the existence of large Muslim populations in Africa and Iran's perception that it could find a receptive audience for its revolutionary Islamic ideology. As a result of its active African diplomacy, Iran's relations on the African continent have expanded, it has opened several new embassies, and it has signed agreements on economic and cultural cooperation with a number of countries.[10]

Yet the record of Iran's African diplomacy has, at best, been mixed, when judged in terms of its success in improving Iran's image, in gaining support on such issues as the Iran-Iraq war, and in spreading ideology. On the one hand, Iran's image has been helped by its severing of ties with South Africa; by its unconditional support for African national liberation movements such as the African National Council (ANC) and the South West Africa People's Organization (SWAPO); and by its financial assistance to a number of African countries, such as Zimbabwe, Tanzania, and Sierra Leone. Moreover, many Africans have been inspired by the fact that Iran has defied the superpowers and, despite their pressures, has survived.[11] On the other hand, however, some African countries find troublesome Iran's efforts to spread its Islamic ideology. Some, such as Senegal, have even broken diplomatic relations with Iran over this issue. Other differences, including divergent positions on relations with the West and on the Iran-Iraq war, have been even more responsible for such ruptures.[12] And even those African countries that do not feel particularly threatened by Iran's Islamic message have found aspects of its ideology distasteful.[13]

For Iran's part, its principal interest in Africa, especially for the long term, mirrors that of the Shah: the importance of African states as sources of raw materials and potential export markets. Islamic Iran claims that its interest, unlike that of the great powers, is not exploitative. Iran has also been interested in Africa as a potential market for its oil and its burgeoning arms industry. For example, in January 1989, Iran took part in the International Arms and Safety Equipment Exhibition held in Gabon and displayed some of its domestically produced military equipment.[14] Nevertheless, Iran's financial difficulties have limited its ability to increase its influence or spread its views in Africa because many countries have largely seen Iran as a possible source of aid.

Conclusions

The Third World focus of Iranian diplomacy reflects a continuation and enhancement of a trend that had been set by the 1960s, as well as the impact of Iran's new global vision and its self-image as a champion of the oppressed. It also reflects a broader trend—the emergence of better opportunities for intra-Third World economic cooperation—because of the industrial development of a number of Third World countries. This focus is likely to survive even a change of regime in Tehran. However, depending on Iran's political developments and those in the Third World, its intensity may diminish, and the identity of Iran's favored partners may also change.

11. Iran and International Organizations

Iran's policy toward international organizations provides a good illustration of the process of adjustment in Iran's diplomatic relations to the international political system. Historically, as a small and weak country faced by encroaching great powers, Iran put great store in the international organizations as a means of protecting its interests. Like most small states, at first it did not fully realize that these organizations had reflected global power realities and thus had been incapable of acting independently from the requirements imposed by these realities.[1] The League of Nation's failure to prevent World War II dispelled many illusions about international organizations and thus, like other small states, Iran approached the United Nations with greater realism.

The Charter of the United Nations took a more realistic approach to facts of global power than had the Covenant of the League, dramatically reflected in the Charter's granting veto power in the Security Council to its five permanent members. Yet, despite its built-in inequalities, the U.N. system was, and is, the only instrument through which small states could voice their grievances, express their views, and seek redress.

Since the creation of the United Nations, both small and large powers have applied its principles selectively and whenever expedient, thus weakening it and undermining its efficiency. Meanwhile, the U.N. system has become an easy target of criticism for big and small countries alike. The big powers, especially those of the West, have complained about the so-called tyranny of the majority, referring to the predominance of Third World nations in the U.N. General Assembly. And the small states have complained about the domination of the Security Council by the larger powers and their widespread disregard for General Assembly resolutions.

At first, however, the smaller states welcomed the creation of the United Nations. Iran was among the original signatories of the U.N. Charter at San Francisco and its early experience with the United Nations was positive. During the Azerbaijan crisis of 1945–46, the United Nations provided an important venue for Iran to press for the withdrawal of Soviet troops. Within a few years, however, Iran gained a different experience, as international organizations—including the United Nations—proved ineffective in vindicating its claims against Britain over the dispute about the nationalization of the Anglo-Persian Oil Company.

As the decades of the 1950s, 1960s, and 1970s progressed, Iran's faith in the United Nations as a component of its security policy declined. It relied instead on its alliance with the United States and, increasingly, on building its own military capabilities. Nevertheless, under the Shah, Iran remained committed—at least rhetorically—to the U.N. Charter and to its principles, as an important part of the ideological framework of Iranian foreign policy. Throughout the 1960s and the 1970s, Iran remained active within the United Nations and its affiliated agencies, although it did have problems with parts of the U.N. system, especially with the Human Rights Commission, which probed into the Iranian record.

Post-Revolution Era

The Islamic regime has taken a different view of international organizations. According to Iran's Muslim revolutionaries, the existing organizations are part of the unjust international order dominated by the "arrogant" powers. To prove their case, Iranian officials have focused on the greater powers' veto in the U.N. Security Council. For example, Foreign Minister Ali-Akbar Velayati spoke out against the United Nations for having accepted the balance of power rather than the rule of law as the basis for safeguarding security. According to Velayati, this fact is reflected in the U.N. Charter, which has an unjust tendency to preserve the interests of big powers. Those with veto power want to carry their influence into the General Assembly by employing financial leverage.[2]

Iranian revolutionaries also believe that most international rules were laid down by the dominant powers without concern for the interests of small states and without taking into account the latter's legal and philosophical traditions.[3] Thus Iran has argued that, in many instances, other countries cannot be bound by these rules. For example, when attacked on its human rights record at the U.N. Commission on Human Rights, the Islamic regime has responded that it abides by its own Islamic code of justice and is not bound by the tenets of the Universal Declaration of Human Rights. This stance has not meant total rejection of the Declaration's principles, however. Rather, Iranian officials suggested that the principles should be amended on the basis of Islamic law.[4]

The Islamic regime was confirmed in its belief that the international system is inherently unfair because of its experience with international organizations throughout the Iran-Iraq war. The Iranians were especially piqued by the unwillingness of the U.N. Security Council to condemn Iraq's aggression and to call for the withdrawal of Iraqi troops from Iranian territory. Also frustrating was the council's failure to condemn Iraqi attacks on shipping in the Persian Gulf while condemning Iran for retaliating, and by its unwillingness to condemn Iraq's use of chemical weapons. This attitude was particularly difficult for Iran to accept because it had rightly been condemned and punished for its violation of international regulations.

Yet despite its negative view of the nature of international organizations and its disappointing experience, Iran did not withdraw from the United Nations or affiliated agencies. The same pragmatic streak in Iranian foreign policy which helped it maintain reasonably friendly relations with a large number of countries, despite deep ideological differences, also argued against its full-scale defection from international organizations. Indeed, the regime has gradually come to appreciate the potential usefulness of these institutions. Even Iran's foreign minister has acknowledged the relatively constructive role of the United Nations and its importance in certain complicated situations in the world today.[5] As a result, Iran has continued limited cooperation with such organizations as WHO, UNDP, UNHCR, UNESCO, and the United Nations Economic and Social Commission for Asia and the Pacific (ESCAP).[6]

In general, in recent years Iran has concluded that, to help reform international organizations, it must work within the system, although its contributions so far have been limited. In fact, they have mostly consisted of exhortation at plenary meetings. Even here, statements by Iran's representatives have increasingly come to resemble standard Third World language, except for harsh criticism of the U.N. Security Council and its attitude toward the Iran-Iraq war. For example, Iran's representatives at the IMF and World Bank meetings have criticized the limited role of Third World nations in these institutions, and the imposition of burdens of adjustment on them that are more onerous than the requirements levied on more powerful countries.[7]

There has been nothing especially militant about these statements. In fact, the Shah's representatives had made harsher statements about the inequities of the international economic system and its institutions. Furthermore, the view that the World Bank and the IMF have essentially served the interests of Western industrialized countries is pervasive in the Third World and among Western critics of these organizations. In the words of one Third World expert, the principal function of the World Bank is the promotion of " . . . capitalist development in the Third World countries in such a way as to make those countries as receptive, as safe, and as profitable as possible. . . . "[8] Nevertheless, even in regard to the World Bank and the IMF, Iran appeared to be adopting a more positive approach which could eventually lead to the renewed involvement of these institutions in Iran's economic reconstruction and development.

On some occasions, however, the comments of Iranian officials about international organizations have betrayed naivete. When, in 1984, the United States decided to leave UNESCO because of disagreements with its secretary general, the Senegalese Amadou M'bow, the Iranian minister of education sent a message of congratulation to the secretary general and said that U.S. withdrawal was a sign of decline in the power of "oppressor world powers." He expressed hope that "all oppressor world powers would be expelled from international organizations and forums in order that the smaller nations would be able to operate in a free and independent atmosphere." He added that those member countries that obviously wish to secure their autonomy for voting in such organizations will certainly compensate for any financial needs of UNESCO, thereby preventing any adverse effects upon the operations of the organizations.[9] Of course, the minister did not say how small states would be able to compensate for the loss of the contributions of the big powers, especially if this were to apply to all international organizations.

On another occasion, at a meeting of the Food and Agriculture Organization

(FAO), Iran's minister of agriculture urged the Islamic countries to expand the exchange of agricultural products in order to reduce dependency on the superpowers. Yet his statement ignored the fact that none of the Muslim countries is among the principal producers of grain and other agricultural products. Further, one of the superpowers, the Soviet Union, is partly dependent on grain imports, and the principal grain exporters include Australia, Canada, and Argentina, none of whom are superpowers.[10]

The Non-Aligned Movement and the Organization of the Islamic Conference

In a significant departure from the Shah's policy, Islamic Iran joined the Non-Aligned Movement (NAM) and has since consistently supported strengthening it.[11]

There is a contradiction, however, between the Islamic and Third World dimensions of Iran's ideology, reflected in its approach toward the NAM. The Ayatollah Khomeini did not think much of the non-aligned countries. Other Iranian leaders, however, have understood the importance of the NAM in the context of Iran's efforts to reach out to Third World nations. The Iranian regime has resolved these contradictions by urging the movement to expel those members who are not truly non-aligned.[12] In sum, Iran's impact on the NAM has been minimal, largely because of other members' fears about its efforts to spread its militant ideology, plus concern over its image as a sponsor of terrorism.

Organization of the Islamic Conference (OIC)

The one organization within which Iran should have felt at home is the Organization of the Islamic Conference (OIC). Yet because of the OIC's unwillingness to condemn Iraq's invasion, its political domination by Saudi Arabia, and, at the time, Iran's provocative attitude, the Islamic regime's relations with the organization has been troubled. In 1986, for example, the OIC insisted on holding its summit conference in Kuwait, despite Iranian opposition. Iran argued that holding the summit in Kuwait was unsafe because of its proximity to the war zone, and pro-Iranian groups in Lebanon threatened retaliation. Yet Iran was unsuccessful, and even Syria attended, underscoring Tehran's defeat. Later, during the OIC's 1988 meeting in Amman, Iran's representative walked out because he was mistreated by Jordanian authorities upon his arrival and later was not allowed to read a message from Foreign Affairs Minister Velayati on the massacre of thousands of Iraqi Kurds by chemical warfare. Instead, the OIC praised the Iraqi regime for its war against Iran and encouraged the United States to exert more pressure to make Iran accept U.N. Resolution 598.[13]

This experience was not much different from Iran's past troubled relations with the OIC. Its origins lay in the alliance between the Shah of Iran and King Faisal of Saudi Arabia against the influence of Nasser's Egypt. But in the 1970s—as Nasser was removed from the scene, and as Iran and Saudi Arabia became rivals for regional influence—Iran lost some interest in the OIC. Also, as countries such as Libya tried to gain influence in the organization and to use it for their own ends, Iran's disillusionment intensified. In 1974, the Shah refused to take part in the first Islamic summit in Lahore because of Qadhafi's presence.

Iran's experience both in the pre- and post-revolutionary periods has reflected its basic handicap in interacting with and influencing the largely Sunni Muslim world. Nevertheless, despite its disappointments and tribulations, Iran has retained its membership in the OIC and has joined the Islamic Development Bank, which the Shah shunned. Following the cease-fire in the Iran-Iraq war and relative improvement in Arab-Iranian relations, OIC officials have expressed hope for better ties with Iran.

Conclusions

Despite its deep ideological mistrust of current international organizations, the requirements of international life have led Iran to bend its ideological beliefs and principles and to maintain its ties with international organizations. Thus, beneath the rhetoric, there has not been a drastic departure from the past pattern of Iran's interaction with these organizations.

12. Terrorism and Subversion
Impact on Foreign Policy

During the last ten years, the most significant departure both from Iran's own past pattern of behavior and from what could be characterized as normal state behavior has been its involvement in what is variously called subversion, terrorism, or the export of revolution. That Iran has been involved in all these activities cannot be denied. Its world view, along with its self-image as the vanguard of an Islamic revolution and defender of the rights of the oppressed, have provided the framework for Iranian behavior that many observers have viewed as subversive—although Iran has always emphatically denied wanting to export its revolution by the use of force, whether direct or indirect.

But legitimate questions need to be asked about the nature, magnitude, and record of Iran's subversive activities. For example, it is legitimate to ask whether all of Iran's efforts to spread its political message can be strictly characterized as subversive. And if the answer is positive, it is also legitimate to ask whether similar activities by other states should not also be characterized as subversive.

Three further issues should be addressed—namely: (1) How have Iran's subversive and terrorist activities been affected by its internal political evolution, including differences of opinion within its leadership, and by the regime's gradual and painful adjustment to the international political system? (2) How has this aspect of Iran's external behavior fit within the overall pattern of its foreign policy and to what extent has it helped or hindered the achievement of its diplomatic goals? And (3) to what extent has Iran itself become the target of what could be called retaliatory subversion and terrorism?

Iran and Terrorism

Iran has been responsible for, or implicated in, several acts which could unconditionally be qualified as terrorist. The most significant of these have been the taking hostage of 52 diplomats and employees of the U.S. embassy in Tehran on November 4, 1979; the truck bombings of the U.S. embassy in Beirut on April 18, 1983, and of the U.S. Marine barracks in Beirut on October 23, 1983; and the attempted truck bombing of the U.S. embassy compound in Kuwait City in December 1983. During 1989, there was also suspicion that Iran was implicated in the bombing of Pan Am flight 103 over Scotland on December 20, 1988.[1] In addition, Iran has been implicated in a series of kidnappings of Western nationals in Lebanon.

Iran's responsibility for the hostage-taking of the U.S. diplomats is beyond doubt. There is strong circumstantial evidence that it was implicated in the planning of the truck bombings in Lebanon, although at the time several Iranian officials denied any responsibility and condemned these terrorist acts.[2] However, the available circumstantial evidence in the case of the bombings and the nature of the resolution of some of the hostage issues—such as the freeing of a number of French hostages in 1985 and 1987 in the context of a political and financial deal with Iran—support the thesis of a significant Iranian role in the hostage-taking and terrorist operations in Lebanon.

At times, statements by some Iranian officials have also indicated Iran's involvement, such as during intra-Shi'a fighting in Lebanon in 1988 and the Syrian-Iranian disagreement over the deployment of Syrian troops in Beirut's southern suburbs. At the time, Iran's deputy foreign minister stated that Iran would agree to Syrian intervention, provided the hostage situation were resolved "in a way that serves the objectives for which they were kidnapped."[3]

With this background, however, it is important to try to understand how these operations were related to Iran's domestic political conditions, especially to the power struggles among its different factions. As discussed earlier, the U.S. hostage crisis was directly linked to Iran's domestic politics and the post-revolution struggle for dominance among its diverse political tendencies. The hostage crisis reflected Iran's political chaos and was aimed as much at undermining the government of Prime Minister Mehdi Bazargan as at harming the United States and American interests in Iran. Indeed, this crisis—at least in its initial stage—cannot be characterized as a terrorist act undertaken by the Iranian government of Prime Minister Bazargan because its sanction was clearly lacking. Yet after Bazargan fell and the Ayatollah Khomeini sanctioned the operation, the Iranian government became directly and unequivocally involved.

The culmination of the crisis was also inextricably linked to Iran's internal power struggle. The crisis did not serve any clearly defined foreign policy goal, but Khomeini and a variety of Islamic and leftist groups did use it to undermine U.S. prestige and regional influence. Thus, in this sense, it became linked to Iran's long-term goals of challenging the superpowers and eliminating their influence from the Islamic world.

Iran's involvement in terrorist actions in Lebanon and Kuwait against U.S. and European nationals and interests could be more directly linked to its foreign policy objectives and the state of its relations with different countries. For example, Iran's involvement in terrorist activities in Lebanon against France and the United States was related to the Persian Gulf war and was a form of retaliation for French and American support for Iraq, as well as for their intervention in support of the Christian forces and Israel. These actions were also aimed at a more long-term objective that derived from Iran's ideological aspirations—namely, the spread of revolutionary Islam and the weakening of the influence of what it viewed as the arrogant powers. For example, by resorting to these acts, Iran hoped to eliminate U.S. and French influence from Lebanon and to create conditions for the establishment of an Islamic republic on its own model.

Iran's perceptions of the degree of public receptivity in Muslim countries to its revolutionary message and thus the prospects for a successful repetition of its own example have also played a role in its willingness to engage in such terrorist or subversive acts that it has judged likely to help speed the process of revolutionizing the Middle East. By the same token, Iran's failure to transform into concrete revolutionary action the vague sympathy that its revolution had generated among segments of Muslim populations, plus the effect of the containment policies of regional states and the great powers, contributed to its reassessment of the usefulness of such tactics as instruments of policy.

From the very beginning of the revolution, because of the lack of a clear center of decision making in Iran and the multiplicity of unofficial or semi-official revolutionary organizations, it has been difficult to pinpoint responsibility for the conduct of Iran's terrorist activities or to assess the degree to which they have enjoyed the support of principal figures within the Iranian leadership. Since 1984–85, however, when a moderate trend within the Iranian leadership asserted itself, there have been differences of opinion among leading figures. These have included the advisability of resorting to terrorist actions and of supporting extremist elements elsewhere in the Middle East, as well as the best approach to take in Lebanon. The existence of these divisions was illustrated when the leader of the less radical pro-Syrian Shi'a movement, AMAL, complained that the "woes afflicting Lebanon's Shi'ite community stemmed from conflict between the Iranian Foreign Ministry—headed by Ali-Akbar Velayati—and Mr. Mohtashemi's Interior Ministry."[4] Although referring to a later period, this complaint reflects a fact that had existed for some time. For example, before becoming the minister of interior, Mohtashemi was Iran's ambassador in Damascus and is strongly suspected of having been involved in planning the 1983 bombings in Lebanon.

Also, the disclosure of the secret U.S.-Iranian contacts and the Beirut kidnapping of three U.S. citizens in January 1987 were the work of Iranian radical factions, their Lebanese allies, and, according to some analysts, Syria—each for its own reasons. The Iranian radicals and their Lebanese allies wanted to undermine the moderates and their efforts at ending Iran's hostility with the United States, and in general, improving its relations with the West. For its part, Syria seems to have been angered at Western attacks on its own role in terrorism while dealing secretly with Iran.[5]

In like manner, the Iranian radicals manipulated the Rushdie affair in order to elicit the Ayatollah Khomeini's death sentence on Salman Rushdie (one of Iran's most flagrant departures from the established norms of international conduct); and they may have been involved in the Pan Am bombing, in cooperation with the radical Palestinian group headed by Ahmad Jibril (the Popular Front for the Liberation of Palestine, General Command). These events, too, related both to Iran's domestic power struggle and to the radicals' efforts to sabotage the moderates' policy of lessening tensions between Iran and the West.

The moderate elements, by contrast, have not only tried gradually to disengage Iran from terrorist actions, but they have also occasionally helped to resolve incidents in which Iran was not even implicated. This happened with the hijacking of TWA flight 847 in June 1985. It is generally agreed that Iran did not have any role in the conception and execution of the plan, but it may have played a significant role in ending the hijacking. The United States has said that it had "no direct evidence of Iran being involved in the inception of the hijacking." And although the United States at the time did not acknowledge Iran's positive role in the resolution of the crisis, some U.S. officials characterized Rafsanjani's discussions with various Muslims suspected of implication in the event as "tough talk." At the height of the crisis, he flew to Damascus on his way back from Tripoli specifically to help resolve the crisis. Yet Syria and the AMAL leader, Nabih Berri, received all the credit.[6]

Because of these diverging attitudes within the Iranian leadership, it has been difficult to pinpoint the responsibility of the Iranian government in terrorism, just as it has not been easy to determine which individuals or which organizations should be seen as representing the Iranian government. The following illustrates this difficulty:

> . . . It is often misleading to speak of the Iranian government having taken this or that action. The reality is generally much more complex as different factions compete for power and try to impose their views on policies. . . . It is often not the Iranian government which acts, but a small inner ring of senior clerics who answers directly to the Imamate (i.e., Ayatollah Khomeini and his immediate advisers). Sometimes, factions outside the control of even this powerful group act on their own. . . . [7]

Even more revealing is the complaint of Iran's former Prime Minister Moussavi— a hardliner on domestic and foreign policy but skeptical about the advisability of resort to terrorism—that subversive and terrorist acts have been committed by certain elements without his knowledge. In a letter to President Ali Khamenei submitting his resignation, he complained that "extra-territorial operations" were carried out without his knowledge. He also said these acts had had "catastrophic" results for Iran.[8]

However, for victims of Iranian-sponsored terrorism, the fact of the existence of such differences and complexities has made little difference. Nor is Iran absolved of responsibility for such acts by the fact that certain elements of its leadership may not have condoned its involvement in terrorism or have not been involved in carrying out such actions.

Yet this situation has complicated the response of other countries to Iranian-supported terrorism. Often, the retaliatory measures which countries that have been subjected to terrorism have felt impelled to take against Iran have only served to strengthen the radical tendency. Indeed, Iranian radicals are aware of this connection. Thus, at sensitive moments during the evolution of Iran's domestic scene and foreign relations, especially whenever Iran has tried to ease tensions with the West, the radicals have engaged in terrorist actions or indulged in inflammatory rhetoric— as during the Rushdie affair—in order to trigger a retaliatory Western response and consequently to undermine the moderates and to halt improvement in Iran's relations with the West.

Iranian Subversion

Iran has also been involved in what is generally called subversion. The primary focus of Iranian subversion has been the Persian Gulf Arab states and Iraq. But many observers have believed that Iran's subversive network has also covered Muslim countries from North Africa to the Pacific.[9] An accurate assessment of Iran's subversive activities is very difficult because of the paucity of reliable data. But a number of factors—most important, the record of Iran's limited success— tends to dispute the exaggerated view of its subversive activities.

A further point is also important in judging the significance of Iran's subversive activities. As opposed to terrorist actions that are relatively clear-cut, such as hostage-taking or bombings, it is much more difficult to define precisely the nature of "subversion." For example, should the exaltation of the virtues of a particular ideology and efforts to attract others to it be considered subversive? Should mere verbal attacks on other states' policies or even leadership be considered subversion? In many respects, the answer to these questions is "yes", especially when viewed from the perspective of those governments that are the targets. In this sense, revolutionary Iran has indeed been engaged in subversion. By the same standard, however, so have almost all other nations as, at times, was Iran under the Shah. Thus, in the context of the Cold War, Western and Eastern bloc countries have each viewed the other's radio broadcasts and other forms of propaganda as subversive. Likewise, in the Middle East, propaganda warfare has a long history. In the past, Iran engaged in such warfare against radicalism in the region and was itself targeted by radicals—as best illustrated by Egypt's propaganda warfare in the 1960s. Following the revolution, those Middle East countries that have been the target of Iran's subversive propaganda have retaliated in kind.

In addition, Iran's efforts to lure young Muslims to its religious seminaries in Ghom and to indoctrinate them with the principles of its revolutionary ideology, plus its holding of seminars and other gatherings for similar purposes, have been characterized as subversive. Again, if the term is defined broadly, this assessment is correct. But other states—particularly those professing revolutionary ideologies—have also done so. For years, the Soviet Union attracted Third World students to Patrice Lumumba University in Moscow, trying to imbue them with socialist ideas and values. Other countries try to attract new adherents to their ideas and values, a practice that opponents may view as subversive.

Therefore, insofar as subversion through the spread of ideas is concerned, Iran's behavior has not been much different from that of many other countries. Iranian authorities have often referred to the double standard used against Iran, as illustrated in comments by its prime minister: "The U.S. and other countries spread their message and influence all over the world and say and do what they deem right. Why should not we"?[10]

In this sense of the term, the very occurrence of the Iranian revolution was a subversive event. Even if Iran had done or said nothing, its revolution, by its very existence, would send the wrong message to many people and create anxiety for existing governments. In other words, even without any action, Iran would have been guilty of "subversion by example."

Subversion can also consist of manipulating a country's ethnic, religious, or other divisions, providing arms and financial aid to insurgents or anti-government forces, or encouraging *coups d'etat* against legal and sometimes even popular governments.

The Islamic regime has been guilty of this type of subversion. It has manipulated the Shi'a populations of the Persian Gulf Arab states, Iraq, and Lebanon, and it has provided arms and financial aid to anti-government elements in these countries. Iran may have been implicated in a *coup* attempt against Bahrain in 1981, and it was suspected of being behind the assassination attempt against the Emir of Kuwait in 1985.[11]

By the same token, however, these countries and others have engaged in similar actions against Iran. Iraq and other Gulf Arab governments have helped Iran's ethnic insurgents and financed and armed its opposition forces. Some of these opposition groups have engaged in acts inside Iran, such as planting bombs in public places and killing innocent people—acts that should correctly be characterized as terrorism. In Lebanon, Christian forces kidnapped and—it is widely believed—killed four Iranian diplomats. This event occurred before the Beirut bombings and before the wave of kidnappings in which Iran was implicated.

The fact is that a wide range of subversive activities has become a feature of international life since the end of World War II, when the systemic changes caused, in part, by the nature of new weaponry and, in part, by the East-West conflict made the open use of force more problematic, thus putting a greater premium on the use of proxies and a panoply of so-called covert operations.

In this sense, at one time or another almost every country has practiced some of these tactics, from staging *coups d'etat* or backing different parties in a civil war or supporting ethnic insurgencies. In the Middle East, Egypt's and Saudi Arabia's involvement in the Yemeni civil war, Iran's and Iraq's manipulation of each other's Kurdish problems, and Iraq's agitation among Iran's Arab and Baluch minorities are examples that predate the Iranian revolution.

By no means are these points intended to justify Islamic Iran's subversive actions or to absolve it of its responsibilities; they are intended instead to put these actions in their proper historical and systemic context. Iran has also engaged in certain activities that have gone far beyond the normal practices of states. These have included the abuse of the extra-territoriality of embassies and of the diplomatic privileges of envoys, mistreatment of foreign diplomats stationed in Iran, and the use of Iranian pilgrims during the Hadj ceremonies to create dissent or occasionally to smuggle firearms to Saudi Arabia's Muslim dissidents. Together with Iran's more starkly terrorist acts, these examples imply that Iranian behavior, even when judged in light of the covert and non-conventional warfare practices of other states, has departed both from Iran's own past behavior and from the normal conduct of international affairs.

Nevertheless, both Iran's potential for subversion and the success of its subversive activities have been limited by a number of factors:

(1) Iran's Persian character. Despite the regime's attempt to minimize Iranian nationalism, the fact of Iran's Persianness has limited its ability to reach the Arab masses. Indeed, ethnicity and nationalism have proved to be much stronger than the appeal of Islamic universalism. Nothing better illustrates the potency of ethnic loyalties than Iran's failure to generate a mass uprising among Iraq's Shi'as. Indeed, many Arab diplomats, journalists, and scholars have commented to me that, had the Islamic revolution occurred in an Arab country, its contagious impact would have been much greater.

(2) Iran's Shi'a character. This has also been a barrier to Iran's ability to appeal to larger groups of Muslims beyond the Shi'a minorities. Indeed, in some cases, such as in Kuwait, Iran's activities have brought Sunni fundamentalist groups closer to their governments. Because of its Persian-Shi'a character, Iran's intellectual influence over Islamic groups—its natural constituency—has been limited, as most of these groups have been influenced by Egyptian and other Arab and Pakistani fundamentalist thinkers. Thus Iran has not been able to use these groups effectively as a means of either subverting their governments or spreading its revolutionary message.[12] Indeed, Iran has been forced to focus most of its attention and energies on those areas where the existence of Shi'a majorities or sizable minorities creates a relatively more receptive environment for its ideas and influence.

(3) Iran's financial limitations and the demands of the Persian Gulf war. These factors have also restrained Iran's ability to expand its subversive activities. Again, this is not to suggest that Iran has no links with Islamic groups or has not tried to recruit supporters and agents among them. Rather, it is to emphasize that its ability to do so and its rate of success have been severely limited.

Moreover, facing the Iranian challenge, those countries with either large Shi'a minorities or substantial fundamentalist Islamic groups have, through a mixture of cooptation and repression, successfully managed their Muslim discontents and thus have reduced Iran's ability to use them as instruments to challenge governments or to advance its national or Islamic goals. In addition, Iran's potential for subversion has been limited by the containment policy of other powers—which itself has been a natural reaction to Iran's revolutionary challenge to the existing system, similar to other examples of revolutionary challenge and systemic response.

The best proof of this point is the failure of either Islamic groups or Iran seriously to threaten existing governments, let alone to cause their downfall. Nor, as was clearly illustrated during the Persian Gulf war, has Iran succeeded in its efforts to intimidate the Arab states and to force them to be responsive to its concerns, through threatening to subvert them by manipulating their Shi'a or other Muslim dissident groups.

Iran's subversive potential has been even more limited in areas beyond its immediate vicinity and in countries with Sunni majorities. Indeed, many Western diplomats—including the French, who have been particularly concerned about the Islamic challenge in North Africa—have told me that Iran's reach and influence are far more limited than is generally perceived. If this is so, as the record of the last ten years seems to indicate, then why do the more exaggerated views of Iran's subversive activities persist? Four factors help to explain this phenomenon:.

(1) Given the upsurge of Islamic feeling that followed the Islamic revolution, all Islamic movements, even those predating the Iranian revolution, have become somehow identified with Iran.

(2) Iran has reaped the harvest of its self-appointed role as the leader of the Islamic world and its propensity to exaggerate its own influence among Islamic movements.

(3) Some governments have manipulated the Iranian role in order to crack down on their fundamentalist movements and to undermine their legitimacy with the public, by pointing to their foreign connections. This was done, for example by the government of Tunisia.[13]

(4) The Iranian threat has been exaggerated by the West, and even by the Soviet Union, in order to justify certain policies, ranging from support for Iraq and arms sales to the Persian Gulf states to the pursuit of a punitive policy towards Iran.

Iranian Subversion: Impact on Foreign Policy

As discussed above, Iran's subversive activities have been related to the conduct of its external relations. In particular, its propaganda efforts have stemmed from its Islamic ideology and from its self-perception as the vanguard of Islamic revolution. Like many other governments—not just revolutionary ones—it has also felt that it can only be safe if it is surrounded by like-minded regimes. Initially, the Iranian leadership felt that, if the revolution did not expand, it would die. Thus, Iran's efforts to export its revolution also had a security dimension. Similarly, the Iranian regime, in the pattern of others, has believed that it could spread its influence through the spread of its revolutionary message. Indeed, the Iranian leadership has been united in believing that its message should be exported, but there has been disagreement on the means. The radicals have not excluded the arming and training of opposition groups, plus active subversion, whereas the moderates have preferred only non-violent means. In practice, both methods have been applied.

As discussed above, most Iranian-inspired violent acts have in some way been related to the Iran-Iraq war—e.g., to Iran's efforts to influence the attitude of regional countries and external powers toward the war, or to retaliate against them for supporting Iraq. These acts, rather than reflecting Iran's power and ambitions, have generally demonstrated its weakness and desperation in the face of superior foes.

This has brought it little profit, however. In fact, the record of the last ten years shows beyond doubt that Iran's resort to terrorism and subversion has not only failed to help it to achieve its national and ideological goals or to enhance its security, but it has also been highly damaging in all three respects. This is best illustrated by international attitudes toward the Iran-Iraq war and the almost universal failure to condemn Iraq's aggression against Iran. Iran's words and deeds also created tensions in its relations with nearly all Muslim countries, plus those with substantial Muslim minorities, leading them to limit their contacts. Indeed, Iran's extremism and inflammatory rhetoric have reduced rather than increased its chances of spreading its Islamic message and of achieving its goal of raising the Muslims' Islamic consciousness.

Iran's terrorist actions thus both failed to intimidate anyone and prompted Iran's neighbors to forge close ties among themselves and with outside powers. The result was growing political, economic, and military pressures on Iran, which finally led to its defeat in the war with Iraq. Iran's international prestige has also suffered grievously.

The Iranian leadership has been aware of the negative consequences of this behavior, as illustrated by the aforementioned comment of its prime minister. Indeed, the failure of subversive and terrorist tactics to advance Iran's goals, along with disastrous consequences, have been among the most potent factors behind Iran's gradual adjustment to the international system. Realistic and moderate elements and even the less extreme hardliners in the Iranian leadership have recognized this fact and have argued against the use of such methods. They have tried to mitigate the negative consequences of the subversive dimension of Iran's behavior. As illustrated earlier, during the last several years, a principal task of the Iranian foreign ministry has been to reduce tensions arising from Iran's rhetoric and the activities of extremist personalities and groups. Because of the influence of the extremist factions, the realists have had only partial and transitory success. Nevertheless, their influence, strengthened by knowledge of the defeats Iran has suffered, has led to a gradual reduction in the incidence of Iranian-inspired terrorist and subversive actions.

Conclusions

The extent of Iran's involvement in subversive and terrorist activities during the post-Khomeini period depended at any time on the evolution of its political scene. Today, however, the high price that Iran has paid for this behavior is clear, as is its need to gain access to sources of capital and military supplies from abroad, especially from the West—an involvement that is not likely to be forthcoming so long as Iran maintains its image as a "terrorist" state. The end of the Iran-Iraq war and the relative improvement in Arab-Iranian relations across the Persian Gulf should also help reduce the incidence of Iranian-inspired subversion and terrorism. There have also been indications that Iran has been trying to distance itself from the more radical factions in Lebanon and in general trying to disentangle itself from the morass in Lebanon, while maintaining a political presence there.[14] Thus it is fair to assume that Iran will continue the process of adjusting to the international system and that the subversive dimensions of its behavior will greatly diminish, although—depending on domestic developments—the occurrence of such incidents cannot be ruled out.

Indeed, all signs in the immediate aftermath of the Ayatollah Khomeini's death have pointed to Iran's wanting to focus on its domestic problems. It also seems to understand, as its new spiritual leader has indicated, that it can be a source of emulation for other Muslims only by building an economically advanced and socially just country, thus presenting a successful Islamic model.

Conclusions

The purpose of this book has been to demonstrate four basic points and then to draw some conclusions about Iran's future foreign policy:

• complex and multiple factors have determined Iran's behavior since the Islamic revolution;

• there has not been a complete breach with the Iranian past in its external behavior;

• Iran's world view has neither been purely Islamic nor entirely novel, especially when viewed in terms of Third World intellectual trends; and

• its behavior has not been radically different from that of "normal" states, especially Third World states at a revolutionary stage of development.

This survey of Iran's interaction with the outside world has clearly confirmed these points. It has illustrated that many factors that traditionally affected its behavior—factors related to Iran's history, cultural traits, geopolitical characteristics, and external realities—have also affected its behavior during the revolutionary decade. Even the impact of Iran's Islamic ideology has not diminished their importance. And as the revolution has gradually settled down, the role of these traditional factors has grown in significance, a phenomenon that accounts for considerable continuities in the pattern of Iran's international behavior, despite some dramatic changes.

Moreover, Iran's Islamic ideology and revolutionary world view have not been a totally novel phenomenon unrelated to, and unaffected by, its past, its national ethos, or the broader milieu and intellectual trends of the Third World. On the contrary, as demonstrated in this study, they have reflected both the impact of Iran's own past and the recent history of the Third World.

Iran's geopolitical situation and its ethnic and religious characteristics have also made their imprint on its policy, despite the Islamic regime's efforts to break out of their constraining impact by resorting to Islamic universalism. For example, despite the early fires kindled in the region by Iran's revolution, historic patterns of resistance to Iranian influence and hyper-activism have persisted and become stronger. This was proved by Iran's interaction with the Arab world where the revolution, instead of bridging the Arab-Iranian ethnic and sectarian chasm, has deepened and intensified it—as best illustrated in the Iran-Iraq war. In the Persian Gulf, the traditional pattern of Arab-Iranian relations has remained valid in the post-revolution period. As in the past, Iraqi-Iranian and Saudi-Iranian competition has continued, whereas Iran's relations with the United Arab Emirates and with Oman have remained friendly. Yet the same ethnic and religious characteristics which, both before and after the revolution, have limited Iran's options and acted as barriers to its activism have offered it other options. Thus Iran's Shi'a character, a barrier to its influence in the Sunni Muslim world, has given it opportunities to gain influence in countries with substantial Shi'a minorities.

Meanwhile, geopolitical factors and common vulnerabilities have led Iran to maintain working relationships with Turkey and Pakistan, despite political and ideological differences. In its approach toward East Asia and the Pacific regions, Iran has been motivated by the same strategic and economic considerations that prompted the eastward thrust of its diplomacy during the 1970s. And in the broader international context, Iran's geopolitical conditions and the fact that the distant superpower (the United States) has no intrinsic interest in it have continued to shape its relations with the two superpowers.

Yet the revolution has added new complexities to these relations. For example, it has magnified Iran's underlying systemic problem in dealing with the great powers—emanating from its position as a core regional power—by intensifying the perception, if not the reality, of the challenge it poses to their interests. Their historic tendency to contain Iran and to limit its influence and activism have been enhanced. Nothing demonstrates this better than the support that both the United States and the Soviet Union gave to Iraq during the Persian Gulf war. Yet both Iran's behavior and the great power reaction to it have been in the traditional mold of revolutions and responses. All revolutions since that of France in 1789 have had expansionist and proselytizing dimensions, and all have triggered policies of containment on the part of powers who have felt threatened. The Napoleonic wars were as much about checking France's territorial expansion as about containing its revolutionary message. Western and Soviet support for Iraq was also principally aimed at checking the spread both of the Islamic revolution and of Iranian power.

Nor did the revolution end Iran's vulnerability to the vagaries of international politics—in particular, to changes in the nature and character of great power relations. On the contrary, by posing a common challenge of revolutionary Islam, Iran's vulnerability to changes in superpower relations created new incentives for superpower cooperation at its expense. Indeed, the improvement in relations between the United States and the Soviet Union, plus their tacit agreement in 1987–88 that Iran should not be allowed to win the war, profoundly affected its position both in the war and more broadly in the Persian Gulf. Iran found itself unable to play one superpower off against the other. At the same time, however, the relative *détente* in superpower relations did not end their global competition for influence, and thus Iran's geopolitical position moderated their reaction towards it.

Because of the same factors, Iran's relationship with the Soviet Union in the post-revolution period have retained its special characteristic, which is a function of Soviet proximity and overwhelming power. Thus despite periods of acute tension in Soviet-Iranian relations, Iran did not break relations or stop all communications with the Soviet Union. By the same token, Iran's historical memory of Russia—as both Tsarist and socialist—kept it from moving too close to the Soviet Union.

On balance, the basic changes taking place in the Soviet Union, changes in its approach toward Iran, and the reduction in the Soviet security threat, indicate that the nature of Soviet-Iranian relations could change drastically in the months and years ahead. Nevertheless, even under the best of conditions, the facts of proximity and power would argue for Iran to maintain some degree of distance from the Soviet Union, or at least to offset its influence by having ties with other states that could act as countervailing forces. To be sure, during the last decade Iran has used countries like China, Japan, Turkey, and some in Europe as counterweights, in order to avoid dependence on the Soviet Union. Yet its revolutionary ideology also introduced a fundamental change in its relations with the superpowers and challenged the logic of geopolitical imperatives. Thus Iran's hostility and defiance towards the United States has belied strategic logic concerning the need to balance Soviet proximity with at least reasonable ties with the other superpower.

Nevertheless, as underlying forces have reasserted their influence, along with the requirements of Iran's economic, technological and other needs, it has gradually adapted itself to the international system and its foreign policy has steadily grown more pragmatic. This process of adjustment has been slow, however. Under the impact of its revolutionary ideology and in pursuit of related goals, Iran has tried to resist the influence of traditional factors shaping its foreign policy. In the process, it has often narrowed its options and incurred considerable costs.

Nothing better illustrates this aspect of Iran's behavior and its resistance to systemic pressures than its refusal to accept a negotiated peace with Iraq, despite tremendous odds against its winning the war. This behavior reflected a trait common to revolutions—namely, the belief in their power to change the world by the sheer force of faith in the justness and strength of their ideals.

But reluctance to adjust to reality has also betrayed deeply rooted traits of Iranian character and political culture, such as an emotionalism and unrealism that have so often affected Iran's external behavior and caused it damage. These should not be dismissed as mere character flaws but rather seen as reflecting a national psychological problem: Iran's inability to come to terms with its decline and loss of power; to overcome its intense feelings of having been wronged; and thus to control the urge to seek redress. Over the years, therefore, Iran's behavior has shifted periodically, from quietism to over-activism. Certainly, its behavior during the last decade—including its involvement in subversive activities (its "other diplomacy")—reflects the conflicting and contradictory effects of its limited power and its psychological problem in trimming its aspirations to meet its limitations. It is not unique, however, in having aspirations which outstrip indigenous capabilities.

Nevertheless, despite its national propensity to be unrealistic about its possibilities—intensified during the last ten years by Islamic revolutionary fervor—Iran has been able to put the requirements of national survival above its ideological aspirations, thereby proving the rule that states have an irresistible urge to survive. In the future, as well, the imperative of national survival is likely to prevail.

At the same time, Iran's external behavior under the Islamic regime has been characterized by inconsistency, contradictions, and sudden shifts in direction. These also reflect, at least in part, the natural course of a revolutionary movement's adaptation to the international system, as well as the inherent tension between Iran's state interests and its revolutionary ambitions. Partly, however, they also reflect both internal power struggles and differences of opinion within the leadership about the directions that Iran's foreign policy should take. Here, too, Iran has not been unique, nor has its behavior in the past ten years been as dramatic a departure from "normal," as is often assumed, especially in the West. Indeed, differences of opinion within European chancelleries, struggles within the U.S. government, and the demands of domestic politics in democratic nations have had a major impact on the making of policy toward Iran and thus on the state of Iran's relations with the West.

As with Iran's difficulty in adjusting to reality, the vacillations and inconsistencies in its foreign policies have masked underlying national divisions and contradictions that only came to the fore after the revolution. And unless and until they are resolved, within a broad national consensus, Iran's external behavior could continue to be erratic.

The most important of these contradictions is the dichotomy between Islam and nationalism, both of which are integral parts of Iran's national and cultural character and both of which will continue to influence its behavior. Yet, based on the past, even a minor shift in favor of one or the other can have significant implications for its behavior.

Other dichotomies in Iranian society that are most important pit economic efficiency against social justice and modernization against religious and cultural autonomy and spirituality. These underlying divisions were highlighted during the national debate that took place following the August 1988 cease-fire. Formally, the terms of debate centered on how much foreign involvement to permit in the Iranian economy; on what level and what kind of technological dependence is acceptable; on how much self-sufficiency must be preserved; and on how far Iran can open itself to outside cultural influences. So long as the more basic issues are not resolved, however, Iran will not gain a clear and broad-based image of itself and thus will fail to settle on a sustainable notion of its international role. Meanwhile, of course, the outcome of debate—even if not conclusive—will have a major impact on Iran's external behavior and its choice of economic and political partners.

Iran's ethnic and cultural isolation is also unlikely to end in the near future. It will continue to face the problem of finding a role in the region beyond which Iran can satisfy its desire for independence and influence without either threatening its neighbors and clashing too strongly with their aspirations.

It is particularly difficult to predict what Iran will do abroad because of the role played by domestic developments. Furthermore, it will not act in a vacuum. For example, a drastic change in the Soviet Union's approach toward Iran, including the elimination of its threat to Iran's security, would dramatically alter the traditional context of Iran's foreign policy and could prompt significant changes in its international and regional outlook. The attitudes of both Western and regional states toward Iran and its interests in the Persian Gulf and South Asia will also have a major impact on its approach to the Soviet Union, to the West, and to regional politics.

Despite these cautions, however, Iran's experience both historically and during the past decade provides the basis for making some basic predictions about its future behavior, regardless of the kind of regime ruling the country. As with other states—provided that Iran does not plunge into chaos or disintegrate, a development that seemed unlikely in the aftermath of Khomeini's death, the imperatives of national survival and the maintenance of territorial integrity and political independence will ultimately overcome other considerations.

Given a choice, it is unlikely that Iran will develop a dependent relationship with any great power, although it may favor some over others. Most likely, it will try to broaden its economic and political options by establishing ties with a wide range of countries. The Persian Gulf will remain a priority focus of Iran's foreign policy, as the window to the world. In that relationship with other Gulf states, some Arab-Iranian competition is inevitable; but Arab-Iranian relations need not be conflictual. Indeed, both Iran and its Arab neighbors share a major foreign policy challenge to create a new framework for their interaction that will minimize tensions and maximize the potential for cooperation. In view of Iran's size, ethnic and religious barriers between it and the Arabs, and limits imposed by the Arab nationalist ethos, cooperative programs that are too ambitious will fail, even under the best of circumstances. But mutual efforts must be made to develop enough economic and political cooperation to give Iran a sense of involvement in the region and a stake in the stability of its Arab neighbors.

The worst policy would be to exclude Iran from the region's economic and political setting or constantly to view it as an active or potential threat. There is potential disaster in efforts to give the Persian Gulf an exclusively Arab character and to deny the legitimacy of any Iranian aspiration for an active presence. The temptation must be resisted to brand even limited Iranian aspirations as hegemonic and expansionist—whether of imperialist or Islamic variety. By the same token, countries beyond the region need to recognize Iran's political, economic, and cultural weight within the region and to deal with it accordingly.

For its part, Iran must control its unrealistic impulses. It must fashion a role that takes into account its neighbors' fears and vulnerabilities and does not threaten the vital interests of others—provided that these interests are defined reasonably and do not serve as a cover for domination. In any event, the global importance of the Persian Gulf region means that Arab-Iranian relations will also continue to be affected by the impact of global politics.

It is also important to understand that Iranian foreign policy will remain activist even though, as in the past, its character and intensity will depend on domestic conditions and the external setting. Some underlying resentment toward the West, rooted in an Iranian historical experience that was strengthened when the West sided with Iraq, will continue to limit the improvement and expansion of relations. This will be especially true if Iran finds other viable economic partners. Yet Iran's domestic politics—in particular, factional rivalry for power—may change this equation if some faction uses the promise of improved relations to gain Western support. Although Iran's range of possible partners are wider today, its economic reconstruction would still require access to the West's financial and technological resources, thus forcing it to overcome its historic resentment.

For the foreseeable future, Iran's foreign policy will also continue to be affected by economic and military needs. Because of its weaknesses following the Gulf war, it will likely have to curb the most ambitious and controversial aspects of its behavior, especially its urge to export revolution, in order to gain access to trade and technology needed for economic and military reconstruction.

The Islamic and Third World dimensions of Iran's foreign policy are also likely to survive—though at reduced intensity—because they have deep national roots. And its belief in its innate right to be active both in the region and on the international scene will not be eliminated. Yet unless there are major political upheavals or a change in regime following the Ayatollah Khomeini's death, during the 1990s Iran is likely to experience a period of relative quietism in foreign policy, concentrating instead on economic reconstruction and political consolidation. This inward-looking mood will lead Iran increasingly to behave as a state rather than as a revolutionary movement, giving priority to state interests rather than to the pursuit of revolutionary aspirations.

During this period, Iran's foreign policy will likely be concerned mostly with its immediate surroundings, and it will lose some of the expansionist dimensions of the 1970s and 1980s—unless, of course, it gains opportunities that cannot be overlooked, either from external developments or from a dramatic improvement in its economic conditions because of tightening energy markets and rising oil prices. If Iran succeeds in resolving its internal problems and reconciling its national dichotomies, it will increasingly behave like a "normal" state, subject to the prevailing rules of international life and ready to play a role in global politics to which other nations can relate.

Epilogue

This book was completed in August 1989. Since then, momentous changes have occurred in many parts of the world. These have included the opening of the Berlin Wall and the movement toward German unification, the evident collapse of Communist regimes in Eastern Europe, the wholesale retreat of Soviet strategic power from the heart of the European continent, and rumblings of independence among Soviet nationalities, not least among those resident in its Asiatic empire.

These and other events are fundamentally altering the nature of the international political system that was established after World War II. Indeed, the world is experiencing a period of transition when the old rules of international politics no longer apply and when the disciplining and organizing functions of such paradigms as the "Cold War," "security blocs," and "non-alignment" have become irrelevant.

Yet, in this period of transition, it is not clear what kind of new international system will replace the one whose basic character and rules were determined by global ideological competition between the forces of socialism and those of liberal democracy. At the economic level, the international system is moving toward multipolarity while, at the ideological level, liberal democracy appears to be unrivaled—hence, at least the appearance of a unipolar system.

Meanwhile, some pre-1945 patterns of interstate and intrastate relations and conflicts, which had been subordinated to the rules of the Cold War, are reappearing, thus adding to the uncertainties and confusion of international politics. Indeed, forces unleashed by changes in the Soviet Union and the dissolution of the socialist bloc will leave no region or country unaffected.

The consequences of these changes will be more far-reaching and profound for some countries than for others. For Iran, with its special geopolitical position, its close proximity to the Soviet Union, and its ethnic and religious composition, the impact of these changes, both positive and negative, will be particularly consequential. Indeed, these changes will have an impact beyond the realm of foreign policy and, depending on how they develop, may even have implications for Iran's borders. As discussed in this book, Iran's geostrategic situation has historically made its foreign policy options—and indeed its national fate—acutely vulnerable to the vagaries of international politics, especially the nature of Great Power relations.

Thus, the end of the Cold War and the dramatic reduction—if not the complete elimination—of East-West competition will have a great impact on Iran's foreign policy options and behavior. Yet, it is still too early to determine whether, for Iran, the ultimate result of these changes will be positive or negative.

In the foreseeable future, these recent developments are likely to affect Iran negatively, by rendering its regional and international position more precarious, narrowing its options, and limiting its maneuverability. This is so because the changes in superpower relations are accompanied by a crisis in the Soviet Union's Asian empire, which lies perilously close to Iran and many of whose ethnic and linguistic groups overlap those of Iran.

For example, the reduction of the Soviet threat to the Persian Gulf–Southwest Asia region will drastically reduce, if not eliminate, Iran's value to the West as a buffer. This fact, coupled with Iran's inherent competitive potential—based on its size, resources, and population—will enhance the Western predisposition to contain Iran's influence in the Persian Gulf, even if Iran were to abandon completely its revolutionary pretensions.

More serious from Iran's perspective, the Western powers will be tempted to exaggerate an Iranian threat to Persian Gulf security—or to the security of Gulf Arabs—in order to justify a projection of their own power in the region, a situation which, in the absence of a Soviet threat, would otherwise be less defensible.

The same pattern may also hold true in the case of some of the region's other countries, which see their strategic significance and usefulness being eroded by the end of the Cold War. This situation means that Iran will have an increased need to come to terms with the West.

By contrast, the elimination of the Soviet threat will open up new possibilities for cooperation between Iran and Russia, thus mitigating the negative consequences of Iran's loss of importance as a buffer state and hence the undermining of its bargaining position vis-à-vis the West. Indeed, this seemed to be happening during the fall and winter of 1989–90.

Better relations with the USSR would also help reduce Iran's ethnic and cultural isolation by facilitating contacts with kin in the Soviet Asian republics. Still, turmoil in these republics and the possible dissolution of the Soviet Asian empire would pose serious dilemmas for Iran and could nullify the potential benefits of a less threatening Russia. It could even create new strains in Soviet-Iranian ties.

A suggestion of what could happen in the future emerged during the upheavals in Soviet Azerbaijan and their spillover into Iran during the winter of 1990, when Soviet troops quelled the Azerbaijani-Armenian dispute. Iran was faced with a critical dilemma: how to safeguard its newly improved relations with the Soviet Union while remaining true to its commitment to defend Muslim rights throughout the Islamic world.

The Azerbaijan crisis also had—and will continue to have—domestic implications for Iran. If an independent and perhaps nationalist, irredentist republic of Azerbaijan should emerge, it could—by trying to incorporate Iranian Azerbaijan—threaten Iran's territorial integrity. By the same token, because of the deep religious and cultural affinities between Iran and Azerbaijan (80 percent of Soviet Azerbaijanis are Shi'a) and the fact that until 1828 this area was part of Iran, an independent Azerbaijan might want to have close ties with Iran, perhaps including some form of confederal relations.

Such a prospect, however, would be highly disquieting to the Soviet Union, the West, and other countries in the region because it would enhance Iran's regional weight and its competitive potential. Such ties would therefore be actively discouraged. Similar situations could arise in other Soviet Asian republics, especially Tadjikistan, where linguistic and cultural links with Iran are very strong.

Changes in the Soviet Union will also deeply affect Iran's regional ties because, at least for the last seven decades, a shared fear of the Soviet Union has been the principal determinant of Iran's relations with its neighbors—especially Turkey and Pakistan. Indeed, reconciliation between Turkey and Iran in the 1920s, their co-operation during the post–World War II years, and their uneasy accommodation since the Islamic revolution have largely resulted from their common concern over Soviet domination. With the elimination of this common threat, and in light of developments in the Soviet Asian empire, the competitive aspects of Turko-Iranian relations could reemerge. This is so because the elimination of the Soviet threat means that Turkey's importance to the West will also diminish, along with its chances of becoming an integral part of the European community.

Turkey could thus be faced with something close to an identity crisis, which could lead it to search for a new regional and international role. As a result, Turkey may once again find pan-Turanism to be an attractive concept by which to define its role and to rationalize the expansion of its influence. It might, for example, play a more active role in developments in Azerbaijan and the other parts of Soviet Central Asia where Turkic ethnic elements are dominant.

Such a development could bring Turkey into competition, and possibly even conflict, with Iran. Indeed, a glimpse of possible Turko-Iranian competition was evident during the Azerbaijan crisis. While both Ankara and Tehran tried to avoid antagonizing the Soviet Union, they expressed their concern for the fate of the Azerbaijanis: Turkey emphasized the bonds of ethnic and linguistic kinship—reflecting its pan-Turanist impulses—and Iran highlighted Shi'a solidarity. By contrast, Turkey's failure to become a part of Europe could prompt it to seek closer economic relations with Iran and other Islamic countries, thus reducing the effect of competitive forces.

The elimination of the Soviet threat, along with developments in the Soviet Asian empire, will also be felt in Iran's relations with Pakistan and Afghanistan, although it is not yet possible to discern in what ways. That will depend in part on what impact these changes will have on the internal conditions and regional position of those countries. Here, too, there will be potential for increased conflict and competition, but also for more cooperation within the region.

In sum, whatever transpires in the immediate future, changes in the Soviet Union—along with their international and regional consequences—will complicate Iran's foreign-policy choices by presenting new challenges and new opportunities. These changes will enhance the regional focus of Iran's diplomacy. They will make it imperative for Iran to improve its relations with its Arab neighbors and their Western allies, albeit from a bargaining position of diminished strength.

Iran will also need to speed the process of rejoining the international community. Indeed, Iran's national fate and territorial integrity may depend on the skill of its diplomacy and its correct understanding of emerging regional and international forces during a period of deep systemic changes and transition to a new world order.

Statistical Appendix

TABLE I   Iranian-U.S. Trade

	'78	'79	'80	'81	'82	'83	'84	'85	'86	'87
Exports to U.S.:	4345	3904	435	60	556	1061	664	693	556	1592
Imports:	4053	1191	25	330	134	209	178	81	38	59

Source: U.S. Department of Commerce

Information for Tables II-VIII is from International Monetary Fund, Bureau of Statistics, *Direction of Trade Statistics Yearbook,* 1988. Figures are quoted in millions of U.S. dollars.

TABLE II   Iranian-Soviet Trade

Years	'78	'79	'80	'81	'82	'83	'84	'85	'86	'87
Exports to USSR:	64	68	116	649	259	509	298	195	26	u
Imports from USSR:	419	565	712	712	712	676	608	548	438	394

TABLE III   Iranian-Arab Trade

Years	'78	'79	'80	'81	'82	'83	'84	'85	'86	'87
Exports to:										
Kuwait	25	32	19	9	13	12	14	11	10	10
Libya	2	1	u	1	1	u	u	u	u	u
Oman	4	2	1	1	1	u	u	u	u	u
UAE	26	30	29	28	10	48	34	26	24	24
Syria	3	29	2	3	717	1080	849	642	169	2
Not spec.	76	72	37	50.1	41.8	41.4	40.2	28.8	23.7	25.8
Imports from:										
Kuwait	97	126	301	134	74	213	73	55	52	52
Libya	u	—	—	—	—	—	—	—	—	—
Oman	u	.1	5.2	2	1	1	1	1	1	1
UAE	161	253	402	230	90	72	75	57	54	54
Syria	u	u	1	u	45	113	46	10	13	53
Not spec.	164	42	50	52	18	15	14	14	10.3	10.3

Not specified: Iraq, Qatar, Saudi Arabia, Bahrain, Egypt, Israel, Jordan, Lebanon, Yemen

TABLE IV   Iranian-Subcontinent Trade

Years	'78	'79	'80	'81	'82	'83	'84	'85	'86	'87
Exports to:										
Afghanistan	104	147	1	1	u	u	u	u	u	
Bangladesh	46		36	3	12		19		12	17
India	509	408	1227	1655	1232	1047	942	801	561	652
Pakistan	7	9	2	3	38	90	48	108	63	130
Turkey	4	165	701	439	680	1111	1423	1150	201	628
Imports from:										
Afghanistan	u	u	1	1	u	u	u	u	u	u
Bangladesh	17	19	53	48	18	73	78	86	35	28
India	153	118	148	155	155	139	125	107	80	86
Pakistan	39	62	219	169	107	539	298	63	66	67
Turkey	49	21	93	257	870	1197	826	1187	621	484

TABLE V   Iranian-West European Trade

Years	'78	'79	'80	'81	'82	'83	'84	'85	'86	'87
Exports to:										
Austria	154	52	28	85	49	19	42	59	36	65
Belgium	707	353	246	389	267	152	170	252	163	343
Denmark	171	109	9	6	34	29	57	4	8	10
Finland	86	196	154	128	51	114	51	147	32	4
France	1093	940	630	434	804	881	710	730	328	577
W. Germany	1910	2110	1710	612	639	561	589	584	470	455
Greece	195	108	35	1	15	47	u	49	47	2
Ireland	19	36	75	.3	6	53	67	54	35	—
Italy	1421	374	309	637	2523	2389	1713	1366	783	954
Netherlands	1362	862	274	140	1592	1357	1631	800	388	878
Norway	134	77	34	2	1	11	1	2	3	7
Spain	829	657	973	1226	970	1652	1101	807	367	605
Sweden	259	208	137	6	150	132	42	16	69	66
Switzerland	74	43	75	38	66	39	48	25	4	47
UK	928	471	226	285	356	138	433	73	132	283
Not spec.	145	152	53	180	192	294	197	71	69	—
Imports from:										
Austria	134	76	237	202	148	304	215	193	141	153
Belgium	358	175	297	281	160	283	254	196	237	169
Denmark	102	97	115	109	124	142	163	79	111	109
Finland	104	50	138	124	107	87	83	39	28	48
France	970	468	793	735	367	408	201	176	108	198
W. Germany	3719	1413	1657	1766	1536	3310	2518	1812	1649	1740
Greece	17	16	111	69	17	29	53	52	13	5
Ireland	33	17	29	11	7	57	75	60	38	77
Italy	1173	455	632	829	796	994	1039	672	715	556
Netherlands	346	261	386	430	298	460	417	298	254	315
Norway	37	21	24	30	24	32	15	12	19	10

TABLE V   Iranian-West European Trade

Years	'78	'79	'80	'81	'82	'83	'84	'85	'86	'87
Spain	285	133	360	371	361	452	327	312	188	112
Sweden	247	75	207	215	219	462	522	210	125	100
Switzerland	423	245	304	260	211	336	311	219	256	244
UK	1585	542	1006	888	635	1047	1030	745	645	556
Not spec.	17	7	2	32	2	8	27	73	54	—

Not specified: Cyprus, Iceland, and Portugal

TABLE VI   Iran-East Asia, and Pacific Trade

Years	'78	'79	'80	'81	'82	'83	'84	'85	'86	'87
Exports to:										
Japan	3869	3854	3745	1732	2331	3852	2606	2296	1281	1426
China	49	29	53	2	81	25*	14*	7	5*	4
Australia	67	68	81	12	95	2	3	13	3	4
New Zealand	75	41	17	1	1	20	1	1	1	u
Indonesia	—	—	—	—	—	1	—	—	1	—
Malaysia	65	25	—	90	52	88	—	—	15	1
Thailand	34	15	31	10	5	—	—	34	9	—
S. Korea**	154	307	247	—	—	—	—	—	—	—
N. Korea**	—	—	—	—	—	—	—	—	—	—
Imports from:										
Japan	2991	1013	1697	1629	1033	3102	1862	1496	1270	1160
China	72	40	133	179	45	294	170	92	55	104
Australia	218	146	311	220	219	258	411	235	297	276
New Zealand	68	38	195	253	123	284	260	213	169	150
Indonesia	1	—	1	1	1	1	1	—	4	8
Malaysia	19	10	25	18	17	68	36	36	17	12
Thailand	41	6	115	233	109	114	136	72	45	134
S. Korea	181	204	119	—	—	—	—	—	—	—
N. Korea	—	—	—	—	—	—	—	—	—	—

* Data extrapolated for the entire year.

** There is a paucity of information on trade statistics between Iran and North and South Korea due to the delicate nature of the transactions. North Korea is reported to be the second largest supplier of weapons to Iran. South Korea has extensive dealings with Iran, but little is published in this regard due to Iran's friendly relations with North Korea.

TABLE VII   Iranian-African Trade

Years	'78	'79	'80	'81	'82	'83	'84	'85	'86	'87
Exports to:										
Africa	254	208	157	82	58	137	189	173	123	146
Imports from:										
Africa	16	13	46	26	17	48	41	38	25	26

TABLE VIII   Iranian-Latin American Trade

Years	'78	'79	'80	'81	'82	'83	'84	'85	'86	'87
Exports to:										
Bahamas	640	928	144	144	123	104	99	84	59	68
Brazil	520	804	696	u	47	383	168	98	76	338
Venezuela	1			1						
Cuba										
Argentina		6		9						
Nicaragua										
Imports from:										
Bahamas	1	1	1	1	1	16	15	13	11	10
Brazil	133	79	263	214	231	382	328	234	199	179
Venezuela	—	5	—	—	—	73	3	—	2	2
Cuba	—	—	—	—	—	—	—	—	—	—
Argentina	49	18	95	34	148	436	473	345	282	206
Nicaragua	—	—	—	—	—	—	—	—	—	—

Notes

1. Determinants of Iran's Foreign Policy

1. On factors affecting state behavior, see, among others, Hans J. Morgenthau, *Politics among Nations,* New York: Alfred A. Knopf, 1985; James N. Rosenau, *The Scientific Study of Foreign Policy,* New York: The Free Press, 1971; James N. Rosenau (ed.) *International Politics and Foreign Policy,* New York: Wolfram F. Hanrieder, 1971, *Comparative Foreign Policy: Theoretical Essays,* New York: David McKay Company Inc., 1971; Robert Lieber, *No Common Power: Understanding International Relations,* Boston: Scott Foresman, Little Brown, 1988.

2. On Iran's physical characteristics and their impact on its social, cultural, and political characteristics, see Roman Ghrishman, *Iran,* Harmondsworth, England: Penguin Books Ltd., 1959, pp. 21–26.

3. There is, of course, a certain irony here, because the Safavids who united Iran in A.D. 1499 and challenged the Ottoman Empire were themselves Turkic and close ethnic and linguistic kin of the Ottomans.

4. For a study of these issues from the earlier times, see various volumes of *The Cambridge History of Iran,* Cambridge: Cambridge University Press, 1975. Also Abol Hassan Pirnia, *The History of Ancient Iran* (4 vols., in Persian), Tehran: Donyay-e-Ketab, 1362 (1983).

5. On the security dilemmas and foreign policy choices of small states, see Robert L. Rothstein, *Alliances and Small Powers,* New York: Columbia University Press, 1968; John F. Triska (ed.), *Dominant Powers and Subordinate States,* Durham, N.C.: Duke University Press, 1986; John Chay & Thomas E. Ross (eds.), *Buffer States in World Politics,* Boulder, Colo.: Westview Press, Inc., 1986. On Iran's special case see Shahram Chubin and Sepehr Zabih, *The Foreign Relations of Iran,* Berkeley: University of California Press, 1974, pp. 27–35.

6. In recent years, for example, both the United States and the Soviet Union have behaved toward Islamic Iran with some degree of restraint because their relations in the region are still competitive. Nevertheless, certain changes in the Soviets' foreign-policy priorities under Gorbachev and the beginning of a new era of Soviet-American détente have increased the chances of U.S.-Soviet understanding over Iran and thus have rendered Iran's position more precarious. Indeed, during the last two centuries Iran has not only been preoccupied with the impact of great power rivalry on its destiny, it has also been fearful of the effect of their collusion.

7. On the history of the Russo-Iranian wars, see R. K. Ramazani, *The Foreign Policy of Iran: A Developing Nation in World Affairs,* Charlottesville: University Press of Virginia, 1966, pp. 44–47; and from the same author, *History of Persia Under Qajar Rule,* translated from the Persian by Hassan Fasai. New York: Columbia University Press, 1972, pp. 107–143, 174–90.

8. For an Iranian account of Anglo-Iranian relations, see Mahmud Mahmud, *The History of Anglo-Iranian Relations in the Nineteenth Century,* Tehran, 1336 (1957–58). The British used their naval supremacy in the Persian Gulf to pressure Iran during the Anglo-Iranian wars over Herat. When the combined forces of Iran and the Emir of Herat—who wanted to remain under Iranian suzerainty—seemed to succeed, in 1856 the British fleet bombed the Iranian port of Khoramshahr (Mohammarah), thus forcing Iran to relinquish its claim to Herat. For a detailed account of the Anglo-Persian war of 1856–57, see Barbara English, *John Company's Last War,* London: Collins Clear-Type Press, 1971.

9. Iran, however, for some time resisted British pressure. In 1836 the Iranian prime minister, Ghaem Magham Farahani, argued with the British envoy that if Britain had Iran's interest at heart it would help it revise the discriminatory treaty of Turkmanchai rather than demanding the same privileges. He told the British envoy that this kind of trade would lead to Iran's gradual annihilation. See Fereydoun Adamiyat, *Andisheh Taraghi va Hokumat Ghanoun: Asr-e-sepahsalar* [*The Idea of Progress and the Rule of Law: The Era of Sepahsalar*] Tehran: Entesharat-e-Kharazmi, 1351, (1973).

10. See Dennis Wright, *The Persians Amongst the English,* London: I. B. Taurus & Co. Ltd., 1985, pp. xiii–xix. See also by the same author, *The English Amongst the Persians,* London: William Heinemann Ltd., 1977, pp. 1–4.

11. For example, the British envoy in Iran, Scheel, in his letter of 4 August 1850 to Foreign Secretary Lord Palmerston, opposed the idea of building a railroad in Iran and linking it to the proposed Europe-Asia railroad which was to begin in Vienna and end in the Sind Province. He thought this would increase Iran's economic and military power and thus would damage British interests. Passages of this letter read as follows:

"It would take another hundred years before the poor and weak Iran and its lethargic and coward government and people deserve to be part of the railroad plan. Of course, the building of the railroad would awaken Iran's talents which, because of need and poverty, have remained dormant. The movement of part of the European trade with India would increase Iran's importance and its dependence on Britain. However, this would also put the fate of Britain's enormous trade with the East all the way to China in the hands of this treacherous and hypocrite nation. Thus, there is no balance between the benefit that Iran would derive from the railroad and that which would incur to the British. From a military perspective, the railroad would bring Iran closer to the Indian border. An Iran which would be more active and more powerful. This would increase the threat of aggression against British possessions in India. Of course, currently there is no threat from Iran. But we cannot be sure of its behavior in time of war. Let us not forget that in this land there is no sign of honor, faith or gratitude. Greed determines the behavior of its people. . . . If once Iran and Russia were to form an alliance the railroad which extends to India's borders would increase our difficulties. . . . Devastation, impotence, poverty and barbarianism are the characteristics of all countries to the west of India. These characteristics have enabled Britain to consolidate its power in India. Of course, the British government does not intend to perpetuate this general state of Eastern societies. But it also does not have any moral commitment to try to end this state of devastation, impotence, poverty and barbarism."

Quoted in Fereydoun Adamiyat, *Andisheh Taraghi,* pp. 338–39. The last passage illustrates the hollowness of the so-called civilizing mission of imperialism. The Russians also consistently opposed the building of a railroad in Iran. Finally, the Persian king promised Russia that it would not grant a railroad concession to any other country. Since Britain would not allow this, in reality it meant that Iran would never have a railroad.

12. In 1883, popular opposition, combined with Russian opposition, forced the cancellation of concessions granted to an English baron, Julius Reuter. See Ibrahim Teymuri, *Asr-e-Bikhabari ya Tarikh-e-Imtiyazat dar Iran,* Tehran: Chap-e-Eghbal, 1332 (1953–54). Even Lord Curzon viewed this concession as "the most extraordinary surrender of the entire industrial resources of the country." See George N. Curzon, *Persia and the Persian Question,* London: Cass, 1982, p. 480. In 1890–91, massive popular outbursts against the concession granted by the Iranian government to Major G. Talbot for the exclusive sale and export of tobacco forced the cancellation of the concessions—the precursor of the Iranian constitutional revolution. See Ibrahim Teymuri, *Asr-e-Bikhabari.* Three prominent clerical leaders, Mirza Javad Mojtahed of Tabriz, Agha Najafi of Isphahan, and Hajd Mirza Mohammad Hassan-e-Shirazi of Najaf, played the leading role in gathering opposition. They called on the faithful

to refrain from smoking until the concessions were revoked, a call which was heeded by most Iranians.

13. On the Islamic regime's views on foreign borrowing, see *Middle East Economic Digest (MEED)*, Vol. 30, No. 19, 10 May 1986, p. 14, and Vol. 30, No. 35, 30 August 1986, p. 12. Iran's financial difficulties and enormous reconstruction problems have been changing attitudes toward foreign borrowing.

14. Professor Ramazani effectively shows instances of Iran's failure to adapt its goals to its means. See his *Iran's Foreign Policy.*

15. See Jalal Al-Ahmad, *Gharbzadeghi [Westoxication]*, Islamic Students Association of Europe and U.S. and Canada, 1979, p. 105

16. *Ibid.*, pp. 71–80.

17. The following statement by the Ayatollah Hossein-Ali Montazeri illustrates the view that the loss of cultural independence and authenticity has been at the root of Iran's and the Muslim world's scientific and technological backwardness and their dependent state. "Despite their glorious history and scientific traditions, Muslims became estranged from their Islamic personality as a result of colonialism. Colonialism thus convinced the Muslims that they could not survive independently. . . . " See *Keyhan Hawai*, 8 May 1985.

18. See Shireen T. Hunter (ed.), *The Politics of Islamic Revivalism: Diversity and Unity,* Bloomington: Indiana University Press, 1988.

19. Some believe Iran's language should be called Persian and not Farsi. However, Farsi is not limited to Iran. It is also spoken in Afghanistan and Tadjikistan.

20. Prominent Shi'a clerics have produced *Hadith* regarding the Iranians' special place in Islam. According to the prominent Shi'a cleric, Kulayni, the Shi'as' eighth Imam (Ali-Ibn Musa-ar-Reza) said that, since the Prophet Muhammad's death, the Iranians had been accorded a special status among the Muslims. Mohammad Baghir Majlesi, the great religious leader of seventeenth century Iran, went even further and claimed that, in matters of faith, the Iranians are superior to the Arabs. In support of this claim, he quoted the sixth Imam, Ja'far as-Sadiq, as having said that: "If the Qu'ran had been revealed to the Iranians, the Arabs would not have believed in it. So it was revealed to the Arabs, and the Iranians came to believe in it." Ibid., p. 33.

21. See Fereydoun Adamiyat, *Andishehay-e Mirza Agha Khan Kermani,* Tehran: Chap-khaneh Pirouz, 1346 (1967–68), pp. 176–97.

22. Ibid., pp. 252–68. This excessive Persian cultural nationalism grew stronger in the first four decades of the twentieth century, and many Iranian intellectuals came to believe that the restoration of Iran's Persianness was the remedy for its decline. A good representative of this intellectual trend is Taghi Arani, although he later turned to Marxism-Leninism as the answer to Iran's problems. While a native of Azerbaijan, he advocated the eradication of the Turkic language, seeing it as the legacy of the Mongol and Turkic invaders in the land of Zoroaster. Ahmad Kasravi, another native of Azerbaijan, had the same feelings and wrote a book on the pre-Turkic Iranian language of the region: *Azeri ya Zaban Bastan Azerbaijan (Azeri or the Ancient Language of Azerbaijan)*. Fereydoun Adamiyat cites an unknown author's work in which he argues that Iran's decline has been the result of their abandoning Islam to the point that the Iranians want to impose Christian laws on the Muslims, although they have the best law, namely the Holy Qur'an. See *Fakr Azadi va Nehzat Mush-rutiat [The Idea of Liberty and the Constitutional Movement]*, Tehran: Entesharat Sukhan, 1340 (1962), pp. 35–36

23. Shahrough Akhavi, *Religion and Politics in Contemporary Iran: Clergy, State Relations in the Pahlavi Period,* Albany: SUNY Press, 1980, pp. 60–90.

24. The year 1963, the beginning of the Shah's so-called White Revolution, was a watershed in this regard. From then on intellectual clerics such as Mir Motaheri began to systematically attack Iranian nationalism. On Mir Motaheri's views, see Hamid Enayat, *Modern Islamic Political Thought,* pp. 115, 122–25.

25. For an elaboration of the Ayatollah Khomeini's views on these and other issues, see

Islam and Revolution: Writings and Declarations of Imam Khomeini, translated by Hamid Algar, Berkeley: Mizan Press, 1981.

26. There were rare exceptions, such as U.S. intervention in the First World War and Woodrow Wilson's proclamation of his Fourteen Points.

27. For example, Fereydoun Adamiyat recounts that nineteenth century Iranian Constitutionalists all had a copy of the Declaration of the French Revolution. *Fakr-e-Democracy-e-Ejtemaie dar Nehzat Mashrutiatet-e-Iran* [The Idea of Social Democracy in Iran's Constitutional Movement], Tehran: Payam, 1354 (1975), p. 3

28. For details, see Sepehr Zabih, *The Communist Movement in Iran*, Berkeley: University of California Press, 1966, pp. 8, 9, 11, 14, 22–23.

29. See Morgenthau, *Politics Among Nations*, p. 92. Of course, other scholars have emphasized the concept of national interest as the primary impulse of state behavior.

30. See Zbigniew Brzezinski, *Ideology and Power in Soviet Politics*, Westport, Conn.: Greenwood Press, 1976, pp. 4–5.

31. F. S. Northedge, "The Nature of Foreign Policy," in F. S. Northedge (ed.), *The Foreign Policies of the Powers*, London: Faber and Faber, 1968, p. 13.

32. During this period, certain ideological currents within the Third World, such as non-alignment, also influenced the Iranian outlook and behavior.

33. See F. S. Northedge, *Op.cit.*, p. 10. On the linkages between domestic conditions and foreign policy, see James N. Rosenau, *Linkage Politics: Essays on the Convergence of National and International Systems*, New York: The Free Press, 1969. Also see David S. Geller, *Domestic Factors in Foreign Policy: A Cross-National Statistical Analysis*, Cambridge, Mass.: Scharkman Books, 1985.

34. See Jalal Al-Ahmad, *Gharbzadeghi*, pp. 87–90. He complains that in fact 54 percent of Iran's budget is spent on the military. He also refers to several articles published in the Tehran daily, *Etela'at*, authored by Dariush Homayoun.

35. See Chubin and Zabih, *The Foreign Relations of Iran*, pp. 89–90.

36. Ibid.

37. However, this policy did not prove successful and the radical Arabs continued their support for the anti-Shah forces. The Palestine Liberation Organization played an important role in training Iranian guerrillas, especially the Mojahedin-e-Khalgh. For detailed information on this with excellent sources, see Shoja-ed-Din Shafa, *Crimes and Punishments: Iran 1977–1985*, vol. II (in Persian), Washington D.C.: Inter-Collegiate Press, 1988, pp. 966–979. See also Jerrold D. Green, *Revolution in Iran: The Politics of Countermobilization*, New York: Praeger, 1982.

38. For a detailed discussion of the French Military Mission to Iran headed by General Gardane, see Sa'id Nafisi, *Tarikh-e-Siyasi va Ejtemai Iran* [The Political and Social History of Iran] Tehran: Intisharat-e-Bonyad 1335 (1956–57), pp. 100–21.

2. The Evolution of Iran's Diplomacy

1. See Mohammad Reza Pahlavi, *Mission for My Country*, London: Hutchinson & Co. Ltd., 1968, pp. 66–81.

2. See Shireen T. Hunter, "The Iran-Iraq War and Iran's Defense Policy," in Thomas Naff (ed.), *Gulf Security and the Iran-Iraq War*, Washington D.C.: National Defense University Press, 1985, pp. 169–72. Also William F. Hickman, *Ravaged and Reborn: The Iranian Army*, Washington D.C.: The Brookings Institution, 1982. In addition to rehabilitating the remnants of the Shah's military, the Islamic regime has created a strong para-military force in the form of the Revolutionary Guards, and it has tried to make Iran militarily self-sufficient. See Vahe Petrossian, "Iran Stocks Up its Armory," *MEED*, Vol. 31, No. 18, 2 May 1987, p. 11. Also *MEED*, various issues in September and November 1987, and April 1988.

3. On one such occasion, the Safavid king, Shah Abbas, enlisted British support in his

efforts to dislodge the Portuguese from the Iranian port of Gombrun in the Persian Gulf, later renamed Bandar Abbas after the king.

4. The impact of British naval supremacy was felt far beyond the Persian Gulf. During the Anglo-Iranian wars in 1856–57 over Herat—which Iran, with the assistance of the local Emir of Herat, was winning—British naval forces bombed the Iranian port of Khoramshahr, thus forcing it to concede defeat.

5. He was one of Iran's most-admired political personalities and its prime minister from 1846 until his removal from office in 1851 and assassination in 1852. See Fereydoun Adamiyat, *Amir Kabir Va Iran,* Tehran: Chapkhaneh Payam, 1323 (1944–45), pp. 281 and 492.

6. Ibid., pp. 112–150 and 240–66.

7. See Sepehr Zabih, *The Mossadegh Era,* Chicago: Lakeview Press, 1982, p. 88.

8. For example, writing in 1957, L. P. Elwell-Sutton observed that "Neutralism is stronger today in Iran than it has ever been; one can hardly speak with anyone who would not prefer his country to be free from all entanglements. . . . " "Nationalism and Neutralism in Iran," *The Middle East Journal,* Vol. 12, No. 1, Winter 1958, pp. 20–21.

9. See Sepehr Zabih, "Iran's International Posture: De Facto Non-Alignment Within a Pro-Western Alliance," *The Middle East Journal,* Vol. 24, No. 3, Summer 1970.

10. On Iran's early efforts to interest the United States in its development and to use it as counterweight to Russia and Britain, see Abraham Yeselson, *United States-Persian Diplomatic Relations 1883–1921,* New Brunswick, N.J.: Rutgers University Press, 1956.

11. On Franco-Iranian relations in this period, see Said Nafisi, *Tarikh-e-Siyasi va Ejtemai Iran,* Also Peter Avery, *Modern Iran,* New York: Praeger, 1965, pp. 33–39.

12. The U.S. Secretary of Defense, James V. Forrestal, believed that the United States must control Saudi Arabia's oil. This was a principal factor in forging close ties with Saudi Arabia first initiated by the meeting between President Franklin Roosevelt and King Abdulaziz in 1945. See William B. Quandt, *Saudi Arabia in the 1980s: Foreign Policy, Security, and Oil,* Washington D.C.: The Brookings Institution, 1981, pp. 47–48.

13. In 1919, therefore, the Iranian parliament rejected a treaty of alliance with Great Britain that, in effect, would have made Iran a British protectorate. This act, while totally in line with Iran's political culture and realities, was diplomatically a mistake. Had Iran agreed to British protection, it may very well have gotten a better deal in defining its territorial borders with the newly created state of Iraq. As it happened, Britain used its power and defined these borders as well as the regime of Shat-al-Arab in Iraq's favor. See Asghar Ja'far Valdari, "Barrasi Tarikhi Ekhtelafat Marzi Iran Va Aragh," *The Journal of Foreign Policy* (Tehran), Vol. 1, No. 4, October, November 1987.

14. For a brief but excellent study of Iran's regional diplomacy, see R. K. Ramazani, *The Foreign Policy of Iran* pp. 258–76. Also see his "The Instruments of Iran's Foreign Policy," in *Iran: Past, Present and Future,* Jane E. Jacqz (ed.), New York: Aspen Institute for Humanistic Studies, 1976, pp. 387–96.

15. This understanding was embodied in the landmark 1937 Sa'ad Abad Pact. Ramazani, *The Foreign Policy of Iran,* 272–76.

16. See R. K. Karanjia, *The Mind of a Monarch,* London, George Allen and Unwin, 1977, p. 236.

17. For examples of such statements, see *The Sayings of H. I. M. The Shah About Oil, July 1953–July 1975,* (In Persian). Tehran: Ministry of Information and Tourism, August 1975.

18. Ibid.

19. See Ibid., also for examples, see Shireen T. Hunter, *OPEC and the Third World: Politics of Aid,* Bloomington: Indiana University Press, 1984, pp. 106–123.

20. See Samuel Segev, *The Iranian Triangle: The Untold Story of Israel's Role in the Iran-Contra Affair,* New York: The Free Press, 1988, pp. 47–48.

21. See R. K. Ramazani, *Iran's Foreign Policy, 1941–1973,* Charlottesville: University Press of Virginia, 1975, pp. 298–299.

22. On the impact of Iran's economic needs on the Shah's foreign policy, see R. M. Burrell & Alvin J. Cottrell, *Iran, Afghanistan, Pakistan: Tensions and Dilemmas*, Washington D.C.: Center for Strategic and International Studies, Georgetown University, 1974, pp. 17–35. Also, on the question of export promotion as a consideration in foreign policy, see Firouz Vakil, "Iran's Basic Macro-Economic Problems," in *Iran: Past, Present and Future*, p. 84, and also Mohsen Fardi, "Iran's International Economic Outlook" in *Ibid.*, p. 350.

23. See Selig Harrison, "Dateline Afghanistan: Exit Through Finland," *Foreign Policy*, No. 41, Winter 1980–81.

24. Shahram Chubin has summed up this view well in the following way: "Few [Iranians] understood why a $10 billion defense budget had become a necessity overnight or why a war on the Horn of Africa threatened them. Nor could the majority of Iranians comprehend why large loans were being made to other countries when Iran's own countryside was deteriorating." See Shahram Chubin, "Local Soil, Foreign Plants," *Foreign Policy*, No. 34, Spring 1979, p. 22.

3. Iran's Islamic World View and Its Impact on Foreign Policy

1. For an elaboration of these points, see Farhang Rajaee, *Islamic Values and World View: Khomeini on Man, the State, and International Politics*, New York: University Press of America, 1983, pp. 45–46.

2. Following the end of World War II, the international system itself became polarized along many lines, political, ideological, and economical. During the last two decades this rigid ideological bipolarity has been eroded. Nevertheless, the world is still polarized at many other levels. The few newly industrializing countries (NICs) notwithstanding, the world is still divided into the rich, technologically advanced, industrialized countries, and the poor and technologically backward—the so-called developing nations. In other words, the North-South divide between the haves and the have-nots persists and is widening.

3. See M. Schwartz, "The Old Eastern Iranian World View According to the Avesta," and "The Religion of Achaemenian Iran," in *The Cambridge History of Iran* (Vol. 2)., pp. 640–97.

4. See Hamid Enayat, "Iran and the Arabs," in Sylvia Haim, ed., *Arab Nationalism and a Wider World*, New York: American Association for Peace in the Middle East, 1971, p. 15.

5. For an excellent study of Iranian impact on the development of Shi'a philosophy and mysticism, see Henry Corbin, *En Islam Iranian* (4 volumes), Paris: Gallimard, 1972.

6. See *Foreign Broadcasting Information Service (FBIS)/South Asia*, 24 July 1984, pp. I-3, I-4.

7. See Jalal Al-Ahmad, *Gharbzadeghi*, pp. 60–70.

8. *Ibid.*, pp. 73–80. It is also important to note that variations of this theme are widely believed in the Third World. In fact, the theory of dependency as an explanation for the Third World's problems was first developed in Latin America. During the last two decades, Third World rhetoric has emphasized the search for means to end this state of dependence and to achieve greater national and collective self-sufficiency. The views of the non-clerical Islamic ideologues have been greatly influenced by these Third World philosophical trends, which have contributed to their new interpretation of Islam. See, for example, "South-South: A Necessary Alliance," *South: The Third World Magazine*, No. 9, July 1981, pp. 13–18. Also see various documents of the United Nations Conference on Trade & Development (UNCTAD) on intra-Third World cooperation. The views of the non-clerical Islamic ideologues have also been greatly influenced by these Third World philosophical trends. Ali Shari'ati is the most famous representative of this group of intellectuals.

9. See Ismail Rai'n, *Hoghough Beghiran Engilis Dar Iran* [In the Pay of the English], Tehran: 1347 (1968). However, Khomeini and other leaders of the Islamic regime would not admit that many prominent religious figures in the nineteenth and twentieth centuries

were an important part of this corrupt elite. In other Third World countries, a history of *coups d'etat* and cover operations against a number of national governments and the perpetuation of a quasi-colonial relationship adds further credence to this theory.

10. See, for example, "France's Role in Africa: The Colonial Master Who Did Not Go Home," *The Wall Street Journal*, 22 July 1981, p. 1.

11. See Farhang Rajaee, *Islamic Values and World View*, p. 86.

12. Juan Jose Arevalo, *The Shark and the Sardines*, New York: El Stuart, 1961, p. 34.

13. See Farhang Rajaee, *Islamic Values and World View*, pp. 85–88; also for the Ayatollah Khomeini's talk on the unity of the Muslims, see *Keyhan*, 16 January 1982.

14. On Al-Afghani's views and tactics, see Eli Kedourie, *Afghani and Abduh*, London: Frank Cass & Co. Ltd., 1966, pp. 23–70.

15. See Richard Cottam, *Nationalism in Iran*, p. 153.

16. Elwell-Sutton, "Nationalism and Neutralism in Iran," pp. 20–21.

17. Farhang Rajaee, *Islamic Values and World View*, p. 83.

18. Ibid., pp. 88–91.

19. He further urged for an active foreign policy for Iran, in general, despite its enormous internal problems.

20. Quoted in "Sad Magaleh," a collection of Bani Sadr's articles, 1358 (1979), p. 84.

21. *Keyhan*, 11 January 1982, p. 4.

22. Shahrough Akhavi, "The Power Structure in the Islamic Republic of Iran," in Shireen Hunter, ed., *Internal Developments in Iran*, Washington: CSIS, 1985, pp. 1–10.

23. Shireen T. Hunter, "After the Ayatollah," *Foreign Policy*, No. 66, Spring 1987, pp. 77–97.

24. Ibid.

25. See the Iranian president's statement regarding the superpowers' fear of Islamic revolution and Iran's quest for Muslim unity, *Keyhan*, 9 January 1982.

26. On Rafsanjani's comments, see *MEED*, Vol. 32, No. 45, 1988, pp. 2–3, and on Montazeri's comments, see "Text of Montazeri's Speech on Revolution's Tenth Anniversary, *FBIS/MESA*, 10 April 1989, pp. 58–59.

27. "Khomeini Stresses Importance of Foreign Relations," *FBIS/SA*, 29 October 1984, p. I-1.

28. Ibid.

29. Ibid.

30. "Iranian Minister Defends Policy," *The Washington Post*, 27 November 1986, p. A-25. Iran's Foreign Minister, Ali-Akbar Velayati, has on many occasions said that having relations with other countries does not mean "accepting their hegemony."

4. Iran and the Superpowers: The United States

1. The idea, like many other reformist ideas, originated with Mirza Taghi Khan Amir Kabir. A principal reason for his interest in the United States was his desire to purchase warships to protect Iran's shores and trade in the Persian Gulf. See Mahmoud Foroughi, "Iran's Policy Towards the United States," in Abbas Amirie and Hamilton A. Twitchell (eds.), *Iran in the 1980's*, Tehran: Institute for International Political and Economic Studies, 1978, p. 339. Later Iran sought the use of American naval forces to protect the Iranian merchant marine and certain islands and ports "from the preponderance" of an unnamed power. Ibid.

2. Ibid. See Abraham Yeselson, *United States-Persian Diplomatic Relations*, p. 22. The first official contacts between Iran and the United States were undertaken between the diplomatic envoys of the two countries in Constantinople in 1851, and a Treaty of Friendship and Commerce was signed between the two countries on 13 December 1856. But it was

soon allowed to lapse because of British intrigues in Iran but, more important, the United States' own internal preoccupations.

3. For example, the American Minister in Constantinople maintained this view and argued that " . . . pressure could be applied secretly by the adroit use of Russian intrigue in Teheran." Ibid.

4. In 1919, the Americans told the British that Iran's representatives should be allowed to address the Paris Peace Conference, but abandoned this effort rather quickly in the face of British opposition. And during the Tehran Summit in 1943, the United States helped obtain the commitment of the Allied Powers occupying Iran to respect its independence and territorial integrity, a step which proved valuable in forcing the Soviet troop withdrawal in 1946.

5. U.S. Secretary of Defense James Forrestal's comment in the early 1940s that " . . . I don't care what American companies develop the Arabian reserves, but I think most emphatically that it should be Americans. . . . " illustrates Saudi Arabia's intrinsic value to the United States. See William B. Quandt, *Saudi Security in the 1980s: Foreign Policy, Security, and Oil,* Washington D.C.: The Brookings Institution, 1981, p. 48.

6. See R. K. Ramazani, *The United States and Iran,* New York: Praeger, 1982, pp. 37–38.

7. Ibid.

8. During the period 1953–61, Iran received a total of $548.1 million in economic loans and grants and $506 million in military aid. During the same period, India received $2,407.5 million in economic loans and grants but no military aid; Egypt received $302 million in economic aid; Pakistan received $1,418.7 million in economic aid and $508.2 million in military loans and grants; and Turkey received $1,093 million in economic aid and $1,463.4 in military loans and grants. Source: U.S. Senate Foreign Relations Committee: *U.S. Overseas Loans and Grants,* (CONG-R-0105). Some authors have argued that the low level of U.S. aid was due to Iran's low absorptive capacity. But surely, Iran's capacity was not less than Turkey's or Pakistan's. See Amir Taheri, *Nest of Spies: American Journey to Disaster in Iran,* New York: Pantheon Books, 1989, pp. 27, and 44–45.

9. According to a number of sources, all Amini needed was $250 million, based on personal conversations.

10. The Alliance for Progress was to bring about agrarian reform, but political vacillation by some countries, outright desertion by others, and shifting priorities in the United States have delayed the integration of the rural masses into Latin American society. . . . The Kennedy administration's political emphasis on changes in land tenure to prevent violent agrarian upheavals has given way to an economic emphasis on expansion of agricultural production. See Jerome Levinson and Juan De Onis, *The Alliance That Lost its Way,* A Twentieth Century Fund Study, Chicago: Quadrangle Books, 1972, pp. 247–48.

11. For an excellent account of this period and how the United States' other preoccupations related to handling of the Iranian problem, see Gary Sick, *All Fall Down: The United States' Tragic Encounter with Iran,* New York: Random House, 1985.

It is also instructive to contrast the U.S. handling of Iran and the Shah in 1978 with its handling of Ferdinand Marcos and the Philippines in 1986. Turkey's military regime was also treated more gently because of its vital role in NATO, especially in view of uncertainties with Greece and Spain. Indeed, human rights abuses in Turkey have continued in the 1980s. According to Amnesty International, 250,000 political prisoners have been detained in Turkey in the 1980s and "almost all of them were tortured," *The Washington Post,* January 4, 1989, p. A-14.

12. The United States has not been alone in this predicament. For example, after the expansion of the Soviet presence in Egypt in the 1960s, anti-Soviet feelings rose among the Egyptians and led to the eventual expulsion of the Russians by President Sadat.

13. The following quote from African scholar Ali Mazrui illustrates this point: "Israel

Was a Piece of the Western World deposited in the Heart of the Third World." Mazrui, ed., *Africa's International Relations,* p. 136.

14. It is interesting that not all of this analysis originated from Moscow or Peking. Many European leftist intellectuals also promoted such theories.

15. In addition to these fundamental factors that explain the evolution of Iranian attitudes toward the United States, over the years some U.S. officials and private citizens living and working in Iran have disregarded the Iranians' national and religious sensitivities, thus contributing to the rise of anti-Americanism and providing anti-U.S. forces with effective propaganda tools. The most graphic U.S. *faux pas* was the obtaining in the 1960s of special privileges and immunities for U.S. military personnel in Iran. This act had great symbolic significance for the Iranians because it reminded them of the era of capitulation.

16. However, Iran did not join the NAM. See Shapur Bakhtiar's interview reprinted in *FBIS/ME & NA,* 15 January 1979, pp. R5–R7.

17. See the text of comments by Karim Sanjabi, Iran's first post-revolution foreign minister. *FBIS/ME & NA,* 5 February 1979, p. R16.

18. These were over the delivery of military spare parts, as well as other difficulties largely emanating from canceled contracts and disputes over compensation—as was also the case with Iran's other major trading partners. Cheryl Benard and Zalmay Khalilzad, *The Government of God: Iran's Islamic Republic,* New York: Columbia University Press, 1984, pp. 160–62.

19. Ibid., pp. 160–61.

20. According to Professor Richard Cottam, the State Department was against this action, fearing that it would cause a setback in U.S.-Iranian relations, which it did. See Richard W. Cottam, *Iran and the United States,* Pittsburgh: The University of Pittsburgh Press, 1988, p. 209.

21. Ibid.

22. In addition to Richard Cottam's book, see Gary Sick, *All Fall Down,* and James Bill, *The Eagle and the Lion: The Tragedy of American-Iranian Relations,* New Haven: Yale University Press, 1988. Also see the memoirs of Zbigniew Brzezinski and Cyrus Vance.

23. Richard Cottam, p. 211. Professor James Bill sees an even more direct link. See Bill, *The Eagle and the Lion,* p. 294.

24. The opposition of other secular, nationalist leaders derived almost solely from personal power considerations.

25. Indeed, some Iranian officials expressed their fear of PLO penetration to U.S. embassy officials. See Benard and Khalilzad, *Government of God,* p. 161.

26. See Richard Cottam, p. 211.

27. The Carter Doctrine, announced in Carter's *State of the Union Address* (1980), stated "An attempt by any outside force to gain control of the Persian Gulf region will be regarded as an assault on the vital interests of the United States of America. And such an assault will be repelled by any means necessary, including military force."

28. This belief seems to have been punctured by developments in 1987–88: the mild Soviet response to the projection of U.S. naval power to the Persian Gulf and to U.S.-Iranian military confrontation and increased Soviet willingness to reach mutually beneficial agreements with the United States on regional issues.

29. In fact, some Iranian moderate figures, such as Foreign Minister Ali-Akbar Velayati, stated categorically that the radicals are " . . . leftists with an Islamic veneer. . . . " See Velayati's speech delivered at Tehran University, *The Washington Post,* 27 November 1986. For their part, the radicals accused the moderates of adhering to what they call "American Islam." See the interview of Hodjat-al-Islam Khoeiniha, *FBIS/MESA,* 28 January 1988, p. 13–4.

30. The following quote sums up Khomeini's view of these connections, quoted in Ledeen and Lewis, *Debacle,* p. 108. " . . . It is America which supports Israel and its well wishers; it is America which gives Israel the power to turn Muslim Arabs into vagrants; it is America

which directly or indirectly imposes its agents on the nation of Iran; it is America which considers Islam and the glorious Qur'an a source of harm to itself and wishes to remove both from its path. . . . "

31. See "Shultz Outlines Policy of Opposing Soviets," *The Washington Post*, 16 June 1983, p. 1.

32. See address by Secretary of State Alexander Haig on 26 May 1982 before the Chicago Council on Foreign Relations, *Transcript in American-Arab Affairs*, No. 1 (Summer 1982), pp. 190–196.

33. See Nader Entessar, "Super Powers and Persian Gulf Security: The Iranian Perspective," *Third World Quarterly* Vol. 10 No. 4, October 1988, p. 1437.

34. On the Beirut bombings, see various issues of *The Washington Post* and *The New York Times*.

35. Soon thereafter, the Lebanese government abrogated the 17 May 1983 treaty it had signed with Israel at U.S. instigation.

36. On sanctions, see "Statement by the President," The White House, Office of the Press Secretary, 26 October 1987, which provides background information on the earlier sanctions.

37. On Iran's fear of a military strike, see the Tehran Radio Commentary, "U.S. Preparation for Confrontation Viewed," *FBIS/SA*, 7 December 1983, p. I-2.

38. "Prime Minister Views Elections, U.S. Bullying," *FBIS/SA*, 19 April 1984, p. I-1. (Tabas was the location of the failed rescue mission in the Iranian desert: "Desert One.")

39. For example, " . . . in January 1984 Geoffrey Kemp, senior director for Near East and South Asian Affairs in the National Security Council and the principal NSC staff officer responsible for the Persian Gulf, wrote a memorandum to Robert C. McFarlane, assistant to the president for national security affairs. . . . He viewed the Khomeini government as a menace to American interests and suggested a revival of covert operations against it. According to Kemp, Teheran's policies and politics enhanced Syria's standing among Arab states and threatened Western access to Persian Gulf oil. . . . He reported that exiled Iranians with whom he regularly communicated, hoped that with foreign help they might install a pro-Western government. Suggestions of divisions in the country and support from Saudi Arabia for the exiles encouraged Kemp to submit his proposal. (Kemp to McFarlane 1, 13, 84)." See Malcolm Byrne, ed., *The Chronology: The Documented Day-by-Day Account of the Secret Military Assistance to Iran and the Contras, The National Security Archive* (New York: Warner Books, 1987), p. 47.

40. *Financial Times*, 12 May 1984, p. 2.

41. See, for example, the Ayatollah's address to the clergy in Tehran, FBIS/SA, 6 October 1983, pp. I1–3.

42. I wrote on 23 August 1984 in *The New York Times*, p. 31, under the title "Inviting Post-Khomeini Moderation," and in Fall 1985 Professor Ramazani wrote "Iran and the United States, Burying the Hatchet," in *Foreign Policy* magazine, No. 60, pp. 52–74.

43. A former U.S. official told me that this approach was adopted in part because some members of the U.S. administration found exaggeration of the Iranian threat to be useful—and even necessary—for the success of their particular policies. At the Defense Department, for example, proponents of arms sales to Saudi Arabia and other Gulf states needed to exaggerate the Iranian threat in order to get congressional approval. According to the same official, even Operation Staunch created its own bureaucracy, which then fought for this approach. Some U.S. officials were also pleased that Iran and the Iranian threat had transcended the Palestinian issue as the most serious problem in the Middle East.

44. Indeed, as one former member of the National Security Council staff told me, no one in the bureaucracy wanted to think about Iran—except occasional and desultory talk of using the Iranian exiles—until and unless it ended the war and clearly denounced terrorism.

45. See Laurie Mylroie, "The Super Powers and the Iran-Iraq War," *American-Arab Affairs*, No. 21, Summer 1987, pp. 15–26. Also see Eric Hooglund, "Factions Behind U.S.

Policy in the Gulf,'' *Middle East Report*, Vol. 18, No. 2, March-April 1988, pp. 29–31. According to Hooglund, '' . . . while the 'Arabists' are unified in their perceptions of the threat posed by Iran, there is less consensus on how that threat should be contained. One camp supports active measures, including the use of military force, in order to convince Iran to cease efforts to export its revolution. . . . ''

46. These comments are based on personal interviews. Similar views were also held by officials at the Defense Department. This was graphically illustrated by Caspar Weinberger's statement in a televised interview, during the Iran-Contra affair, that Iranian "moderates" are dead Iranians. Later, the Defense Department campaigned for a total trade embargo against Iran.

47. See "U.S. Reviews Trade," *MEED*, Vol. 31, No. 26, 3 July 1987, p. 13.

48. The supply of arms as the principal instrument of contact with Iran was indefensible, on practical as well as on other grounds. Any supply of arms should have followed, not preceded, the release of hostages and the moderation of Iranian behavior. The United States should have indicated to Iran that, if it moderated its behavior—including willingness to accept a negotiated peace—the United States would consider such Iranian grievances as Iraqi aggression.

49. While the threat of an imminent Soviet takeover of Iran may have been somewhat exaggerated, the underlying assumption behind the famous Graham Fuller memo of 1985, namely that "the Soviet Union is better placed to affect Iran's evolution through a mix of cooperation and intimidation" was correct. See The National Security Archive, The *Chronology*, p. 78, and "The Report of the President's Special Review Board" (The Tower Commission), 26 February 1987.

50. Michael Ledeen, "How the Iran Initiative Went Wrong," *The Wall Street Journal*, 10 August 1987, p. 26.

51. This study is not designed as a comprehensive analysis of the Iran-Contra affair but discusses only those elements that are germane to the central arguments about Iranian foreign policy. Several good treatments have been prepared on the Iran-Contra affair. See, for example, Michael Ledeen, *Perilous Statecraft: An Insider's Account of the Iran-Contra Affair*. New York: Scribner Press, 1988. Samuel Segev, *The Iranian Triangle*, and Amir Taheri, *The Nest of Spies*.

52. *Chronology*, pp. 72–73.

53. It is, however, clear that different elements had different objectives, with the radicals being essentially after arms. For example, apparently, in one of the secret U.S.-Iranian meetings, someone from the prime minister's office was present. He was a well-known opponent of improvement in U.S.-Iranian relations. See *Chronology*, Ibid.

54. *FBIS/SA*, 5 December 1986, p. I-2.

55. See, for example, Prime Minister Hoseyn Musavi's declaration in *FBIS/SA*, 5 November 1986, and Ayatollah Khomeini's statements in *FBIS/SA*, 20 November 1986, p. I1–2.

56. Note the following in the Tower Commission's Report: "In addition, elements in Israel undoubtedly wanted the United States involved for its own sake so as to distance the United States from the Arab world and ultimately establish Israel as the only real strategic partner of the United States in the region." Part III, Section A, Stage 3: "The Israelis Provide a Vehicle."

57. Statement by Secretary of State George P. Shultz before the Senate Foreign Relations Committee, as transcribed in *Arab-American Affairs*, No. 20 (Spring 1987), pp. 163–165.

58. See the testimony of Assistant Secretary of State for Near Eastern and South-Asian Affairs, Richard Murphy, before the Senate Foreign Relations Committee, 29 May 1987. Michael Armacost said that American interests included the free flow of oil, freedom of navigation, the security and stability of moderate actions in the Gulf, and the limitation of Soviet influence.

59. It is also intriguing that the United States was emphasizing the Soviet threat at a time

when U.S.-Soviet relations were rapidly improving, and there was increasing talk of Soviet-American cooperation to manage, if not resolve, regional conflicts. It is fair to assume that the emphasis on the Soviet threat was an effort to gain domestic support for the reflagging policy.

60. This point was conceded by Undersecretary of State for Political Affairs Michael Armacost in testimony before the Senate Foreign Relations Committee on 11 June 1987.

61. Indeed, as of March 1987 only 12 Kuwaiti ships had been attacked. See *The Washington Post*, 28 March 1987, p. A-13.

62. According to the report prepared by the U.S. Senate Foreign Relations Committee: " . . . Kuwait permitted the use of its airspace for Iraqi sorties against Iran, agreed to open its ports and territory for the trans-shipment of war materiel (mostly of French and Soviet origin) and joined with the Saudis in providing billions of dollars in oil revenues to help finance the Iraqi war effort. In clear and unmistakable terms, Kuwait took sides." U.S. Committee on Foreign Relations, *War in the Persian Gulf, The U.S. Takes Sides*, Washington D.C., 1987, p. 37.

63. The circumstances of this incident were not clear. The United States maintained that it was a deliberate Iranian attack. But there was speculation that it was an accident, and that the missile had been fired at random.

64. According to Gary Sick, the Resolution was written in a way as to make it unacceptable to Iran. See Gary Sick, "What Do We Think We Are Doing in the Gulf?" *The Washington Post*, 24 April 1988, p. D-1.

65. Meanwhile, only two days after the U.S. attack, Iraqi forces captured the Faw peninsula on 20 April 1988.

66. Sick, "What Do We Think We Are Doing in the Gulf?" p. D-1. I was told by a journalist who regularly visits Iran and has good contacts that the Ayatollah Khomeini initially approved of this policy but later was dissuaded by Foreign Minister Velayati and President Khamenei. Moreover, as one former British diplomat with service in Baghdad told me, it is possible that the mine was laid by Iraq. Just as Iraq's apparently accidental attack on the *U.S.S. Stark* in May 1987 had brought U.S. warships into the Persian Gulf, so the attack on the *U.S.S. Roberts* led to the most significant military confrontation between Iran and the United States. It must be remembered that the mere presence of the U.S. Navy had not ended the war nor had it forced Iran to the bargaining table. On Iraqi provocations, see also Peter Grief, "Ship Attacks Reflect Iran's Frustration, U.S. Resolve," *The Christian Science Monitor*, 19 April 1988, p. 1.

67. As *The New York Times* reported, " . . . other officials said that Mr. Larijani's apparently conciliatory messages constituted an authentic offer of dialogue on behalf of the Iranian governments." "Iran Sought Talks in April, U.S. Says," *The New York Times*, 8 July 1988, p. A-6.

68. See Youssef M. Ibrahim, "As Iran Mourns, Khomeini Urges 'Real War' on U.S.," *The New York Times*, 5 July 1988, p. A-9.

69. See Edward Cody, "Tehran Official Cautions Against Hasty Revenge." *The Washington Post*, 6 July 1988, p. A-1.

70. However, ICAO's report later faulted the United States for grave negligence. See "World Aviation Panel Faults U.S. Navy on Downing of Iran Air Jet," *The New York Times*, 4 December 1988, p. 3.

71. See "Iranian Minister Calls on U.S. to Lessen Hostility," *The Christian Science Monitor*, 28 July 1988, p. 8.

72. For example, after the release of the Pentagon report, Admiral William Crowe, chairman of the Joint Chiefs of Staff, commented: "I believe that the actions of Iran were the proximate cause of this accident and would argue that Iran must bear the principal responsibility for the tragedy." See *The Washington Post*, 20 August 1988, p. A-18.

73. See "Bush Terms Strike at Plane Self-Defense," *The Washington Post*, 15 July 1988, p. A-1.

74. For example, Gary Sick wrote in "Failure and Danger in the Gulf," *The New York Times*, 6 July 1988, p. A-23, that: "Over the past few months our forces have been deployed aggressively and provocatively in the hottest part of the Persian Gulf. We have assumed responsibility not only for ships that fly our flag—including the 11 reflagged Kuwaiti tankers—but for any ship that finds itself under attack. This expansion of the United States' role was a disaster waiting to happen. Over the past weekend it did. . . . "

75. For example, *The New York Times* published a report that the Iranians had been cleaning the American Embassy compound in Tehran. The United States answered that "We are not moving in." 18 October 1988, p. 6.

76. The Democratic Party's candidate for president, Governor Michael Dukakis, attacked the Republican candidate, Vice President George Bush, for having dealt with Iran, for having "sold arms to the Ayatollah," and for compromising on the issue of dealing with terrorists. Thus the Reagan administration feared that any response to Iranian overtures would be exploited as another dishonorable dealing with terrorists.

77. This debate dates back to at least 1986. After the Iran-Contra affair, articles were written attacking continuous U.S. preoccupation with Iran and its strategic importance. See Frederick W. Axelgard, "Mistaken Nostalgia About Iran," *The Christian Science Monitor,* 21 November 1986, p. 20.

78. However, many oil industry analysts do not agree with this assessment. One oil industry executive told me that their geological surveys indicate significant untapped reserves in Northern Iran, on the Caspian Sea, and parts of the south which puts their estimates of Iran's potential very close to those of Iraq.

79. See "A Sharp Divergence Over Sanctions for Iraq: Shultz Counters Hard-Line Hill Approach," *The Washington Post,* 18 August 1988, p. 1.

80. See "Daily on U.S. Spies, Algiers Accord Violations," *FBIS/NESA,* 3 May 1989, p. 59.

81. See: "Iran Broke CIA Spy Ring, U.S. Says," *New York Times* 8 August 1989.

82. See "Iranian Advocates Killing: Rafsanjani Says Palestinians Should Attack Westerners," *The Washington Post,* May 6, 1989, pp. Al and A8.

83. See the commentary by Rowland Evans and Robert Novak in *The Washington Post,* 12 June 1989. Also "U.S.: Diplomatic Ball is in Tehran's Court," *The Christian Science Monitor,* 13 June 1989, pp. 1–2.

84. There is a suspicion, however, that he was killed earlier. See "US Says CIA Believes It Is Probable Higgins Was Killed before Monday," *New York Times,* 3 August 1989, p. A8.

85. See "US Sees Long Process in Hostage Negotiations," *Washington Post,* 7 August 1989, p. A16.

86. The fact is that while at least rhetorically the U.S. has portrayed Iran as responsible for all the actions of radical Lebanese Shi'as, a variety of motives have been behind their actions, as illustrated by the following comment by an Egyptian columnist quoted in the *New York Times*: " . . . The issue of the hostages is tied to the wider Arab confrontation with the West. . . . It cannot be divorced from Israel's occupation of a slice of southern Lebanon where many Shiites live, nor from the resentment among Arabs of American support for Israel . . . " See "Hostages Are the Victims of Chaos as Well as Rage," *New York Times,* 6 August 1989, p.1. The Syrians also made it clear that their cooperation had a price. Indeed, the Syrian foreign minister told the U.N. mediator, Marrack Goulding, that a solution to the hostage crisis "depended on a change in American policies in the area." See "Syrian Help on Hostages Has a Price," *Christian Science Monitor,* 11 August 1989, pp. 1, 2.

87. See "Iran, Syria Offer to Help in Hostage Swap, sources Say," *Washington Times,* 4 August 1989, p. 9. Indeed, the behavior of Iran's new president was quite conciliatory despite challenges from his radical rivals. He expressed his regret and condemned the killing of Colonel Higgins.

88. "Hashemi Rafsanjani 'Ready to Help' in Lebanon," *FBIS ME/SA*, 4 August 1989, p. 43.

89. See "Rafsanjani Will Help if Washington Scrubs 'Hostile' Stance," *Washington Times*, 18 August 1989, p. 9.

90. "U.S. and Iran Face Political Constraints," *Washington Post*, 7 August 1989, p. 1.

91. "See "Rafsanjani Will Help if Washington Scrubs 'Hostile Stance'," *Washington Times*, 18 August 1989, p. 9.

92. See "Iran Suggests Talks through Pakistan," *Washington Post*, 11 August 1989, p. 1.

93. Among the three different types of claims—government-to-government, corporate, and private, the first has proved easiest to resolve. On the private claims, the Iranians have shown sensitivity to claims lodged by Iranians with dual nationality.

94. This information is based on personal interviews.

5. Iran and the Superpowers: The Soviet Union

1. See Rouhallah K. Ramazani, *The Foreign Policy of Iran: A Developing Nation in World Affairs, 1500–1941*, pp. 21–22.

2. In 1723 when Tahmasb Ghuli (Nadir Shah Afshar) was fighting the Ottomans, Russia offered to help Iran in exchange for Gilan, Mazandaran, Astarabad, and Darband. Ibid., p. 22. But in 1729, it agreed to the partition of Iran with the Ottomans.

3. The first round of Russo-Iranian wars lasted from 1804 to 1813. The war was interrupted because of the start of the Napoleonic wars in Europe. British mediation resulted in the signing of a highly discriminatory treaty, called the Treaty of Gulistan, ceding to Russia most of Iran's trans-Caucassian possessions, as well as the exclusive right to have warships on the Caspian Sea, although Russia was soon to be invaded by Napoleon and thus forced to withdraw from Iran, leaving no need for Iranian concessions.

4. For the text of the treaty, see J. C. Hurewitz, *Diplomacy in the Near and Middle East*, Vol. I, Princeton, N.J.: Princeton University Press, 1956, pp. 96–102.

5. Russia's continued southward advance during the nineteenth century eliminated Iran's traditional links with Central Asia, many of whose peoples are ethnically and culturally related to the Persians. In fact, a large part of what is now Soviet Central Asia, and large parts of what is now Afghanistan, plus Khorasson—which is still part of Iran—are where the post-Arab invasion of Persian literary and linguistic renaissance occurred. It was in this geographic area that a new Persian known as "Farsi-e-Dari," as opposed to Pahlavi Persian, emerged. Bokhara was the seat of the local Samanid dynasty, which traced their ancestry to one of the most illustrious generals of the Sassanid period, Bahram Chubin. Later, recurring Turkic and Mongol invasions numerically weakened the ethnic Iranian element. However, most of the invaders—like the Arabs before them—became culturally Persianized. The Tadjiks, however, maintained a greater degree of ethnic purity and their language remained Persian. Indeed, Soviet writers had developed a history and cultural heritage for Tadjikistan derived from Iran's heritage. A book entitled *Tadjikistan*, published in French by the Novosti Press Agency, builds up a history for Tadjikistan on the basis of Iranian history without, however, even once mentioning Iran or the fact that this area was once part of Iran. It talks about the conquest of Central Asia by Alexander of Macedonia and the Arabs. But it never mentions the Achamenid or Sassanid Persian empires. In one passage of the book it says that "in the IXth and Xth centuries A.D. the true master of this territory was the state in which reigned the Samanid Dynasty." Yet even in this respect, not once is the name of Iran mentioned, although the Samanids considered themselves Persians. However, this denial of the Iranian element in Tadjikistan reaches a flagrant and almost ridiculous level when the book talks about the Tadjiks' literary and scientific heritage. Not only are poets such as Roudaki Samarqandi considered Tadjiks, but Firdowsi Tusi (Tus is a city in

the present-day Iranian province of Khorasson), the author of *Shahanameh,* who chronicles Iran's pre-Islamic history from the mythological era until the Arab invasion, is considered Tadjik. According to this book, Abu-Ali Sina (Avecenna), the Iranian philosopher and scientist (born in Nishapur and died in Hamadan, Iran), Jalal-ed-in Rumi, Omar Khayyam, Sa'adi (born in Shiraz in southern Iran), Djami (born in Kirman, Iran), and Nasser-e-Khosrow are Tadjiks (pp. 50–51).

According to this interpretation of history, there never was an Iran or an Iranian literary and scientific tradition. This conscious falsification of history is intended for political purposes, so that Iran can never claim any special relationship to this area and its people. Another example of this conscious elimination of any Iranian connection illustrates the point: The book says that for twenty-seven centuries "Now Rouz" (the mythical Iranian New Year) has been celebrated in Tadjikistan without making any reference to its origins in Iran. This usurpation of Iran's cultural and historical heritage is not limited to Tadjikistan. In large parts of Afghanistan, Persian is spoken. The Afghans, however, like to call their language "Dari" to emphasize their linguistic and cultural distinctiveness from Iran, without admitting to the historical beginnings of the language noted before. Similarly, the Afghans also claim Firdowsi, although he never once mentioned the words Tadjik or Afghan in connection with the people or history that he was writing about.

6. See R. K. Ramazani, *The Foreign Policy of Iran, 1500–1941,* p. 148.

7. See Mohammad Taghi Bahar (Malek-e-Sho'ara), *Tarikh-e-Ahzab-Siasi* [The History of Political Parties], Tehran: 1323 (1945), Vol. I, p. 27.

8. Bolshevik repudiation of Tsarist privileges enabled Iran to extract similar concessions from other foreign powers and to free itself from capitulatory treaties.

9. On the Gilan Republic and the beginnings of the Communist movement in Iran, see Sephr Zabih, *The Communist Movement in Iran,* pp. 13–45.

10. R. K. Ramazani, *Iran's Foreign Policy 1971–73: A Study of Foreign Policy in Modernizing Nations,* Charlottesville: University Press of Virginia, 1975. Also see Sephr Zabih and Shahram Chubin, *The Foreign Relations of Iran: A Developing State in a Zone of Great Power Conflict,* Berkeley: University of California Press, 1974; Shireen T. Hunter, "The Soviet Union and the Islamic Republic of Iran," in Hafeez Malik (ed.), *Soviet-American Relations with Pakistan, Iran and Afghanistan,* New York: St. Martin's Press, 1987, pp. 244–66.

11. These parties include the Kurdish Democratic Party (KDP), the Democratic Party of Azerbaijan, and the Communist Party of Baluchistan.

12. These changes included its withdrawal from CENTO, the severing of its links with Israel and South Africa, the establishing of close ties with such Soviet allies as Syria, Libya, and the PLO.

13. They had noticed strains in U.S.-Iran relations, and the view in influential quarters in the United States of the Shah as more of a liability than an asset. This view was best illustrated by the characterization of the Shah by the then U.S. Secretary of the Treasury, William Simon, as a "jerk."

14. Ibrahim Yazdi, in particular, had been instrumental in selling a positive image of Khomeini to American political and academic circles. Ghotbzadeh and Bani-Sadr also have had secret contacts with the Americans. See, for example, Dilip Hiro, *Iran Under The Ayatollahs,* London: Routledge & Kegan Paul, 1985, pp. 197–98.

15. Sadegh Ghotbzadeh was perhaps the most outspoken anti-Soviet member of this group. But Bani-Sadr also was highly suspicious of the Soviet Union. The following passage from Bani-Sadr illustrates his sentiments toward the Soviet Union and betrays pan-Iranist feelings. "Soviet Russia contains Asian Republics which were historically a part of our territory, that is, Turkmenistan, Azerbaijan, Tadjikistan, etc. . . . and which were taken from us as a result of two wars between Iran and Tsarist Russia. From a cultural and even from an economic point of view, these regions are a part of Iran. . . . As far as I can see, the Russians would never want an independent regime in Iran." Interview with *Le Quotidien du Peuple,* 19

September 1978, quoted in Ali-Reza Nobari (ed.), *Iran Erupts,* Iran-America Documentation Group, Stanford University, 1978, p. 283.

16. Moscow had extensive contacts with other Iranian leftists, many of whom were trained in PLO camps in Lebanon, where Soviet influence is strong. There is also evidence that there had been extensive contacts between leftist and Islamic opposition groups, as well as some Soviet infiltration of religious students in Qom. For example, Hodjat-el-Islam Khoei-niha, once the Iranian prosecutor general, and one of the most radical and pro-Soviet elements of the current regime, was the liaison between the Tudeh Party and the religious opposition.

17. Leonid Medvedko, "Islam and Liberation Revolution," *New Times,* No. 43, October 1979, pp. 18–21.

18. Ibid.

19. Medvedko further stressed that progressive components of Islam are stronger in Shi'ism than in Sunnism. Ibid.

20. These articles allowed the Soviets to intervene militarily in Iran if they felt that their security was threatened by a third country.

21. Soviet behavior in Azerbaijan and Kurdistan underscored this Soviet proclivity. The Soviet Union was also irritated by some pan-Iranist claims to parts of the USSR with Persian-speaking peoples. See "Ex-Envoy To Iran on Paper's Territorial Claims," *FBIS Soviet Union/ International Affairs,* 9 January 1987, p. 87. Radio Moscow was commenting on an article in the Iranian paper, *Jomhuri-e-Eslami,* claiming that some Soviet border areas belonged to Iran.

22. For an elaboration of Soviet views on Iran's national minorities, see Pavel Mezentsev, "Iran: Faced With Complex Problems," *New Times,* No. 33, August 1979, pp. 8–9.

23. For details of Iraqi subversion in Khusistan, see R. K. Ramazani, *Revolutionary Iran and The Middle East: Challenges and Responses,* Baltimore: The Johns Hopkins University Press, 1986, pp. 61, 103.

24. *Le Monde,* 18 April 1980, p. 5.

25. Quoted in Aryeh Yodfat, *The Soviet Union and Revolutionary Iran,* New York: St. Martin's Press, 1984, pp. 65–66.

26. See "Russians are Dangerous, Iranians Say," London *Times,* 22 January 1980, p. 1.

27. *Ettela'at,* 12 May 1980.

28. See Ned Temko, "Is Iran Losing Fear of Soviet Bear Hug?" *The Christian Science Monitor,* 24 April 1980, pp. 1, 7.

29. In its 2 February 1982 issue, the Tehran daily, *Keyhan,* printed an interview with a German journalist in which she alleged that, nine months before the beginning of the war, Helmut Schmidt and Valery Giscard d'Estaing knew about it.

30. For example, in an interview with *An Nahar al-Arabi Wa ad Duwali* in October 1980, the adviser to Bani-Sadr talked of a Soviet-American agreement to divide the region.

31. His other statements, such as his demand that Iran be allowed to open a consultate to Dushanbeh (capital of Tadjikistan) also irritated the Soviets. See "Relations Worsen Between Tehran and Moscow," London *Times,* 3 July 1980, p. 8.

32. The following statement by Mir-Hossein Moussavi to an interviewer on his view of the Soviet Union illustrates the pro-Soviet tendency within the regime. Asked why there has been less criticism of the Soviet Union and Eastern bloc countries, he said: "We did not sustain as much damage from them as we did from the United States in the last fifty years." See *Joint Publications Research Service* (JPRS), 23 June 1986, p. 53.

33. The Tudeh Party hoped to seize power in cooperation with the so-called followers of the Imam's line. See " 'Red Plot' Sparks Off Anti-Russian Frenzy," London *Sunday Times,* 8 May 1983, p. 18.

34. See various issues of SIPRI annual reports on details of sources of Iran's arms supplies.

35. See Shahram Chubin, "Gains for Soviet Policy in the Middle East," *International Security,* Spring 1982, Vol. 6, No. 4, pp. 122–52.

36. Trade was conducted mostly through barter agreements. Many joint Soviet-Iranian economic ventures were carried over from the Shah's time and no major new industrial or other ventures were set up. Some of the most important of these joint ventures are the following: The Isphahan Steel Mill, Ahwaz Power Station, Aras Dam, Arak Machine Building Factory, and the installation of several grain elevators. Iran has constructed eleven grain elevators with Soviet cooperation since 1963.

37. For example, in June 1981 the one-time prosecutor general of Iran, the Ayatollah Mohammad Sadiq Khalkhali, visited Baku and Tashkent as head of an Iranian religious delegation, at the invitation of the Muslim Board of Transcaucasia—one of the four religious boards responsible for the administration of Islam in the Soviet Union. Other contacts with Soviet Muslims and authorities in charge of Muslim affairs in the Soviet Union have continued. For example, after the Mecca incident, Iran's ambassador to Moscow met Muslim officials in Baku and explained Iran's positions. See *FBIS Soviet Union/International Affairs,* 27 August 1987, pp. 7–8.

38. Quoted in Aryeh Y. Yodfat, *The Soviet Union and Revolutionary Iran* p. 94.

39. Ibid.

40. See Muriel Atkin, "Moscow's Disenchantment with Iran," *Survey,* Autumn/Winter, 1983, pp. 247–60.

41. Yet Iranian Islam is not the greatest threat to Soviet Asia because, except for Azerbaijan, most of its populations are Sunni. In fact, propaganda coming from Pakistan and Saudi-Wahabi infiltration is more insidious. For example, Tadjikistan's Muslim extremists are Wahabi, not Khomeinist. Iran's challenge is more cultural, ethnic, and linguistic, and that is why the Soviets focus on Iran. See, for example, Alexander Benningsen, "Mullahs, Mujahedin & Soviet Muslims," *Problems of Communism,* November/December 1984, pp. 28–44. On Wahabi infiltration in Tadjikistan, see Alexandre Beningsen, "Unrest in the World of Soviet Islam," *Third World Quarterly,* Vol. 10, No. 2, April 1988, pp. 770–87.

42. See "Islam Rejects Violence," an interview with Shaikh-ul-Islam Alla Shukur Pasha-Zade, chairman of the Muslim Board for Transcaucasia, *New Times,* 9 April 1987, p. 5.

43. Among the forces armed by Iran are the following Shi'a groups: Harakat-e-Islami (Islamic movement), which is located in the Central Hazara region; and Nasr, another Hazara Party active in Central and Northern Afghanistan. In addition, Iran has good connections with certain Sunni groups as well. See "Afghan Resistance Groups," *Defense Journal,* Vol. XII, No. 12, 1987, pp. 43–44. On the conditions of Afghan refugees in Iran, see "Iran: Sanctuary for Millions," *MEED,* Vol. 30, No. 4, 25 January 1985, p. 5.

For example, the morning edition of Izvestia on 2 December 1986, in a long article attacking Iranian involvement with Afghan rebels, said the following: "In rendering support to the bandits, supplying them with weapons and setting camps for Afghan counter revolutionaries on its territory, the Iranian government bears full responsibility for the bloody crimes perpetrated by the dushmans (dushman, meaning enemy in Farsi, is the term used by the Soviets to define the Afghan Mojahedin). Other known facts also confirm that Iran is carrying out flagrant interference in the internal affairs of Democratic Afghanistan. In this year alone, the Iranian Air Force and ground forces have carried out over 60 acts of aggression against the DRA. . . . " See *FBIS USSR/International Affairs,* 3 December 1986, p. H1. Also "Afghan Rebels Describe Training in Iran," *FBIS USSR/International Affairs,* 6 January 1988, p. 11.

44. In an important speech, Iran's Foreign Minister, Velayati, referred to this view and attacked it. See *FBIS/South Asia,* 26 November 1986, p. 11.

45. In fact, in early 1987 there was a rumor that Iran and the USSR might be working out a deal: Iran would help the Soviets exit from Afghanistan, and the USSR would prevent an arms embargo on Iran and would reduce assistance to Iraq. See *MEED,* Vol. 32, No. 8, 20–26 February 1988, p. 8.

46. For example, the leftist National Voice of Iran Radio operating from Soviet territory

criticized economic cooperation between Iran, Pakistan, and Turkey. See *FBIS/South Asia,* 19 March 1985, p. 5.

47. Among those executed were the commander of the Iranian navy, Captain Bahram Afzali, and a special assistant to the speaker of Parliament, Hashemi Rafsanjani. See "Iran Tries Ex-Navy Chief," *The Washington Post,* 7 December 1983, p. A22, and "Iran Executes 10 Communists," *The Washington Post,* 26 February 1984, p. A25.

48. "Red Plot Sparks Off Anti-Russian Frenzy," the London *Times.* Amir Taheri reported that "The plot appears to have been based at least partly on an assumption that radical elements within the present regime would eventually support a new coalition linked to Moscow. The so-called Imam's-line group which dominated Iranian politics until a year ago was regarded by the pro-Soviet parties as their main potential partner."

49. See *FBIS/South Asia,* 3 May 1983, pp. I1–I3.

50. See *Iran Times,* 16 November 1984, p. 1.

51. V. Komarov, "Reign of Terror Against Patriots," *New Times,* No. 21, May 1983, pp. 10–11.

52. "Red Plot Sparks Anti-Russian Frenzy," London *Sunday Times,* 8 May 1982, p. 18.

53. Ibid.

54. For example, Iran has reacted rather mildly to certain Soviet transgressions of its air space and land frontiers. Some reports have also alleged that Iran allowed a Soviet listening station in Baluchistan, enabling the Soviets to assess activities on the Soviet-Afghan border. See *Time,* 8 March 1982, p. 32.

55. "Gromyko and Iranians Meet on U.S. Moves in Gulf," *The New York Times,* 9 June 1984, p. 5.

56. See A. Stepanov, "The Gulf: Threat of Intervention," *New Times,* No. 22, May 1984, p. 13.

57. See *The New York Times,* 23 July 1984, p. A1.

58. See "Iran-Soviet Cooperation to Start," *Keyhan,* 21 February 1985, p. 2.

59. See *MEED,* 1–7 February 1986, Vol. 30, No. 5, p. 18.

60. Particularly damaging was Saudi Arabia's policy of defending its market share, which pushed oil prices as low as ten dollars per barrel, with the threat of five dollars per barrel looming in the horizon. Increasingly effective Iraqi bombing of Iranian oil installations added to Iran's already acute economic and financial problems. On Iran's economic problems, see various issues of *MEED.*

61. Despite these developments, this period was also marked by incidents which, on occasion, led to temporary outbursts of anti-Soviet statements by some Iranian authorities. These remarks led Soviet commentators to complain of anti-Soviet hysteria in Iran. *FBIS USSR/International Affairs,* 4 June 1987, p. E6.

62. See "Iranian Minister Defends Policy," *The Washington Post,* 27 November 1986, p. A25.

63. See "Izvestia Views Speech by Iran's Velayati," *FBIS USSR/International Affairs,* 8 December 1986, p. H1.

64. For report on this visit, see *FBIS USSR/International Affairs,* 19 February 1987, pp. 13–14.

65. *FBIS USSR/International Affairs,* 24 August 1987, p. E3.

66. *FBIS/SA,* 12 May 1987, pp. I2–I3.

67. See, for example, the reportage on Mohammad Larijani, Iran's Deputy Foreign Minister's trip to Moscow. *FBIS USSR/International Affairs,* 20 July 1987, pp. E1–E3.

68. See *FBIS/SA,* 19 June 1987, p. 51.

69. "Iran and Soviet Draft Big Projects Including Pipelines and Railroad," *The New York Times,* 5 August 1987, pp. A1, A13.

70. For example, the Kuwaiti paper, *Al-Ray-Al'Am,* reported Iran and the USSR were on the verge of concluding a joint defense pact. See *FBIS/SA,* 25 November 1987, p. 43.

71. *FBIS/SA,* 15 June 1987, p. S2. See also "Rafsanjani to Visit Moscow," *MEED,* Vol. 31, No. 36, 5 September 1987, p. 11.

72. For example, during his trip to Moscow in 1987, King Hussein of Jordan expressed Arab unhappiness with an apparent Soviet tilt toward Iran. See "Soviets Cite Arms Ban As Topic for Gulf Talks," *The Washington Post,* 23 December 1987, p. A7.

73. U.S. Secretary of State George Shultz and the British Foreign Secretary on several occasions expressed their unhappiness over Soviet foot-dragging. See "Shultz is Chiding Russians Over Iran," *The New York Times,* 16 January 1988, p. 1.

74. On the Soviet proposal, see "Soviets Urge UN Flotilla in Mideast," *The Washington Post,* 16 December 1987, p. A1.

75. The following passage from a commentary published in the Tehran daily, *Keyhan,* referred cryptically to this possible Iranian role: "Perhaps the best decision for Moscow is to choose an Asian capital whose spiritual presence in Afghanistan has given it an automatic place in the formula. The wisest thing for the Soviets is to remove the barricades that are preventing that Asian capital from blocking any U.S. influence in the future of Afghanistan— something the Soviets can no longer guarantee." *MEED,* 20–26 February 1988, Vol. 32, No. 8. See also 26 May 1988. Needless to say, the "Asian capital" that the commentator had in mind was Tehran and the "barricades" were the Iran-Iraq war.

76. *FBIS/MESA,* 25 March 1988, p. 60. However, there have been some press reports that a West German firm helped Iraq expand the range of its missiles. See "Fusees: Les allemand de Baghdad," *Le Point,* 27 March 1987, p. 38.

77. *FBIS/MESA,* 13 July 1988, pp. 54–55.

78. "Musavi Welcomes USSR Proposal To End Cities War," *FBIS/NES,* 9 March 1988.

79. *FBIS/MESA,* 22 July 1988, p. 48.

80. *MEED,* Vol. 32, No. 47, 9 November 1988, p. 19. "Moscow Wants Role in Re-construction." The visiting Soviet deputy foreign minister, Alexander Bessmertnykh, admitted that "mistakes had been made in the last decade."

81. See "Iranian Trade Exhibition Comes to Moscow," *FBIS/SOV,* 13 October 1988, p. 19.

82. An especially vocal critic of past mistakes was Ayatollah Hossein-Ali Montazeri.

83. During this visit, the Ayatollah Amali delivered Ayatollah Khomeini's letter in which, according to Western reports, he had urged him to study the Qur'an. But he had also expressed his joy at the reopening of some mosques. See "Khomeini Aides Meet With Gorbachev," *The Washington Post,* 5 January 1989, p. A27.

84. For example, in an interview with the London-based Arabic publication, *Al-Hawadith,* Yuriy Vinogradov clearly stated that Iraq was obstructing the signing of a peace agreement by insisting that the 1975 Algiers agreement be considered invalid. See "Foreign Affairs Official on Mideast Policy," reprinted in *FBIS/SOV,* 31 January 1989, p. 33. Meanwhile, Iran's Deputy Foreign Minister, Javad Larijani, during a visit to Cuba, said that Gorbachev's speech at the United Nations made a "superb impression." See "Iran Welcomes Soviet Policy, Will Aid Pullout," *FBIS/SOV,* 1 December 1988, p. 20.

85. On Shevardnadze's visit to Tehran, see "Shevardnadze Meets Iran's Rafsanjani, Musavi," *FBIS/SOV,* 28 February 1989, p. 25–26, and "Shevardnadze, Khomeini Meet in Tehran," *The Washington Post,* 27 February 1989, pp. 1 and 14. The article citing Tehran Times said that there are discussions on significant arms deals and that in December an Iranian military delegation visited Moscow as part of the meeting of the Joint Economic Commission. Also, "US Aides Critical of Soviet on Iran," *The New York Times,* 3 March 1989, p. A7.

86. See "Gorbachev Invites Rafsanjani," *MEED,* Vol. 33, No. 14, 14 April 1989, pp. 11–12.

87. See "Rafsanjani Meets Gorbachev," *MEED,* Vol. 33, No. 25, 30 June 1989, p. 23.

88. Ibid.

89. The areas covered in the framework agreement include the following: energy, oil and

gas, petrochemicals and chemicals, metallurgy, machine manufacturing, transport, and building materials. For details of the projects, see "Iran: Soviet Deal to Expand Power Generation," *MEED*, Vol. 33, No. 28, p. 18.

90. See "Moscow Indicates Iranian Shift on Afghanistan," *MEED*, Vol. 33, No.23, 18 August 1989, p. 17.

91. See Roderic Pitty, "Soviet Perceptions of Iraq," *Middle East Report*, Vol. 18, No. 2, March–April 1987, pp. 23–27. On U.S.-Iraqi relations, see Frederick W. Axelgard, *U.S.-Arab Relations: The Iraq Dimension,* National Council on U.S.-Arab Relations, 1985, pp. 1–31.

92. These fears were not unfounded. Saddam Hussein certainly wanted to topple the revolutionary regime, and his contacts with Iranian exiles indicated his objective.

93. For example, *New Times* wrote: "Imperialist powers have done a great deal to turn the long-running Iran-Iraq disputes into a full-scale armed conflict. Shortly before the hostilities began, the media in the United States and Western Europe started discussing the 'deadly threat' from the Islamic revolution to Iraq and from Iraq to Iran. *Le Quotodien de Paris* goaded the two countries on, claiming that the emotional and bloodthirsty Shi'ite faith professed by the Ayatollah Khomeini threatened the leaders in Baghdad. The Western media played up the territorial claims. The U.S. press commented that the United States would not oppose Iraqi claims to the Shat-al-Arab waterway or the possible formation of the Republic of Arabistan on the territory of the Iranian province of Khusistan. . . . " See Yuri Sedov, "War of Attrition: No End in Sight," *New Times*, 7 February 1988, p. 14.

94. See Dennis Ross, "Soviet Views Toward the Gulf War," *ORBIS*, Fall 1984, pp. 437–47.

95. Ibid., pp. 442–43.

96. Ibid., pp. 443–44.

97. Although that treaty strained Moscow's relationship with Iran by exacerbating the Shah's fears of Soviet encirclement, the Soviets judged the payoffs to be higher in Iraq than the costs in Iran. They knew then that they could not replace the United States in Iran, but they could obtain a privileged position in Iraq.

6. Iran, the Arab World, and Israel

1. Iran's Islamization was not a smooth process. For nearly two centuries after the Arab invasion there were pockets of resistance to Arab rule. In the third century, together with a literary renaissance, a number of local dynasties developed in Iran, some of which challenged the Khalif in Baghdad, one being the Shi'a dynasty of Al-Buyeh (the Buyids). For details, see *The Cambridge History of Iran*, Cambridge: Cambridge University Press, 1975, Vol. 4.

2. The third khalif, Omar, condoned and encouraged this practice. For example, he prohibited marriage between the Arabs and the Iranians. See Hamid Enayat, *Modern Islamic Political Thought,* Austin: University of Texas Press, 1982, p. 33.

Also, one of the reasons for the Iranians' attachment to the House of Ali was that, unlike Omar, they treated them with kindness and respect. *Ibid.,* pp. 115–25. The spread of Shi'ism in Iran is often traced to the late fifteenth century and the establishment of the Safavid dynasty. The systematic Shi'ization of Iran began with the Safavids, but the influence of Shi'ism in Iran dates to earlier times. For example, the "Buyids" were Shi'a. See Hamid Enayat, "Iran and the Arabs" in Sylvia Haim (ed.), *Arab Nationalism and a Wider World*, New York: American Association for Peace in the Middle East, 1971, pp. 13–25.

3. Many Iranians believe that Shi'ism is nothing but an Islamic reinterpretation of old Iranian concepts, while many Arabs dismiss Shi'ism as "an Iranian conspiracy against Islam." Ibid.

4. Iran's basic complaint has been that the Arabs equate Islamic culture with Arab culture and ignore Iran's very significant contributions.

5. See King Fahd's statement that Iran should stop imposing its alien ideas on the Arab world. *The Washington Post,* 28 December 1987, p. A29.

6. On the impact of these factors on Iran's ability to influence the Arab world, see Shireen T. Hunter, "Iran and the Spread of Revolutionary Islam," *Third World Quarterly,* Vol. 10, No. 2, April 1988, pp. 730–49.

7. See Adeed Dawisha, "Invoking the Spirit of Arabism," in *Islam in Foreign Policy,* Cambridge: Cambridge University Press, 1983, pp. 112–27. Also the editorial in Al-Qabas "In a Confrontation Between Arabs and Persians, the Arab is True to Himself," reprinted in *FBIS/ME & NA,* 11 April 1980, p. C2.

8. Some Arabs, however, have believed that the Islamic regime's abandonment of Persian nationalism as the core of its political ideology and its emphasis on Islamic solidarity has created a unique opportunity for ending the historic Arab-Persian rivalry. See "Syria Turns to Iran as Political and Financial Ally," *The Washington Post,* 29 December 1983, pp. A1, A23. Also see Shireen T. Hunter, "Islamic Iran and the Arab World," Middle East Insight, Vol. V, No. 3, August-September 1987, p. 17.

9. See Majid Khadduri, *Political Trends in the Arab World: The Role of Ideas and Ideals in Politics,* Baltimore: The Johns Hopkins University Press, 1970, pp. 194–95 and 205–07.

10. For example, Prince Hassan, Jordan's crown prince, in an article in *The Washington Post* on August 6, 1982, p. A23, wrote that the Arab nation has two enemies—Iran in the East, and Israel in the West.

11. Nasser's Egypt, for example, accused Iran of wanting to create another Palestine in the Persian Gulf and condemned Iranian immigration to the Arab side of the Persian Gulf.

12. Shireen T. Hunter, "Arab-Iranian Relations and Stability in the Persian Gulf," *The Washington Quarterly,* Vol. 7, No. 3, Summer 1984, pp. 67–76.

13. For examples, see the statements by the commander of the Iranian navy in *FBIS/SA,* 24 October 1984, p. 8, and the speaker of the Iranian Parliament, Ali-Akbar Hashemi Rafsanjani, *FBIS/ME & NA,* 29 December 1982, p. C4.

14. See the *Ettela'at* editorial on the summit decision regarding the Shat-al-Arab in *FBIS/NES,* 14 June 1989, p. 14. See also the editorial in *Jomhuri-ye-Eslami* on the Algerian position, ibid.

15. On the Arab nationalists' views on oil, see Émile Bustani, *Marche Arabesque,* London: Robert Hale Ltd., 1961 and David Hirst, *Oil and Public Opinion in the Middle East,* London: Faber and Faber, 1966.

16. See Judith Perera, "Together Against the Red Peril: Iran and Saudi Arabia, Rivals for Super Power Rule," *The Middle East,* No. 43, May 1978, pp. 16–25.

17. For a brief, but excellent discussion of these issues, see R. K. Ramazani, *Iran's Foreign Policy 1500–1941.* On Bahrain, Fereydoun Adamiyat, *Bahrain Islands: A Legal and Diplomatic Study of British-Iranian Controversy,* New York: Praeger, 1955.

18. Iran's news media, in discussing the causeway, has characterized it as the annexation of Bahrain by Saudi Arabia. *FBIS/SA,* 28 January 1982, pp. I3–I4.

19. For example, during the 1970s Iraq established the so-called "Front for the Liberation of Ahwaz" as part of its anti-Iranian strategy. The Front is still active in Baghdad. See the interview of the leaders of the Front, FBIS/MENA, 6 October 1981, p. E4.

20. For example, while both Iraq and Iran were monarchies, and especially after they were members of the Baghdad Pact, they maintained friendly relations and even tried to resolve their disputes. After the 1958 revolution in Iraq, and later the Ba'athist takeover and Iraq's pro-Soviet stand, however, cooperation turned into hostility. Meanwhile, tense Egyptian-Iranian relations became friendly once President Anwar al-Sadat abandoned Nasser's Arab socialism and its pro-Soviet stand. See Shahram Chubin and Sepehr Zabih, *The Foreign Relations of Iran,* p. 171.

21. The current situation is somewhat different from that in the past in that what has

linked Iran's Islamic regime to Syria and Libya has been their common anti-Americanism rather than their common attraction to the USSR. However, in addition to common friendship with the United States, shared animosity toward the USSR tied Iran to conservative Arab regimes. Also, in the past, Iran and conservative Arab governments held similar views on the structure of their respective societies, whereas Islamic Iran has had deep ideological differences with its Arab allies.

22. R. K. Ramazani, "Iran and the Arab-Israeli Conflict," *Middle East Journal*, Vol. 32, No. 4, Autumn 1978, p. 415.

23. See Ali Mazrui, *Africa's International Relations: The Diplomacy of Dependency and Change*, p. 136.

24. R. K. Ramazani, "Iran and the Arab-Israeli Conflict," p. 415.

25. See Amir Taheri, *Nest of Spies*, p. 100.

26. The Shah first met Arafat in October 1969 when they were both taking part in the Islamic Summit Conference in Rabat, Morocco. He complained to him about the developing cooperation between the Palestinians and opposition to his regime. But Arafat denied any knowledge and refused to give any assurances. See Samuel Segev, *The Iranian Triangle*, pp. 115–16.

27. See, for example, Nita M. Renfrew, "Who Started the War," *Foreign Policy*, No. 66, Spring 1987, pp. 98–108.

28. Iraq's Shi'a problems, however, long predate Iran's Islamic revolution. On Iraq's Shi'a problems see Hanna Batatu, "Iraq's Underground Shi'a Movements: Characteristics, Causes, and Prospects," *The Middle East Journal*, Vol. 35, No. 4, Autumn 1981, pp. 578–94. Also Chibli Mallat, "Iraq," in Shireen T. Hunter (ed.) *The Politics of Islamic Revivalism*, pp. 71–87. Also by the same author, "Religious Militancy in Contemporary Iraq: Muhammad Baqer as-Sadr and the Sunni-Shi'a Paradigm," *Third World Quarterly*, Vol. 10, No. 2, April 1988, pp. 699–729.

29. At the time, Iraq had $30 billion in foreign reserves, and the fall of the Shah and Egypt's isolation after the Egyptian-Israeli peace treaty had turned Iraq into the new regional power. On assessments of Iraq in this period, see Philippe Rondot "L'Irak: Une Puissance Regionale en Devenir," *Politique Etrangere*, Vol. 45, No. 3, Septembre 1980, pp. 637–52. Also Claudia Wright, "Iraq: New Power in the Middle East," *Foreign Affairs*, Vol. 58, No. 11, Winter 1979–80, pp. 257–77.

30. This attitude on the part of Saddam Hussein is quite understandable since Arab nationalists, particularly the Ba'athists, equate Islam with Arabism. Quoted in R. K. Ramazani, *Revolutionary Iran: Challenge and Response in the Middle East*, Baltimore/London: The Johns Hopkins University Press, 1986, pp. 65–66.

31. See *FBIS/ME & NA*, 1 August 1980, pp. E5 and E6.

32. On the Bani-Sadr-IRP conflict and its impact on the conduct of the war, see Dilip Hiro, *Iran Under the Ayatollahs*, pp. 178–79.

33. On the performance of the Iraqi military and other lessons of the war, see Anthony H. Cordesman, "The First Round: Lessons of the Iran-Iraq War," *Armed Forces Journal International*, April 1982, pp. 32–47, and "The Iran-Iraq War: Attrition Now, Chaos Later," *Armed Forces Journal International*, May 1983, pp. 36–43, 116–17.

34. See "Iranian Official Admits Little Progress in War," *The New York Times*, 15 February 1983, p. A5. Also "Iran Issues Warning on Shipping," *The New York Times*, 28 September 1983, p. A4; "Oil States in Gulf Fear Threat to Vital Strait," *The New York Times*, 11 November 1983, and "Iraq Again Warns Shipping to Avoid End of Gulf," *The New York Times*, 26 November 1983, p. 8.

35. See *FBIS/SA*, 17 October 1983, pp. I1, I3.

36. See "Iraq Proposes Accord with Iran to Ban Attacks on Civilians," *The New York Times*, 26 May 1983, p. A3; and "Iran and Iraq Bar Attacks on Cities," *The New York Times*, 13 June 1984, p. A9.

37. "If You Can Think of Something Even Beastlier, Do It," *The Economist*, 26 March 1988, p. 33.

38. See, among others, "Iraq Displays the Battered Remnants of Fighting in Fao," *Financial Times*, 22 April 1988, p. 1, 24; Iraqis Bulldoze Bodies, Dance on Faw," Washington Times, 21 April 1988, p. A9; "Iraq's Swift Stunning Victory," *The Christian Science Monitor*, 26 April 1988, p. A1; "The Balance Tilts Against Iran," *Financial Times*, 27 April 1988, p. 27.

39. "Khomeini Accepts Poison of Ending the War with Iraq," *The New York Times*, 21 July 1988, p. A1.

40. " . . . Council's refusal, explicitly or implicitly, to condemn Iraq's action was due to the members' prejudice against Iran. At the very least they were prepared to give Iraq more leeway than might otherwise have been expected. . . . " See R. P. H. King, *The United Nations and the Iran-Iraq War*, New York: Ford Foundation, 1987, p. 16.

41. Ibid., pp. 20–21.

42. Ibid., p. 17.

43. This plan was an elaboration of plans developed by Prime Minister Olaf Palme and called for incremental agreements to be implemented on specific dates and covering such areas as an end to attacks on civilian centers, civil aviation, shipping, port and oil facilities, and the use of chemical weapons. Ibid., p. 21 and personal conversations with officials involved in negotiations.

44. These include the setting up of a committee to investigate the beginning of the war and the withdrawal of Iraqi troops from the Iranian territory.

45. *FBIS/ME & NA*, 22 October 1980, p. A1.

46. *FBIS/ME & NA*, 13 April 1982, pp. E2–E4.

47. See Stephen R. Grummon, *The Iran-Iraq War: Islam Embattled*, The Washington Paper No. 92, Washington D.C.: The Center for Strategic and International Studies, 1982, pp. 73–79.

48. Thus Iran doubted the OIC's impartiality, and Iranian officials such as Seyyed Ali Khamenei called the OIC Peace Committee the committee in support of Saddam.

49. Based on personal interviews with officials directly involved in negotiations.

50. Based on personal interviews. For example, Palme was simultaneously speaking to President Bani-Sadr and the Ayatollah Beheshti.

51. See, for example, "PRC Reportedly Set to Mediate in Gulf War," *FBIS/ME & NA*, 27 March 1984, p. C1; "Japan's Undeclared Mediation Role," *FBIS/ME & NA*, 17 May 1984, p. A4.

52. For example, Kuwait rebuffed the Shah's offer of help when it was attacked by Iraq in 1972, partly out of concern for its impact on the Palestinian population.

53. This has been the case in Dubai where Sheikh Rashid, the old ruler, was particularly well-disposed toward the Iranian community and many of his advisers were Dubai citizens of Iranian origin.

54. See the interview of an Iranian Majlis deputy, Mahmud Yazdi, with Ash-Shariqah-al-Khalij, 18 February 1981. Also the interview of the UAE minister of foreign affairs in which he said that "the fact is that these islands are Arab . . . we want to regain our rights through peaceful and brotherly means and in an Islamic spirit." *FBIS/ME & NA*, 19 January 1981, p. C7.

55. See R. K. Ramazani, *Revolutionary Iran: Challenge and Response in the Middle East*, p. 49.

56. Ibid.

57. In December 1981 a coup plot was uncovered in Bahrain, and Bahraini officials accused Iran of having trained the plotters. However, it is important to note that all those who actually were responsible for carrying out the plot were Arabs. The Iranian government denied any involvement, but there is strong circumstantial evidence that Iran was involved.

58. In Bahrain, for example, a Najdi-Sunni tribal family rules over an overwhelmingly

Shi'a population, and both in economic and political spheres this situation favors the Sunnis. In addition, at least 40 percent of Bahrain's indigenous population is of Iranian origin, although not all Iranian Bahrainis are Shi'a, and many of them are Sunni.

In Kuwait, the majority of Shi'as, who are of Iranian and Iraqi origins, constitute one of the lowest levels of society doing mostly menial jobs.

The Saudi Shi'as' living standard has been, and still is, far below that of the rest of the population, and they are politically under-represented.

59. For example, Iran has accused Saudi Arabia of involvement in the coup attempt against the regime in 1981, in which Ayatollah Shariat-Madari and former Foreign Minister Sadegh Ghotbzadeh were also implicated. The Iranian news agency reported that Kuwait has been assisting Iranian counterrevolutionaries, especially the monarchists. See *FBIS/SA*, 26 February 1985, p. I6. Iraq, of course, has been the principal supporter of the Iranian opposition, Mojahedin-e-Khalgh.

60. After the attempt on the life of the Emir of Kuwait on 25 May 1985, there was a rumor that Syria was behind this attack, because Kuwait had decided to stop aid to Syria in retaliation for its support of Iran. See "Iraq Forms Terrorist Squads Against GCC Countries," *FBIS/SA*, 9 January 1986, p. I4; "Iraqis in UAE Dismissed for Suspect Actions," *FBIS/SA*, 29 May 1985, pp. I6–I7; and "Tehran on Iraqi Agents Arrested in Bahrain," Ibid.

61. Musavi Interviewed on "War, Relations, Economy," *FBIS/SA*, 22 December 1981, I1 and *FBIS/SA*, 29 January 1982, p. I2.

62. In this period, Iraq developed the so-called Arab charter, setting the guidelines for Arab conduct, especially in the Persian Gulf. One of the principles in this charter was to keep the two superpowers out of the Gulf. See Shireen T. Hunter and Robert E. Hunter, "The Post-Camp David Arab World," in Robert O. Freedman (ed.), *The Middle East Since Camp David*, Boulder: Westview Press, 1984, pp. 83–84.

63. Estimates on the exact amount of Gulf Arab assistance to Iraq varies, but a plausible figure is $50 to $60 billion.

64. See Shahram Chubin and Charles Tripp, *Iran and Iraq at War*, Boulder: Westview Press, 1988, pp. 160–161, 177.

65. See R. K. Ramazani, *Revolutionary Iran, Challenge and Response*, pp. 42–48.

66. On these occasions, the Ayatollah Khomeini instructed his representative to "acquaint Muslims with what is taking place in dear Lebanon, in crusading Iran, and in oppressed Afghanistan," and to inform them of their great duties in confronting aggressors and international plunderers. See *The Guardian*, 15 September 1982, pp. 1, 14.

67. "U.S. Blamed for Mecca Toll," *The Washington Times*, 3 August 1987, pp. A1, A10. Also, "Iran Promises to Avenge Deaths of Mecca Pilgrims," *Financial Times*, 3 August 1987, p. 1.

68. See "Besharati Blames Saudi Arabia for Oil Market Glut," *FBIS/SA*, 30 June 1986, p. I1.

69. See the commentary of IRNA in *FBIS/SA*, 18 October 1982, pp. I10, I11.

70. See Shireen T. Hunter and Robert E. Hunter, "The Post-Camp David Arab World," in Robert O. Freedman (ed.), *The Middle East Since Camp David*, p. 90.

71. For example, in an article in the Kuwaiti daily, Al-Anbaa', a senior Kuwaiti diplomat, Abdullah Hussein, called for the inclusion of Iraq in the GCC and argued that if the Gulf states " . . . do not consider seriously the inclusion of Iraq in the Council and the formation of a unified Arab army to be deployed along the Gulf shores to confront the Islamic revolution, then any talk about Arab security is without avail." See *Financial Times*, 19 March 1984, p. 2.

72. For example, when in 1986 Kuwait, partly under Saudi pressure, closed its Parliament, one representative said, "We are now really part of the Gulf Cooperation Council." See *MEED*, Vol. 30, No. 28, 12 July 1986, p. 17.

73. *FBIS/SA*, 19 October 1983, p. 12. See President Khamenei's comments on the then U.S. Secretary of Defense Caspar Weinberger's visit to the Persian Gulf Arab states. *FBIS/*

SA, 16 February 1982, pp. I3, I4. The following comment by the Tehran daily, Jomhuri-e-Islami, illustrates this point: " . . . The setting up of the G. C. C. is the brainchild of the Arabs of the area and the product of the propaganda machinery and power network of the West."

74. *FBIS/SA*, 29 January 1982, p. I1, I2.

75. See the Rafsanjani comment on the use of AWACs.

76. "Gulf Arabs Seek Better Iran Ties," *The New York Times*, 17 October 1988, p. A1. Also see *Keyhan*, 17 September 1988, p. 4.

77. Ibid.

78. See Patrick Seale, *Asad: The Struggle for the Middle East*. Berkeley: University of California Press, 1989, p. 353.

79. In fact, during the period of 1982–83, when Saddam Hussein's regime seemed faltering, strains were reported in Syrian-Iranian relations because of disagreements over Saddam Hussein's successor. Iran favored the leader of Iraq's Islamic opposition, Ayatollah Hakim, and Syria favored a pro-Syrian Ba'athist colonel.

80. See Patrick Seale, *Assad*, p. 352.

81. See "Majlis Speaker: No Anti-Arab Sentiment in Iran," *FBIS/SA*, 6 May 1985, p. I2, I3.

82. According to one report, a Syrian military official suggested that "15,000 elite troops would be required to defeat Hizb-ul-Allah." See "Ties with Iran Paralyze Syrians in Lebanon," *The Washington Post*, 25 May 1988, p. A27.

83. "Precarious Syria-Iran Truce Holds in Beirut," *Financial Times*, 13 May 1988, p. 4.

84. While visiting Beirut, General Tlas said that, "The deployment will take place sooner or later. After that, even if a cat dares to breathe in the suburbs, it will be strangled." See "Beirut Suburbs-War Sparks Regional Tensions," *The Washington Post*, 24 May 1988, A18.

85. Ibid.

86. "Daily Criticizes Syrian Policy on Lebanon, Egypt," *FBIS/NESA*, 16 May 1989, p. 45. Also "Iran's Velayati Sends Message to Al-Huss," and "Al-Huss Receives Iranian Delegation," *FBIS/NESA*, 22 May 1989, p. 41.

87. In 1983 Syria agreed to receive 300,000 Iranian tourists, many of them families of war dead. This was a lucrative business for Syria, but the Iranian tourists also seem to have been propagandists carrying the Ayatollah Khomeini's pictures and insisting on displaying them, including at the airport. This attitude angered Syrian authorities, and they tried to keep the Iranian tourists separated from the public and housed them in a special hotel. See "Iranian Tourists Cause Airport Disturbances," *FBIS/ME & NA*, 23 March 1983, pp. H4, H5.

88. On this, see Fouad Ajami, *The Vanished Imam: Musa al Sadr and the Shi'a of Lebanon*, Ithaca, New York: Cornell University Press, 1986.

89. Ibid. Also Patrick Seale, *Asad*, p. 352.

90. Ibid.

91. See "The Ayatollah's Benevolent Hand," *Financial Times*, 25 July 1987, p. 4.

92. These included such organizations as Al-Sadr Brigade, Islamic Jihad, and the Hussein Suicide Squad. For details, see Augustus Richard Norton, *AMAL and the Shi'a: Struggle for the Soul of Lebanon*, Austin: University of Texas Press, 1987, pp. 99–101.

93. Ibid., p. 103. According to Norton, Fadh al-Allah's refusal in 1985 to demand the immediate establishment of an Islamic republic in Lebanon led to a cool reception by the Iranians when he visited Tehran.

94. *The Washington Post*, 25 May 1988, p. A28.

95. For example, it is believed that George Habbash's group trained members of the Iranian opposition group, Mojahedin-e-Khalgh. See Jerrold Green, *Revolution in Iran*, pp. 127–28. See also Samuel Segev, *The Iranian Triangle*, pp. 114–17.

96. Jerrold Green, p. 110.

97. See *FBIS/SA*, 21 February 1979, p. R9.
98. Some Arab sources have even accused Iran of wanting to assassinate Arafat. "Iranians Arrested for Plotting Against Arafat," *FBIS/ME & NA*, 1 March 1982, p. A3.
99. "Khamenei Urges End to Lebanon Conflict," *FBIS/SA*, 10 June 1985, p. I2.
100. "Libyan Foreign Minister Denies Arms Sale to Iran," *FBIS/SA*, 8 August 1985, p. I3, I4.
101. "Iranian Oil Experts Cooperate with Libya," *Keyhan*, 3 January 1982, p. 1.

7. Iran and Its Neighbors: Pakistan, India, and Turkey

1. Most of the people of Iran and the subcontinent are from the same Indo-European stock and the result of the influx of Aryan tribes. Old Persian and Sanskrit are linguistically close.
2. Indian works translated into Pahlavi were once more translated into Arabic by the Persians. One of the most famous of these books is the *Kalile va Damneh*, which is about politics and statecraft, but discussed through the intermediary of animals. The Arabs, however, seldom acknowledge the Indo-Persian origins of the *Kalile va Damneh*. Iran's cultural and linguistic influence in India greatly expanded during the Safavid rule in Iran and Mogul rule in India. Nothing symbolizes Persian influence in India more than the jewel of the Mogul art, the Taj Mahal. Prime Minister Jawaharlal Nehru once generously said that "Persia's soul came to India and found an eternal dwelling place in Taj Mahal." For a brief but excellent overview of Iran's cultural impact on India in this period and in earlier Islamic periods, see H. Goetz, "Persia and India After the Conquest of Mahmud," A. J. Arberry (ed.), *The Legacy of Persia*, Oxford: Clarendon Press, 1953, pp. 89–115.
3. Even today, there is a great affection for the Persian language in the subcontinent, and Urdu is quite close to Persian. This point was emphasized by Pakistani officials during the ceremonies marking the formation of the Pakistan Persian Society in Lahore. See The *Pakistan Times: Overseas Weekly*, 7 January 1987, p. 4.
4. The overwhelming majority of Pakistanis are Muslims, and the country has a substantial Shia's minority of 20 percent. Urdu and Persian are very closely related. Iran and Pakistan share a security interest in Baluchistan, which straddles the two countries. For a brief, but good analysis of Iran-Pakistan relations, see Shirin Tahir-Kheli, "Iran and Pakistan: Cooperation In An Area of Conflict," *Asia Survey*, Vol 17, May 1977, pp. 474–90.
5. After the Iranian revolution, because of Iran's desire to dissociate itself from the symbols of the Shah's policies, the organization was renamed the Economic Cooperation Organization (ECO). The revitalization of the RCD under its new name was harshly criticized by the Soviet Union and the clandestine radio of Iranian leftists operating from Soviet territory. The National Voice of Iran called the creation of ECO a "first step toward the establishment of an Iranian-Turkish-Pakistani military pact." See FBIS, 19 March 1985, p. 13. See also "Distrust of Soviets will Outlast That of Satan," *Far Eastern Economic Review*, 4 July 1985, pp. 22–23.
6. See K. R. Singh, *Iran: Quest for Security*, New Delhi: Vikas, 1988, pp. 162–63.
7. See Amir Taheri, "Policies of Iran in the Persian Gulf Region," in Abbas Amirie (ed.), *The Persian Gulf and Indian Ocean in International Politics*, Institute for International Political and Economic Studies, Tehran, 1975, p. 262. Also see Shaul Bakhash, "Iran is Looking Eastward," *Keyhan International*, 10 April 1974, p. 4.
8. This also intensified and accelerated Iran's and Pakistan's loss of interest in CENTO, which was only revived in the mid-1970s because of increased Soviet activities in the Indian Ocean and Red Sea.
9. Iran tried to resolve the long-standing dispute between Afghanistan and Pakistan over the "so-called Pashtunistan." This area covers most of Pakistan's northwest frontier to which Afghanistan has laid claim on an ethnic basis.

10. See Bhabani Sen Gupta's "The View From India" in *The Persian Gulf And Indian Ocean In International Politics*, p. 193.

11. Another part of Iran's aid consisted of its contributions to the development of the Kudrumeh iron ore deposits and their exports to Iran to be used in its steel industry. Iran committed $600,000 to this project. There were also plans for the expansion of trade, particularly an increase in Iranian imports from India. Iran also offered India oil at concessional prices and became involved in a number of development projects therein, the most important of which is the Kudrumeh Iron Ore Project. For a study of Iran's use of aid for political and security purposes, see Shireen T. Hunter, *OPEC And The Third World: The Politics of Aid*, pp. 106–123.

12. This effort may have contributed to his fall and to the installation of a communist government. See Selig Harrison, "Dateline Afghanistan: Exit from Finland?" pp. 165–66.

13. Dieter Brown, "Implications of India's Nuclear Policy for the Region," in *The Persian Gulf And Indian Ocean in International Politics*, 210.

14. For example, in an interview with the Indian journalist, R. A. Karanjia, the Shah said that "India has undertaken to train Iranian cadets in the training ship *Rajandra*, and other facilities for maritime training have also been extended to Iran." Illustrating Iran's need for trained medical personnel, in the same interview the Shah said that " . . . do not be surprised, however, if we drain you of nurses as England has done." See R. A. Karanjia, *The Mind of a Monarch*, pp. 232–33.

15. See Shireen T. Hunter, *OPEC and the Third World* on Arab aid on the subcontinent, pp. 107–123.

16. Hundreds of thousands of Pakistanis went to work in the region, and their remittances, amounting to hundreds of millions of dollars, became the mainstay of Pakistan's economy. On Pakistan's relations with the Persian Gulf Arab states, including its economic dimension, see Craig Baxter, "Pakistan and the Gulf" in Thomas Naff (ed.), *Gulf Security and the Iran-Iraq War*, Washington D.C.: National Defense University Press, 1985, pp. 103–126. According to *The Christian Science Monitor*, 20 February 1981, p. 14, "Pakistani Air Force and Army units already are stationed in Saudi Arabia. The Air Force units are based toward the northern end of the Saudi Gulf coast between the oil fields and the head of the Gulf. . . . The Pakistani Army units reportedly are based on the Saudi Eastern province, site of the oil fields. . . . "

17. Iraq, which like India had a friendship treaty with the Soviet Union, provided India with financial aid and oil at concessional prices. A large number of Indian enterprises became involved in Iraq's development programs.

18. For an elaboration of these points, see Mohammed Ayoob, "Indo-Iranian Relations: Strategic, Political, and Economic Dimensions," *India Quarterly*, Vol. 33, January-March 1977, pp. 5–10.

19. Bhabani Sen Gupta, "View From India," in *The Persian Gulf And Indian Ocean in International Politics*, p. 183.

20. See R. K. Ramazani, *The Foreign Policy of Iran: A Developing Nation in World Affairs 1500–1941*, pp. 15–19.

21. For details of Iran's good neighbor policy and the Saad Abad pact, see Ibid., pp. 258–76.

22. The Kurdish issue and how to keep it under control has always been a concern of Iran and Turkey—as well as Iraq. In fact, some commentators have argued that the Saad Abad Pact and later the Baghdad Pact included implicit agreement between Iran, Iraq, and Turkey to "cooperate in suppressing any Kurdish nationalist movement intent on altering the political status quo in the region." See J. M. Abdulghani, *Iran and Iraq: The Years of Crisis*, London: Croom Helm, 1984, p. 13.

23. See "Paper Criticizes Turkish Restrictions," *FBIS/NES*, 2 May 1989, p. 50.

24. During the 1987 U.S.-Iranian confrontation in the Persian Gulf, which coincided with a sharp improvement in Soviet-Iranian relations, Pakistan expressed its anxiety over the

possible outcome. Pakistan also criticized the U.S. military buildup, which reportedly irritated the Reagan administration. See *The New York Times,* 1 November 1987, p. 26.

25. For example, Pakistan could cause problems for Iran by manipulating autonomist and other anti-regime forces, especially in Iranian Baluchistan, and it could permit Iranian opposition forces to operate from its territory.

26. The announcement of the establishment of an interim government was made on February 18, 1989, with Mohammed Mohammedi as president and Ahmad Shah as prime minister. However, these appointments reportedly disturbed certain moderate factions, and the negotiations had still failed to resolve the question of involvement of Iranian-based guerrilla groups. See *The New York Times,* 19 February 1989, p. 1. A second report indicated that the appointments represented a compromise among the seven guerrilla factions based in Pakistan, four of which are fundamentalist and three of which are moderate. See *The Washington Post,* 19 February 1989, p. A44. For further details on the interim government, see The Washington Post, 20 February 1989, p. A29, and *The New York Times,* 20 February 1989, p. A6.

27. Shireen T. Hunter, "In Afghan Act II, Let U.S. Be Wary of Friends' Aims," *Los Angeles Times,* 3 April 1989, p. 5.

28. Pakistan answered that its army is representative of its population, and thus inevitably contains some Shi'as. Iranian sources have alleged that the Pakistani brigade was sent home because it refused to shoot at demonstrating Iranian pilgrims during the Hadj ceremonies of 1987. The Iranians also claimed that the Saudis wanted to replace the Pakistanis with Turkish units. See *The Washington Post,* 28 November 1987, p. A1 & A22, also *FBIS/NES,* 11 May 1988, p. 51.

29. "A Military Consensus with Iran, Afghanistan," *Pakistan Profile,* No. 6, 24 February 1989, pp. 1–2. "Irano-Pak Defense Weaponry Talks Due" *Tehran Times* 19 July 1989, p. 4.

30. See *FBIS/NEA,* 21 April 1988, p. 58. On the other hand, an Iranian Deputy Foreign Minister predicted that the Kabul regime would not survive long after the Soviet withdrawal. See *FBIS/NES,* 21 October 1988, p. 46.

31. For example, in November 1984 the Friday Prayer Imam of the New Delhi Jame Mosque, Sayyed Abdulah Bokhari, visited Tehran. Bokhari has on many occasions been critical of India's treatment of its Muslims. As a result, such visits are not to the liking of the Indian government.

32. This was confirmed to me during a visit to India in 1987.

33. The following statement by the Iranian Foreign Minister illustrates this point: "India is one of the few Third World countries which has achieved a high level of self-sufficiency and in many respects resembles our country, its experiences in various scientific, technical, and agricultural areas can be communicated to us. See *FBIS,* 4 December 1984, p. 12. However, trade and economic relations between Iran and India have not always been smooth. To regulate economic relations, in 1983 they set up a joint commission. But because of Iran's financial problems and the Gulf war, the volume of Indo-Iranian economic exchanges has remained limited. Yet the Iranians have stressed the great potential for increased Indo-Iranian economic relations. During a visit to Tehran by an Indian delegation, the speaker of the Iranian parliament, Ali Akbar Hashemi Rafsanjani, referred to this point and said that Indo-Iranian economic relations could expand tremendously once the war was over. Iran's major investments in India are a smelter and an oil refinery in Madras. There is also talk that the Kudrumeh Iron Ore Project might be revived. And there is a joint Indo-Iranian shipping company that operates 14 vessels.

34. Shireen T. Hunter, "In Afghan Act II."

35. For example, during a visit to Turkey, Iran's prime minister, Mir Hossein Musavi, refused to visit Ataturk's tomb and instead visited the tomb of the Iranian poet and mystic, Jalal-ed-Din Balkhi (known as Molana), thus arousing anger and criticism. Some Iranian newspapers wrote derogatory articles about Ataturk, and Turkish newspapers retaliated by

writing derogatory articles about Ayatollah Khomeini. However, the official reaction was muted. See "Turkish Trade Rises Despite Press Row," *MEED,* Vol. 31, No. 25, 20 June 1987, pp. 12–13. On another occasion, the Iranian embassy refused to fly its flag at half mast on the anniversary of Ataturk's death. On the head scarf issue, see *Tehran Times,* 18 January 1987, p. 2. Turkey's so-called "head scarf law" was established by a decree issued by Turkey's President Evran.

36. See "Iranians Flee to Turkey and Dream of US," *The New York Times,* 26 May 1987, p. A1.

37. Of the three countries with substantial Kurdish populations, Turkey has the largest, an estimated 8 to 10 million. Turkey calls its Kurdish population "Mountain Turks," thus in a way denying their existence. Nevertheless, Turkey has a Kurdish insurgency problem, although currently it is not as serious as that of Iraq and Iran. Their manipulation of each other's Kurdish problem worsened Turkey's Kurdish problem by establishing links between them and the Iranian and Iraqi Kurdish insurgents.

38. Ali-Fuat Borovali, "Kurdish Insurgencies, the Gulf War and Turkey's Changing Role," *Conflict Quarterly,* Vol. VII, No. 4, Fall 1985, p. 39.

39. Turkey has had a long-standing claim to this area, and it could have also used the issue of Iraq's one million Turkmen to justify its actions. Indeed, as one observer put it, "There is no shortage of excuses for Turkey's possible intervention." Ibid., p. 38. Some observers have speculated that there have been plans by the United States that Turkey should capture the Kirkuk area in the event of a significant Iranian victory in the south. On this and other speculation see John Siegler, "The Iran-Iraq Conflict: The Tragedy of Limited Conventional War," *International Journal,* Spring 1986, p. 445. See also Talal Halman, "Satan's Battle," *Milliyet,* 17 November 1986, p. 10.

40. See *Keyhan,* 8 November 1986. On other occasions, as well, Iranian authorities had sent thinly veiled warnings to Turkey. One such occasion was a conference held in Tehran in December 1986, among different Iraqi opposition groups. During this conference, President Khamenei reiterated Iran's commitment to an independent Iraq within its internationally recognized borders, thus indirectly warning Turkey to suppress any territorial ambitions it might have against Iraq. Also, after the Turkish bombing of Iraqi Kurdish insurgents, a Kurdish member of the Iranian Parliament accused Turkey of collaborating with the Iraqi regime despite its declared neutrality. He also warned Turkey not to covet Iraq's oil-rich province of Kirkuk, adding that Iraq's natural resources belong to the Muslim Iraqi nation. Ibid.

41. According to some reports, at some point the Saudis asked Turkey to stop trading with Iran and promised that they would make up any losses that Turkey might suffer. See *MEED,* Vol. 30, No. 6, 19–25 April 1986, p. 29.

42. On several occasions, certain elements in Iran have questioned the value of having good relations with Turkey, given its position on the Iran-Iraq war and its attitude toward its Islamic movement. See the interview of the minister of heavy industries, Behzad Nabavi, with the correspondent of *Keyhan.* In this interview, the minister said that, if Iran wanted to break relations with all those countries which supported Iraq or mistreated their Islamic movements, " . . . there will be no room for trade, economic and technical relations, or exchange," *Keyhan,* 11 June 1987, pp. 6 and 19.

43. Some observers have argued that Turkey has tolerated aspects of Iran's behavior because of Prime Minister Turgut Ozal's pragmatism. Ozal, himself a devout Muslim who at one point was sympathetic to the Islamic-oriented "National Salvation Party," reportedly does not view Islamic fundamentalism as an imminent threat to Turkey. The Turkish generals, by contrast, view the Islamic movement as an immediate threat, more dangerous than communism or neo-fascist nationalism. Thus if Ozal loses power or the generals' anxieties deepen, Turkish-Iranian relations may seriously deteriorate. It seems that the generals have been particularly alarmed by the infiltration of the armed forces by Islamic elements. See *Ali-Fuat Borovali,* "Kurdish Insurgencies," p. 41. On Turkey's Islamic movement, see Feroz

Ahmad, "Islamic Reassertion in Turkey," *Third World Quarterly,* Vol. 10, No. 2, April 1988, pp. 750–69.

8. Iran and Europe

1. J. H. Iliffe, "Persia and the Ancient World," in A. J. Arberry (ed.), *The Legacy of Persia,* p. 1.
2. Quoted in C. Elgood, "Persian Science" in A. J. Arberry (ed.), *The Legacy of Persia,* p. 292.
3. See the aforementioned letter of Scheel to Palmerston.
4. Both Presidents Ronald Reagan and George Bush have called the Iranians barbarians. See George Bush's speech at the United Nations Security Council after the U.S. Navy downed an Iranian civilian aircraft, killing 290 passengers. *The Washington Post,* 15 July 1988, p. A1.
5. This results from the Iranians' long philosophical tradition in pre- and post-Islamic eras. Ernest Renan, the French philosopher, has noted this fact in the case of Seyed Jamal-ed-din Asad Abadi (known as al-Afghani). See Eli Kedourie, *Afghani and Abdul: An Essay on Religious Unbelief and Political Activism in Modern Islam,* New York: Humanities Press, 1966.
6. A retired British ambassador who also served as the British political agent in the Persian Gulf admitted to me that during the last century and a half, the West has always sided with the Arabs against Iran. Also, after conquering India, the British banned the use of Persian, which was the official language of the Moghul Court.
7. Contrast this with the West's attitude toward Arab expansionism. Iran renounced its claim to Bahrain in 1970 and was accused of hegemonism, but for all practical purposes Saudi Arabia has annexed that island without any complaints about Saudi hegemonism.
8. See references in Chapters I and II. Also see Mahmoud Mahmoud, *Tarikh-e-Siyasi-yi Ravabet Iran va Inglis Dar Qarne Nouzdahom* [*The History of Anglo-Iranian Relations in the Nineteenth Century*], Tehran: Chaph Khanhe-e-Shargh, 1960.
9. To sacrifice material benefits for emotional satisfaction has been an important trait of Iranian foreign policy during the last several decades. The episode of the Anglo-Iranian oil dispute and many of the Islamic regime's policies only make sense if judged in this context. The British policy toward Iran during the nineteenth century is a good example. Had the Iranian parliament ratified the 1919 Anglo-Iranian Treaty making Iran a British protectorate, Iran's destiny might have been different. But the Iranians' extreme nationalism and their desire for independence, even at great cost, ruled out such an option.
10. See *The Relations of the Imperial Government of Iran with The Countries of Western Europe,* pp. 3–6, 3rd Political Department, Ministry of Foreign Affairs, February 1976. These were Germany in 1887, Italy in 1886, Spain in 1841, Belgium in 1889, Denmark in 1896, and Switzerland in 1918. But because of financial difficulties, it did not maintain legations in all of them and relied upon its ambassadors to France, Russia, or Britain.
11. During the nineteenth century, Iranian students went to France and were influenced by French political ideas. Many of these students later took part in Iran's constitutional movement. During the reign of Reza Shah, the government itself each year sent 100 students abroad, mostly to France, and there were a number of French schools in Iran, operated by missionaries and secular groups.
12. The Nazi-Soviet pact somewhat eroded the German image and worried Iranian authorities. In fact, they asked the German ambassador in Iran for clarification. For details see R. K. Ramazani, *Iran's Foreign Policy 1941–1973,* 1975, p. 26.
13. Their potential as export markets for Iranian goods, including light consumer industries, was an added motive, and a number of economic-cooperation agreements signed between Iran and East European countries in the mid-1970s included provisions for the

export of non-oil Iranian goods. During 1975, Iran signed trade agreements with Poland, Hungary, Czechoslovakia, Romania, and Yugoslavia. Most of these agreements included provisions regarding the export of Iranian goods to these countries. See *Iran Economic News,* Vols. 1, 2, and 5, February, March, and May 1975.

14. For example, see various issues of *Tehran Times, Keyhan International, FBIS/MESA,* and *MEED* on visits of Iranian officials to these countries and their return visits. Greece's minister of energy visited Iran in 1984 at the head of a delegation to discuss trade issues. In December 1985, a "Greco-Iranian Friendship Society" was formed as a result of private initiative. See "Austria Makes Barter Deal," *MEED,* Vol. 28, No. 38, 21 September 1984; "Tehran Seeks 'Ceiling for Trade' with Athens," *Tehran Times,* 1 August 1984; "Greco-Iranian Friendship Society Formed," *Tehran Times,* 19 December 1985, p. 4.

15. Ibid.

16. The expansion of economic ties was slowed because Sweden refused to complete certain projects such as the unfinished Iranian nuclear power plant. But Iran did obtain some speedboats from Sweden which it used in the Gulf war. See "Sweden Rejects Nuclear Job," *MEED,* Vol. 28, No. 45, 9 November 1984, p. 12.

17. See *FBIS/ME & SA,* 20 April 1988, p. 50.

18. See "Talks with Italy Agreed." *MEED,* Vol. 32, No. 33, 19 August 1988. According to this report, nearly 40 large- and medium-sized Italian companies are either working in Iran or negotiating contracts. To be sure, there are a number of outstanding problems between the two countries, mostly disputes over payments to Italian companies. Nevertheless, these difficulties should be resolved through negotiations to which both parties have agreed.

19. On Musavi's trip to Italy, see "Prime Minister Musavi Departs for Italy," *FBIS/NES,* 17 January 1989, p. 70. During this trip Iran and Italy signed an economic trade protocol. Included in the protocol was an increase in Iran's crude oil exports to Italy and its purchase of more non-oil goods. It was also agreed that Italy would help Iran to build two power plants, complete four units of the Mobarakeh steel complex, and transfer technological know-how. See "Trade and Construction Protocol Signed with Italy," *FBIS/NES,* 19 January 1989, p. 54.

20. On the European Community's decision see "Les Occidentaux sont indignes et embarassés par les ménaces contre Salman Rushdie," *Le Monde,* 18 February 1989, p. 1. Among visits which were cancelled was that of the Dutch foreign minister. Ibid. However, commenting on the Dutch foreign minister's decision, the French foreign minister, Roland Dumas, commented that he would have gone to Iran because one "cannot judge the whole Iranian scene on the basis of one verdict." Ibid.

21. On Iran's reaction, see "Musavi on EEC Decision," *FBIS/NESA,* 21 February 1989, p. 80. Iran's Speaker of Parliament Rafsanjani and Foreign Ministry officials tried to distance Iran from the Ayatollah Khomeini's decision. There was also some criticism of the edict in the Iranian press. See "Ettela'at Deplores Bounty," *FBIS/NES,* 21 February 1989.

22. See "Iran Says it Shifts Assets From Europe," *The New York Times,* 24 April 1980, p. A11.

23. This dependence on East European countries has been promoted by Iran's inability to obtain weapons from Western sources (this does not include arms bought on the black market). There are no exact figures regarding the amount of Soviet-made arms supplied by East European countries, but that there have been such transfers is not in doubt.

24. See "Pour ses Partenaires économique occidentaux l'Iran reste un Pays à risques," *Le Monde,* 3 March 1989, p. 3.

25. The number of Eastern European experts and nationals in Iran has increased somewhat. During the period from 1980–1982 when Soviet-Iranian relations had improved considerably and the Soviets had infiltrated Iranian military and security organizations, a number of East European countries, especially East Germany, apparently made inroads into Iran's civilian and military organizations. For examples of Iran-East European economic and trade relations, see various issues of *MEED.*

26. *Keyhan*, published in London (not to be confused with Tehran Daily), reported that Iran had reached long range agreements with Czechoslovakia and Romania for the joint production of tanks, anti-aircraft and anti-tank missiles, and the training of the Iranian military and the Guards Corps. See "Eastern Bloc Rebuilding Military Forces," *FBIS/NES*, 4 May 1989, pp. 50–51. *MEED* also confirmed these reports. See Vol. 33, No. 22, 9 June 1989, p. 29. On Rafsanjani's trip, see Ibid.

27. On the Musavi and Khamenei trips, see "Musavi Interviewed on Trips to Poland and Italy," *FBIS/NES*, 26 January 1989, p. 62. Also "Joint Communique on Musavi's Visit to Poland," *FBIS/NES*, 27 January 1989, p. 65. Also, "Khamenei to Visit Yugoslavia 20 Feb.," *FBIS/NES*, 14 February 1989, p. 47; "President Khamenei to Visit SFRY, Romania," *FBIS/NES*, 16 February 1989, p. 67. There were also visits to Iran during January and February of 1989 by East European officials. For example, on 30–31 January the Czechoslovak prime minister visited Tehran. *FBIS/NES*, 31 January 1989, p. 53, and on 10 February, Romania's deputy foreign minister visited Tehran, *FBIS/NES*, 14 February 1989, p. 48.

28. Romania has agreed to buy $560 million worth of crude oil and oil products and $30 million worth of non-oil goods from Iran. Tehran has also proposed fresh Romanian investment in rubber industries, ship-building, and other ventures. But while Romania has expressed its readiness to take part in Iran's post-war reconstruction, no specific projects have yet been finalized. See "Billion Dollar Trade Deal Signed with Romania," *MEED*, Vol. 23, No. 31, 5 August 1988, p. 26. The two sides agreed to increase bilateral trade to $400 million annually on a barter basis. Yugoslavia is to purchase 330,000 tons of Iranian crude oil and to help it in buliding power stations, oil refineries, petrochemical plants, and food processing plants. *MEED*, Vol. 32, No. 50, 4 November 1988, p. 42. For examples, see various issues of *MEED*.

29. After the Rushdie affair, Iranian papers warned that if the EC continued its hostile attitude toward Iran, the Soviet Union and the Pacific nations would replace it as Iran's major trading partners. See "Editorial on EEC Relations, Soviet Union," *FBIS/NES*, 1 May 1989, p. 47.

30. A Swedish diplomat who served in Iran after the revolution told me that he was surprised to find out that there were more anti-British feelings in Iran than anti-American sentiments.

31. The Shah himself, as a sign of British complicity, referred to the BBC's reporting of Iranian events during the fateful months of the summer and fall of 1978. See William Shawcross, *The Shah's Last Ride: The Fate of An Ally*, New York: Simon and Schuster, 1988, pp. 16–17, 116, 343.

32. Anthony Parsons, *The Pride and the Fall: Iran 1974–1979*, London: Jonathan Cape, 1984.

33. Roger Cooper, long-time resident of Iran, was jailed on charges of spying. In a letter to *Keyhan*, while discussing British policy toward Iran, he refers to this split. Although there may be some doubt as to the authenticity of the letter, the thesis itself is plausible. See "*Keyhan Hawai* Publishes Text of Cooper Letter," *FBIS/NES*, 31 January 1989, p. 49. But this is not a too novel phenomenon. Since the nineteenth century there had been a debate in Britain on how to deal with Iran: to strengthen it and use it as a buffer against Russia or to weaken it and nibble at it territorially. The latter view has generally won.

34. On the occupation of the British embassy by Iranian demonstrators, see *Daily Telegraph*, 6 November 1979, p. 1. The Iranian embassy in London, in turn, was occupied in May 1980 by gunmen who claimed to be Khusistan Arabs. But there was reasonable evidence to suggest that Iraq was implicated in the incident. The crisis was finally defused after British police stormed the embassy. In the process, serious damage was done to the embassy building. See "Iranian Gunmen Hold 20 Hostages in London Embassy," The London *Times*, 1 May 1980, p. A1, and "Suspicions Harden on Iraqi Involvement in Siege of Embassy," The London *Times*, 12 May 1980, p. 2.

35. "Interview: Prime Minister Hossain Moussavi," *MEED*, Vol. 32, No. 37, 16 September 1988, pp. 4–5.

36. See "The Ayatollah Welcomes British Businessmen Back to Tehran," The London *Times*, 3 June 1983, p. 21. A member of the visiting British trade team said: "Iran is a country of 40 million people that now has a much more realistic appraisal of its needs. . . . With the United States, Russia, and France out in the cold the prospects for Britain look even better." However, Britain's position later eroded; by 1989 it controlled 6 percent of Iran's export market. See "l'Iran reste un pays à risques," *Le Monde*, 3 March 1989.

37. "Mrs. Thatcher Backs Boycott on Iran," The London *Times*, 18 December 1979, p. 1. Also "Iran Boycott: Britain May Set the Pace," London *Sunday Times*, 23 December 1979, p. 20.

38. "Arms Ban on Tehran Soon," The London *Times*, 29 February 1988, p. 7. Also "Senior British Envoy in Iran is Kidnapped," The London *Times*, 29 May 1987, p. A 1.

39. "Iran and U.K. Look for Way Out of Diplomatic Deadlock," *MEED*, Vol. 31, No. 23, 6 June 1987, pp. 10–11.

40. *Ibid.*

41. "Iran: Looking for a Showdown with the 'Old Vulture'," *MEED*, Vol. 31, No. 25, 20 June 1987, p. 12. According to *MEED*, the Iranian news media in their commentary vowed "to disabuse the old vulture of its 19th century dreams."

42. See *MEED*, Vol. 31, No. 41, 10 October 1987, pp. 12–13. The NIOC offices were closed in September.

43. The sympathy shown by some of the more left-wing British politicians to the Iranian opposition group, Mojahedin-e-Khalgh, and criticism of Iran's human rights record have been other causes of strain.

44. "British Envoy Vetoed by Iran," The London *Times*, 16 May 1986, p. 6.

45. "Talks Over Iran Embassy Agreement," *Financial Times*, 6 June 1988, p. 2, and, for the final agreement, see *MEED*, Vol. 32, No. 28, 15 July 1988, p. 28.

46. "Britain-Iran Talks May Yield Diplomatic Thaw," *The New York Times*, 28 September 1988, p. A 1, and "Britain and Iran Agree to Resume Relations," *The Washington Post*, 1 October 1988, p. 13.

47. The dominant view in the British Foreign Office, as explained to me by one diplomat, was that the best way to help Iranian moderates was by pressuring Iran, proving that extremism does not pay. However, a purely "stick" policy with no "carrots" also helped the radicals argue that, with the West moderation does not pay.

48. See "A French Overture," *MEED*, Vol. 32, No. 26, 1 July 1988, p. 11.

49. General De Gaulle first visited Iran and met the Shah in 1944 on his way to Moscow. At the time, Iran had recognized the general's Free French Government headquartered in Algeria. The general paid an official visit to Iran in 1963. See *The Relations of the Imperial Government of Iran with the Countries of Western Europe*, pp. 57–58.

50. In 1974, the Shah paid an official visit to France and discussed France's role in implementing Iran's Fifth Development Plan. Following this meeting, in 1975 the French minister of industry, Michel d'Ornano, visited Iran, and Jean-Pierre Fourcade, the French minister of economy and finance, followed suit in May 1976. Extensive economic agreements were reached between the two countries, including one regarding Iran's $1 billion loan to France's Atomic Energy Agency. Ibid. Other arguments included the construction of a steel mill in Ahwaz, the purchase of two nuclear power plants, the adoption by Iran of the French color television system (SECAM), the assembly of Renault cars in Iran, and a number of other industrial, agricultural, and cultural projects.

51. Initially, France's hospitality to the Ayatollah Khomeini after his ouster from Iraq, plus the long association with France of some of Iran's revolutionary figures, such as Abol-Hassan Bani-Sadr, offered France a unique opening into revolutionary Iran. But these positive factors were offset by all-out French support for Iraq in the war.

52. See *FBIS/ME & NA*, 25 February 1981, p. I9.

53. See, for example, the article in the French magazine *L'Express*, "Comment Khomeini Veut Conquerir le Monde," 6–12 July 1984, pp. 23–29.

54. In recent years, the French have been very concerned about the resistance of their Arab population to assimilation into French culture and society. The enhancement of Islamic feelings has made assimilation even more difficult. As a reuslt, the French have become extremely concerned about the possibility of Iranian infiltration and subversion among France's Arab population. See Dominique Moisi, "A European Perspective," *Great Power Interests in the Persian Gulf,* New York: Council on Foreign Relations, 1988, pp. 62–63.

55. Expressing this view, a French Foreign Ministry analyst told me that "we [the French] are able to talk to the communists but not to the Muslim fundamentalists."

56. This view is often attributed to one-time French Foreign Minister Claude Cheysson and was explained to me by a number of French journalists.

57. Before that, in 1981, France had delivered Mirage aircraft to Iraq and had refused to deliver to Iran some gunboats bought and paid for by the Shah. This French action led Iranian President Bani-Sadr to cable Valery Giscard d'Estaing, expressing "astonishment and regret." Unofficial commentaries used much harsher language and accused France of sacrificing humanitarian values for commercial gains. See *FBIS/ME & SA,* 6 February 1981, p. I2, and *FBIS/NESA,* 25 February 1987, p. I3.

58. See *MEED,* Vol. 27, No. 46, 18–24 November 1983, pp. 17–18. Also, "Iran Issues Reprisals in French Jet Dispute," *The Washington Post,* 11 November 1983, p. A19.

59. Ibid., and "French Jets Strike Shi'ite Position in Eastern Lebanon," *The Washington Post,* 18 November 1983, p. A1.

60. These included the wounding of the French cultural attaché in Beirut and some members of the French peace-keeping forces. Then on 8 March 1985, the so-called Organization of Revolutionary Justice abducted two French journalists, Phillip Rochat and George Hansen, together with two other French nationals, Aurel Cornea and Jean-Louis Normandin. This incident was followed by the abduction of three French diplomats, Marcel Fontain, Marcel Carton, and his daughter, Danielle Perez. Islamic Jihad claimed responsibility for these abductions. The kidnappings were followed by the abduction of Camille Sontag on 7 May 1985 and of the French scientist Michel Seurat and journalist Jean-Paul Kaufman on 22 May 1985. Again, Islamic Jihad claimed responsibility. See *FBIS/MESA,* 30 May 1985, p. i.

61. "French Concerned About Losses," *MEED,* Vol. 28, No. 5, 3 February 1984, p. 15. Also see "French Continues Power Scheme," *MEED,* Vol. 30, No. 13, 29 March 1986, p. 11.

62. For example, French businessmen and bankers have, on occasion, complained about their government's policy on the Iran-Iraq war. According to one banker, "whether of the right or left, French governments have conducted a disastrous policy for business [by] openly backing Iraq." Ibid.

63. This was partly due to the fact that there was a strong pro-Iraq lobby centered around the prime minister's office.

64. "French Delegation in Tehran," *Keyhan,* 5 January 1986, p. 4. During this period, the French Foreign Ministry was the main coordinator of Franco-Iranian contacts.

65. See *Politique étrangère de la France: Textes et documents,* November 1986, p. 37.

66. Ibid., September 1986, p. 13.

67. The French government claimed that he did not have official diplomatic rank and thus could not benefit from diplomatic immunity. The Iranian government, by contrast, claimed that Gordji was a bona fide member of the Iranian diplomatic representation in Paris.

68. For a good account of the French case against Gordji, see "France's Iran Dilemma: Juggling Ties to Iran with Antiterrorist Policy," *The Christian Science Monitor,* 7 July 1987, p. 9.

69. "Affaire Gordji: Teheran nargue Paris," *Le Point,* 7 July 1987, No. 772, pp. 34–35, and "France-Iran: Le bras de fer," *Le Point,* 20 July 1987, No. 774, pp. 34–35.

70. However, the French authorities claimed that the new evidence about Gordji's activities came to light when a young Tunisian defected from the pro-Iranian groups and provided information to the French. See "How France Links Iran to Terror," *The Christian Science Monitor,* 31 July 1987, p. 15.

71. Some French experts on terrorism continued to believe that the Lebanese Christian Abdullah family was responsible for the September 1986 killings. Ibid.

72. Vahid Gordji briefly appeared before the judge and was then sent to Pakistan, where he was delivered to Iranian authorities in exchange for the French diplomats.

73. Some of the Mojahedin members went on a hunger strike and the UN's High Commission for Refugees appealed to France.

74. See *MEED,* Vol. 32, No. 25, 24 June 1988, p. 20.

75. In July 1988 an Iranian trade team visited Paris. Among the deals signed with France was a barter trade agreement worth $500 million and a deal with Peugot for the assembly of cars in Iran.

76. *MEED,* Vol. 32, No. 28, 15 July 1988, p. 28.

77. "Paris has also recommended that companies show moderation in buying from Iran, to avoid upsetting Iraq. . . . " "France Lifts Oil Embargo to Open Way for Business," *MEED,* Vol. 32, No. 50, 16 December 1988, p. 16. A few issues still remain in Franco-Iranian relations. For example, Iran claims the accumulated interest on the EURODIF loan, which could be close to $1 billion, while French companies have claims against Iran. The French have suggested that the interest be paid as compensation to French companies, and meetings apparently have been held in Vienna between representatives of French companies and the Iranians.

78. On Dumas's visit, see "The New French Connection," *MEED,* Vol. 33, No. 6, 17 February 1989, pp. 15–16.

79. On the Dumas's comments see: "Les Douze rappellent en consultations leurs ambassadeur à Teheran," *Le Monde,* 21 February 1989, p. 3.

80. Roland Dumas said that "I have seen it first hand that the Mullah's regime is not all of Iran and that Iranian officials have tried to distance Iran from Khomeini's religious edict." Ibid.

81. Iran has been particularly worried about French involvement in the building up of Iraq's military industries. See "Editorial Assails French Support for Iraq," *FBIS/NES,* 10 May 1984, pp. 51–52.

82. See "Iran reste un pays à risques," *Le Monde,* 3 March 1989, p. 3.

83. "W. Germany Says It Made No Deals for Hostages," *The Washington Post,* 14 September 1988, p. A20.

84. *FBIS/NESA,* 18 February 1987, p. I1. In February 1988, West German television aired a program in which the Ayatollah Khomeini was satirized in rather lurid terms and images. The Iranian government vigorously protested to Bonn, the German Cultural Institute in Tehran was closed, and two West German diplomats were expelled from Iran. However, the crisis was diffused reasonably soon after the head of the German television network expressed its "deep regret" to the Iranian ambassador in Bonn and said that "The show was not meant to hurt the religious feelings of the Iranian people."

85. See "Bonn Agrees to Consider Financing Request," *MEED,* Vol. 32, No. 49, 9 December 1988, p. 19.

86. Based on interviews in Bonn in February 1989.

87. "*Tehran Times* on U.S. Spy Network," *FBIS/NES,* 1 May 1989, p. 51; "ABRAR Urges Government to Cut Ties with FRG." *Ibid.,* p. 52; and "Tehran Commentary Assails FRG Support for Iraq," *FBIS/NES,* 4 May 1989, p. 51.

9. Iran, East Asia, and the Pacific

1. It is believed that there were contacts between Iran and China as early as the Achamenid Period or even before. However, the first historical evidence of political contact is dated to 115 B.C. Since that time, there have been regular contacts, albeit with some significant gaps. What is interesting in the history of Sino-Iranian relations is that they were often prompted by the challenge posed to both of them by a third power. This factor has continued to be important, even in modern times. In fact, the Sino-Iranian rapprochement in the last two decades was largely the result of their concern over Soviet power and influence. Sino-Iranian cultural interaction continued and even intensified in the Islamic era. In fact, Islam's penetration in China was largely the work of the Persians. This is evidenced by the fact that Persian words, even today, are used by Chinese Muslims. For more details, see A. H. H. Abidi, *Iran-China Relations: A Historical Profile,* pp. 33–49. See also the Persian translation of an article by a professor of Persian Studies at the University of Beijing: "Friendly contacts between Iran and China in Ancient Times," published in *Journal of Foreign Policy,* Vol. 1, No. 4, October-December 1987, which itself is published by The Institute for Political and International Studies associated with the Iranian Foreign Ministry.

2. Ibn Batutah, the famous traveler, mentioned a number of prominent Iranians residing in Java and northern Sumatra, including Amir Said Shirazi, Tajd-ed-Din Isphahani, and a seafaring man named Behrouz.

3. In fact, since the sixteenth century, the tombs of some of these leaders have become places of pilgrimage.

4. For example, in the seventeenth century, Shah Suleiman Safavi sent a delegation to the court of Siam, headed by Mohammad Hassan Beg Ilchi. Prior to this visit, the King of Siam had sent an envoy to the Safavid court, Hadji Salim, who was originally from Iran. According to the accounts of the rapporteur of the Iranian delegation to Thailand, several hundred Iranian residents in the capital took part in the welcoming ceremonies. During the fourteenth and fifteenth centuries, Iranian sailors, merchants, and even religious and literary figures had been in contact with what is now called Malaysia. This period is known as the Malay's Golden Age, and during this period a number of Persian literary works were translated into the Malay language. See *Iran's Relations with the Countries Under the Purview of the Seventh Political Department,* Ministry of Foreign Affairs, Tehran, 1976, (in Persian), pp. 19–24, and 30–31.

5. Ibid., pp. 6–7.

6. This is so because the Russians were supporting the then-Iranian king Mohammad Ali Shah Qajar.

7. Abidi, pp. 44–45. The first Japanese diplomatic representative, Shunsure Naruse, who held the rank of *chargé d'affaires,* arrived in Tehran. A year later, in June 1930, the first Iranian envoy, Avanes Khan Mossaed-al-Saltaneh, who held the rank of Minister Plenipotentiary, went to Tokyo and opened the first Iranian legation in Japan. See *Iran's Relations with the Countries under the Purview of Seventh Political Department,* p. 8. Before that, in 1926 Japan had set up economic representation in Iran. Ibid.

8. For example, in 1958 the Shah of Iran visited Japan. Later the same year, the two countries signed an economic and technical cooperation agreement, followed by a cultural agreement. In 1960, Japan's Crown Prince visited Tehran. Ibid., p. 9.

9. In June 1968, the first agreement for the expansion of Nippo-Iranian trade was signed. In 1972, a 66-member Japanese economic delegation, including the head of the committee to encourage Japanese investment in Iran, visited Tehran. Ibid., pp. 10–11.

10. The plant was 80 percent complete on the eve of the revolution. The plant, which involved massive Japanese investment, was severely damaged by the Iran-Iraq war and may have to be abandoned. For a detailed description of the project, see *Keyhan International,* 7 September 1978 article, "Iran-Japan leads world in petrochemicals," p. 4.

11. For example, during a visit to Iran by the Japanese prime minister, Takeo Fukuda, in September 1978, the Iranians expressed the hope that Japan would help Iran "produce such intermediate goods as are needed by Japan and whose production in Iran will be more economical."

12. However, during the premiership of Mossadegh and the nationalization of Iranian oil, the Chinese hailed Iran's efforts in trying to gain control over its own natural resources. See Rosemary Foot, "China's New Relationship with Iran," *Contemporary Review,* Vol. 226, Feb. 1975, p. 100.

13. *Beijing Review,* July 1966, p. 5.

14. Pakistan, an ally of both Iran and China, played the most important role. In 1966, the Iranian Council of Ministers issued a decree freeing trade between Iran and China. And in January 1969 the Shah of Iran, in an interview with the Pakistani daily, *Dawn,* declared that the PRC should be accepted into the United Nations. See Nader Entessar, "The People's Republic of China and Iran: An Overview of the Relationship," *Asia Quarterly,* 1978, No. 1, pp. 79–88.

15. See various issues of *FBIS/China,* during August and September 1976.

16. For example, the volume of trade between Iran and China on the eve of the revolution was only around $60 million. Nor was China significantly involved in Iran's development projects. The reason for this was that the Shah was interested in obtaining state-of-the-art technology and in encouraging capital investment in Iran. In all these respects, Western countries and Japan seemed to be much more attractive partners.

17. At the ambassadorial level, these countries were Thailand, Indonesia, Malaysia, the Philippines, the Republic of Korea (South Korea), the Democratic Peoples' Republic of Korea (North Korea), Singapore, Vietnam, Cambodia, and Laos. See *Iran's Relations with the Countries Under the Purview of the Seventh Political Department,* pp. 37–38, 45–48.

18. See Nick Cumming Bruce, "Need for Supply Sources Broadens World Outlook," *MEED,* Vol. 9, No. 14, 4 April 1975, pp. 6–7. Also, " . . . The strategy of export promotion had become a no-choice policy for Iran's long-term development strategy." Firouz Vakil, "Iran's Basic Macroeconomic Problems: A 20-year Horizon" in Jane V. Jacqz (ed.), *Iran: Past, Present and Future,* New York: Aspen Institute for Humanistic Studies, 1976, p. 89.

19. In 1970, the Shah visited Australia where he talked about his idea of an Asian Common Market.

20. The Iranian revolutionaries found China's so-called "rejection of hegemony" quite attractive. See "Teheran Views Hashemi-Rafsanjani's PRC Visit," *FBIS/South Asia,* 5 July 1985, p. I 2.

21. The Iranian side expressed its desire for Chinese participation in dam-building projects, construction of fishing ports, and other industries in Iran. Ibid. Prior to that visit, a Chinese delegation, led by State Councillor Zhang Zingfu, had visited Tehran in March 1985. During that trip, the two countries had agreed to increase the volume of trade from $250 million to $600 million. See *Far Eastern Economic Review,* 4 July 1985, p. 22.

22. Certain U.S. sources have claimed that Iran and China agreed to an arms deal worth $1 billion. See *MEED,* 22 August 1987, Vol. 31, No. 34, p. 11.

23. *New York Times,* 28 May 1987, p. I 13; London *Times,* 20 May 1987, p. 9; see also *MEED,* 15 August 1987, Vol. 31, No. 33, p. 9.

24. This was quite worrying to the Chinese and prompted them to strenuously deny having supplied Silkworms to Iran. *New York Times,* 7 June 1987, p. I1; *MEED,* 15 August 1987, Vol. 31, No. 33, p. 9.

25. The trade potential of Arab countries is considerable, and China desperately needs foreign exchange. Arab capital could also contribute to China's economic modernization and development. For example, Libya recently announced that it was investing in a Chinese silk factory. Kuwait and Tunisia also have set up a joint venture with China to produce fertilizers. See "Arab Lands Said to be Turning to China for Arms," *New York Times,* 24

June 1988, p. A3. On China-Arab arms trade see also "China Missile Sale Report Concerns U.S.," *Washington Post*, 23 June 1988, p. A33.

26. The Saudi missile sale should also be seen in light of Soviet advances in the Persian Gulf region since 1985 and growing expectations about the establishment of diplomatic ties between Saudi Arabia and the Soviet Union.

27. *FBIS/NESA*, 11 April 1989, p. 55.

28. *FBIS/NEA*, 4 April 1989, p. 55.

29. By the end of 1988, there were signs of improvement in both Sino-Soviet and Sino-Indian relations. On November 1988, there was a Sino-Soviet foreign ministers' meeting, and on 21 December 1988, Prime Minister Rajiv Gandhi visited China. See *Washington Post*, 22 December 1988, p. A28.

30. "China, One of our Real Friends—Rafsanjani," *Keyhan*, 20 August 1988, p. 4.

31. "Trade, Cultural Exchanges," see *FBIS/NES*, 9 May 1989, p. 521, and "Teheran Commentary on Visit," ibid.

32. See "Japanese Get Oil Offer," *MEED*, Vol. 31, No. 48, 28 November 1987, p. 10.

33. See Michael M. Yoshitsu, "Iran and Afghanistan in Japanese Perspective," *Asian Survey*, Vol. XXI, No. 5, May 1981, pp. 501–512.

34. "Tokyo's Envoy to Ask End of Iran-Iraq War," *Washington Post*, 29 July 1983, pp. 21–26.

35. "Japanese to Support Gulf Effort: Many More Ships Will Be Provided," *Washington Post*, 7 October 1987, pp. 23–24.

36. According to some reports, for example, during a visit to Japan in July 1985 the speaker of the Iranian Parliament, Hodjat-al-Islam Hashemi Rafsanjani, said that Japan had reduced its oil purchases in order to pressure Iran into accepting a peaceful settlement to the Iran-Iraq war. The Japanese denied the accusation and responded that the fall in Japanese oil purchases was due to the high price of Iranian oil compared to other crude.

37. In 1982–84, for example, when Iran was experiencing an economic mini-boom, Japanese-Iranian trade reached $4,561 million, and Japan occupied first place among Iran's trading partners.

38. Based on interviews with Japanese businessmen and Middle East experts in Spring of 1989.

39. For example, the foreign minister of Iran, Ali-Akbar Velayati, in an interview published by the *Indonesia Times*, said the following:

"Interference in the internal affairs of other countries is contrary to the Islamic Republic of Iran's foreign policy or its constitution. We therefore refrain from interfering in other countries' internal affairs. All accusations against Iran so far had their sources from the imperialists and zionists and were intentionally launched to discredit Iran."

See *FBIS/SA*, 18 June 1984, p. I1.

40. An Iranian foreign ministry official aid that the South Asian countries should not worry so much about us. . . . Some of our enthusiasts have caused us problems. But proper communication at the top level is slowly putting matters right. See "Dispelling fear with Proper Diplomacy," *Far Eastern Economic Review*, 4 July 1985, p. 29. Also "Ministry Official Denies Meddling in Malaysia," *FBIS/SA*, 29 December 1983, p. I1.

41. Since 1984 there have been a number of visits by Iranian officials, including the foreign minister, to Indonesia, Malaysia, and South Korea, and return visits by the officials of these countries to Iran. The Malaysian foreign minister visited Teheran from 21–23 January 1984 and met with Iranian officials. See *FBIS/SA*, 27 January 1984, p. 13. Dr. Velayati, the Iranian foreign minister, paid a return visit to Malaysia in April of 1984. In October of 1984 the Indonesian trade minister visited Tehran.

42. See "South Korea May Expand Economic Role," *MEED*, Vol. 33, No. 27, 14 July 1988, p. 13.

43. During a visit to Tehran in April 1987, the South Korean assistant minister of foreign affairs, Park-Soo-Gil, expressed the hope that relations between Iran and South Korea could be upgraded from the level of *chargé d'affaires* to that of ambassador. He also said that South Korea would like to help Iran's development through transfer of technology within the framework of the South-South dialogue. South Korean companies are active in a number of industrial projects in Iran, such as the Shiraz Petrochemical Plant, the Tabriz power plant, natural gas distribution in Ahwaz, and the Bafg-Bandar Abbas railway construction. There are approximately 2,000 South Koreans working in Iran. See *Tehran Times,* Vol. IX, No. 9, 9 April 1987, p. A1. Iranian Deputy Foreign Minister Mohammad Javad Mansur visited South Korea and discussed South Korean companies' participation in its war rehabilitation project. *Korea Times,* 26 January 1989, p. 2.

44. For example, it was reported that Iran was interested in obtaining aircraft from Indonesia. See *MEED,* Vol. 32, No. 42, 21 October 1988, p. 23. Iran and Malaysia agreed to increase the volume of bilateral trade, signed agreements for the exchange of Iranian oil for Malaysian palm oil, and set up a direct shipping line between the two countries. See "Iran-Malaysia to Increase Bilateral Trade," *FBIS/NES,* 10 April 1989, p. 60.

45. For example, President Kim Il Sung said to the visiting Iranian Deputy Foreign Minister that "North Korea will always stand by the Islamic Republic." See *MEED,* Vol. IX, No. 9, 9 April 1987, p. 8.

46. However, in the 1970s Iran had offered to help Vietnam with oil refinery development. For example, the general director of the Iranian Foreign Ministry's Asia-Oceania Department visited Laos and Vietnam in December 1983 to pave the way for the reestablishment of diplomatic ties. *FBIS,* 29 December 1983, p. 11.

47. *MEED,* Vol. 29, No. 27, 6–12 July 1985, p. 10.

10. Iran and the Third World

1. In fact, because of its efforts, the Iranian representative to the United Nations was chosen to introduce U.N. Resolution 1560 on decolonization in the General Assembly.

2. By 1976, Iran had established diplomatic relations with 31 African countries.

3. For example, the Shah gave military assistance to Somalia and promised further help should Ethiopia attack. It also tried to shore up Sudan through economic assistance and helped Zaire during the Shaba uprising. Senegal was another recipient of Iran's aid. See Fred Halliday, "U.S. turns blind eye on Iran's aid to Somalia," *The Middle East* No. 40, February 1978, p. 23. On Iran's aid, see *Keyhan International,* 18 April 1979, and *Iran Economic News,* Vol. II, No. 1, pp. 6–7.

4. For example, Cuba had links with Libya and the PLO, both of which were actively engaged in subversion against the Shah's regime. For details, see Damian J. Fernandes, *Cuba's Foreign Policy in the Middle East,* Boulder, Col.: Westview Press, 1988, p. 85.

5. For example, a Brazilian team visited Iran to discuss supplying equipment for several power plants. See *MEED,* Vol. 32, No. 41, 14 October 1988, p. 19. Also the Iranian Industries Minister visited Brazil in October 1988 and announced that trade between the two nations would expand to $1.5 billion. See *FBIS/SA,* 4 October 1988, p. 51.

6. For example, in June 1986, Iran's foreign minister visited both countries. On 28 January 1985, the Iranian prime minister paid a visit to Managua. And in May 1987, the Cuban foreign minister visited Tehran. Iran had sent an ambassador to Cuba in 1984. See *MEED,* Vol. 30, No. 25, 21–27 June 1987, p. 15, and *MEED,* Vol. 29, No. 5, 1 February 1985, p. 8. Also *FBIS/SA,* 29 May 1987, p. I2–I3; "Nicaraguan Education Minister Visits," *Keyhan,* 12 May 1983, p. 1, and also "Iran Premier Visits Nicaragua," *New York Times,* 24 January 1985, p. A6.

7. Castro, for example, has expressed the hope that "Marxists and Christians can be strategic allies. . . . " See "An Interview with Fidel Castro," *Time,* 4 February 1980, p. 48.

8. Damian J. Fernandez, *Cuba's Foreign Policy in the Middle East,* pp. 85–88.

9. The following statement by the Ayatollah Khomeini to the visiting Nicaraguan minister of education illustrates this point. " . . . As you say, your country is very similar to our country; but ours has more difficulty. We are faced with the plots of all world powers. . . . We should all try to create unity among the oppressed, regardless of their ideology and creed. Otherwise, the two oppressors of East and West will infect everyone like a cancerous tumor." See *Keyhan*, 12 May 1983, p. 1.

10. During a visit by the Iranian president to Tanzania, the two countries agreed to set up interstate committees or cooperation in cultural, health, trade, rural development, and petroleum sectors. Similar agreements were signed with Ghana. Iran had opened an embassy in Sierra Leone and opened an Islamic library there. Iran has given financial assistance to Tanzania and Zimbabwe. See "Frontier Identity," *Africa Events*, February 1986, p. 9:

" . . . Iran's ties with Africa, especially East Africa, go back a long way. Long before the Gulf oil boom, sailors and traders from Iran (especially from Shiraz) sailed down to East Africa with the North-East monsoons in their magnificent giant wood hulled ships, gorgeously sculptured from stem to stern. Mogadisho in Somalia; Bagamayo Kilwa, and Zanzibar in Tanzania; and Beira in Mozambique were their ports of call."

As a result of Iranian settlers, "Kiswahili, the language of the East African Coast, now widely spouted in most countries in East and Central Africa, sports many a word that have their origin in old Persia." Also the descendants of the Persian settlers were one element of the Afro-Shirazi Party. Also "Ghanaian Delegation Departs," *Tehran Times*, 11 April 1987, p. 2. Also see "President Elect Calls for Iranian Oil Aid," *FBIS/ME&AL*, 6 November 1985, p. T6, also "Vice President Discusses Ties with Iranian Envoys," *FBIS/ME&A*, 12 May 1987, p. T7. Also "Sierra Leone Seeks Iran Aid," *Financial Times*, 23 August 1983, p. 6. Some have alleged that Sierra Leone has become the center of Iran's intelligence activities. See *Africa Confidential*, 7 September 1983. Also Patrick Van Roekeghem, "AFP: Iranian Influence Increasing in Country," *FBIS/ME&A*, 15 August 1984, p. T4.

Also Iranian officials have visited Burkino Faso (22 May 1987), Congo (27 August 1987), Gabon (foreign minister, 6 August 1986), Madagascar (22 May 1984), Guinea (29 March 1984), Mali (23 May 1987), Ethiopia (21 April 1987 and 25 August 1987). Source: *FBIS*, various issues. Iran's foreign minister visited Niger in August of 1983. *FBIS ME&A*, 24 August 1983, p. T2.

11. The following quote from an article entitled "Frontier Identity" and comments by Radio Kauns in Nigeria illustrate this point. "Cultural and trade ties apart, the new Iran has something else to offer Africa, especially to those fighting apartheid in South Africa. They once held Vietnam as their symbol. As the teeny-weeny nation that shoved the mighty United States to the wall, Vietnam has an unparalleled renown in the annals of resistance. It provided a global focus of the anti-imperialist struggle. But the Vietnamese had both the material and moral support of the Soviet Union, China, and other Communist nations. The Iranian revolution, however, only had its own internal resources in the shape of mass resistance to pit against the U.S. hubris. In this sense, therefore, Iran stands out as a natural inspirer, whose revolutionary fire the oppressed peoples of Southern Africa should fittingly emulate." *Africa Events*, p. 9. So, really, the contemporary world must now address the Iranian situation much more realistically. Iran will not go away, as it represents a renewed struggle for social justice; the only difference this time around being that it is being fought by a whole country against U.S. imperialism. And in this respect, Iran has sparked a reaction in Haiti, Panama, Sri Lanka, the Philippines, South Korea, and perhaps, in many other countries of the world where the struggle for self-determination may have been temporarily suppressed. *FBIS/West Africa*, 6 August 1987, p. D11. For example, Senegal broke diplomatic relations with Iran in January 1984. It justified this decision on the grounds that "Iranian Embassy personnel were involved in activities that violate international norms. The embassy personnel were engaged in "fundamentalist propaganda" in Senegalese Moslem

associations, and the Shi'a Lebanese Moslem community in the country financed publications, organized trips to Mecca, and increased its Dakar staff without authorization. See *FBIS/ME&A*, 6 February 1984, p. T4. Also Senegal-Iran "Dakar Embassy Closed," *Africa Research Bulletin*, February 1984, Vol. 21, No. 2, p. 7160.

12. See "Mauritania-Iran: Diplomatic Rupture," *Africa Research Bulletin*, 15 August 1987, Vol. 24, No. 7, p. 8581. Mauritania's excuse for breaking relations was Iran's refusal to accept a negotiated peace with Iraq.

13. For example, Ali Khamenei's otherwise successful visit to Zimbabwe was marred by his refusal to attend a reception in his honor because it was attended by women whose hair was not covered, and he refused to greet the female Zimbabwean cabinet members. See "Iranians RSVP," *Africa News*, 10 February 1986, p. 16.

14. For Brigadier General Jalali's visit to Gabon and the display of Iranian equipment, see *FBIS/NES*, 26 January 1989, p. 70. There seems to be a rivalry between Iran and Egypt for African arms markets. See "Arms Sales to Some African States Rejected," *FBIS/NE/SA*, 22 January 1988, p. 9. This is in fact an Egyptian effort to pressure African states not to expand their ties with Iran. According to this report, Egypt is concerned about the Iranian influence in Africa and it views Iran's offer of oil, trade, and economic cooperation as a cover for military cooperation.

11. Iran and International Organizations

1. But when it was unable to get a fair hearing by the League of Nations concerning either its dispute with Great Britain over Bahrain or that with Iraq and Britain—as the protecting power—over the Shat-al-Arab, it was cured of some of its illusions. Iran appealed to the League of Nations on the Bahrain issue in 1928 and on the Shat-al-Arab in 1935.

2. See UNGA Records No. A/41/PV.19 1987.

3. Note, for example, the following remark by Velayati:

"There is no doubt that the life of every organization is dependent upon its value system. . . . But the question is: How and by whom these value judgments are made? The founding of the United Nations and the structure of its organs were overshadowed by the special circumstances and conditions of the political and military balance prevailing after the Second World War. Thus the basic values of this organization, as maintained in the charter of the United Nations, were all formulated within the framework of the historical and cultural values of victors in the Second World War. That is why they do not represent the shared values of the majority of the members of the world community . . . " [emphasis added]. See UNGA records No. A/40/PV.20 1985.

4. For example, during the March 1988 session of the U.N. Commission on Human Rights, Iran's representative made the following remarks and suggestions;

"When the declaration of human rights and other conventions were written, Islamic countries were not present and did not have an active role in preparing them. . . . Inasmuch as conforming with Islamic principles amounts to belief in Muslim countries and nations, it is desirable that international assemblies find a way to incorporate Islamic principles into the conventions on human rights. The Islamic Republic of Iran is ready to supply the necessary assistance and to cooperate in any consultations. . . . "

See "UN Envoy on Amending Human Rights Declaration," *FBIS/NES*, 15 March 1988, p. 67.

5. See UNGA Records No. A/40/PV.20 1985.

6. For example, the Iranian government and the UNDP in 1983 agreed on a three-year

country program for Iran to cover the period of 1983–86, according to which UNDP would assist Iran in areas of agriculture, industry and mines, transport, telecommunications, and other projects. Iran also has had limited cooperation with WHO on a number of health-related projects. See "Approval of UNDP Assistance To A Project of The Government of The Islamic Republic of Iran," *DP/Projects/5273 (IRA/82/002)*, 16 June 1986. Also *DP/CP/IRA 3*, 31 March 1983.

In 1989 Iran signed a joint agreement with the UNDP and the International Association of Meteorology and Atmospheric Physics. Eleven UNDP specialists are in Iran. See *MEED*, Vol. 33, No. 16, 28 April 1989, p. 15. The UNDP has also agreed to provide $400,000 toward setting up a graduate course in oil exploration at Abadan Institute of Technology. ESCAP is also helping Iran to research desert encroachments, *MEED*, Vol. 33, No. 22, 9 June 1989, p. 30.

7. See speeches of Iran's representatives on the *Summary Records of IBRD/IMF Annual Meetings, of 1980 and 1988*.

8. Mansour F. Fawzi, "Restructuring The World Bank" in Khadija Haq (ed.), *Dialogue for a New Order*, New York: Pergamon Press, 1980, p. 109.

9. "Minister on U.S. Decision to Quit," *FBIS/SA*, 3 January 1984, p. I2.

10. "Agricultural Minister Departs for Rome Meeting," *FBIS/SA*, 10 November 1983, p. I6.

11. See Velayati's speech noted in *UNGA records No. A/38/PV.13, 1983*.

12. According to Velayati, the success of the Non-Aligned Movement is dependent on its ability to purge its ranks categorically of those stooges of the superpowers that make a superficial claim to being non-aligned but in reality only serve the interests of world imperialism. Ibid.

13. The press conference was given in Damascus, Syria. See "OCI Delegate Tashiri Explains Walkout," *FBIS/NES*, 28 March 1988, p. 49. Furthermore, the Iranian representative attributed this situation to "Saudi manipulation."

12. Terrorism and Subversion: Impact on Foreign Policy

1. Initially, Western experts on terrorism thought that Iran had not been involved in this incident. They reached this conclusion on the basis of the nature of the operations. According to U.S. terrorism experts, only two terrorist groups have a history of using the kind of sophisticated explosives that caused the Pan Am crash. One is the 15 May Organization, a Palestinian group, and the other is the Damascus-based Popular Front for the Liberations of Palestine—General Command, headed by Jibril. Later on, however, the evidence seemed to indicate that, although the operation was carried out by the Jibril group, it was done in complicity with Iranian hardliners. See "U.S. Thinks Pro-Iran Group Was Probably Not Involved," *New York Times*, December 28, 1988, p. 2, and "Palestinian Group and Iran Tied to Pan Am Bomb," *New York Times*, February 8, 1989, p. A10.

2. Both Iran's Foreign Minister and its speaker of parliament, Hashemi Rafsanjani, denied any Iranian involvement. See: *FBIS/SA*, 24 October 1983. Others, however, have argued that the movements of members of the Iranian embassy in Damascus and telephone communications between the embassy and Syrian officials monitored by the U.S. National Security Agency indicate Iran's involvement. See David C. Martin and John Walcott, *Best Laid Plans*, New York: Harper & Row, 1988, p. 106.

3. See "Iran Smooths Way for Syrians to Enter Bloody Slums of Beirut", *Washington Times*, May 23, 1988, p. A10.

4. See "Lebanon Senses Change in Tehran," *Christian Science Monitor*, 26 July 1989, p. 3.

5. On Syria's role, see Patrick Seale, *Asad: The Struggle for the Middle East*, pp. 489–490. According to Seale, Assad was angry that the pro-Iranian kidnappers of David Jacobsen

did not release him to Syrian troops, and thus in a "snub aimed at Iran and the U.S.", he leaked the news of McFarlane's visit and secret U.S.-Iranian contacts to *Al-Shira*.

6. For an elaboration on Iran's role in defusing this crisis, see R. K. Ramazani, *Revolutionary Iran: Challenge and Response in the Middle East*, pp. 190–93.

7. See Alex Von Dornoch, "Iran's Violent Diplomacy," *Survival*, Vol. XXX, No. 3, May/June 1988, pp. 253–54.

8. See "Musavi - Admission of Involvement in Hijacking," *FBIS/NES*, October 5, 1988, p. 3.

9. For an exaggerated account of Iran's subversive reach, see Amir Taheri, *Holy Terror,* Bethesda, Md.: Adler & Adler, 1987, and "Comment Khomeiny Veut Conquerir le Monde" *L'Express,* July 1984.

10. See "Interview: Prime Minister Hossain Moussavi," *MEED*, Vol. 32, No. 37, September 16, 1988, p. 5.

11. However, as far as the assassination attempt on the Emir of Kuwait's life is concerned, there is also suspicion that other countries—namely, Iraq or Syria—were implicated. At the time, Iran was trying to improve its relations with the GCC countries, with the hope of persuading them to stop helping Iraq. An Iranian-sponsored attempt to kill Kuwait's ruler could only have derailed this process. But such a prospect was extremely disturbing to Iraq. The assassin was an Iraqi by the name of Riyad Mufti Aqil, apparently belonged to the Al-Dawa Party, a dissident Shi'a movement with ties with Iran. But given the suspicions generated against Iraq, its ambassador to Kuwait had to deny any Iraqi connection and to claim that the Al-Dawa Party "is an Iranian party a hundred percent." See "Iraq Envoy Denies Connection," *FBIS, ME & Africa,* May 29, 1985, p. C-1. It must be noted that the Al-Dawa Party was formed in Iraq in the late 1950s, long before the Islamic revolution. Syria had its own grievance against Kuwait because, shortly before the incident, Kuwait's parliament had decided to cut aid to Syria for supporting Iran.

12. On Iran's ties with Islamic groups, see various chapters in Shireen T. Hunter (ed.), *The Politics of Islamic Revivalism: Diversity and Unity.* Also see Shireen T. Hunter, "Iran and the Spread of Revolutionary Islam," *Third World Quarterly,* Vol. 10, No. 2, April 1988.

13. See "Tunisia Claims Iranian Hand Stirring Up Islamic Fundamentalism," *Christian Science Monitor,* March 3, 1987, p. 6.

14. See "Lebanon Senses Change in Tehran," p. 3.

Selected Bibliography

Books

Abdulghani, J. M. *Iran and Iraq: The Years of Crisis*. London: Croom Helm, 1984.
Adamiyat, Fereydoun. *Andishehay-e-Mirza Agha Khan Kermani* [The Ideas of Mirza Agha Khan Kermani]. Tehran: Chapkhaneh Piruz, 1346 (1967–68). (Farsi)
Adamiyat, Fereydoun. *Amir Kabir va Iran* [Amir Kabir and Iran]. Tehran: Chapkhaneh Payam, 1323 (1944–45). (Farsi)
Adamiyat, Fereydoun, ed. *Andisheh-E-Taraghi Va Hokoumat-e-Ghanoun: Assr-e-Sapahsalar*. [The Idea of Progress and the Rule of Law: the Era of Sephsallar]. Tehran: Entesherat-e-Kharavmi, 1351 (1973).
Adamiyat, Fereydoun. *Bahrain Islands: A Legal and Diplomatic Study of British-Iranian Controversy*. New York: Praeger, 1955.
———. *Fakr-e-Azadi Va Nehzat-e-Nashrutiat* [The Idea of Liberty and the Constitutional Movement. Tehran: Entesharat-e-sokhan, 1340 (1962).
———. *Fakr-e-Democracy-e-Ejtemaie dar Nehzat-e-Mashrutiat-e-Iran* [The Idea of Social Democracy in Iran's Constitutional Movement]. Tehran: Payam, 1354 (1975).
Al-Ahmad, Jalal. *Gharbzadeghi* [Westoxication]. Islamic Students' Association of Europe and U.S. and Canada, 1979.
Ajami, Fouad. *The Vanished Imam, Musa al Sadr and the Shi'a of Lebanon*. Ithaca, N.Y.: Cornell University Press, 1986.
Akhavi, Shahrough. *Religion and Politics in Contemporary Iran: Clergy, State Relations in the Pahlavi Period*. Albany: SUNY Press, 1980.
Amirie, Abbas, ed. *Persian Gulf and Indian Ocean in International Politics*. Tehran: Institute for International Political and Economic Studies, 1975.
Amirie, Abbas and Hamilton A. Twitchell, ed. *Iran in the 1980s*. Tehran: Institute for International, Political, and Economic Studies, 1978.
Amirsadeghi, Hussein, ed. *Twentieth Century Iran*. New York: Holmes and Meier Publishers, Inc., 1977.
Arberry, A. J., ed. *The Legacy of Persia*. Oxford: Clarendon Press, 1953.
Arevalo, Juan Jose. *The Shark and the Sardines*. New York: El Stuart, 1961.
Avery, Peter. *Modern Iran*. New York: Praeger Inc., 1965.
Axelgard, Frederick W. *Iraq in Transition: A Political, Economic, and Strategic Perspective*. Boulder, Colo.: Westview Press, 1986.
———. *U.S.-Arab Relations: The Iraq Dimension*. National Council on U.S.-Arab Relations, 1985.
Azhary-El, M.S., ed. *The Iran-Iraq War: A Historical, Economic, and Political Analysis*. New York: St. Martin's, 1984.
Bahar, Mohammad Taghi. *Tarikh-E-Ahzab-Siasi* [The History of Political Parties]. Tehran, 1323 (1945).
Bakhash, Shaul. *The Reign of the Ayatollahs*, New York: Basic Books, 1984.
Bani-Sadr, Abol Hassan. *Sad Magaleh* [One Hundred Essays], published by the Organization of Iranian students in the United States. 1359 (1979).
Benard, Cheryl, and Khalilzad, Zalmay. *The Government of God: Iran's Islamic Republic*. New York: Columbia University Press, 1984.
Bill, James. *The Eagle and the Lion: The Tragedy of American-Iranian Relations*. New Haven: Yale University Press, 1988.

Brzezinski, Zbigniew. *Ideology and Power in Soviet Politics*. Westport, Conn.: Greenwood Press, 1976.

Byrne, Malcolm, ed. *The Chronology: The Documented Day-by-Day Account of the Secret Military Assistance to Iran and the Contras: The National Security Archive*. New York: Warner Books, 1987.

Burrell, R. M. and A. J. Cottrell, *Iran, Afghanistan, Pakistan: Tensions and Dilemmas*. California: Sage Publications, 1974.

Bustani, Emile. *Marche Arabesque*. London: Robert Hale Ltd., 1961.

Chay, John and Thomas E. Ross, eds. *Buffer States in World Politics*. Boulder, Colo.: Westview Press, 1986.

Chubin, Shahram and Sepehr Zabih. *The Foreign Relations of Iran*. Berkeley: University of California Press, 1974.

Chubin, Shahram and Charles Tripp. *Iran and Iraq at War*. Boulder, Colo.: Westview Press, 1988.

Corbin, Henry. *En Islam Iranian*. (IV Volumes). Paris: Gallimard, 1972.

Cordesman, Anthony M. *The Iran-Iraq War and Western Security, 1984–1987*. London: Jane's, 1987.

Cottam, Richard. *Iran and the United States: A Cold War Case Study*. Pittsburgh, Pa.: University of Pittsburgh Press, 1989.

Cottam, Richard. *Nationalism in Iran*. Pittsburgh, Pa.: University of Pittsburgh Press, 1979.

Dawisha, Adeed (ed.). *Islam in Foreign Policy*. London: Cambridge University Press for Royal Institute of International Affairs, 1983.

Enayat, Hamid. *Modern Islamic Political Thought*. Austin: University of Texas Press, 1982.

English, Barbara. *John Company's Last War*. London: Collin Clear-Type Press, 1971.

Fasai, Hasan. *Farsnama-Ye-Naseri* [Nasseri's History of Persia], translated by Heribert Busse. New York: Columbia University Press, 1972.

Fernandez, Damian J. *Cuba's Foreign Policy in the Middle East*. Boulder, Colo.: Westview Press, 1988.

Fischer, Michael M. J. *Iran: From Religious Dispute to Revolution*. Cambridge, Mass.: Harvard University Press, 1980.

Freedman, Robert O. *The Middle East Since Camp David*. Boulder, Colo.: Westview Press, 1984.

Fukuyama, Frances. *The Soviet Union and Iraq Since 1968*. Santa Monica, Calif.: Rand, N-1524, AFI, 1980.

Geller, Daniel S. *Domestic Factors in Foreign Policy: A Cross-National Statistical Analysis*. Cambridge, Mass.: Scherkman Books, Inc., 1985.

Ghrishman, Roman. *Iran*. Harmondsworth, England: Penguin Books, Ltd., 1959.

Green, Jerrold D. *Revolution in Iran: The Politics of Countermobilization*. New York: Praeger, 1982.

Grummon, Stephen R. *The Iran-Iraq War: Islam Embattled*. Washington Paper 192. Washington D.C.: Center for Strategic and International Studies, 1982.

Haim, Sylvia, ed. *Arab Nationalism and a Wider World*. New York: American Association for Peace in the Middle East, 1971.

Hanrieder, Wolfram F., ed. *Comparative Foreign Policy: Theoretical Essays*. New York: David McKay Company Inc., 1971.

Haq, Kadija, ed. *Dialogue for a New Order*. New York: Pergaman Press, 1980.

Hickman, William F. *Ravaged and Reborn: The Iranian Army*. Washington D.C.: The Brookings Institution, 1982.

Hiro, Dilip. *Iran Under the Ayatollahs*. London: Rutledge and Kegan Paul, 1985.

Hirst, David. *Oil and Public Opinion in the Middle East*. London: Faber and Faber, 1966.

Hunter, Shireen T. *OPEC and the Third World: The Politics of Aid*. Bloomington: Indiana University Press, 1984.

————, ed. *The Politics of Islamic Revivalism: Diversity and Unity.* Bloomington: Indiana University Press, 1988.

————, ed. *Internal Developments in Iran.* Washington, D.C.: Center for Strategic and International Studies, 1984.

Hurewitz, J. C. *Diplomacy in the Near and Middle East.* Princeton, N.J.: Princeton University Press, 1956.

Jabber, Paul, ed. *Great Power Interests in the Persian Gulf.* New York: Council on Foreign Relations, 1989.

Jacqz, Jane W., ed. *Iran, Past, Present and Future.* New York: Aspen Institute for Humanistic Studies.

Karanjia, R. K. *The Mind of a Monarch.* London: George Allen and Unwin, 1977.

Katz, Mark. *Russia and Arabia: Soviet Foreign Policy and the Arabian Peninsula.* Baltimore: Johns Hopkins University Press, 1985.

Kedourie, Elie. *Afghani and Abduh: An Essay on Religious Unbelief and Political Activism in Modern Islam.* New York: Humanities Press, 1966.

Khadduri, Majid. *Political Trends in the Arab World: The Role of Ideas and Ideals in Politics.* Baltimore: The Johns Hopkins University Press, 1970.

Khomeini, Imam Ayatollah Ruhollah. *Islam and Revolution: Writings and Declarations of Imam Khomeini,* translated by Hamid Algar. Berkeley: Mizan Press, 1981.

King, R. P. H. *The United Nations and the Iran-Iraq War.* New York: Ford Foundation, 1987.

Ledeen, Michael. *Perilous Statecraft: An Insider's Account of the Iran-Contra Affair.* New York: Scribner, 1988.

Ledeen, Michael and William Lewis. *Debacle.* New York: Knopf, Inc., 1980.

Levinson, Jerome and Juan de Onis. *The Alliance That Lost its Way.* A Twentieth Century Fund Study. Chicago: Quadrangle Books, 1972.

Lieber, Robert. *No Common Power: Understanding International Relations.* Boston: Scott Foresman, Little Brown, 1988.

Limbert, John W. *Iran: At War With History.* Boulder, Colo.: Westview Press, 1987.

Mahmud, Mahmud. *Tarikh-E-Ravabet Iran va Inglis Dar Gharn Nouzdaham* [The History of Anglo-Iranian Relations in the Nineteenth Century], Tehran: Chap-e-Eghbal, 1949.

Malik, Hafeez, ed. *Soviet-American Relations with Pakistan, Iran, and Afghanistan.* New York: St. Martin's Press, 1987.

Mazrui, Ali. *Africa's International Relations: The Diplomacy of Dependency and Change.* Boulder, Colo.: Westview Press, 1977.

Naff, Thomas, ed. *Gulf Security and the Iran-Iraq War.* Washington D.C.: National Defense University Press, 1985.

Nafisi, Said. *Tarikh-E-Siyasi Va Ejtemai Iran* [The Social and Political History of Iran]. Tehran: Entesharat-e-Bonyad, 1335 (1956–57).

Nobari, Ali-Reza, ed. *Iran Erupts.* Stanford: Iran-America Documentation Group, 1978.

Northedge, F. S., ed. *The Foreign Policies of the Powers.* New York: Praeger, 1968.

Norton, Augustus R. *Amal and the Shi'a: Struggle for the Soul of Lebanon.* Austin: University of Texas Press, 1987.

Pahlavi, Mohammad Reza. *Answer to History,* translated by Michael Joseph. Scarborough House, N.Y.: Stein and Day Publishers, 1980.

————. *Mission for My Country.* London: Hutchinson and Co. Ltd., 1968.

Parsons, Anthony. *The Pride and the Fall: Iran 1974–1979.* London: Jonathan Cape, 1984.

Pirnia, Abol Hasan. *The History of Ancient Iran.* (4 vols. in Persian), Tehran: Donyay-e-Ketab, 1362 (1982–83).

Quandt, William B. *Saudi Arabia in the 1980s: Foreign Policy, Security, and Oil.* Washington D.C.: The Brookings Institution, 1981.

Rai'n, Ismail. *Hoghough Beghiran Engilis Dar Iran* [In the Pay of the English]. Tehran: 1347 (1968).

Rajaee, Farhang. *Islamic Values and World View: Khomeini on Man, the State, and International Politics.* New York: University Press of America, 1983.

Ramazani, R. K. *Iran's Foreign Policy 1941–1973: A Study of Foreign Policy in Modernizing Nations.* Charlottesville: University Press of Virginia, 1975.

―――. *The Foreign Policy of Iran: A Developing Nation in World Affairs, 1500–1941.* Charlottesville: University Press of Virginia, 1966.

―――. *The Persian Gulf: Iran's Role.* Charlottesville: University Press of Virginia, 1973.

―――. *The United States and Iran.* New York: Praeger, 1982.

―――. *Revolutionary Iran and the Middle East: Challenges and Responses.* Baltimore: Johns Hopkins University Press, 1986.

Rosenau, James N., ed. *International Politics and Foreign Policy.* New York: The Free Press, 1969.

Rosenau, James N. *Linkage Politics: Essays on the Convergence of National and International Systems.* New York: The Free Press, 1969.

―――. *The Scientific Study of Foreign Policy.* New York: The Free Press, 1971.

Rothstein, Robert L. *Alliances and Small Powers.* New York: Columbia University Press, 1968.

Seale, Patrick. *Asad: The Struggle for the Middle East.* Berkeley: University of California Press, 1988.

Segev, Samuel. *The Iranian Triangle: The Untold Story of Israel's Role in the Iran-Contra Affair,* New York: The Free Press, 1988.

Shafa, Shoja-ed-Din. *Crimes and Punishments: Iran 1977–1985.* (Vol. II - Farsi), Washington D.C.: Inter-Collegiate Press, 1988.

Shawcross, William. *The Shah's Last Ride: The Fate of an Ally.* New York: Simon & Schuster, 1988.

Sick, Gary. *All Fall Down: The United States' Tragic Encounter with Iran.* New York: Random House, 1985.

Singh, R. K. *Iran: Quest for Security.* New Delhi: Vikas Publishing House Pv. Ltd., 1981.

Stempel, D. John. *Inside the Iranian Revolution.* Bloomington: Indiana University Press, 1981.

Taheri, Amir. *The Nest of Spies: America's Journey to Disaster in Iran.* New York: Pantheon Books, 1988.

―――. *Holy Terror: The Inside Story of Islamic Terrorism,* London: Hutchinson, 1985.

Teymuri, Ibrahim. *Asr-E-Bikhabari Ya Tarikh-E-Imtiyazat dar Iran* [The Era of Ignorance or the History of Concessions in Iran]. Tehran: Chap-e-Eghbal, 1332 (1953–54).

Triska, Jan F., ed. *Dominant Powers and Subordinate States.* Durham, N.C.: Duke University Press, 1986.

Waltz, Kenneth N. *Theory of International Politics.* Addison, Mass.: Wesley Publishing Company., 1979.

Wright, Dennis. *The English Amongst the Persians.* London: William Heinemann Ltd., 1977.

Wright, Dennis. *The Persians Amongst the English.* London: I. B. Taurus and Co. Ltd., 1985.

Yeselson, Abraham. *The United States-Persian Diplomatic Relations, 1883–1921.* New Brunswick, N.J.: Rutgers University Press, 1956.

Yodfat, Aryeh. *The Soviet Union and Revolutionary Iran.* New York: St. Martin's Press, 1984.

Zabih, Sepehr. *The Communist Movement in Iran.* Berkeley: University of California Press, 1966.

―――. *The Mossadegh Era.* Chicago, Ill.: Lake View Press, 1982.

Articles

Ahmad, Feroz. "Islamic Reassertion in Turkey." *Third World Quarterly,* Vol. 10, No. 2, April 1988.

Ayoob, Mohammed. "Indo-Iranian Relations: Strategic, Political, and Economic Dimensions," *India Quarterly,* Vol. 33, January-March 1977.

Axelgard, Frederick W. "The Tanker War in the Gulf: Background and Repercussions," *Middle East Insight,* Vol. 3, No. 6 (November-December 1984).

Atkin, Muriel. "Moscow's Disenchantment with Iran." *Survey.* Vol. 27, Autumn/Winter 1983.

Batatu, Hanna. "Iraq's Underground Shi'a Movements: Characteristics, Causes, and Prospects." *Middle East Journal,* Vol. 35, No. 4, Autumn 1981.

Bennigsen, Alexandre. "Mullahs, Mujahedins and Soviet Muslims." *Problems of Communism,* Vol. 33, November/December 1984.

Bennigsen, Alexandre. "Unrest in the World of Soviet Islam." *Third World Quarterly,* Vol. 10, No. 2, April 1988.

Borovali, Ali-Fuat. "Kurdish Insurgencies: The Gulf War and Turkey's Changing Role." *Conflict Quarterly,* Vol. VII, No. 4, Fall 1987.

Chubin, Shahram. "Gains for Soviet Policy in the Middle East." *International Security* [Vol. 6] Spring 1982.

———. "Iran Between the Arab West and the Asian East." *Survival,* Vol. 16, No. 4, July-August 1974.

———. "Local Soil Foreign Plants," *Foreign Policy,* No. 34, Spring 1979.

Cordesman, Anthony H. "Lessons of the Iran-Iraq War: The First Round." *Armed Forces Journal International,* Vol. 119, April 1982.

———. "The Iran-Iraq War: Attrition Now, Chaos Later." *Armed Forces Journal International,* Vol. 120, May 1983.

Dawisha, Adeed. "Iran's Mullahs and the Arab Masses," *Washington Quarterly,* Vol. 6, No. 3, Summer 1986.

Dornach, Alex Von. "Iran's Violent Diplomacy." *Survival,* Vol. XXX, No. 3, May/June 1988.

Elwell-Sutton, L. P. "Nationalism and Neutralism in Iran." *Middle East Journal,* Vol. 12, No. 1, Winter 1958.

Entessar, Nader. "The People's Republic of China and Iran: An Overview of the Relationship." *Asia Quarterly,* No. 1, 1978.

Foot, Rosemary. "China's New Relationship with Iran." *Contemporary Review,* Vol. 226, February 1975.

Halliday, Fred. "U.S. Turns Blind Eye on Iran's Aid to Somalia." *Middle East,* No. 40, February 1978.

Harrison, Selig S. "Dateline Afghanistan: Exit Through Finland." *Foreign Policy,* No. 41, Winter 1980–81.

Hunter, Shireen T. "After the Ayatollah." *Foreign Policy,* No. 66, Spring 1987.

———. "Arab-Iranian Relations and Stability in the Persian Gulf." *Washington Quarterly,* Vol. 7, No. 3, Summer 1984.

———. "Iran and the Spread of Revolutionary Islam." *Third World Quarterly.* Vol. 10, No. 2, April 1988.

———. "Islamic Fundamentalism: What It Really is and Why It Frightens the West." *SAIS Review,* Vol. 6, No. 1, Winter 1986.

———. "Islamic Iran and the Arab World." *Middle East Insight,* Vol. V, No. 3, August-September 1987.

————. "Syrian-Iranian Relations: An Alliance of Convenience or More." *Middle East Insight,* Vol. 4, No. 2, June-July 1985.

————. "Terrorism: A Balance Sheet." *Washington Quarterly* Vol. 12, No. 3, Summer 1989.

Ja'afari, Maldari Asghar. "Barrasi Tarikhi Ekhtelafalt Marzi Iran Va Aragh" [The Historical Analysis of Border Disputes between Iran and Iraq]. *Journal of Foreign Policy,* Vol. 1, No. 4, October/November 1987 (published by the Institute for Political and International Studies, Tehran).

Malat, Chibli. "Religious Militancy in Contemporary Iraq: Muhammad Baqer as-Sadr and the Sunni-Shi'a Paradigm." *Third World Quarterly,* Vol. 10, No. 2, April 1988.

Paul, Jim. "Insurrection at Mecca." *MERIP Reports,* No. 86, October 1980.

Pitty, Roderic. "Soviet Perceptions of Iraq." *Middle East Report,* Vol. 18, No. 2, March-April 1988.

Ramazani, R. K. "Iran and the Arab-Israeli Conflict." *Middle East Journal,* Vol. 32, No. 4, Autumn 1978.

————. "Iran: Burying the Hatchet." *Foreign Policy,* No. 60, Fall 1985.

————. "The Iran-Iraq War and the Persian Gulf Crisis." *Foreign Policy,* Vol. 87, No. 526, February 1988.

Renfrew, Nita M. "Who Started the War." *Foreign Policy,* No. 66, Spring 1987.

Rondot, Philippe. "L'Irak: Une puissance regionale en devenir." *Politique Etrangère,* Vol. 45, No. 3, 1980.

Ross, Dennis. "Considering Soviet Threats to the Persian Gulf." *International Security,* No. 2, Fall 1982.

————. "Soviet Views Towards the Gulf War." *ORBIS,* Vol. 18, No. 3, Fall 1984.

Rouleau, Eric. "Khomeini's Iran." *Foreign Affairs,* Vol. 59, Fall 1980, pp. 1–20.

Siegler, John. "The Iran-Iraq Conflict: The Tragedy of Limited Conventional War." *International Journal,* Spring 1986.

Tahir-Kheli, Shirin. "Cooperation in an Area of Conflict." *Asian Survey* Vol. 17, May 1977.

Wright, Claudia. "Iraq: New Power in the Middle East." *Foreign Affairs,* Vol. 58, No. 11, Winter 1978–80.

Yoshitsu, Michael M. "Iran and Afghanistan in Japanese Perspective." *Asian Survey,* Vol. XXI, No. 5, May 1981.

Zabih, Sepehr. "Iran's International Posture: De Facto Non-Alignment within a Pro-Western Alliance." *Middle East Journal,* Vol. 24, No. 3, Summer 1970.

Index

Abu Musa (island), 101–2, 115, 219 n.54
Afghan civil war, 28, 58, 86–87, 213 n.43; Soviet intervention, 83–87, 89–94, 96, 215 n.75
Afghanistan, 65, 67, 90, 95, 136–37, 224 n.26; as concern of Iran and China, 159, 160; as concern of Iran and Pakistan, 132, 135–36, 222 n.9, 224 n.26; history and cultural heritage, 199 n.19, 210–11 n.5; Iran's relations with, 7, 8, 27, 28, 33, 34, 132, 192
Africa, 165, 167, 235 nn.2, 3, 236 n.10, 236–37 n.11, 237 nn.13, 14
Al-Ahmad, Jalal, 9, 38
Algeria, 53, 76, 99, 128
Algiers Agreement: *1975*, 105, 112, 113, 215 n.84; *1981*, 74, 76
Alliance for Progress, 51, 53, 204 n.10
AMAL (Lebanese Shiʻa group), 124–27, 176
Amini, Ali, 31, 32, 49–50
Amir Kabir, Mirza Taghi, 22–23, 39, 201 n.5, 203 n.1
Anti-Americanism, 53, 57, 86, 128, 166–67; in post-revolution Iran, 53, 89, 205 n.15; role in Arab-Iranian relations, 102, 217–18 n.21
Anti-British feelings, 102, 228 n.30
Arab-Israeli conflict, 51, 53, 62, 102–4, 122
Arab-Israeli war (1973), 100, 103
Arab League, 113, 125
Arabs, 52–53, 131, 140, 199 n.20, 209 n.86, 222 n.2, 226 n.6; in France, 149, 230 n.54
Arab states, 28, 42, 67, 94, 136, 156; China's relations with, 161, 233–34 n.25, 234 n.26; France's relations with, 149, 150; Iran's relations with, 6–7, 98–130; Iran's relations with under the Shah, 31, 32, 34, 98–105, 200 n.37; and U.S. policies, 62, 67, 68, 73, 77–78, 207 n.56. *See also countries by name*
Arab states, Persian Gulf, 100, 122–23, 127, 145, 179, 191; assistance to Iraq, 107, 108, 110; as focus of Iranian subversion, 178, 179; relations with India, 132–33; relations with Iran, 99, 108, 109, 114–21, 184, 188; relations with Pakistan, 132, 223 n.16; Soviet concern over, 87, 90, 92. *See also countries by name*
Arafat, Yasser, 104, 127–28, 218 n.26, 222 n.98
Argentina, 165, 166
Arms supplies: for Africa, 167, 237 n.14; for Arab states from China, 161, 234 n.26; indirectly reaching Iran, 63; for Iran from East Europe 144, 227 n.23; for Iran from U.S., 49, 60, 64; and the Iran-Contra affair, 65–66, 207 nn.48, 53; for Iraq from France, 150, 230 n.57. *See also* Military assistance
Ataturk, Mustafa Kemal, 133, 137, 224–25 n.35

Australia, 159, 163–64, 233 n.19
Azerbaijan: Iranian, 8, 80, 169, 191, 211 n.11, 212 n.21; Soviet, 82, 94, 191, 192, 211–12 n.15, 213 n.41
Azerbaijanis as Shiʻites, 11, 213 n.41

Baʻathist regime (Iraq), 60, 105, 217 n.20, 218 n.30
Baʻathists, 15, 100, 114
Baghdad Pact, 27, 100, 131, 217 n.20, 223 n.22
Bahrain, 114, 116, 117, 219 n.57, 226 n.7, 237 n.1; Arab-Iranian dispute over, 99, 101; relations with Iran, 114, 115, 219 n.67; Shiʻas in, 115, 219–20 n.58
Bakhtiar, Shapour, 3, 54, 153–54
Baluchistan, 84, 211 n.11, 222 n.4, 224 n.25
Bani-Sadr, Abol-Hassan, 1, 36, 55, 106, 115, 219 n.50; France's relations with, 149, 229 n.51, 230 n.57; on need for activism, 41, 203 n.19; and relations with USSR, 81, 83–85, 86, 211 nn.14, 15
Bazargan, Mehdi, 1, 36, 54–56, 57, 142, 175; relations with Gulf Arabs, 115; relations with USSR, 81–83
Belgium, 142, 143, 226 n.10
Berri, Nabih, 126, 177
Bombings, 90, 91, 118, 150, 174–75, 176; by Iraq, 66, 88–89, 92, 108, 110, 111, 214 n.60
Brazil, 165, 166, 235 n.5
British Embassy (in Tehran), 145–46, 147, 148, 228 n.34
Brzezinski, Zbigniew, 16, 55, 81
Bush, George, 72, 73, 209 n.76, 226 n.4
Bush administration, 74, 75–76

Carter, Jimmy, 51, 55, 58–59, 205 n.27
Carter doctrine, 58–59, 205 n.27
Castro, Fidel, 165, 166, 235 n.7
CENTO (Central Treaty Organization), 27, 32, 54, 132, 133, 222 n.8; Iran's withdrawal from, 134, 211 n.12
China, 15, 113, 161, 234 n.29; post-revolution Iran's relations with, 43, 89, 159–62, 233 nn.20, 21, 22, 24; pre-revolution Iran's relations with, 25, 34, 133, 157, 158–59, 232 n.1, 233 nn.12, 14, 16
Chirac, Jacques, 151–53
Clergy, 12, 13, 38, 199 n.24
Clerical (religious) factions, 57, 59, 61, 83, 85, 86, 145
Colonialism, 40, 52–53, 141, 199 n.17, 204–5 n.13, 205 n.14

Constitutionalist movement, Iranian, 15, 28, 157, 200 n.27, 226 n.11, 232 n.6
Containment policy, 180, 185, 191
Cottam, Richard, 56, 57–58, 205 n.20
Coups d'etat, 179; 1953 Iranian, 8, 46–47, 48, 50–51, 53, 145
Cuba, 111–12, 165–67, 235 n.6

Danesh case, 155
Dari (language), 210–11 n.5
Decolonization, 27, 165, 235 n.1
Denmark, 143, 226 n.10
Dubai, 117, 219 n.53
Dumas, Roland, 154, 231 n.80

East European countries, Iran's relations with, 142, 144, 226–27 n.13, 227 nn.23, 25, 228 nn.26, 28
Economic assistance
—from Iran, 34, 132, 222 n.11
—to Iran, 18, 24; from the U.S., 31, 49–50, 204 nn.8, 9; from USSR, 91–92
—to Iraq from Gulf states, 107, 117, 220 n.63
Economic attrition, war of, 107–8
Economic relations: between Arab countries and China, 233–34 n.25; between Iraq and France, 149
—between Iran and: Africa, 165, 167, 235 n.3, 236 n. 10; East Asian countries, 158–63, 232 nn.8, 9, 10, 233 n.21, 235 n.43; East European countries, 144, 226–27 n.13; India, 224 n.33; Pakistan, 135; USSR, 84, 85, 89, 213 n.36; West European countries, 143, 148–49, 151, 154, 155, 227 nn.18, 19, 229 n.50
Economy, 32, 34, 42, 47, 86, 89; role in foreign policy decisions, 17, 22, 23, 28, 31, 189
Egypt, 120, 172–73, 178, 179, 204 n.14, 237 n.14; economic aid from U.S., 49, 52, 204 n.8; relations with Iran, 100, 101, 128–29, 217 nn.11, 20; support for Iraq, 62, 73, 107, 129
Egyptian-Israeli peace treaty (1979), 122, 123
Elite, the, 15, 38, 202–3 n.9
Embargoes, 86, 146, 153; by U. N., 91–92, 161; by U.S., 70, 74, 77, 143
Equilibrium, 22–24, 29, 81
Ethnicity, 10, 11, 98–99, 123, 180
EURODIF loan, 151, 153, 231 n.77
Europe, 22, 25, 84, 139–56, 212 n.29. *See also countries by name*
Extremists, Iranian. *See* Radicals, Iranian

Farahani, Ghaem Magham, 39, 198 n.9
Farsi, 11, 199 n.19. *See also* Persian language
Farsi-e-Dari (language), 210–11 n.5
Faw peninsula 92, 109–10, 208 n.65
Forrestal, James V., 201 n.12, 204 n.5
France, 18, 25, 124, 126, 175; pre-revolution Iran's relations with, 141, 148–49, 226 nn.10, 11; re-lations with Islamic regime, 107, 148, 149–54, 227 n.20
French Embassy (in Tehran), 153
Friendship and Commerce, U.S.-Iranian Treaty of (1856), 48, 203–4 n.2
Fuller, Graham, 207 n.49

Gadhafi, Muammar. *See* Qadhafi, Muammar
Genscher, Hans Dietrich, 88, 154, 155
Germany, 16, 18, 24, 141–42, 226 nn.10, 12; East, 144, 227 n.25; West, 154–56
Ghotbzadeh, Sadegh, 83, 84–85, 115, 220 n.59; and relations with U.S. and USSR, 81, 85, 211 nn.14, 15, 212 n.31
Gorbachev, Mikhail, 6, 91, 93, 94, 97, 197 n.6
Gordji, Vahid, 152–53, 230 n.67, 231 nn.70, 71, 72
Great Britain, 22, 25–26, 70, 131, 200–201 n.2, 201 n.4, 210 n.3; approach to Mossadegh, 46, 60; 19th- and 20th-century Persian Gulf policies, 19, 140, 226 n.6; relations with Iran in 19th and early 20th centuries, 8, 22–23, 80, 197 n.8, 198 nn.9, 11, 198–99 n.12, 201 n.13; re-lations with Iran under the Pahlavis, 8, 23, 24–25, 30, 141–42, 144–45, 169, 226 nn.9, 10, 237 n.1; relations with Islamic regime, 142, 145–48; role in creation of Baghdad Pact, 27; withdrawal of military presence from Persian Gulf, 28, 33
Greater Tunbs (islands), 101–2, 105, 115, 219 n.54
Guerrilla groups, Afghan. *See* Mojahedin; Rebels, Afghan
Guerrillas, Iranian, 104, 127, 200 n.37
Gulf Cooperation Council (GCC), 61, 87, 109, 112–13, 114, 120–21

Hadj ceremonies, 118–19, 224 n.28
Hague Process, 86, 210 n.93
Haig, Alexander, 61
Hansen, Georges, 151, 230 n.60
Headdress, Islamic, 137, 224–25 n.35
Herat, 197 n.8, 201 n.4
Higgins, William, 75, 209 nn.84, 87
Hijacking of TWA flight 847, 177
Hizbullah, 75, 124–27, 221 n.82
Hormuz, Strait of, 63, 69, 107–8
Hostage crisis, U.S., 1, 56–59, 73–74, 129, 174–75; European reaction to, 143, 146, 153; failure of rescue attempt, 58; as isolating Iran, 44, 105; seeds of in 1953 *coup d'etat,* 46; and Soviet-Iranian relations, 83–84
Hostages, 73–74, 155, 174–75; British, 127, 147–48; French, 150–52, 153, 175, 230 n.60; and the Iran-Contra affair, 65–66, 207 n.48; in Lebanon, 72–73, 75–76, 124–25, 209 n.86
Human-rights record, Iran's, 140, 170, 237 n.4;

European criticism of, 142, 143, 149, 155, 156, 229 n.43; U.S. policy applied to, 51, 204 n.11
Hussein (king of Jordan), 123, 129, 215 n.72

Ideology, 10, 14–17, 37, 41, 102. *See also* Islamic ideology; Islamic revolutionary ideology; Revolutionary ideology
Iliffe, J. H., 139
Independence: as an imperative for Iran, 21–22, 24, 30, 37, 188
India, 22, 32, 136–37, 198 n.11, 226 n.6; conflict with Pakistan, 27, 131–32; economic aid from U.S., 49, 204 n.8; historical background to relations with Iran, 28, 131–33, 222 n.2, 223 nn.11, 14; Iran as buffer state for, 7, 8, 25–26; relations with China, 161, 234 n.29; relations with Gulf Arab states and Iraq, 132–33, 223 n.17; relations with Islamic regime, 134–35, 136–37, 224 nn.31, 33
Indo-Pakistan wars: *1965*, 32, 91, 131–32, 159; *1971*, 33, 131–32, 159
Intellectuals, secular Iranian, 37, 38, 39, 53, 202 n.8
Iran Air jet, downing of, 71–73, 93
Iran-Contra affair, 65–67, 104, 110, 146, 207 nn.46, 48; effect on Franco-Iranian relations, 152, 153; impact on Soviet-Iranian relations, 89–93; leaking of U.S.-Iranian contacts, 176, 238–39 n.5; as U.S. election issue, 73, 209 n.76
Iranian Embassy (in London), 147, 228 n.34
Iranian (Islamic) revolution, 1–5, 16, 41, 46, 105, 142, 203 n.19; effects on Iran's relationship with India, Pakistan, and Turkey, 134–38, 225 n.43; goals compared with China's, 160; Gulf states' fear of, 115–17, 120, 220 n.71; Nigerian praise for, 236–37 n.11; Soviet hopes about, 81–82; Western overreaction to, 140–41
Iran-Iraq war, 2, 21, 28, 104–14, 126, 167, 181–82, 184; Algeria's posture toward, 128; capture of Faw peninsula, 92, 109–10, 208 n.65; as dilemma for PLO, 127; effect on Franco-Iranian relations, 140–50, 153, 230 n.62; effect on Iran-Gulf relations, 116, 117–19, 121; effect on Iran's relations with Turkey, 134, 137–38, 225 n.42; effect on Sino-Iranian relations, 160–61; effect on Soviet-Iranian relations, 88–89, 90–93, 95–97, 215 n.75; European perception of, 140, 143–44, 154; Iran's criticism of Security Council's attitude toward, 170, 171; Japanese posture toward, 162; as limiting Iran's subversion, 180–81; mediation efforts, 93, 110–14; negotiated peace, 8, 17; OIC's unwillingness to condemn Iraqi actions in, 172; proposed policy for Israel in, 104; Syrian views on, 122; tanker war of 1983, 63, 69–70, 107–8, 110, 111, 150; U.S. policy on, 9, 19, 60–64, 65, 66–72, 90, 91–92, 206 n.43, 209 n.74; West accused of provoking, 84, 95, 216 n.83
Iraq, 27, 105, 184, 201 n.13, 218 n.29, 228 n.34,

239 n.11; calls for inclusion in GCC, 120, 220 n.71; claim to Shat-al-Arab, 99, 101, 105, 112; Cuba's ties with, 166; Egypt's support for, 129; failure of mediation efforts to condemn, 110–14, 172, 219 n.40; as focus of Iranian subversion, 178, 179; French relations with, 126, 141, 149–50, 151–52, 154, 229 n.51, 231 nn.77, 81; guidelines for Arab conduct, 117, 220 n.62; international support for, 44, 140, 141, 175; Jordan's support for, 129; Kurdish issue, 134, 137, 223 n.22, 225 n.37; 1958 revolution, 32, 217 n.20; occupation of Khusistan, 11; PLO's relations with, 127; relations with Gulf states, 114, 116–17, 208 n.62; relations with India, 132–33, 223 n.17; relations with Iran in 1950s, 101, 217 n.20; relations with Turkey, 137–38, 225 nn.39, 40; relations with USSR, 32, 83, 86, 90, 92, 93–94, 95–97, 132, 185, 215 n.84, 216 n.97; Syrian relations with, 122–23; territorial integrity affirmed by Iran, 138, 225 n.40; U.S. debate on relative importance of Iran and, 73, 209 n.77; U.S. relations with during 1980s, 61–65, 67–70, 72, 73, 185; use of chemical weapons, 71, 73, 108, 110, 143, 172; use of missiles, 92, 215 n.76; use of subversion, 116, 179; West German relations with, 155; withdrawal of forces from Iran, 86, 96, 106
Islam, 3, 4–5, 15, 41, 98, 123; as core of national culture, 9; equated with Arabism by Arab nationalists, 218 n.30; Iran as transmitter of to China and the Indian subcontinent, 131, 232 n.1; Iranians as holding special place in, 11–12, 199 n.20; Iran's position on Afghanistan as showing solidarity of, 84; Iran's seen as threat to Soviet Muslims, 86, 213 n.41; Iran's world view based on, 36–45; Lebanon receptive to message and influence of, 124, 125–26; relationship to nationalism in Iran, 10, 11–14, 187; role in Khomeini's animosity toward the U.S., 59, 205–6 n.30; Soviet view of revolutionary potential, 82, 212 n.19. *See also* Shi'a Islam; Sunni Islam
Islamic fundamentalism, 64–65, 68, 111, 112, 149, 150, 181–82
Islamic ideology, 14, 15, 140, 167, 172, 184; role in Iran's foreign policy, 15, 16–17, 36–45, 189
Islamic movement, 36, 115, 149, 163, 230 n.54; suppression of in Syria, 122
Islamic regime, 1, 104, 141, 184–89, 216 n.9; China's relations with, 159–62, 233 nn.20, 21, 22, 24; diplomatic strategies, 24–26; foreign policy, 18, 19–20, 28, 29–30, 34–35; Japan's relations with, 162–63, 234 nn.36, 37; military buildup, 52, 200 n.2; rejection of Iranian nationalism, 99, 217 n.8; relations with European countries, 142–56; relations with Gulf Arab states, 114–20; relations with India, Pakistan, and Turkey, 134–38; relations with Third World 166–68; relations with U.S., 59–78; relations

Islamic regime—(*continued*)
   with USSR, 81–97; view of international organizations, 170–73, 237 n.3; world view, 36–45
Islamic republic: possibility of in Lebanon, 124, 126, 175, 221 n.93
Islamic Republican Party, 85, 106
Islamic revolution. *See* Iranian revolution
Islamic revolutionary ideology, 41, 43–44, 129; Iran's attempts to spread seen as subversion, 174, 175–76, 178–79, 181; Iran's use of Hadj to spread, 118–19
Islamization: of Iran, 1–2, 6–7, 98, 216 n.1; of Pakistan, 134, 135
Israel, 10, 67, 100, 127, 150, 207 n.56, 230 n.56; abduction of Sheikh Obeid, 75; invasion of Lebanon, 61, 123, 126, 150; Iran's relations with, 31, 102–4, 115; Iran's severing of links with, 2, 54, 211 n.12; Lebanon's abrogation of 1983 treaty with, 206 n.35; role in hostage problem, 209 n.86; seen as military threat by Syria, 122; U.S. relationship to, 53, 56, 59, 61, 62, 204–5 n.13, 205–6 n.30
Italy, 142, 143, 226 n.10, 227 nn.18, 19

Japan, 113; post-revolution Iran's relations with, 43, 162–63, 234 nn.36, 37; pre-revolution Iran's relations with, 25, 89, 157–58, 232 nn.7–10, 233 n.11
Jordan, 107, 128–29, 172

Kennedy administration, 49–50, 51, 53, 204 n.10
Khamenei, Hodjat-al-Islam Seyyed Ali, 38, 89, 177, 208 n.66, 219 n.48, 225 n.40; visit to China, 162; visit to Zimbabwe, 237 n.13
Khoeiniha, Hodjat-al-Islam, 83, 118, 212 n.16
Khomeini, Ayatollah Rouhollah, 1–2, 3, 11, 160, 208 n.66, 220 n.66, 236 n.9; appeal to OIC, 112; call for Rushdie's execution, 74, 94, 176 (*see also* Rushdie affair); death, 4, 75; France's relations with, 149, 229 n.51; interpretation of Islam, 36–41, 44–45; liberation of Palestine as goal of regime, 127; on non-aligned countries, 172; opposition to nationalism, 13; reaction to downing of Iran Air jet, 71; reaction to hostage crisis, 57–58, 175; Soviet relations with, 83–84, 94, 215 nn.83, 85; on the U.S., Israel, and Islam, 59, 205–6 n.30; West German TV satirization of, 231 n.84
Khusistan (prov., Iran), 11, 83, 95, 105–6, 117, 216 n.93; Arab claims to, 99, 101–2, 105, 217 n.19
Kianuri, Nureddin, 83
Kidnappings, 67, 150–51, 174–75, 176, 179, 230 n.60
Kirkuk (prov., Iraq), 137, 225 nn.39, 40
Korea, North, 163, 235 n.45
Korea, South, 163, 234 n.41, 235 n.43
Kurdistan, 8, 80, 84, 211 n.11, 212 n.21

Kurds, 11, 82–83, 134, 137, 179, 223 n.22, 225 n.37; Iraq's massacre of, 172; rebel factions in Iran-Iraq war, 109–10
Kuwait, 90, 115, 119, 172, 175, 219–20 n.58, 220 n.72; Arab subversion in, 116, 220 n.60; economic relations with China, 233–34 n.25; 1985 assassination attempt on Emir of, 179, 239 n.11; relations with Iran, 114–18, 128, 219 n.52, 220 n.59; support for Iraq, 110, 114, 117, 208 n.62; U.S. naval protection for shipping, 68–70, 208 n.61

Land reform, 43, 50, 51, 204 n.10
Laos, 163, 235 n.46
Larijani, Mohammad Javad, 71, 208 n.67, 215 n.84
Latin America, 39, 51, 165–67, 202 n.8, 204 n.10
League of Nations, 169, 237 n.1
Lebanese Christian forces, 123, 150, 179, 231 n.71
Lebanon, 62, 67, 69, 75, 122, 150–51, 206 n.35; Iran's involvement in, 28, 61–62, 123–27, 174–76, 179, 182–83; Syria's activities in, 123–25, 126
Leftists, Iranian, 1, 23, 55, 57, 81–82, 85, 205 n.30; as challenge to the Shah, 30–31, 142; Soviet contacts with, 80, 82, 97, 212 n.16
Lesser Tunbs (islands), 101–2, 105, 115, 219 n.54
Libya, 57, 90, 101, 102, 155, 165, 173; Cuba's relations with, 166, 235 n.4; economic relations with China, 233–34 n.25; relations with Iran, 101, 102, 123, 211 n.12, 217–18 n.21; relations with Pakistan, 132

McFarlane, Robert, 90
Malaysia, 157, 163, 232 n.4, 234 n.41, 235 n.44
Medvenko, Leonid, 82, 212 n.19
Middle East, 27, 41, 52–53, 100, 178–79; U.S. policy on, 49, 52, 59–72, 204 nn.5, 8, 206 n.43. *See also countries by name*
Military, the (Iranian), 22–23, 28, 41, 74, 189, 200 n.2; buildup, 21, 33, 52, 200 n.2, 202 n.24; expenditures, 17, 31, 200 n.34
Military assistance, 24, 125. *See also* Arms supplies
—from Iran: to Afghan Shi'as, 86, 213 n.43; to Africa, 165, 235 n.3
—to Iran, 18, 31, 85, 96, 230 n.57; from China, 160, 161, 233 n.22, 24; from Eastern Europe, 144, 228 n.26; from North Korea, 163
—to Iraq, 107, 108, from Gulf states, 117, 220 n.63; from USSR, 86, 90, 92, 96
Military intervention
—Syrian, 124–25; threatened by the West, 63
—U.S., 58–59, 75, 83, 84, 88, 205 n.27; effects, 72, 90, 92–93
Mines, 70–71, 90, 208 n.66
Missiles, 69–70, 71, 88, 208 n.63; Chinese sale

of, 160–61, 233 n.24, 234 n.26; Iraq's use of, 69, 92, 150, 215 n.76

Moderates, Iranian, 42–44, 93–94, 143–44, 205 n.29, 207 n.46; and Anglo-Iranian relations, 146, 148, 229 n.47; attitude toward terrorism, 176–78, 182; and the Iran-Contra affair, 66–67, 89, 91; power in late 1980s, 67–68, 72, 74

Mohammed Reza Shah Pahlavi. *See* Shah, the

Mohtashami, Ayatollah, 146, 176

Mojahedin (Afghan), 65, 86–87, 95, 213 n.43. *See also* Rebels, Afghan

Mojahedin-e-Khalgh, 85, 149, 221 n.95, 229 n.43; French expulsion of, 151, 153, 231 n.73. *See also* Opposition groups, Iranian

Montazeri, Ayatollah Hossein-Ali, 44, 199 n.17, 215 n.82

Morocco, 128–29

Mossadegh, Mohammad, 8, 30, 39, 54; Britain's approach to, 60, 145; strategy of negative equilibrium, 23–24, 28–29, 81; U.S. role in toppling, 46–47, 48, 50–51, 53

Mubarak, Hosni, 129

Musavi, Mir Hossein, 116, 138, 177, 178–79, 224–25 n.35; trip to Italy, 143, 227 n.19; on the USSR, 89, 212 n.32

Muslims, 40, 118, 163, 178, 199 n.17, 232 n.1, 234 n.39; African, 165, 167; Khomeini's concern for, 59, 205–6 n.30; Pakistanis as, 222 n.4; Soviet, 86, 94–95, 213 n.37, 222 n.4; treatment by Indian government, 137, 224 n.31

Nasser, Gamal abd-al-, 27, 98, 103, 217 n.20

National Iranian Oil Co., 147, 229 n.42

Nationalism, 2, 10, 15, 23, 53, 187

—Arab, 7, 27, 31, 98–103, 105, 114, 122, 218 n.30; as ethos for PLO, 127; among Gulf Arabs, 117; role in support for Iraq, 123

—Iranian, 10–11, 82, 99, 106, 123, 180, 217 n.8, 226 n.9; growth of cultural, 12, 199 n.22; interaction with Islam, 10, 11–14; Islamic regime's downgrading of, 99, 100, 217 n.8; Mossadegh as symbol of, 47, 50; as state ideology, 16, 29

Nationalization of oil (1951), 4, 8, 29, 60

Nazi-Soviet Pact (1939), 80, 226 n.12

Negative equilibrium, 23–24, 29, 81

Neutrality, 23, 60, 95, 201 n.8. *See also* Nonalignment

New Zealand, 159, 163–64

Nicaragua, 166, 235 n.6, 236 n.9

Nixon doctrine, 28, 33, 52

Non-Aligned Movement (NAM), 15, 29, 40, 166, 200 n.32, 205 n.16; Islamic Iran's approach to, 172, 238 n.12; mediation efforts in Iran-Iraq war, 110, 111–12

Non-alignment, 43, 46, 49, 53, 54, 134; Iran as only example of for Khomeini, 37, 40; and use of negative equilibrium, 23–24

North, Oliver, 66, 90

North Atlantic Treaty Organization (NATO), 49, 134

Obeid Sheikh Abd-al-Karim, 75, 76

Oil, 7, 63, 73, 88, 100, 165, 209 n.78; importance to U.S., 26, 49, 201 n.12, 204 n.5; Iran's nationalization of in 1951, 4, 8, 29, 60; pipelines, 107, 109; price drop, 89, 119–20, 214 n.60; role in French relations with Arab states, 149

Oil exports, Iranian, 86, 107–8, 119–20, 165, 167; to East Europe, 28 n.28; to India, 223 n.11; to Japan, 158, 162, 163, 234 n.36; role in revenue increase under the Shah, 32, 34; to Syria, 123; to USSR, 90–91

Oman, 87, 109, 114, 117, 184

OPEC, 29, 119–20

Operation Staunch, 64, 108, 206 n.42

Opposition groups, Iranian, 116, 149, 155, 220 n.59. *See also* Mojahedin-e-Khalgh

Organization of the Islamic Conference (OIC), 110, 112, 172–73

Ottoman Empire, 7, 26, 79, 133, 197 n.3, 210 n.2

Pahlavi dynasty, 10, 12–13, 16, 18, 21, 23–25. *See also* Reza Shah Pahlavi; Shah, the

Pahlavi Persian (language), 210–11 n.5, 222 n.2

Pakistan, 10, 27, 33, 74, 76, 204 n.8, 213 n.41; as common concern of Iran and China, 159, 160, 233 n.14; relations with Iran under the Shah, 27, 28, 33, 131–33; relations with Islamic regime, 65, 134–37, 185, 222 nn.3, 4, 223–24 n.24, 224 nn.25, 26, 28; relations with Libya and the Gulf Arab states, 132, 233 n.16; relations with Saudi Arabia, 135–36, 137; Soviet displeasure over Iran's relations with, 87, 213–14 n.46. *See also* Indo-Pakistan war

Pakistani brigade, 136, 224 n.28

Palestine, Arab position on, 102–4

Palestinians, 114, 124, 126, 127–28, 150, 219 n.52, 238 n.1

Palme, Olaf, 111, 113, 219 n.43

Pan Am flight 103, bombing of, 174, 176, 238 n.1

Perez de Cueller, Alfonzo, 113

Persian Gulf, 6, 7, 99, 100–101, 203 n.1; Arab nationalism's focus on, 27, 31; British 19th- and 20th-century policies on, 8, 22, 25, 28, 33, 140, 197 n.8, 226 n.6; Iran's interests in, 99, 107; Iran's security role in, 51–52, 54. *See also* Arab states, Persian Gulf; Iran-Iraq war

Persian language, 11, 199 n.19, 210–11 n.5, 222 nn.1–4, 226 n.6

Persian literature, 210–12 n.5, 232 n.4

Persianness, 180, 199 n.22

Persians, 11, 139–40, 210–11 n.5

PLO (Palestine Liberation Organization), 57, 104, 127, 205 n.25, 211 n.12; Cuba's relations with, 166, 235 n.4; role in training Iranian guerrillas, 200 n.37, 212 n.16

Poland, 144, 226–27 n.13
Positive equilibrium, 22–23
Power, 1, 15–16, 25–26, 36, 101, 175; polarization of, 37–39; relations between great powers and core regional powers, 140, 185; shift from U.S. to the Muslims in hostage crisis, 57–58

Qadhafi, Muammar, 98, 128, 132, 173
Qajar dynasty, 11, 38
Qatar, 87, 117

Radicals (Extremists), Iranian, 42–44, 93–94, 97, 107, 111, 144, 152; and Anglo-Iranian relations, 146–48, 229 n.47; attitudes toward terrorism, 176–78; and the Iran-Contra affair, 66, 89, 207 n.53; power in 1980s, 59, 64, 67–68, 72–74, 205 n.29; response to reflagging of tankers, 69, 71
Rafsanjani, Hodjat-al-Islam Hashemi, 44, 45, 74, 89, 123, 224 n.33, 238 n.2; position on hostages and Lebanon, 75, 209 n.87; reaction to downing of Iran Air jet, 71; reassurances to Gulf states, 116; relations with China and Japan, 89, 160, 234 n.36; role in ending TWA flight 847 hijacking, 177; on Soviet approach to the Persian Gulf, 90, 92; on the Strait of Hormuz, 108; trips to USSR and Eastern Europe, 94, 114; on U.S.-Iranian relations, 64, 66
Raimond, Jean-Bernard, 152
Reagan, Ronald, 65, 226 n.4
Reagan administration, 60, 62–63, 75–76. *See also* Iran-Contra affair
Rebels, Afghan, 135–36, 224 n.26. *See also* Mojahedin
Regional Cooperation for Development (RCD), 33, 131, 132, 133, 222 n.5
Religion, 10, 11, 14, 82, 98–99. *See also* Islam
Religious factions. *See* Clerical factions
Revolutionary Guards, 71, 85, 146, 150, 166, 200 n.2; sent to Lebanon, 123, 124, 126; use in Iran-Iraq war, 105, 107, 108
Revolutionary ideology, 166–67, 184–86; bourgeois and socialist, 82, 83, 85. *See also* Islamic revolutionary ideology
Reza Shah Pahlavi, 8, 12, 16, 18, 21, 133, 226 n.11. *See also* Pahlavi dynasty
Roberts, U.S.S., 70–71, 208 n.66
Rocard, Michel, 153–54
Rochat, Phillipe, 151, 230 n.60
Romania, 144, 226–27 n.13, 228 nn.26, 28
Rushdie (Salman) affair, 74, 94, 143, 176, 177, 227 n.30; effect on Iran's relations with the West, 134, 143, 145, 148, 154, 155, 227 n.20
Russia, 8, 15, 25–26, 80, 157, 198 n.11; relations with Iran, 7, 23, 79–80, 141–42, 144, 210 nn.2, 3, 210–11 n.5. *See also* Soviet Union
Russian (Bolshevik) Revolution (1917), 80–81, 211 n.8
Russo-Iranian wars, 8, 22, 25, 79, 210 n.3

Saad Abad Pact, 133, 201 n.15, 223 n.22
Sadat, Anwar al-, 129, 217 n.20
Saddam Hussein al-Takriti, 80, 106–7, 109, 114, 216 n.92; motivations for starting Iran-Iraq war, 105, 218 n.30; Syrian hopes for collapse of, 122, 221 n.79
Safavid dynasty, 11, 13, 14, 197 n.3, 200–201, 216 n.2, 222 n.2
Satanic Verses (Rushdie), 74. *See also* Rushdie affair
Saudi Arabia, 74, 88, 107, 114, 172–73, 179, 214 n.60; Afghanistan policy, 95, 135–36; aid to Iraq, 108, 208 n.62; Chinese sale of missiles to, 161, 234 n.26; connection with Bahrain, 101, 226 n.7; GCC viewed as cover for influence of, 121, 220 n.72, 220–21 n.73; promotion of Wahabism, 41, 213 n.41; relations with Iran, 101, 114, 115, 116–17, 118–20, 184, 220 n.59; relations with Pakistan, 132, 135–36, 137, 223 n.16; sending home Pakistani brigade, 136, 224 n.28; Shi'as in, 219–20 n.58; U.S. policy toward, 49, 52, 88, 204 n.5, 206 n.43, 210 n.12
Seale, Patrick, 122, 238–39 n.5
Secular nationalism (Turkey), 134, 137
Secular nationalists (Iran), 1, 48, 55, 57, 205 n.24
Senegal, 167, 235 n.3, 236–37 n.11
Shah, the (Mohammed Reza Shah Pahlavi), 1, 41, 56, 127, 169–70, 211 n.13; British complicity suspected in deposing of, 145, 228 n.31; Khomeini's hatred of, 59; and the OIC, 172–73; policy of military buildup, 21, 200 n.2; role in conflict between Islam and nationalism, 12, 199 n.24
—foreign relations, 7, 16, 17–18, 134, 142, 232 n.9; with Afghanistan, India, and Pakistan, 131, 132, 133, 223 n.14; with Arabs, 114, 115, 129, 219 n.52; with Australia and New Zealand, 159, 233 n.19; diplomatic strategies, 23–25, 28, 29–35; with France, 148–49, 229 nn.49, 50; with the PLO, 104, 218 n.26; Third World focus of, 165–66, 235 nn.1–3; with USSR, 46, 80–82; with U.S., 46–48, 49–54, 77. *See also* Pahlavi dynasty
Shat-al-Arab, 99, 101, 105–6, 112–13, 237 n.1
Sheikholeslam, Hossein, 124–25, 146
Shevardnadze, Eduard, 94, 215 n.85
Shi'a Islam (Shi'ism), 4–5, 11, 14, 180, 184–85, 212 n.19; influence of pre-Islamic ideas on, 38; Iranians' attraction and conversion to, 98, 216 nn.2, 3; role in Iranian identity, 6–7, 11–13, 199 n.20
Shi'as (Shi'ites), 86, 118, 122, 128, 213 n.43; in Gulf countries, 114, 115–16, 117, 179, 219–20 n.58; Iraqi, 105, 106–7, 218 n.28; Lebanese, 75, 124–27, 150, 176, 209 n.86, 221 n.82; Pakistani, 135, 136, 222 n.4, 224 n.28
Shipping: Iraqi and Iranian attacks on, 88, 108, 170; U.S. protection of in Persian Gulf, 68–72, 90, 91, 110, 153, 207 n.58, 209 n.74

Shultz, George, 62, 67, 215 n.73
Sierra Leone, 167, 236 n.10
Socialism, 37, 42, 82, 83, 85, 86, 158; influence in Iran, 15, 39, 59
Somalia, 34, 165, 235 n.3
South Africa, 2, 54, 165, 167, 211 n.12
Southeast Asia, Iran's relations with, 157, 163, 232 n.2, 233 n.17
South-South cooperation, 40, 163, 166, 235 n.43
Soviet Iranian agreement (1989), 94, 215–16 n.89
Soviet-Iranian relations, 7, 8, 59, 79–97, 185, 187, 190–92; affected by Arab connections, 100, 217–18 n.21; as concern of U.S., 60–62, 64–65, 66, 67, 207 n.49; effect on British policies, 145, 228 n.33; effects of Iran-Iraq war on, 88–89, 90–93, 95–97, 215 n.75; impact of Iran-Contra affair on, 89–93; Iran's attempts to use third-power strategy in, 24–25; Iran's fear of dependence, 143–44; and Iran's sensitivity to attitude of regional states, 102–3; under the Islamic regime, 19, 46, 60–62, 64–65, 66, 69–70, 71, 81–97, 185–86, 187; moderate and radical Iranian leadership on, 43; not prevented by Cuba's and Nicaragua's dependence, 166–67; under provisional government, 54–55; rumored deal over Afghanistan, 86–87, 213 n.45; under the Shah, 17, 23–24, 30–32, 34, 46; West European concern over, 142
Soviet-Iranian treaty (1921), 58, 82, 212 n.20
Soviet-Iraqi Friendship Treaty (1972), 95, 96, 216 n.97
Soviet Union, 58–59, 149, 165, 204 n.12, 222 n.5, 234 n.26; in Afghanistan, 58, 61; as common concern of Iran and China, 158, 160–61, 232 n.1; as common concern of Iran and Pakistan, 135, 223–24 n.24; as common concern of Iran and Turkey, 48, 138; relations with India, 132–33; relations with Iraq, 107, 117, 223 n.17; self-interest and foreign policy, 41, 42; vulnerability to as impetus for regional cooperation, 27, 28. *See also* Russia; Soviet-Iranian relations; U.S.-Soviet relations
Spain, 143, 226 n.10
Stark, U.S.S., 69, 208 n.66
Subversion, 28, 116, 127, 174, 178–83, 186; difficulty of defining, 178–79; use by Iran in Gulf states, 115–16, 117–18
Sunni Islam, 7, 11; fundamentalism, 115, 180
Sunni Muslims, 98, 105, 173, 181, 213 n.43, 219–20 n.58; in Lebanon, 124; in USSR, 213 n.41
Switzerland, 76, 226 n.10
Syria, 57, 62, 106, 172, 177, 239 n.11; activities in Lebanon, 123–25, 126, 150; alliance with Iran, 101, 122–25, 128, 211 n.12, 217–18 n.21; involvement in terrorism, 150, 175, 176, 238–39 n.5; problem of Iranian tourists, 125, 221 n.87; relations with the PLO, 127; role in hostage problem, 75, 209 n.86; use of subversion, 116, 220 n.60

Tadjikistan (S.S.R.), 7, 192, 199 n.19, 210–11 n.5, 211–12 n.15, 213 n.41
Tankers, 68–71, 90; reflagging, 69–70, 90, 91, 110, 153
Tehran Agreement (1971), 32
Tehran Declaration (1943), 30, 204 n.4
Territorial integrity, maintenance of, 8, 11, 21–22, 30, 188
Terrorism, 69, 74, 111, 143, 174–78, 182–83; effect on Anglo-Iranian relations, 147; French policy on, 149, 151–53; U.S. posture on, 62–63, 67, 76; use in Lebanon, 126, 150; West German reaction to, 155
Thailand (Siam), 157, 163, 232 n.4
Third-power strategy, 24–25, 160
Third World, 3–4, 17, 52–53, 158, 163, 184; criticisms of the U.N., 169, 171; dependency, 38, 202 n.8, 202–3 n.9; ideology, 14–15, 172, 189, 200 n.32; Iran's involvement with, 28–29, 34, 43, 134, 137, 165–68, 224 n.33; place in polarized world view, 37, 38, 202 n.2; Soviet policy toward under Gorbachev, 64, 97; world view compared with Khomeini's, 37, 38–40
Tourists, Iranian: in Syria, 125, 221 n.87
Trade relations: between Arab countries and China, 161, 233–34 n.25; between Iraq and France, 149
—between Iran: and Africa, 167, 236 n.10; and East Asian countries, 86, 158, 160, 162–63, 233 nn.11, 14, 16, 234 nn.36, 37, 235 n.44; and East European countries, 226–27 n.13, 227 n.23, 228 n.28; and India, 223 n.11, 224 n.33; and Latin America, 166–67, 235 n.5; and Pakistan, 135; and USSR, 84, 85, 88, 93, 213 n.36; and West European countries, 86, 143, 146, 148–49, 153, 227 nn.14, 16, 18, 19, 229 n.36, 231 n.75
Trans-Iranian railway, 8, 90
Tudeh party, 82, 83, 85, 212 nn.16, 33; banned, 1, 87–88; call for end to Iran-Iraq war, 96, 106
Tunisia, 128–29, 181, 233–34 n.25
Turkey, 7, 25, 33, 48, 87, 192, 213–14 n.46; Iran's pre-revolution relations with, 27, 131, 133–34; Kurdish issue, 109, 134, 137, 223 n.22, 225 n.37; relations with Iraq, 107, 109, 137–38, 225 nn.39, 240–43; relations with Islamic regime, 65, 134, 137–38, 185, 192, 224–25 n.35, 225 nn.37, 39–43; ties with Israel, 103; U.S. policy on, 32, 49, 52, 204 nn.8, 11
Turkic peoples, 11; invasions, 210–11 n.5
Turkmanchai, Treaty of (1828), 79, 198 n.9
Turkmen (in Iran), disturbances among, 82–83
Turkmenistan (S.S.R.), 211–12 n.15
TWA flight 847 hijacking, 177

United Arab Emirates (UAE), 87, 109, 112–13, 114, 116–17, 184
United Nations, 72, 111, 166, 169; Iran's activity in, 102, 165, 169–70, 235 n.1; Islamic regime's

United Nations—(*continued*)
　policy toward, 169–72; mediation efforts in
　Iran-Iraq war, 93, 110–11, 113
U.N. Commission on Human Rights, 170, 237 n.4
U.N. Development Program (UNDP), 171, 237–
　38 n.6
U.N. General Assembly, 39
U.N. Security Council, 169, 170; China's support
　for Iran in, 161; failure to condemn Iraq, 110–
　11, 170, 219 n.40; Iran's criticism of, 170, 171;
　Resolution 1, 30; Resolution 479, 110–11;
　Resolution 514, 111; Resolution 552, 111
—Resolution 598, 70, 73, 111, 154–55, 172; Iran's
　acceptance of, 17, 72, 93, 110, 147; lack of
　pressure to implement, 111, 144, 148, 219 n.44;
　Palme's proposals as basis of, 113; resolution
　on arms embargo as follow-up, 91–92
United States, 95, 100, 102–3, 122, 133, 171;
　accused of provoking Iran-Iraq war, 95, 216
　n.93; alliances formed to protect oil interests,
　26, 201 n.12; global role, 49, 51, 52–54, 204
　nn.8, 10, 11; Iranian terrorism against, 174–
　75; Khomeini's view of, 59, 205–6 n.30; naval
　presence in Gulf, 19, 68–71, 110, 119, 205
　n.78; Nixon Doctrine, 28, 33, 52; Operation
　Staunch, 64, 108, 206 n.42; reflagging of tank-
　ers, 69–70, 90, 91, 110, 153; relations with
　Egypt, Jordan, Morocco, Tunisia, and Sudan,
　129; relations with Iraq, 61–62; relations with
　Turkey and Pakistan, 132, 134, 135, 223–24
　n.24; role in creation of Baghdad Pact, 27; sup-
　ply of technology to China, 160–61; TWA flight
　847 hijacking, 177. *See also* Iran-Iraq war: U.S.
　policy on
U.S. Department of Defense, 206 n.43, 207 n.46
U.S. Department of State, 62, 64, 73, 205 n.20
U.S. Embassy (in Beirut), truck bombings of, 174
U.S. Embassy (in Tehran), 55, 209 n.75. *See also*
　Hostage crisis, U.S.
U.S.-Iranian relations, 43, 111, 128, 154, 185; as
　concern of Soviet Union, 81, 83–84, 95, 211

n.13; effect on Anglo-Iranian relations, 146; effect on Iran's relations with India, Pakistan, and
Turkey, 134; effect on Japan's relations with
Iran, 162; after Islamic revolution, 2, 44, 46,
53, 54–78; pre-Pahlavi, 48–49, 203–4 n.2, 204
nn.3, 4; under provisional government, 54–56;
role in election of 1988, 73, 209 n.76; rupture
over hostage crisis, 56–59; under the Shah, 8–
9, 16, 17, 18, 23–26, 31–33, 46–48, 49–54,
77, 203 n.1, 204 nn.4, 8, 9, 205 n.15; and U.S.
human rights policy, 51, 204 n.11. *See also*
Iran-Contra affair
U.S.-Soviet relations, 68, 197 n.6, 207 n.59; developments in 1987–88, 71, 205 n.28, 207–8
n.59; effects on Iranian diplomatic strategies,
23, 26, 27, 33; as explanation for U.S.-Iran differences, 46–47, 48, 49, 53

Vance, Cyrus, 55, 81
Velayti, Ali-Akbar, 146–47, 205 n.29, 208 n.66,
213 n.44, 234 n.39, 238 n.12; conflict with
Mohtashemi, 176; on foreign relations, 66, 89–
90, 203 n.30; on U.N., 170, 237 n.3; visits to
West Germany, 154
Vietnam, 163, 235 n.46, 236–37 n.11
Vincennes, U.S.S., 71–73
Vorontsov, Yuli, 90, 93

Wahabis, 41, 95, 114, 135–36, 213 n.41
Weinberger, Caspar, 62, 207 n.46
White Revolution, 32, 199 n.24
WHO, 171, 237–38 n.6
World view, 36–45, 59, 202 n.2

Yazdi, Ibrahim, 55, 81, 211 n.14
Yemen, People's Democratic Republic of (South
Yemen), 32, 102, 128
Yugoslavia, 144, 226–27 n.13, 228 n.28

Zia-ul-Haq, 112, 134, 135
Zimbabwe, 167, 236 n.10, 237 n.13